Poolologie
des Wohnens

Poolology
of Housing

PARK BOOKS

pool Architekten

Vorwort / Foreword
Martin Steinmann

Texte / Texts
Raphael Frei
Matthias Heinz
Simone Jeska

4	Vorwort: Knöpfe sortieren	4	Foreword: Sorting Buttons
10	Anleitung zur *Poolologie des Wohnens*	10	Introduction to *A Poolology of Housing*
14	Studierende der TU Berlin: Abbild des Raumes. Historische Interieurs im Modell	14	Students at the TU Berlin: Imaging Spaces. Models of Historic Interiors

48 Das Arbeiten mit Typologien
48 Working with Typologies

68	pool Architekten: Eine Typensammlung. Regelgeschosse im Massstab 1:500	68	pool Architekten: A Type Collection. Standard Floors on a Scale of 1:500

102 Utopien und Erfindungen
102 Utopias and Inventions

120	pool Architekten: Das charaktervolle Haus in der Stadt. Fotografien realisierter Projekte	120	pool Architekten: The Characterful House in the City. Photographs of Realized Projects
154	pool Architekten: Vom Wohnen. Möblierte Grundrisse im Massstab 1:150	154	pool Architekten: On Housing. Furnished Floor Plans on a Scale of 1:150
190	pool Architekten: Interieurs. Das tägliche Leben	190	pool Architekten: Interiors. Daily Life

228 Der spezifische Ausdruck des Materials
228 The Specific Expression of the Material

234	Holz — Stäbe und Platten	234	Wood—Posts and Panels
244	Backstein — vom Weben und Fügen	244	Brick—of Weaving and Joining
262	Beton — das Feine im Rohen	262	Concrete—the Fine within the Rough
280	Stahl — der «unsichtbare» Stoff der unbegrenzten Möglichkeiten	280	Steel—the 'Invisible' Material of Unlimited Possibilities
294	Studierende der TU Berlin: Eine Typensammlung. Regelgeschosse im Massstab 1:500	294	Students from the TU Berlin: A Type Collection. Standard Floors on a Scale of 1:500
324	Studierende der TU Berlin: Vom Wohnen. Möblierte Grundrisse im Massstab 1:150	324	Students from the TU Berlin: On Housing. Furnished Floor Plans on a Scale of 1:150

360 Die Kultur des Interieurs
360 The Culture of the Interior

378	Studierende der TU Berlin: Interieurs. Semesterentwürfe im Modell	378	Students from the TU Berlin: Interiors. Semester Designs in Model Form
412	pool Architekten: Wohnbauprojekte 1998–2018. Ein Werkverzeichnis	412	pool Architekten: Residential Projects 1998–2018. A Catalogue Raisonné
420	pool an der TU Berlin: Entwurfsseminare 2013–2016. Aufgabenstellungen und Projektlisten	420	pool at the TU Berlin: Design Seminars 2013–2016. Assignments and Project Lists
438	Biografien	438	Biographies
439	Bildnachweis	439	Image Credits
440	Dank	440	Acknowledgments

Knöpfe sortieren.
Vorwort von
Martin Steinmann

Sorting Buttons.
Foreword by
Martin Steinmann

Das Buch *Poolologie des Wohnens* zeigt die Entwürfe, die pool Architekten in den vergangenen zwanzig Jahren auf dem Gebiet des Wohnens ausgearbeitet haben, gebaute und noch mehr ungebaute, zudem die Entwürfe der Studierenden von Raphael Frei und Mathias Heinz an der Technischen Universität Berlin. Das Buch enthält nur wenige Fotografien von Bauten, und vor allem von Räumen, denn es geht gewissermassen um ihre Radiografien. Nicht die äussere Form steht im Mittelpunkt, sondern die innere Struktur: Gezeigt werden vor allem Grundrisse im Massstab 1:500.

Ich gestehe, ich bin süchtig nach Grundrissen. Von einem Bauwerk ist seine innere Struktur das erste, was ich verstehen will. «Alles andere ist Beilage», um eine Werbung für Fleisch zu zitieren. Der Grundriss, das ist für mich die Wurst, um die es im Wohnungsbau geht (und das ist auch Fleisch). Für mich ist das Buch also eine *grande bouffe*, um im Genre zu bleiben: Grundrisse, nichts als Grundrisse.

Ich staune über die schiere Menge davon. Zum einen, weil ich mich frage, wie die Architekten* es schaffen, an so vielen Wettbewerben mitzumachen, und zwar mit bemerkenswerten Entwürfen. Dabei ist Wohnungsbau nicht ihre einzige Beschäftigung. Zum anderen aber staune ich über die Bedeutung, die diese Wettbewerbe in den letzten Jahrzehnten gewonnen haben, quantitativ, mehr aber noch qualitativ: Wohnungsbau ist zum wichtigsten Bereich der *recherche architecturale* geworden, zum Bereich, wo die technischen und wirtschaftlichen, die gesellschaftlichen und gelebten Aspekte der Architektur in ihren engen Beziehungen bearbeitet werden.

In dieser Situation ist man an das Neue Bauen erinnert, das den Wohnungsbau zur Grundlage der theoretischen Auseinandersetzung in einem allgemeineren Sinn gemacht hat. Die Siedlungen, die damals entstanden, sind gerade darum zu Monumenten des 20. Jahrhunderts geworden. Ich will nicht so weit gehen und in einer vorweggenommenen Geschichtsschreibung die Wohnanlagen, die heute entstehen, auch schon zu Monumenten erklären. Aber wenn man das Geschehen im Wohnungsbau aufmerksam verfolgt — ich leitete an der ETH Lausanne das *Laboratoire de l'habitation urbaine* —, so spiegelt dieses zwei gegensätzliche Haltungen in der Architektur, nicht nur im Wohnungsbau.

Auf der einen Seite ist da ein Suchen nach immer neuen Grundrissen, nach *nouveautés*, die die Betrachter in Staunen versetzen sollen, den Gesetzen der Konsumgesellschaft entsprechend; auf der anderen Seite gibt es die typologische Arbeit, das Suchen nach Grundrissen, die einige wenige Typen den besonderen Bedingungen einer Aufgabe entsprechend variieren. Das ist — für mich — die sachlich richtige Haltung. Für mich hat Wohnungsbau nichts mit «Erfindungen» zu tun. Wohnungen, hat Bruno Taut gesagt, sollen den elementaren Bedürfnissen der Menschen entsprechen, diese Bedürfnisse aber ändern sich nur langsam.

* Wann immer im Buch zugunsten der Lesbarkeit auf die Nennung der weiblichen Form verzichtet wurde, ist diese selbstverständlich mit eingeschlossen.

Knöpfe sortieren

The book *A Poolology of Housing* features designs produced by pool Architekten over the past 20 years in the sphere of residential development—realized and unbuilt—alongside designs by the students of Raphael Frei and Mathias Heinz from the Technical University Berlin. The book contains very few photographs of actual buildings, and of rooms, in particular, because it's more about the radiographs of buildings. The focus is not so much on external form, but instead on interior structure with particular attention paid to floor plans on a scale of 1:500.

I confess to being obsessed with floor plans. With any building, the inner structure is the first thing I want to understand. "Everything else is a side dish," to cite an advertisement for meat. For me, the ground plan is the sausage, the primary concern in housing development (which also counts as 'red meat'). For me, then, this book is a *grande bouffe*, to remain with food metaphors for the moment: floor plans, nothing but floor plans.

I find myself astonished at their sheer quantity. First, because one has to wonder how these architects manage to participate in so many competitions with such remarkable submissions. Residential development, meanwhile, is not their sole preoccupation. Secondly, I find it astonishing how much significance these competitions have acquired in recent decades. Quantitatively, but even more so qualitatively, housing development has become the most vital area of *recherche architecturale*, a realm where the technical and economic, societal, and experiential aspects of architecture are elaborated in a closely interrelated way.

This situation is reminiscent of the Neues Bauen (New Building), which made housing development the basis of its theoretical activities in a wider sense. And it is precisely for this reason that the housing estates created back then have become monuments of the 20th century. I will refrain from engaging in a kind of anticipatory historiography by declaring the housing estates that are rising today to be monuments. But when one follows current events in housing developments closely (I was head of the *Laboratoire de l'habitation urbaine* at the ETH Lausanne), one discovers that it reflects two antagonistic attitudes in architecture.

On the one hand, there is a search for ever-new floor plans, for *nouveautés*, which are intended—in-keeping with the laws of consumer society—to amaze viewers. On the other hand, we find work on typologies, the search for floor plans which vary only slightly according to the specific requirements of a given commission. In my view, this objective attitude is the correct one. For me, housing development has nothing to do with invention. A home, as Bruno Taut said, should correspond to the basic needs of human beings, and these needs only change very slowly.

Browsing the pages where pool Architekten present their *recherche architecturale* in the realm of housing development, I find childhood memories returning. I loved playing with buttons from my mother's sewing

Wenn ich mir die Seiten ansehe, auf denen pool Architekten ihre *recherche architecturale* im Bereich des Wohnungsbaus vorlegen, so steigt in mir eine Erinnerung aus meiner Kinderzeit auf: Ich liebte es, mit den Knöpfen aus dem Nähkasten meiner Mutter zu spielen, sie nach Grösse, Form und Farbe zu ordnen, die kleinen weissen für Hemden, die mit Stoff überzogenen für Blusen, die grossen dunklen für Mäntel. Dabei waren die kleinen nicht immer gleich weiss, manche waren aus Perlmutt und manche, billigere, aus Glas oder Kunststoff. Trotz solcher feinen Unterschiede liessen sie sich aber nach Typen ordnen.

Warum erzähle ich das? Weil die Seiten des Buches diesem Nähkasten gleichen: Die Grundrisse sind nicht geordnet, sie geben keinen Hinweis auf ihre typologische Verwandtschaft und darauf, wie die Typen den gegebenen Bedingungen entsprechend aktualisiert sind. Hinter dieser Entscheidung von pool steckt eine List, nehme ich an. Sie überlassen es dem Betrachter, in den Grundrissen solche Verwandtschaften zu finden und damit den einzelnen Entwurf *à l'envers* zu wiederholen. Eine gute Strategie, eine Strategie, die dem Besucher eine Arbeit abverlangt, so wie das Bert Brecht in seinem Aufsatz über das Betrachten von Kunst beschrieben hat.

Im Zeitalter der Maschine werde «nur noch das Resultat der Arbeit [...] betrachtet (und eventuell genossen), nicht mehr die Arbeit selber», schreibt Brecht, aber «es genügt ja nicht, lediglich das Resultat einer künstlerischen Produktion [...] konsumieren zu wollen; es ist nötig, sich an der Produktion selbst zu beteiligen», es sei nötig, selbst ein Stück Arbeit zu leisten. «Selbst der nur isst, arbeitet: zerschneidet das Fleisch, führt es zum Mund, kaut es. Das Geniessen von Kunst kann man nicht billiger haben.»[1]

Werknummer, Jahr und Ort sind alles, was man von den Grundrissen erfährt, wie bei einer Ausstellung von Kunst. Und wie dort muss der Betrachter selbst zurechtkommen, er muss sich Fragen zum Wohnungsbau stellen — betriebliche und räumliche — und in den Grundrissen Antworten suchen. Man kann es auch anders herum sagen: Er muss hinter den Antworten, die die Grundrisse geben, die Fragen suchen, auf die sie antworten. Er muss sich, mit anderen Worten, an der Arbeit beteiligen, die ihnen zugrunde liegt. Wie das Brecht fordert. Dafür muss der Betrachter einiges von dieser Arbeit wissen, das ist die Bedingung dieses Buches.

Pool Architekten wurde 1998 gegründet, nach vielen vorbereitenden Gesprächen der acht Partner, und sie hatten 2001 mit dem ersten Preis beim Wettbewerb für eine grosse Bebauung in Zürich-Leimbach einen eindrücklichen Einstand. Wohnungsbau ist für sie bis heute ein besonders wichtiges Arbeitsgebiet geblieben. Die mehr als achtzig Grundrisse von jeweils einem Regelgeschoss zeugen davon. Aber Wohnen ist nicht nur zahlenmässig ein wichtiges Arbeitsgebiet: Es ist sicher das elementarste Bedürfnis des Menschen, die Beschäftigung mit ihm führt somit ins Innerste der Architektur. Bei dieser Beschäftigung aber kommt dem Grundriss der erste Platz zu: Er schafft Räume für die verschiedenen Handlungen, und er ordnet die Beziehungen

1   Bertolt Brecht, «Betrachtung der Kunst und Kunst der Betrachtung», 1939

kit. I arranged them according to size, form, and color; the little white ones for shirts, the fabric-covered ones for blouses, the large dark ones for coats. The small ones were not always white. Some were mother-of-pearl and some of them, the cheaper ones, were glass or plastic. Despite such fine distinctions, they could always be arranged according to type.

Why am I mentioning this? Because the pages of this book resemble that sewing kit. The floor plans are not ordered and we are offered no information as to their typological relationships. Nor on how these types refer to specific contextual conditions. Behind this decision on the part of pool, I assume, is a certain stratagem. It is left to the beholder to discover such affinities between the floor plans, and hence to recapitulate the individual design *à l'envers*. This is a good strategy, and one that calls for a certain amount of effort on the part of the reader. As put by Bertolt Brecht in his essay on looking at art in the machine age: "only the result of work is still [...] looked at (and perhaps enjoyed), no longer the work itself," but "it is not enough to consume the result of an artistic production; one must participate in the production yourself." In other words, one must contribute some work. "Even someone who just eats, works: tearing the meat, carrying it to your mouth, chewing it. The enjoyment of art comes no cheaper than that."[1]

Work number, year, and location: as if at an art exhibition, this is all we learn about the individual floor plans. The viewer must find their own way, must pose their own questions concerning housing development, whether operationally or spatially, and must search for their own answers in the plans. Or the other way around: behind the answers proffered by the floor plans, they must search for the questions. In other words, the viewer must actively engage in the work upon which they are based. Just as Brecht demanded.

Pool Architekten was established in 1998. After numerous preparatory discussions between the eight partners they made an impressive debut in 2001 by winning 1st prize in a competition for a large development in Zurich-Leimbach. Housing development has remained an especially important area of activity for them up to the present. Testifying to this are these more than 80 floor plans, each consisting of a standard floor. But housing is not just important numerically: dwelling is among the elementary human needs and a preoccupation with it exists at the innermost core of architecture. In the context of this preoccupation the floor plan must be accorded priority. It creates spaces for a variety of activities and it organizes the relationships between them. In short: "Le plan est le générateur," as Le Corbusier wrote. The floor plan demands an excellent imagination, and a very stringent organization. "Le plan est la détermination de tout."[2]

The floor plan orients human activity, although it does not dictate human action. And this makes it the social moment of architecture *tout court*. But the floor plans accomplishes even more. Not only does it order spaces, it also orders the perceptions that are associated with the activities which transform them into lived spaces. Asked about the core features that are

1   Bertolt Brecht, "Betrachtung der Kunst und Kunst der Betrachtung," 1939.
2   Le Corbusier, *Vers une architecture*, Paris 1923.

zwischen ihnen. Kurz: «Le plan est le générateur», wie Le Corbusier schreibt. Der Grundriss verlange eine sehr gute Vorstellung, und er verlange eine sehr strenge Ordnung. «Le plan est la détermination de tout.»[2]

Der Grundriss ordnet die Handlungen der Menschen, habe ich gesagt — was nicht heisst, dass er sie diktiert. Das macht ihn zum gesellschaftlichen Moment der Architektur *tout court*. Der Grundriss leistet aber noch mehr: Er ordnet nicht nur die Räume, er ordnet auch die Empfindungen, die mit den Handlungen verbunden sind, die sie zu «gelebten» Räumen machen. Nach den Konstanten in ihrem Wohnungsbau gefragt, sagen die Architekten, dass man ihre Grundrisse ganz allgemein in zwei Kategorien einteilen könne: in «gekammerte», wie sie das nennen, und in «offene». Das entspricht Le Corbusiers Kategorien, wobei er die ersten allerdings als «gelähmt» bewertet hat. Man kennt die zwei kleinen Zeichnungen. Mit anderen Worten gibt es für pool, anders als für das Befreite Wohnen, nicht *die eine* Art von Grundrissen, nicht *den einen* Typ, in dem sich der Geist unserer Zeit manifestieren würde. Es gibt für sie keine Dogmen.

Was es aber gibt, sind elementare Bedürfnisse, körperliche, geistige, seelische, die ich mit den zwei Polen «mit anderen sein» und «allein sein» abstecken möchte. Wie diese Bedürfnisse gewichtet werden, wie sie gewichtet werden können unter Bedingungen, die von Fall zu Fall verschieden sind und die man auch nicht kennt, darüber geben die Grundrisse Auskunft. Und darüber, wie der beschränkte Raum, der dafür zur Verfügung steht, vielfältige Erfahrungen möglich machen kann.

Die Arbeitsweise von pool besteht darin, dass jeweils ein oder zwei Partner für einen Entwurf verantwortlich sind. Sie besprechen ihn regelmässig mit den anderen, müssen deren Kritik aber nicht aufnehmen. (Das ist auch die Arbeitsweise von Atelier 5.) Beim Entwerfen bilden die Erfahrungen der Architekten eine erste Grundlage, angefangen mit den eigenen Entwürfen im Bereich des Wohnungsbaus. Beim Schach würde man von den Zügen sprechen, die sie gespeichert haben und entsprechend der Stellung auf dem Schachbrett nun anwenden. Die Architekten teilen aber nicht alle die gleichen Erfahrungen. So kommen neben geteilten Vorstellungen auch persönliche Erfahrungen ins Spiel und bewirken eine gewisse Breite von Typen oder genauer: von deren Aktualisierung.

pool arbeiten in dem sehr lebendigen Kontext, den die vielen Wettbewerbe für Wohnungsbauvorhaben gerade in Zürich bilden. Sie arbeiten, wie andere Architekten auch, in einer ständigen Konfrontation mit anderen Vorstellungen. Und mit der Versuchung, diese selbst einmal zu testen. Auf die «verwackelten» Grundrisse angesprochen, die gerade *en vogue* sind, sagen sie, dass sie auch einen oder zwei solche Entwürfe gemacht hätten, und sei es, um zu verstehen, was es damit auf sich habe. Im Französischen gibt es einen schönen Ausdruck, der mir hier in den Sinn kommt: Man müsse «sehen, wie weit man zu weit gehen kann».

Auch wenn Wohnungsbau mit Gewohnheiten zu tun hat, so sind diese nicht so fest, dass sie sich jedem Experimentieren widersetzen würden. Experimentieren

[2] Le Corbusier, *Vers une architecture*, Paris 1923

present in their housing projects, the architects argue that their floor plans could be divided into "chambered" floor plans, as they call them, and "open" floor plans. This corresponds to Le Corbusier's categories, the first of which he however always regarded as "paralyzed." We are all familiar with these two small drawings. For pool, in other words, and in contrast to the model of Giedion's so-called "liberated housing," no single type of floor plan, no single typology is held to be the manifestation of the "spirit of the times." For them, there are no dogmas.

What exists instead are elemental needs: the physical, emotional, spiritual. I am fond of considering these by means of two poles which I call "being with others" and "being alone." Between these two poles, a diverse range of experiences can be provided by the floor plan.

According to pool, one or two partners are responsible for each design. The project is discussed regularly with the others but there is no obligation to incorporate criticisms. (The same procedure is in place at Atelier 5.) During the design process, the architects' previous design experiences from a starting point. In chess, one speaks of the moves one has memorized for future use depending upon the current configuration of the board. But architects do not all share the same experiences. Differing personal perspectives create contrasting ideas and these generate a breadth of both concepts and completed designs.

Pool is particularly active in Zurich, where there exists an intense environment of competitions for residential development. As with other architects, their activities involve continual confrontation with varying perspectives. This also involves the temptation to try these out themselves. Asked about the "blurry" floor plan currently *en vogue*, they remark that they produced one or two such designs, if only in order to understand what it's all about. In French, there is a nice expression that seems appropriate here: one ought to "see just how far one can go too far."

Although housing development is bound up with the habitual, this connection is not so rigid that it resists every form of experimentation. Which does not, however, mean that *anything goes*, i.e. arbitrary production that overrides elementary human needs. Experimentation instead means to pose specific questions, to pursue them in the spirit of a *recherche patiente,* and to respond to them with floor plans through which the habitual—to put it paradoxically—acquires a new form.

This book, I believe, addresses this type of work. It constitutes a record of the research in the realm of housing development which pool Architekten has pursued with such commitment since their founding. And with great success.

In the course of day-to-day work, much remains unspoken. The invitation to teach in Berlin for seven semesters called upon the authors to reflect upon their work, probably more than is usual, and probably with greater clarity as well. In doing so, they have selected four areas that shape their design process in equal measures: material, lifestyle, residence type, and interior. The authors introduce the corresponding sections of the book with extended texts which elaborate

aber bedeutet nicht *anything*, es bedeutet nicht, irgendetwas zu machen und dabei die elementaren Bedürfnisse des Menschen ausser Kraft zu setzen. Nein, experimentieren bedeutet, bestimmte Fragen zu stellen, sie im Sinn einer *recherche patiente* zu verfolgen und mit Grundrissen darauf zu antworten, durch die die Gewohnheiten, paradox gesagt, eine neue Form erhalten.

Ich denke, dass das Buch von dieser Arbeit handelt: Es bildet gewissermassen das Protokoll der Recherche im Bereich des Wohnungsbaus, die pool Architekten seit ihrer Gründung mit grossem Engagement betrieben haben. Und mit grossem Erfolg.

In der täglichen Arbeit wird vieles nicht ausgesprochen. Die Einladung, während sieben Semestern in Berlin zu lehren, hat von den Verfassern verlangt, ihre Arbeit zu reflektieren, wahrscheinlich mehr als sonst, und wahrscheinlich klarer. Sie haben dafür vier Bereiche gewählt, die das Entwerfen in wechselseitigen Abhängigkeiten bestimmen. Mit meinen Worten: Material, Lebensform, Wohnungstyp und Interieur. Die Verfasser leiten die entsprechenden Teile des Buches mit längeren Texten ein, die den technischen und wirtschaftlichen, den gesellschaftlichen und kulturellen Kontext entwickeln, in dem sie den Wohnungsbau verstehen und in dem sie diesen betreiben: als Architekten.

Das vorliegende Buch soll also weit mehr sein als eine weitere Sammlung von Plänen und Bildern zum Wohnungsbau, die dann auf Breuer-Tischchen herumliegt zum Blättern oder auf Eiermann-Tischen zum Kopieren. Es ist als ein Arbeitsbuch gedacht, es dient dem entwerferischen Denken, es dient dazu, die Abhängigkeiten der Entscheidungen im Wohnungsbau zu erkennen und die Themen zu setzen, die die Entscheidungen bei der Arbeit leiten.

on the technical and economic, the social and cultural contexts within which they understand housing development, and within which they perform their work as architects.

The present publication is far more than yet another collection of plans and images from the domain of housing development; the kind that lie on Breuer tables waiting to be leafed through or on Eiermann tables waiting to be copied. It is conceived as a working tool; one that facilitates thinking about design, that recognizes the complexities of housing development, and that defines the themes which guide decision-making in design work.

Martin Steinmann ist emeritierter Professor für Entwerfen an der ETH Lausanne und hatte unter anderem eine Gastprofessur am MIT in Cambridge, Massachusetts, inne. Neben seiner Tätigkeit als Redaktor der *archithese* ist er Autor von Texten zur Architektur des 20. Jahrhunderts und der Gegenwart, Kurator von Ausstellungen. 2016 erhielt er den Prix Meret Oppenheim für sein Lebenswerk. Er arbeitet und lebt in Aarau.

Martin Steinmann is an emeritus professor of design at the ETH Lausanne. He has been a guest professor at MIT in Cambridge Massachusetts. Alongside his activities as an editor of *archithese*, he is the author of texts on twentieth century and contemporary architecture, a curator of exhibitions, and the recipient of the 2016 Prix Meret Oppenheim for his lifework. He lives and works in Aarau.

←

Knöpfe sortieren.
Vorwort von
Martin Steinmann

Sorting Buttons.
Foreword by
Martin Steinmann

Anleitung zur *Poolologie des Wohnens*

Introduction to *A Poolology of Housing*

Geschätzter Leser, mit diesem Buch erhalten Sie weder eine fertige Lehre zum Wohnungsbau noch ein Rezeptbuch zum richtigen Wohnen. Dieses Buch bietet keine Lösungen, sondern offeriert Möglichkeiten. Keine Dogmen werden proklamiert, sondern die offene Neugierde wird gepflegt.

Die *Poolologie des Wohnens* streicht über die persönliche Annäherung zum Thema Wohnungsbau das Prozesshafte beim Entwurf heraus. Geprägt von über zwanzig Jahren intensiver Auseinandersetzung von pool Architekten mit dem Thema Wohnungsbau in der praktischen Umsetzung und in der Lehre, unter anderem an der TU Berlin, werden in diesem Buch Arbeiten aus dem Büro mit den studentischen Arbeiten exemplarisch nebeneinandergestellt.

Ziel des Buches ist eine Annährung an das Thema Wohnen über unterschiedliche entwurfstechnische Aspekte. In erster Linie geschieht dies über die Gegenüberstellung von Typologien und Grundrissen eigener und studentischer Arbeiten. Ergänzt durch den Aspekt des Interieurs und der Konstruktion werden die flankierenden Rahmenbedingungen beleuchtet.

Der Grundriss als universelle Sprache

Im Zentrum unserer Arbeit steht immer der Grundriss. Er stellt unsere Leidenschaft dar und als regelrechte Grundriss-Junkies studieren wir bei historischen Vorbildern wie auch zeitgenössischen Arbeiten akribisch den Wohnungsgrundriss, bevor wir uns den anderen Aspekten des jeweiligen Entwurfs zuwenden. Aus diesem Grund haben wir diesem Buch die Grundrisspläne zugrunde gelegt. Sie ziehen sich als immer wiederkehrendes Thema, als Rückgrat durch die ganze Publikation und sind alle im selben Massstab 1:500 oder im grösseren Massstab als möblierter Grundriss und in gleicher Darstellung abgebildet. So wird der Unterschied zwischen ausgeführtem Werk, unrealisiertem Wettbewerbsentwurf und studentischer Arbeit aufgehoben.

Ein Architekturplan und im Speziellen ein Grundriss ist über alle Sprachgrenzen hinweg lesbar und somit universell verständlich. Er dient nicht nur der Darstellung der Raumanordnung, sondern transportiert eine Vielzahl weiterer Informationen. Vergleichbar mit einer Landkarte, in der neben ihren primären Aussagen über Topografie und räumliche Verortung immer auch die Geschichte eines Landes erzählt wird, historische Informationen lesbar sind, sich die Geologie erklären lässt und man herauslesen kann, wie die Bewohner leben und wo sie sich mehrheitlich aufhalten, erzählt auch ein Grundriss vieles über seine zukünftigen Bewohner. Wie sie zusammenleben, über die Art, wie und mit welchem Material das Haus gebaut ist und in welcher klimatischen Region sich das Haus befindet.

Anleitung zur *Poolologie des Wohnens*

Esteemed readers, the book you hold in your hands is neither a final manifesto for residential development, nor a recipe book for producing optimal housing. It provides no solutions, instead proffering possibilities. It proclaims no dogmas, but rather cultivates an open-ended sense of curiosity.

A Poolology of Housing lays out personal approaches to residential development and its design process. For more than 20 years, pool Architekten has been intensively involved in residential development, practically as well as pedagogically—at the TU Berlin, amongst other institutions—in an exemplary way. The present publication thus juxtaposes works from our office with student works.

The aim of this book is to approach the topic of housing in relation to a variety of design techniques. We proceed by presenting and comparing the typologies and plans of our own projects as well as those of our students. A subsequent examination of interiors and of construction methods shed light on two additional conditions that have concerned us over the years.

The Floor Plan as a Universal Language

The floor plan is always central to our work. It's our true passion, and as genuine floor plan junkies we meticulously study the residential plans of both historical and contemporary case studies before turning our attention toward other aspects of architectural design. For this reason, we have based the present book on floor plans. They are the backbone of this book, a pervasive and recurrent topic. All plans are presented in the book at a scale of 1:500, or on a larger scale as furnished floor plans, and are all depicted in a uniform way. This eliminates distinctions between realized projects, unrealized competition designs, and student work.

An architectural plan, and in particular a floor plan, is readable, and hence universally comprehensible, in ways that transcend linguistic boundaries. Not only does it serve to represent a spatial configuration, it also conveys a broad range of additional information. Beyond providing basic information about topography and spatial location, the map of a territory has much to tell us about the history of a country. It renders temporal information legible, elucidating geological aspects and allows the user to infer a great deal about how the inhabitants live their lives. In a way that is directly comparable, a floor plan tells us much about a building's future inhabitants. About how they live together, the way in which the building is constructed, with which materials, and in which climatic region the building is located.

Die Struktur des Buches

Die typologische Sammlung ist das tragende und alles verbindende Element des Buches. Die Grundrisse sind aus ihrem Kontext herausgelöst und im selben Massstab abgebildet, damit die Entwürfe unabhängig vom Bearbeitungsstand vergleichbar werden. Somit geht es weniger um ein tieferes Verständnis des einzelnen Projekts und dessen ganzheitliche Darstellung als um die Assoziationen, die im Nebeneinander oder beim Blättern von Seite zu Seite aufblitzen. Die abstrakte Ästhetik der grafischen Zeichnungen lässt Ähnlichkeiten und Unterschiede, Sympathien und Antipathien, konzeptuelle und strukturelle Prinzipien hervortreten und soll zum skizzierenden Nachvollziehen und Weiterdenken des Gesehenen verleiten.

Neben den büroeigenen Entwürfen von pool Architekten werden die chronologisch gruppierten studentischen Entwürfe aus sieben Semestern Lehre an der TU Berlin zwischen 2013 und 2016 gezeigt. Dabei folgen die Nachbarschaften auf den Doppelseiten keiner zwingenden Logik. Die jeweilige Auswahl vertraut vielmehr auf das geschulte Auge der Grafiker und der Autoren. Somit ist es dem Leser überlassen, seinen eigenen Verknüpfungen und Spuren zu folgen.

Die Textstruktur

Vier Kapitel beleuchten das Wechselspiel unterschiedlicher Faktoren, die den Entwurf eines Wohnprojekts bestimmen. Zuerst wird die Frage nach dem «Arbeiten mit Typologien» behandelt und der produktive Aspekt der typologischen Sammlung untersucht, die das Rückgrat des Buches bildet. Dabei wird, im Zusammenhang mit der Auseinandersetzung mit dem Programmatischen, über das Lesen der Grundrisse reflektiert, die aus den Bedürfnissen der Gesellschaft resultieren. Hierbei spielt das Wissen um die Verankerung in der Tradition und die Inspiration über das Betrachten historischer Referenzen eine tragende Rolle, aus der sich die nachfolgenden Kapitel erschliessen.

Das Kapitel «Utopien und Erfindungen» wendet sich dem Spannungsfeld zwischen gesellschaftlichen Neuerungen und historischen Vorbildern zu und ergründet die Daseinsberechtigung der architektonischen Erfindung. Im folgenden Kapitel «Der spezifische Ausdruck des Materials» wird analysiert, inwieweit das Material auf das Projekt einwirkt und es architektonisch definiert. Dazu werden die Grundbaustoffe Holz, Beton, Stahl und Backstein nach ihrem Einfluss auf Grundrisstypen und nach ihrem atmosphärisch und archaisch wirkenden Potenzial befragt. Im Kapitel «Die Kultur des Interieurs» geht es schliesslich um den Gebrauch der Wohnung und die Geschichten, die anhand des Interieurs erzählt werden, sowie die Geschichten, die aus dem Interieur heraus entstehen. Es geht um die Aneignung des Raumes durch die Bewohner sowie um die räumliche Artikulation — der Raum als Position, als Reibungsfläche und Spiegelbild einer Innerlichkeit.

The Structure of this Book

The typological collection is the primary structural element of this publication. The floor plans are detached from their contexts and illustrated on a uniform scale so that designs can be compared with one another independently of their respective states of realization. It is less a question of acquiring a deeper comprehension of individual projects or of their integrated depiction, and instead of the associations that emerge spontaneously via juxtaposition or by leafing through the pages. The abstract aesthetic of the graphic rendering allows similarities and differences, sympathies and antipathies, conceptual and structural principles to come to the fore, encouraging the reader to engage in exploratory reconstructions and extended reflections on what she has seen.

Presented in conjunction with projects by the office of pool Architekten are chronologically arranged student designs from the seven semesters, between 2013 and 2016, during which we taught at the TU Berlin. The way in which projects are juxtaposed on the double pages follows no compelling logic. The respective choice relies instead on the trained eyes of the graphic designer and the authors. It is left to the initiative of individual reader to generate interconnections, to track down affinities.

The Structure of the Text

The four chapters illuminate the interplay between the interlinking factors that determine the design of a residential project. First we explore the topic of *Working with Typologies*. Here, we reflect upon ways of interpreting floor plans in connection with the programmatic aspects that result from socially determined needs. Fundamental here—and leading directly into the following chapters—is an awareness of the way in which floor plans are anchored in tradition, along with the inspiration that is derivable from historical references.

In the chapter on *Utopias and Inventions*, we turn our attention toward the tension between societal renewal and historical prototypes, while seeking to fathom the *raison d'être* of architectural invention. Then, in the chapter titled *The Specific Expression of the Material*, we analyze the impact of materiality on a given project, and how this factor defines it architectonically. The basic building materials of wood, concrete, steel, and brick are interrogated in relation to their influence on plan types and their atmospheric and archaic potential. In *The Culture of the Interior*, finally, we question the practical use of the dwelling and of the stories that can be narrated with reference to the interior, as well as those that emerge from it. Here, we explore the appropriation of a space by its inhabitants, as well as of spatial articulation; the space as a position, as a source of friction, and as mirror of interiority.

Introduction to *A Poolology of Housing*

Die Bildstrecken

In der Übung «Das Abbild des Raumes» haben die Studierenden historische Innenraumfotografien im Modell nachgebaut und abfotografiert, um die Vorzüge einer vergangenen Interieurkultur nachzuempfinden und die räumlichen Qualitäten von Ikonen des Wohnungsbaus kennenzulernen. Dabei wurde viel über natürliche Lichtführung reflektiert und nicht zuletzt die erzählerische Kraft einer guten Bildkomposition vermittelt.

Bilder sind eines der wichtigsten Kommunikationsmittel der Architekten, denn darin kommen die räumlichen wie auch die atmosphärischen Qualitäten zum Ausdruck. Fotos möblierter Wohnungen geben einen Einblick in die heutige Wohnkultur, Baustellenfotos zeigen die aktuellen Fertigungstechniken und Aussenbilder die Einfügung in den urbanen Kontext. Diesen realen, ausgeführten Bauten sind Modellfotos gegenübergestellt, die die Raum- und Nutzungsvorstellungen studentischer Entwürfe und nicht realisierter Projekte von pool Architekten illustrieren.

Möblierte Grundrisse sind ebenfalls den Bildstrecken zugeordnet. Wie beim fotografischen Material erlauben sie, virtuell durch die Räume zu flanieren und sich eine Vorstellung vom Gebrauchswert der Wohnungen zu machen, den Raum zu lesen und sich in fremde Lebenswelten einzudenken.

Poolologie

Der Titel *Poolologie* schwirrt schon einige Zeit in unseren Köpfen herum. Der Begriff *lògos* aus dem Altgriechischen umfasst einen weiten Bedeutungsspielraum. Im Allgemeinen bedeutet er «das Wort», «die Rede» sowie deren Sinn oder Gehalt. Wir wollen den Begriff in der Neuschöpfung Poolologie im Sinn von «Definition» und «Argument» verstanden wissen. Somit kann man die Poolologie als die Definition und das Argument von pool Architekten verstehen.

Mit der *Poolologie des Wohnens* kommt unser Bedürfnis zum Ausdruck, über den Dienstleistungscharakter des Architekturberufs hinaus das eigene Schaffen inhaltlich zu reflektieren und dieses in einen gesamtgesellschaftlichen Kontext zu stellen. Gleichzeitig wollen wir auch etwas von der Freude und Experimentierlust nach aussen tragen, die unsere Arbeit im Wohnungsbau antreibt.

Da in der Architektur und insbesondere im Wohnungsbau jeder Gedanke schon gedacht und jeder Plan schon mal gezeichnet wurde, setzt sich jede Lösung aus Beiträgen früherer Autoren und Autorinnen zusammen. Diese verschwinden wiederum hinter dem Eigenleben der neuen Kreation, die sich aus unterschiedlichen Einflüssen speist. Diese Tradition wollen wir mit der vorliegenden Publikation weiterführen.

The Image Sequences

In the exercise entitled Imaging Space, students reconstructed historic photographs of interiors in the form of models before photographing them. The aim here was to recreate the interiors of past cultures and acquire greater familiarity with the spatial qualities of certain icons of residential construction. One focus of our reflections was on the utilization of natural lighting, and not least of all a consideration of the narrative power of good visual composition.

For the architect, visual imagery is the most important medium of communication, since images are capable of conveying both spatial as well as atmospheric qualities. Photographs of furnished dwellings offer insights into contemporary domestic culture, construction photos shed light on current production technologies, while images of exteriors highlight the project's integration into the urban context. In this publication, realized projects are juxtaposed with photographs of models which illustrate ideas about space and utilization explored through student designs and in unrealized projects by pool Architekten.

Also included in the image sequences are furnished floor plans. As with the photographic material, they make it possible to stroll, in a virtual sense, through the spaces. They communicate a sense of the use value of a dwelling, rendering the space legible, making it possible to read the space and to think and feel one's way into unfamiliar living environments.

Poolology

The title Poolology has been buzzing around our heads for some time now. The ancient Greek word *logos* embraces a broad range of meanings. In general, it translates to mean "word" or "speech," as well as its "meaning" or content. Poolology, then, is the definition and argument offered by pool Architekten.

The term poolology gives expression to our need—going beyond the service-provision character of architecture as an occupation—to reflect thematically on our own work, and to situate it in a social context. At the same time, we want to convey something of the delight in experimentation that propels our work in the field of housing development.

Given the fact that in architecture, and especially in housing construction, every idea has already been thought, and every plan has already been drawn, every architectural solution necessarily consists of contributions from previous, unnamed authors. These authors disappear behind the independent existence of each new creation, which is, in itself, nourished by a variety of influences. It is this tradition we seek to perpetuate in the present publication.

Anleitung zur *Poolologie des Wohnens*

Studierende der
TU Berlin:
Abbild des Raumes.
Historische Interieurs
im Modell

Students at the
TU Berlin:
Imaging Spaces.
Models of Historic
Interiors

Auguste Perret, Appartement Rue Raynouard, Paris, 1933
Abbild W15/16–02: Tobias Scholz, Tobias Bräunig

Studierende der TU Berlin: Abbild des Raumes.
Historische Interieurs im Modell

← Gio Ponti, Via Dezza, Milano, 1957
Abbild S13—06: Timo Büscher, Olivier Laydevant

↑ Auguste Perret, Rue Franklin, Paris, 1904
Abbild S16—10: Vadim Below, Katharina Zull, Timo Strauch

↑ Alvaro Siza, Casa Beires, Pavoa de Varzim, 1976
Abbild S13–19: Kerstin Krüger, Elisabeth Bork

↗ John M. Johansen, Labyrinth House, Southport/Connecticut, 1966
Abbild S14–07: Myungjin Choi, Elena Schneider
→ Charles Voysey, The Orchard, Winchester, 1899
Abbild W14/15–14: Theodora Constantin, Vanessa Vogel

**Students at the TU Berlin: Imaging Spaces.
Models of Historic Interiors**

← Lux Guyer, Haus Rudolph, Küsnacht, 1931
Abbild W14/15–05: Juan Cequera, Kays Elbeyli, Arthur Schmock, Marc Wendland

↑ Erich Mendelsohn, Russell House, San Francisco/California, 1951
Abbild W14/15–07: Josephine Brillowski, Oskar Ellwanger, Jana Morgenstern

Studierende der TU Berlin: Abbild des Raumes.
Historische Interieurs im Modell

← Kazuo Shinohara, Uehara House, Tokyo, 1976
Abbild W14, 15—12: Ilkin Akpinar, Veronique Baustert, Elena Petkova

↑ Sep Ruf, Kanzler-Pavillon, Bonn, 1964
Abbild S13—16: Marco Migliavacca, Friedrich Neukirchen

Studierende der TU Berlin: Abbild des Raumes.
Historische Interieurs im Modell

↑ Frank Lloyd Wright, Pope Leighey House, Alexandria/Virginia, 1941
Abbild S14—05: Cela Adamescu, Madalina Uram

↗ Rudolph Schindler, Oliver Residence, Los Angeles/California, 1934
Abbild S16—03: Marie-Louise Leeck, Lisa Thürer
→ George Matsumoto, Lipman Residence, Richmond/Virginia, 1957
Abbild W14/15—06: Vera Marie Glas, Rafael Lozykowski, Florian Rizek

Students at the TU Berlin: Imaging Spaces.
Models of Historic Interiors

↖ Berthold Lubetkin, Highpoint II, London, 1938
Abbild S14—10: Sebsatian Genzel, Harald Niessner
← Pierre Chareau, Maison de Verre, Paris, 1931
Abbild S13—04: Cem Baykal, Yuki Hanfeld

↑ Josef Hofmann, Palais Stoclet, Bruxelles, 1911
Abbild S13—07: Veronika Mosser, Nico Steinacker

Studierende der TU Berlin: Abbild des Raumes.
Historische Interieurs im Modell

← Craig Ellwood, Hunt House, Malibu/California, 1955
Abbild S14—04: Thomas Pracht, Guang Xue

↑ Ralph Erskine, Villa Engström, Nynäshamn, 1956
Abbild W13/14—06: Johanna Backhaus, Tetyana Nesterenko

Studierende der TU Berlin: Abbild des Raumes.
Historische Interieurs im Modell

↖ Paolo Soleri, Arcosanti, Arcosanti/Arizona, 1970s
Abbild W15/16—14: Azad Saleem, Martin Ulitzka, Olivia Valenzuela
← Hugo Häring, Haus Schmitz, Biberach, 1950
Abbild W13/14—08: Jennifer Moser, Fabian Trapp

↑ Frank Lloyd Wright, Hanna House, Stanford/California, 1937
Abbild S15—03: Annett Donat, Jakob Pawlowski

**Studierende der TU Berlin: Abbild des Raumes.
Historische Interieurs im Modell**

↖ Luis Barragan, Own House, Ciudad de México, 1948
Abbild S14—02: Patryk Kujawa, Martyna Aleksandra Wojnarowska
← Le Corbusier, Immeuble Molitor, Paris, 1933
Abbild W14/15—04: Marlene Bühner, Cassandra Donath, Anika Weidlich

↑ José Antonio Coderch, Casa Ugalde, Caldes d'Estrac, 1953
Abbild W13/14—05: Ahmed Michael Abd Alla, Eva-Maria Thinius

Studierende der TU Berlin: Abbild des Raumes.
Historische Interieurs im Modell

↑ Josef Frank, Haus Beer, Wien, 1931
Abbild W13/14—07: Sebastian Blatter, Zaneta Choroba

↗ Adolf Loos, Werkbund-Siedlung, Wien, 1932
Abbild S14—09: Ana García Gasquet, Ignasi Querol Diez
→ Atelier 5, Thalmatt 1, Herrenschwanden, 1974
Abbild S15—01: Elsa Albrecht, Nikolaus Schmid

Students at the TU Berlin: Imaging Spaces.
Models of Historic Interiors

↑ John Soane, John Soane House, London, 1792–1823
Abbild W14/15–13, Anna Gert, Cemile Kolgu, Ewa Kostecka

→ Hermann Muthesius, Haus Freudenberg, Berlin, 1908
Abbild W13/14–14: Christopher Sitzler, Kristina Szeifert

Students at the TU Berlin: Imaging Spaces.
Models of Historic Interiors

↖ Jean Prouvé Villa Seynave, Grimaud, 1961
Abbild S13—15: Tatjana Anic, Timo Lück
← Mary Otis Stevens, Thomas McNulty, Own House, Lincoln/Massachusetts, 1965
Abbild S15—05: Fabian Koschowsky, Hanna Rohst

↑ Pierre Forestier, Maison Hexacore, Buthiers, 1954
Abbild W15/16—12: Sarah Meier, Maximilian Quick

Studierende der TU Berlin: Abbild des Raumes.
Historische Interieurs im Modell

← ↑ Alvar Aalto, Villa Mairea, Noormarkku, 1939
Abbild W15/15—06: Elizabeth Beckmann, Catherine Folawiyo, Clara Jereczek

Studierende der TU Berlin: Abbild des Raumes.
Historische Interieurs im Modell

← Ricardo Bofill, La Fábrica, Sant Just Desvern/Barcelona, 1975
Abbild W15/16–01: Niki Apostolopoulou, Johanna Sieberer

↑ Adolf Loos, Villa Müller, Praha, 1930
Abbild W13/14–12, Marlene Bühner, Cassandra Donath

Studierende der TU Berlin: Abbild des Raumes.
Historische Interieurs im Modell

↑ Leonardo Ricci, Casa Ricci, Monterinaldi, 1964
Abbild S16–08: Paul Harries, Ana Richter de Arce, Florian Tropp

→ Charles and Ray Eames, Case Study House N° 8, Los Angeles/California, 1948
Abbild S14–03, Hanna Grabmaier, Julia Henning, Lisa Nagy
→→ Giuseppe Terragni, House for an Artist, Milano 1933
Abbild S16–01: Leonardo Jochim, Lukas Stadelmann, Samuel Yeboa

Students at the TU Berlin: Imaging Spaces.
Models of Historic Interiors

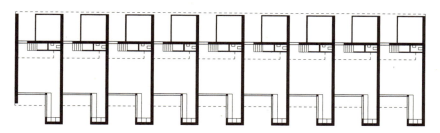

31

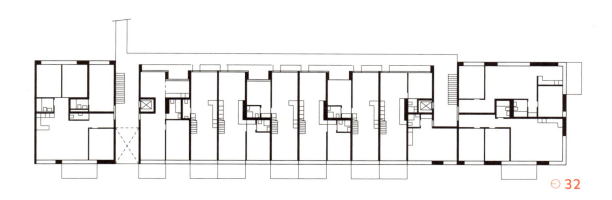

32

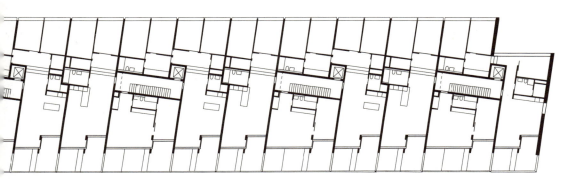

33

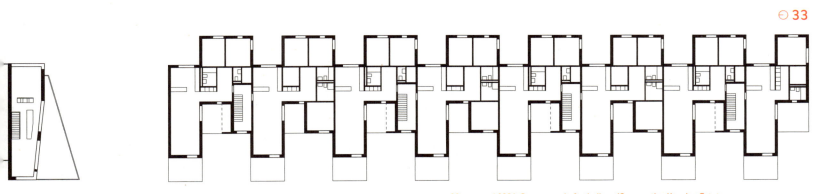

31 pool 0154; Genossenschaftssiedlung/Cooperative Housing Estate, Kronwiesenweg, Zürich-Schwamendingen, 2004

32 pool 0231; Genossenschaftssiedlung/Cooperative Housing Estate, Hunziker Areal, Zürich-Leutschenbach, 2009

33 pool 0007; Genossenschaftssiedlung/Cooperative Housing Estate, Wallisellenstrasse Süd, Zürich-Oerlikon, 1998

pool Architekten: eine Typensammlung.
Regelgeschosse im Massstab 1:500

34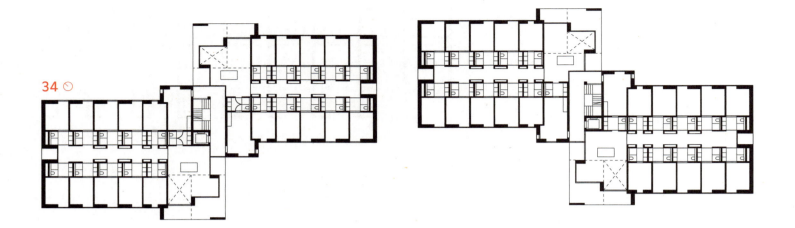

35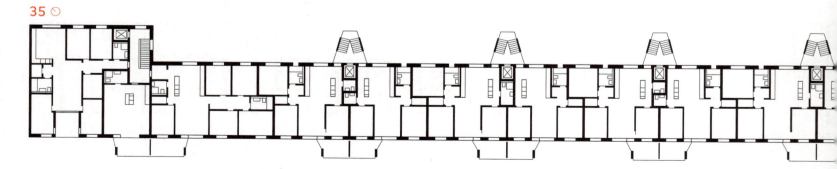

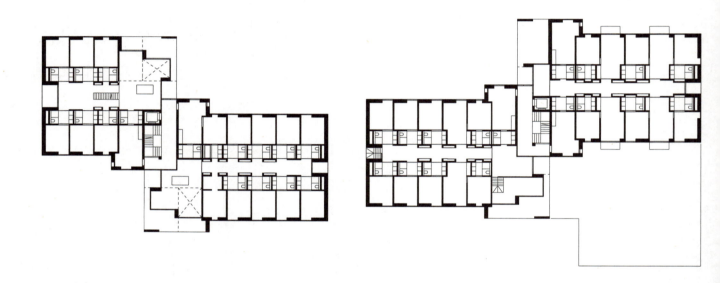

34 pool 0357; Cité internationale du Grand Morillon, Genève, 2017

35 pool 0315; Genossenschaftssiedlung/Cooperative Housing Estate, Glattpark, Opfikon, 2014–2018

pool Architekten: A Type Collection.
Standard Floors on a Scale of 1:500

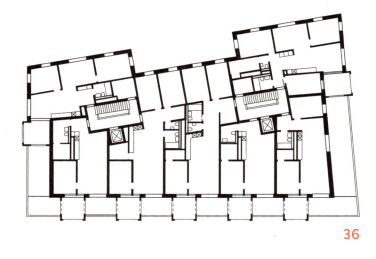

36

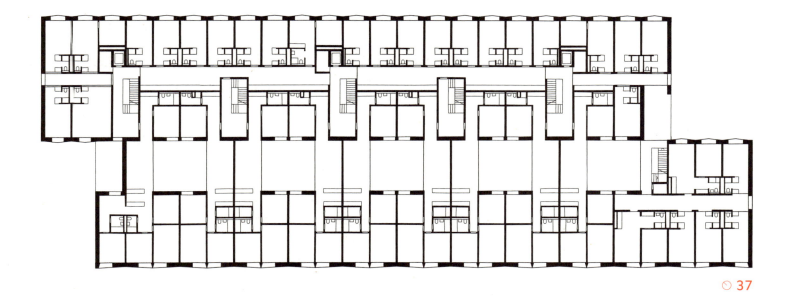

37

36 pool 0243; Genossenschaftliches Wohnhaus/Cooperative Apartment Building, «mehr als wohnen», Haus L, Zürich-Leutschenbach, 2009–2015

37 pool 0309; Studentisches/Student Housing, Wohnen Binz-Ü111, Zürich, 2013

pool Architekten: eine Typensammlung.
Regelgeschosse im Massstab 1:500

38   pool 0159; Wohnüberbauung/Residential Development, Im Blumenfeld, Zürich-Affoltern, 2005–2008
39   pool 0180; Alterswohnungen/Senior Housing Estate, Siedlung Frieden, Zürich-Affoltern, 2006–2013
40   pool 0199; Wohn- und Gewerbeüberbauung/Residential and Commercial Development, Spätzstrasse, Horgen, 2007–2017

pool Architekten: A Type Collection.
Standard Floors on a Scale of 1:500

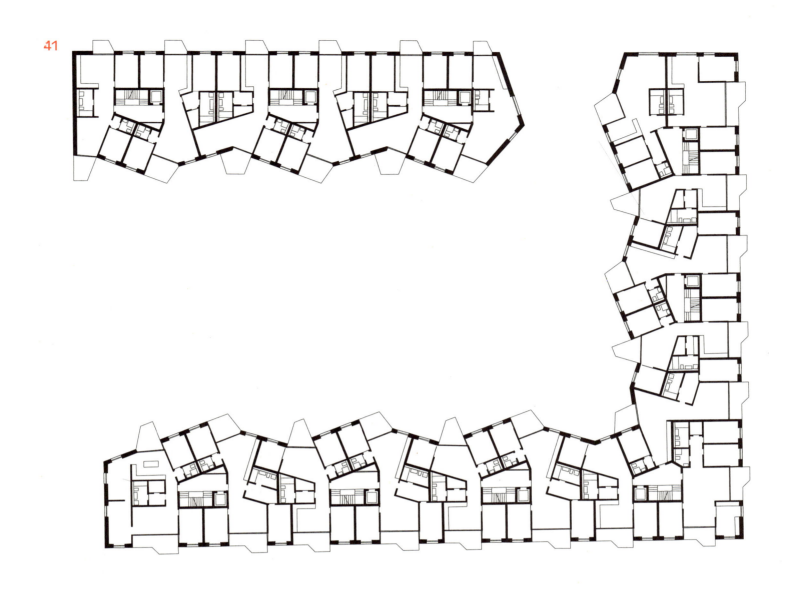

41   pool 0331; Wohnüberbauung/Residential Development, Eggbühl-Areal, Zürich-Seebach, 2014–2020

42   pool 0298; Wohnhochhäuser/Residential High-Rises, Vulcano Areal, Zürich-Altstetten, 2012

pool Architekten: eine Typensammlung.
Regelgeschosse im Massstab 1:500

43

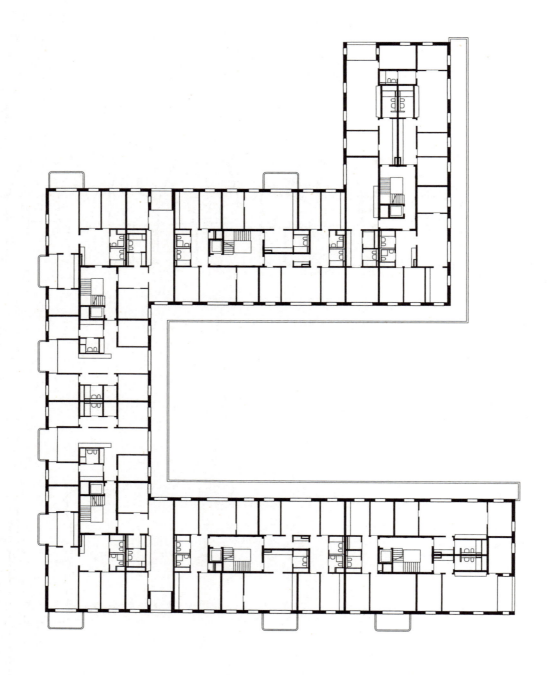

43 pool 0004; Mehrfamilienhaus/Multi-family Dwelling, Kirchdorf, 1998/99

pool Architekten: A Type Collection.
Standard Floors on a Scale of 1:500

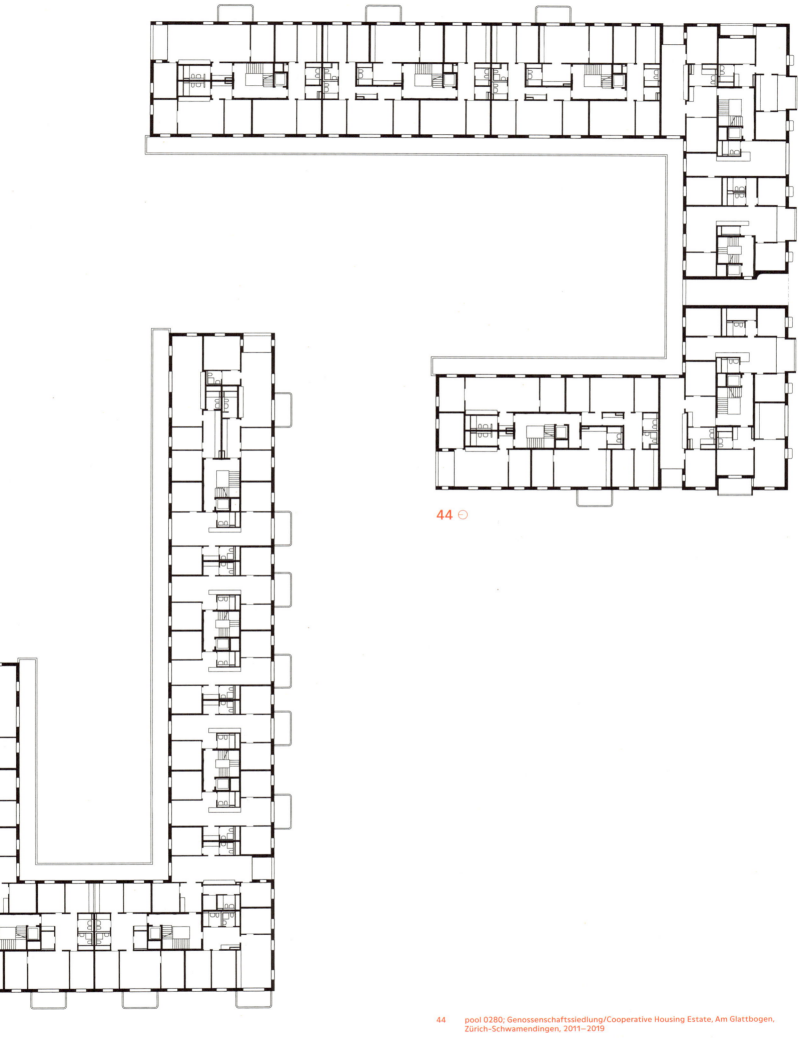

44 pool 0280; Genossenschaftssiedlung/Cooperative Housing Estate, Am Glattbogen, Zürich-Schwamendingen, 2011–2019

pool Architekten: eine Typensammlung.
Regelgeschosse im Massstab 1:500

45

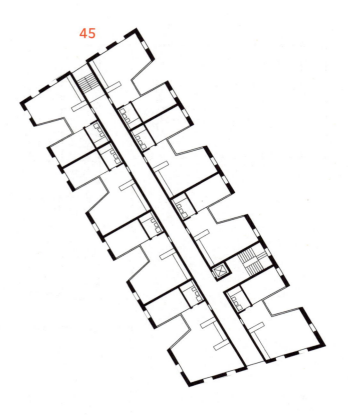
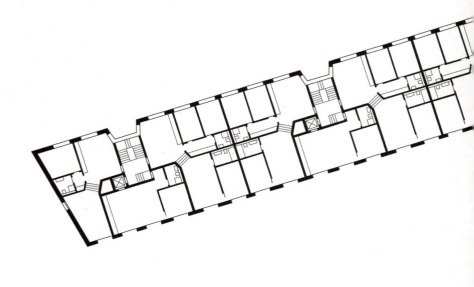

46

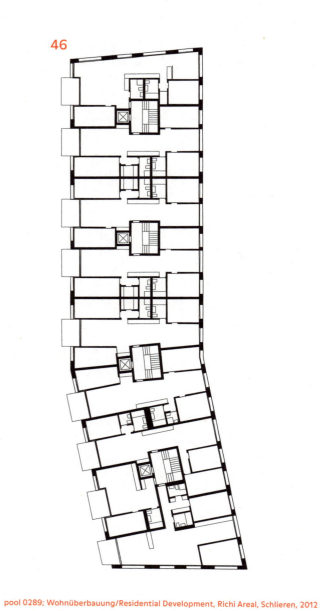
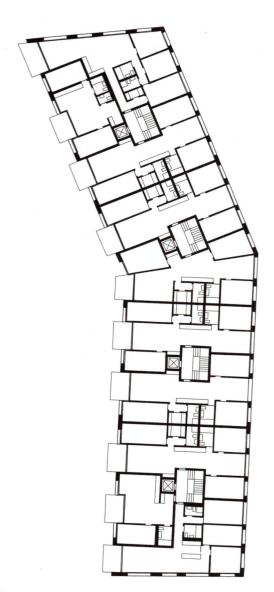

45 pool 0289; Wohnüberbauung/Residential Development, Richi Areal, Schlieren, 2012

46 pool 0251; Genossenschaftssiedlung/Cooperative Housing Estate, Muggenbühl, Zürich-Wollishofen, 2010

pool Architekten: A Type Collection.
Standard Floors on a Scale of 1:500

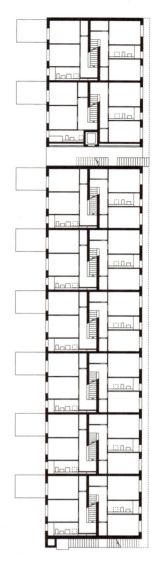

47

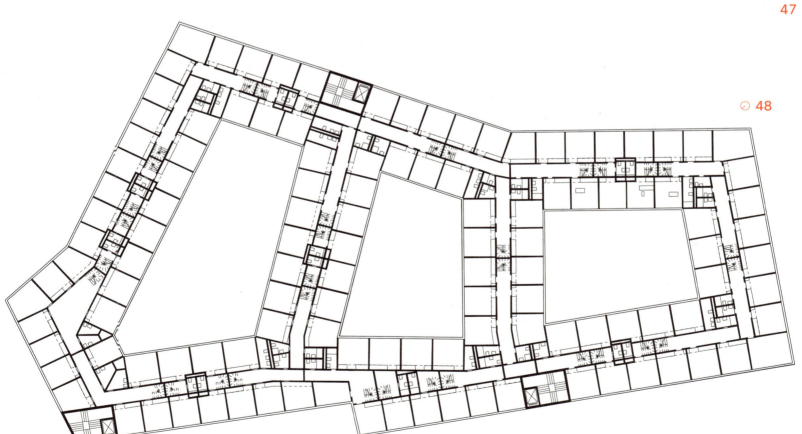

48

47   pool 0239; Genossenschaftsiedlung/Cooperative Housing Estate, Tram-/Funkwiesenstrasse, Zürich-Schwammendingen

48   pool 0025; Siedlung für Studierende/Student Settlement, an der Bülachstrasse, Zürich, 1999

pool Architekten: eine Typensammlung.
Regelgeschosse im Massstab 1:500

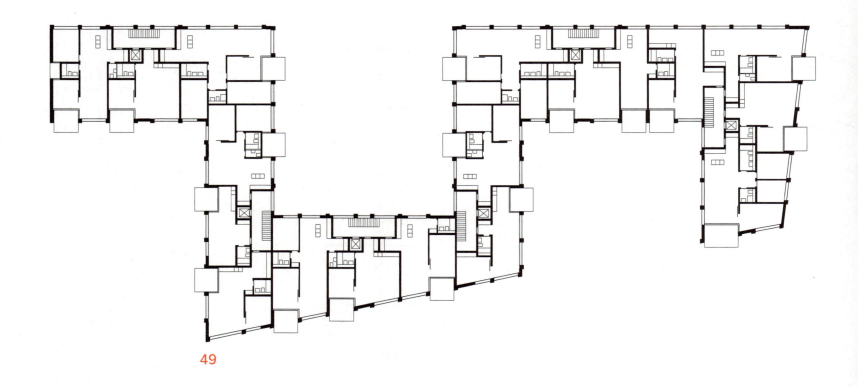

49

50

49 pool 0178; Wohnsiedlung/Housing Estate, Badenerstrasse 707, Zürich-Altstetten, 2006

50 pool 0285; Städtische Siedlung/Municipal Housing Estate, Areal Hornbach, Zürich, 2011

pool Architekten: A Type Collection.
Standard Floors on a Scale of 1:500

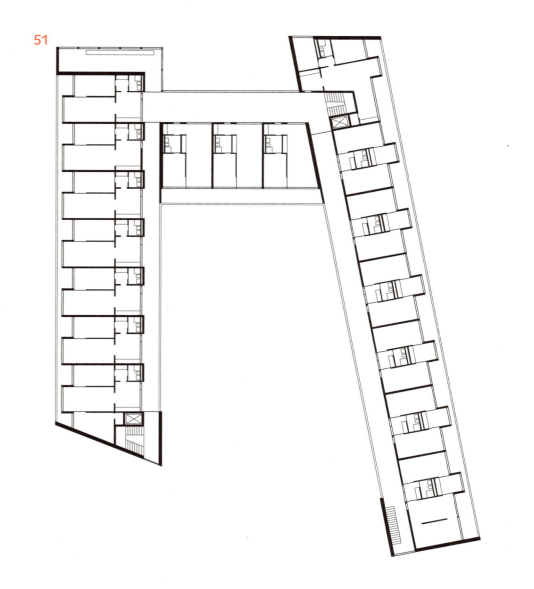

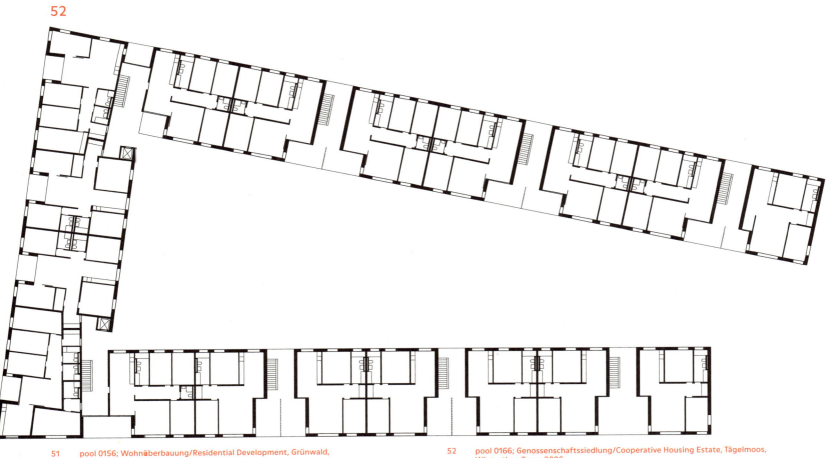

51 pool 0156; Wohnüberbauung/Residential Development, Grünwald, Zürich-Höngg, 2005

52 pool 0166; Genossenschaftssiedlung/Cooperative Housing Estate, Tägelmoos, Winterthur-Seen, 2006

pool Architekten: eine Typensammlung.
Regelgeschosse im Massstab 1:500

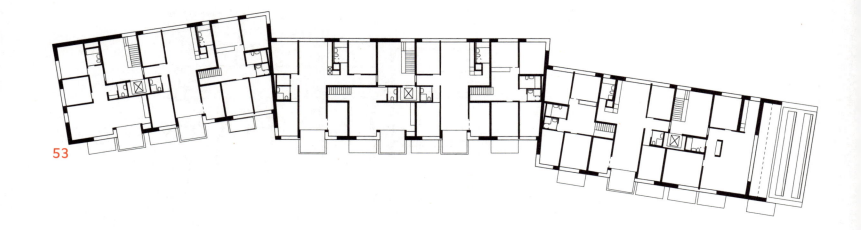
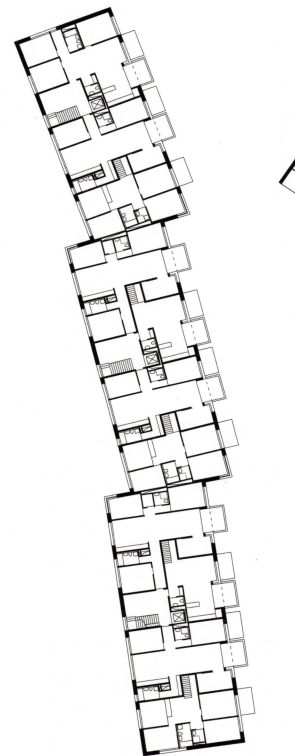
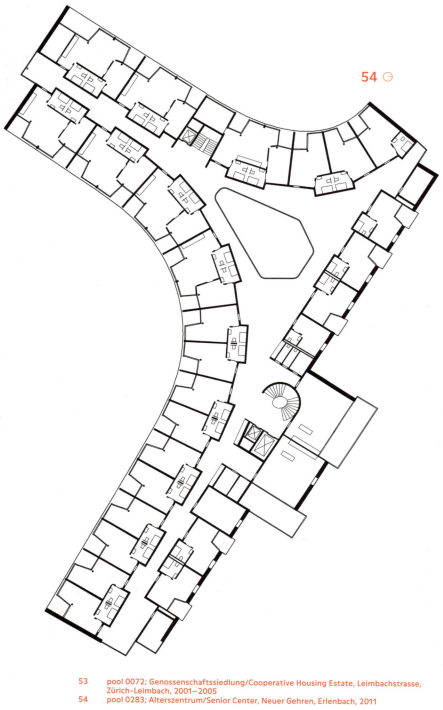

53　　pool 0072; Genossenschaftssiedlung/Cooperative Housing Estate, Leimbachstrasse, Zürich-Leimbach, 2001–2005
54　　pool 0283; Alterszentrum/Senior Center, Neuer Gehren, Erlenbach, 2011

pool Architekten: A Type Collection.
Standard Floors on a Scale of 1:500

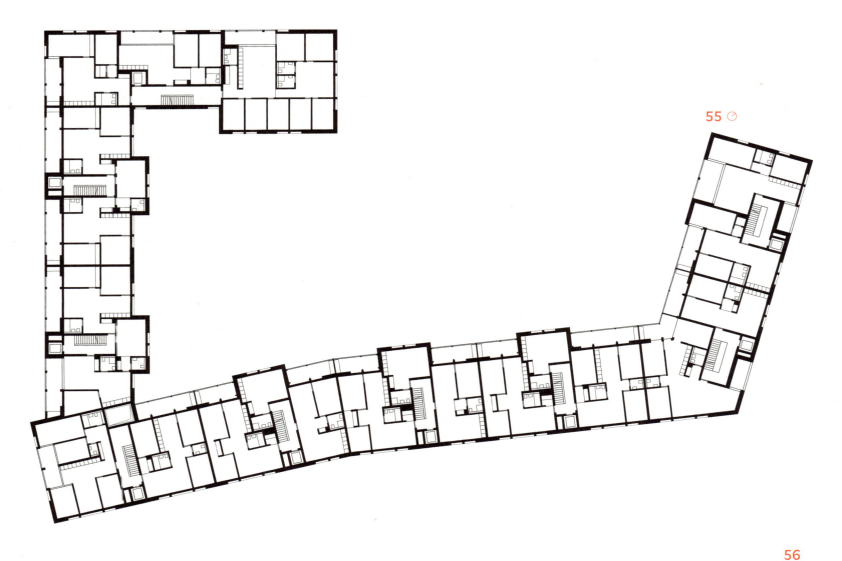

55

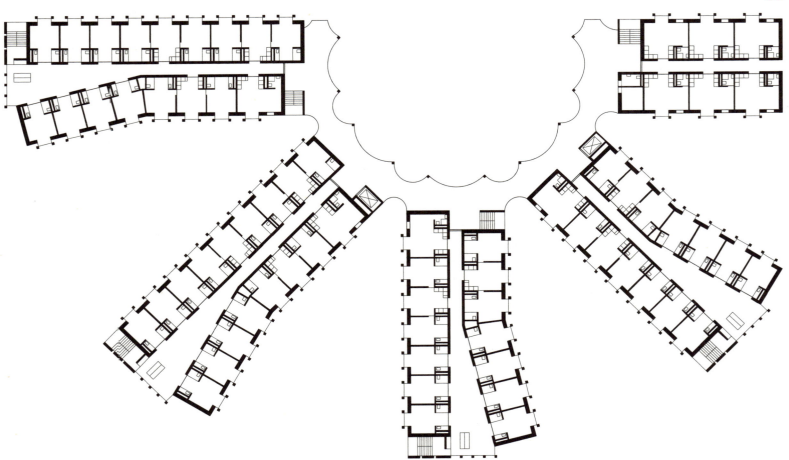

56

55 pool 0364; Gemeinnütziger Wohnungsbau/Nonprofit Residential Construction, Guggach Areal III, Zürich-Oerlikon, 2018

56 pool 0291; Wohnsiedlung für Studierende/Housing Estate for Students, ETH, Zürich-Hönggerberg, 2012

pool Architekten: eine Typensammlung.
Regelgeschosse im Massstab 1:500

57

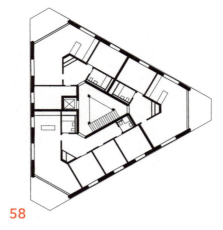

58

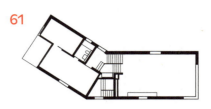

61

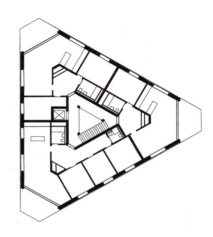

59

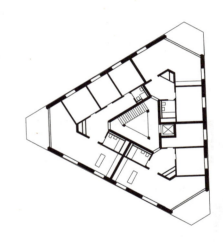

60

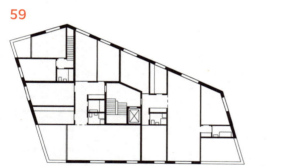

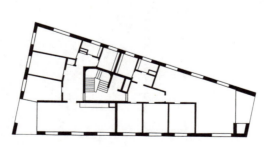

62

57	pool 0079; Haus Buscaglia, Altendorf, 2001–2003
58	pool 0177; Genossenschaftssiedlung/Cooperative Housing Estate, Im Sydefädeli, Häuser/Buildings, A–G, Zürich-Wipkingen, 2006–2016
59	pool 0172; Wohnhaus/Apartment Building, auf der Forch, Küsnacht, 2006
60	pool 0177; Genossenschaftssiedlung/Cooperative Housing Estate, Im Sydefädeli, Häuser/Buildings U–V, Zürich-Wipkingen, 2006–2016
61	pool 0203; Dreifamilienhaus/Three-Family House, Im Dörfli, Oberrieden, 2007–2014
62	pool 0269; Genossenschaftssiedlung/Cooperative Housing Estate, Toblerstrasse, Zürich-Fluntern, 2011

pool Architekten: A Type Collection.
Standard Floors on a Scale of 1:500

63

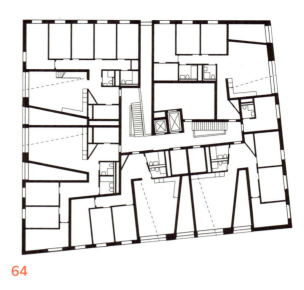

64

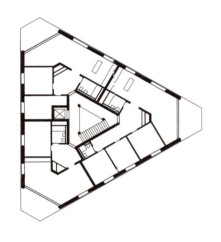

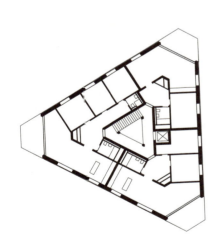

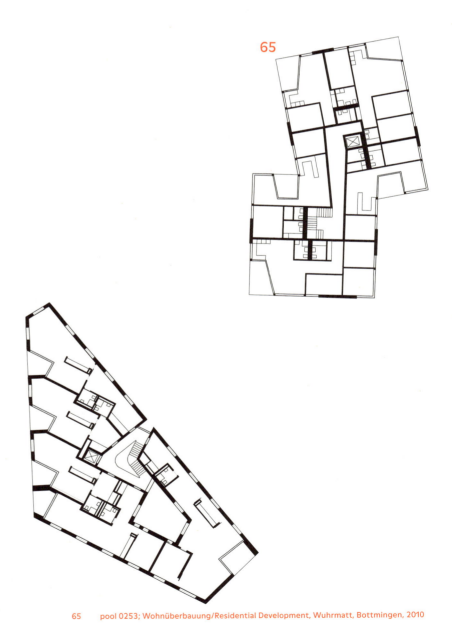

65

63   pool 0151; Genossenschaftssiedlung/Cooperative Housing Estate, Sihlbogen, Zürich-Leimbach, 2005
64   pool 0243; Genossenschaftliches Wohnhaus/Cooperative Apartment Building, «mehr als wohnen», Haus G, Zürich-Leutschenbach, 2009–2015
65   pool 0253; Wohnüberbauung/Residential Development, Wuhrmatt, Bottmingen, 2010

pool Architekten: eine Typensammlung.
Regelgeschosse im Massstab 1:500

93

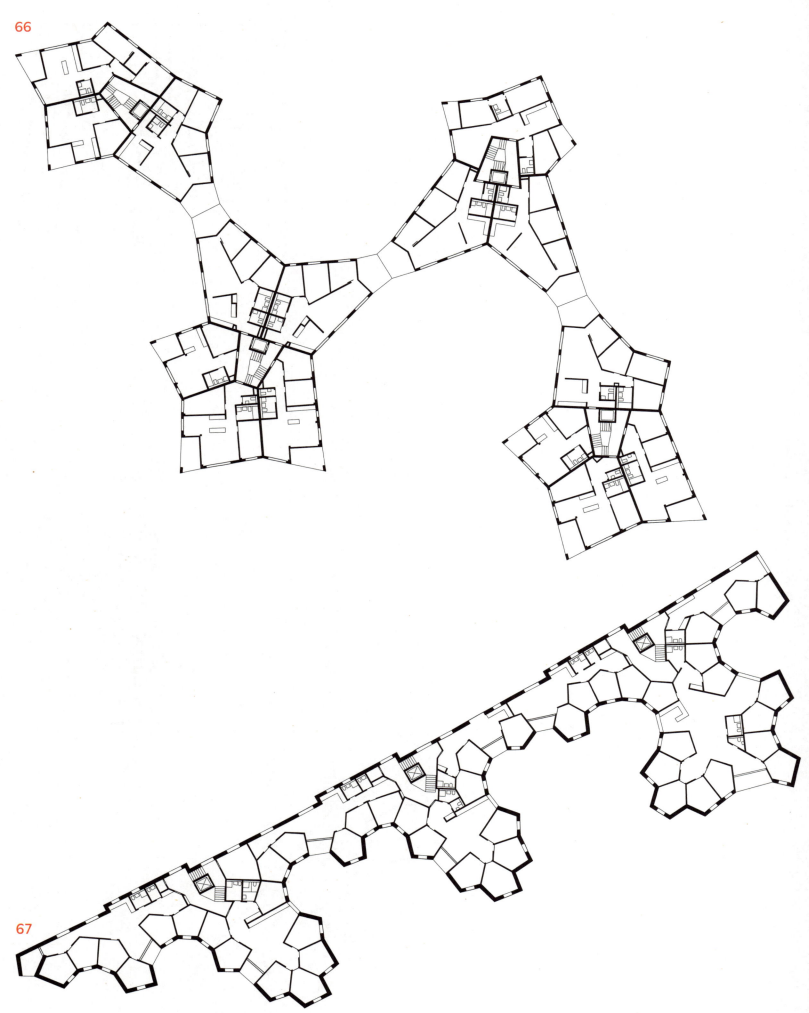

66 pool 0340; Wohnüberbauung/Residential Development, Rütistrasse, Adliswil, 2015
67 pool 0319; Studentisches Wohnen/Student Residences, Areal Rosengarten, Zürich-Wipkingen, 2014

pool Architekten: A Type Collection.
Standard Floors on a Scale of 1:500

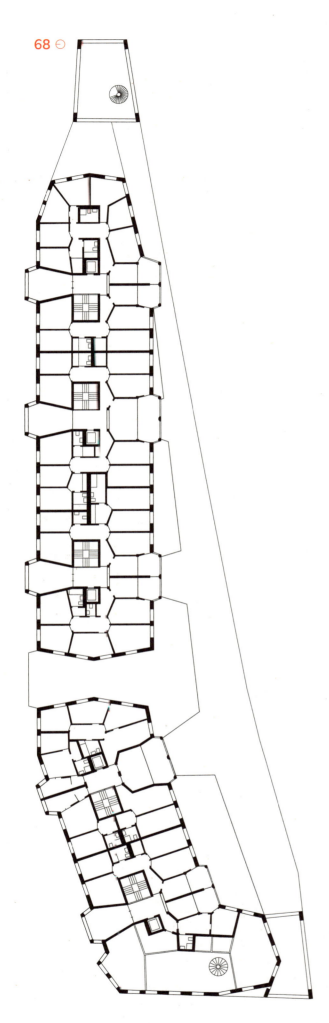
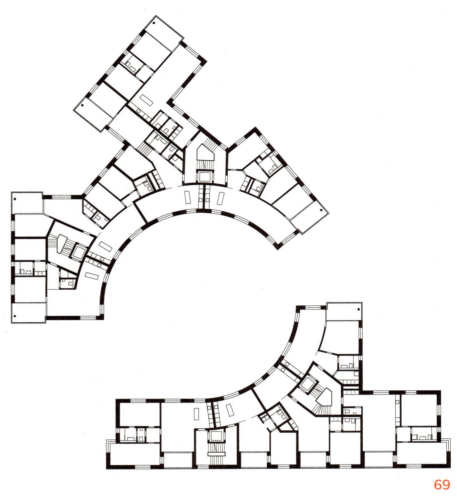
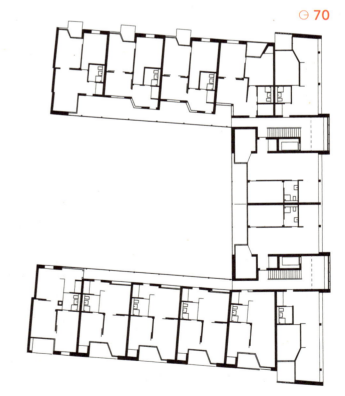

68	pool 0335; Genossenschaftssiedlung/Cooperative Housing Estate, Zollhaus, Zürich, 2015
69	pool 0365; Ersatzneubau/Replacement Construction, Parkend Fonds, Zürich-Hirslanden, 2018
70	pool 0323; Alterswohnen/Senior Housing, Erikastrasse, Zürich, 2014

pool Architekten: eine Typensammlung.
Regelgeschosse im Massstab 1:500

95

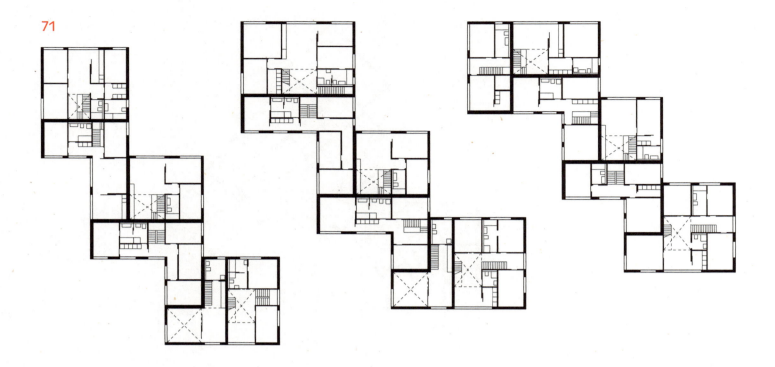

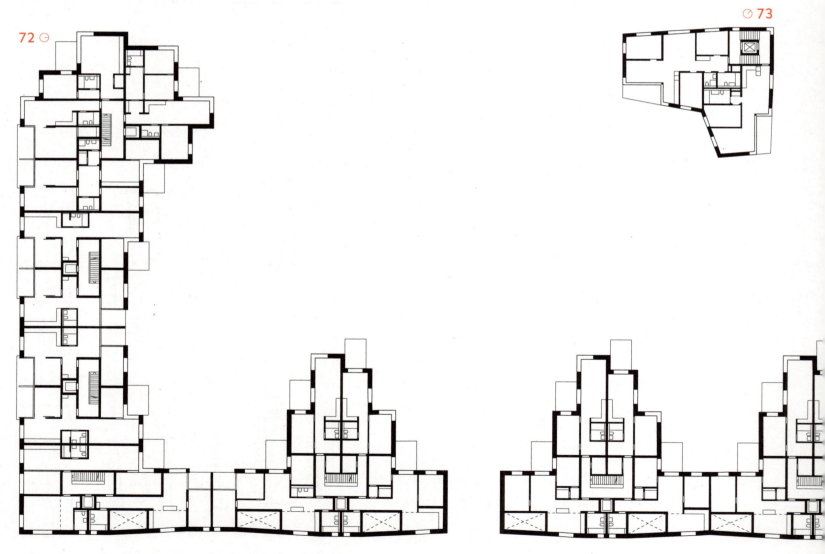

71 pool 0216; Wohnüberbauung/Residential Development, Laufenburg, Aargau, 2008
72 pool 0355; Wohnüberbauung/Residential Development, Manegg, Zürich-Manegg, 2017
73 pool 0276; Mehrfamilienhaus/Multifamily Dwelling, Kosakenweg, Zürich-Oerlikon, 2010–2014

pool Architekten: A Type Collection.
Standard Floors on a Scale of 1:500

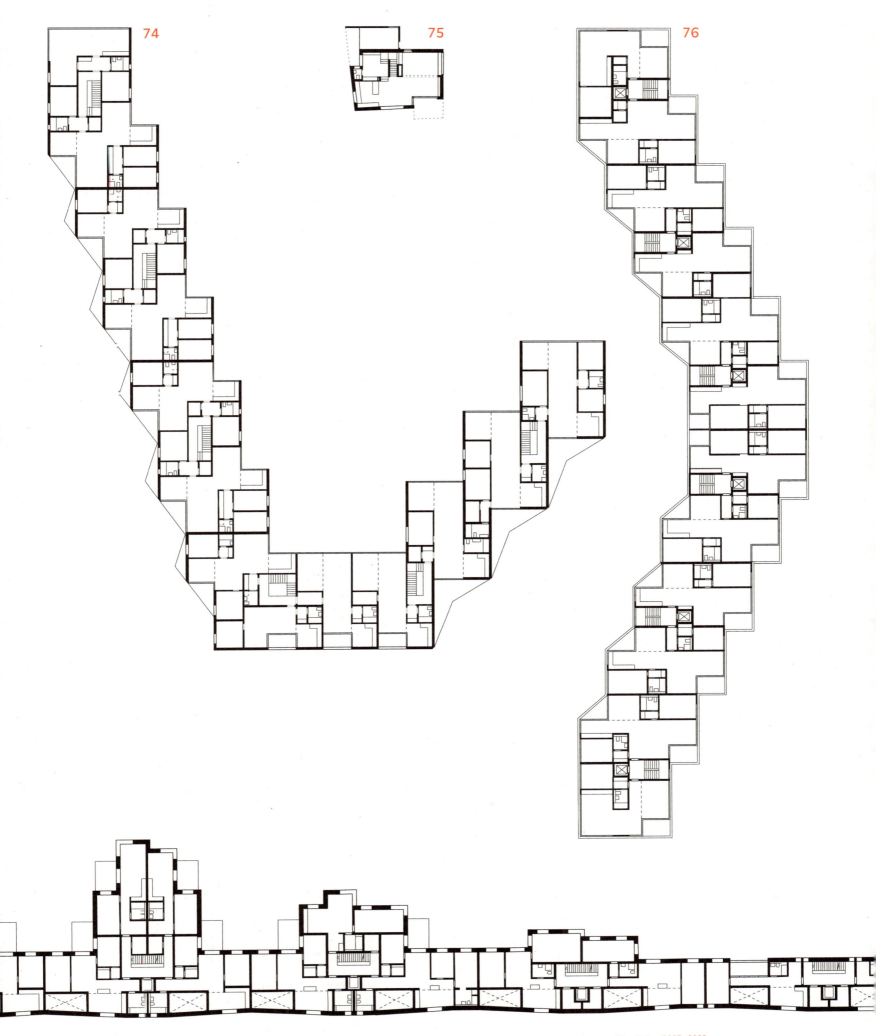

74 pool 0128; Genossenschaftssiedlung/Cooperative Housing Estate, Hofgarten, Zürich-Leimbach, 2004
75 pool 0201; Haus an der Bickelstrasse, Oberrieden, 2007–2009
76 pool 0225; Wohnüberbauung/Residential Development, Zellweger Park, Uster, 2008

pool Architekten: eine Typensammlung.
Regelgeschosse im Massstab 1:500

77

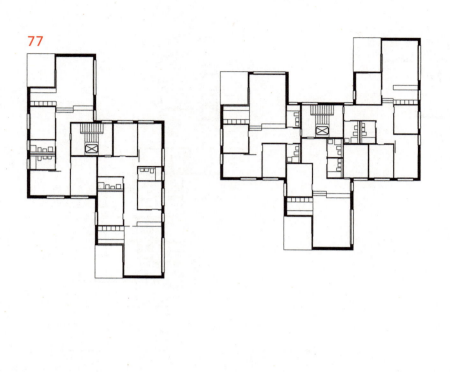

80

78

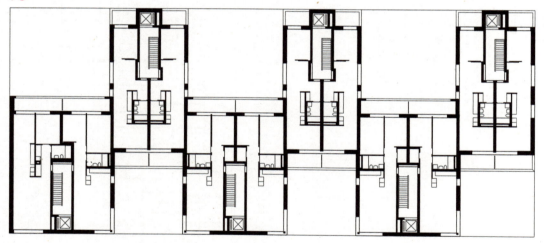

79

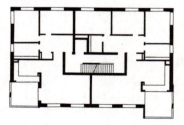 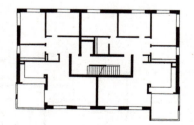 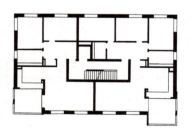

77 pool 0190; Wohnüberbauung/Residential Development, Dammstrasse, Horgen, 2007
78 pool 0176; Genossenschaftliches Wohn- und Geschäftshaus/Cooperative Residential and Commercial Building, Badenerstrasse, Zürich, 2006–2010
79 pool 0177; Genossenschaftssiedlung/Cooperative Housing Estate, Im Sydefädeli, Häuser/Buildings X, Y, Z, Zürich-Wipkingen, 2006–2016
80 pool 0163; Genossenschaftssiedlung/Cooperative Housing Estate, Triemli, Zürich, 2005

**pool Architekten: A Type Collection.
Standard Floors on a Scale of 1:500**

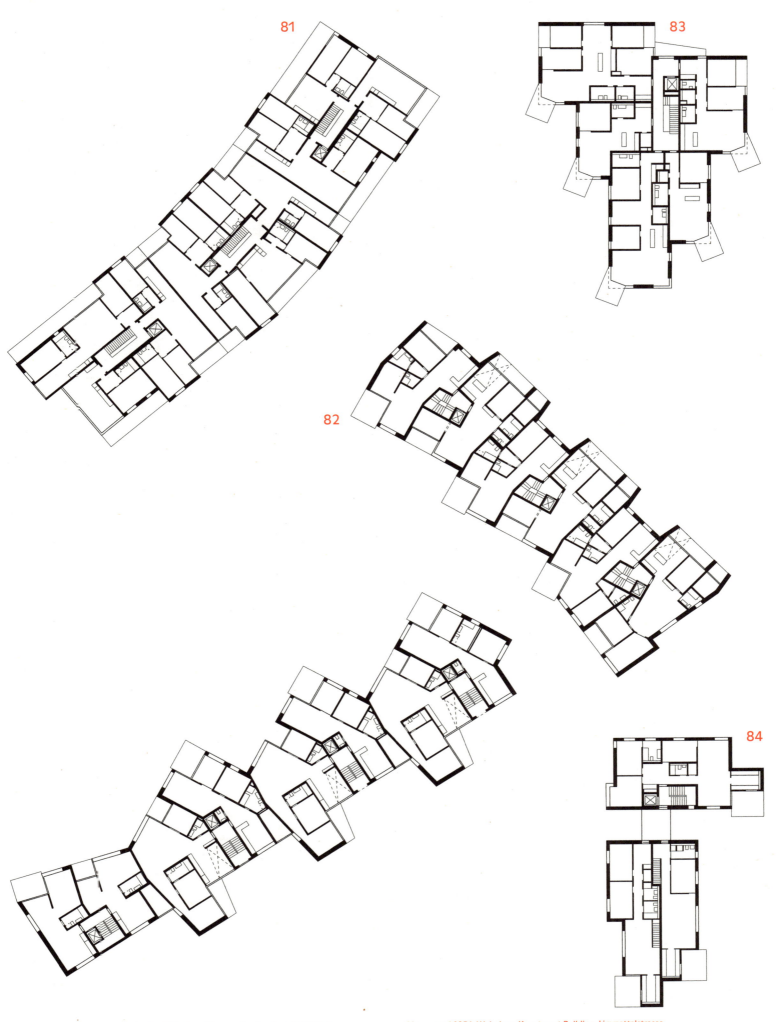

81   pool 0274; Genossenschaftliches Wohnhaus/Cooperative Apartment Building, Seestrasse, Meilen, 2010
82   pool 0282; Wohnüberbauung/Residential Development, Landolt-Areal, Zürich, 2011
83   pool 0254; Wohnhaus/Apartment Building, Limmattalstrasse, Zürich-Höngg, 2010—2013
84   pool 0229; Wohnhaus/Apartment Building, Laur-Park, Brugg, 2009—2012

pool Architekten: eine Typensammlung.
Regelgeschosse im Massstab 1:500

85

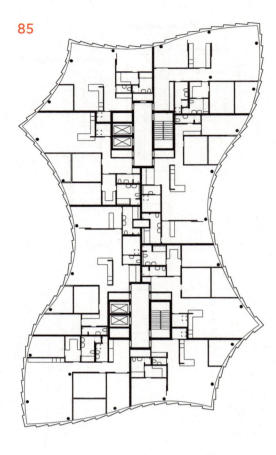

86

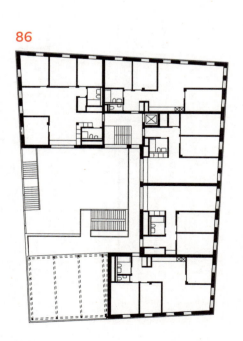

87

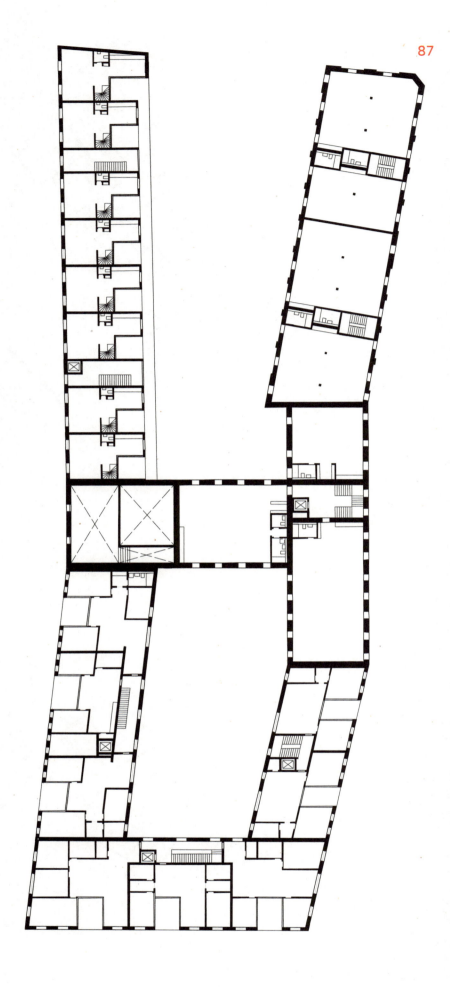

85   pool 0200; Hochhaus/High-Rise, Hardturm-Areal, Zürich, 2007
86   pool 0243; Genossenschaftliches Wohnhaus/Cooperative Apartment Building, «mehr als wohnen», Haus J, Zürich-Leutschenbach, 2009–2015
87   pool 0237; Wohnsiedlung/Residential Development, Areal Teiggi, Kriens, 2009

**pool Architekten: A Type Collection.
Standard Floors on a Scale of 1:500**

←

pool Architekten:
eine Typensammlung.
Regelgeschosse
im Massstab 1:500

pool Architekten:
A Type Collection.
Standard Floors
on a Scale of 1:500

Utopien und Erfindungen   Utopias and Inventions

"How do you grasp something that does not (yet) exist? How is a scenario for the future and for an alternative present to be invented or rendered plausible? The answer is quite simple: You must tell a story. And as banal as this answer appears at first glance, it actually is not, for to tell a good story is by no means banal."[1]

For the science journalist and author Beat Glogger, a literary narrative must be bound up with a certain legality—but not, to be sure, with reality—in order to become plausible. And in particular with a fictional text, we need to investigate its "effect or aftereffect" if it is to retain its relevance. "One of the most effective methods of narration," we read in the conclusion of his essay "Fakten holen die Fiktion ins Leben" (Facts bring Fiction to Life), "consists of maintaining a maximal proximity between fiction and fact. The closer poetry comes to truth, the more the author's fantasy shapes the reader's reality. Facts drag fiction into real life." The transfer of this principle to the activity of architects is well worth considering. In planning a future reality we automatically find ourselves engaging in fictional thought, and—unlike literature—our connection to reality is compulsory rather than optional. Yet not unlike the author, we find ourselves in a ceaseless "skeptical confrontation" with progress. This kind of thinking is a "method for modeling the future."

The architect as storyteller is a somewhat unconventional angle, yet seems thoroughly appropriate provided we regard ourselves as seismographs of societal ruptures and as mediators between today and tomorrow. The urban context in particular requires spaces that accommodate alternative life models which cannot be easily brought into harmony with existing built structures or patterns of thought. To fulfill these needs, concepts need to be found that are capable of breaking with social convention while at the same time generating links to the familiar and the habitual. Only by linking together the past, the present, and the future can our professional activities transfer Utopia as an imaginary place in an indeterminate temporality into the here and now.

Architecture and Utopia

The description of an ideal form of collective human life corresponds to a primary need on the part of the thinking and philosophizing individual who cannot simply satisfy himself with a fate that is ordained by divine or mundane powers. Familiar political utopias such as Plato's *Republic* (367 BCE), Thomas More's *Utopia* (1516) →[1], Francis Bacon's *Nova Atlantis* (1626), and William Morris's *News from Nowhere* (1891) →[2] are devoted to a generalized future. Typically, the settings for such works are "non-places" (ou-topos) in the genuine sense. These "new societies" are situated in foreign places that lack any specific localization, on

---

1   Beat Glogger, "Fakten holen die Fiktion ins Leben," *Archäologie der Zukunft*, ed. Rainer Egloff, Gerd Folkers, Matthias Michel, Zurich 2006, pp. 91–97.

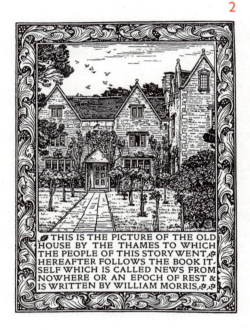

1   Thomas Morus, *Utopia,* Titelholzschnitt der Ausgabe von 1516
2   William Morris, *News from Nowhere,* Titelblatt mit Kelmscott Manor, Kelmscott Press, 1893
3   Charles Fourier, Phalanstère, Perspektive, 19. Jh.
4   Jean-Baptiste André Godin, Familistère, Guise, 19. Jh.
5   Lucius Burckhardt, *Der Sieg der Guten Form — Erfolge des Werkbunds,* 1982
6   Frank R. Paul, Illustration zu *A Story of the Days to Come* von H.G. Wells, 1928

1   Thomas More, *Utopia,* title woodcut for the edition of 1516
2   William Morris, *News from Nowhere,* title page with Kelmscott Manor, Kelmscott Press, 1893
3   Charles Fourier, Phalanstère, perspective, 19th century
4   Jean-Baptiste André Godin, Familistère, Guise, 19th century
5   Lucius Burckhardt, *Der Sieg der Guten Form — Erfolge des Werkbunds,* 1982
6   Frank R. Paul, illustration to *A Story of Days to Come* by H. G. Wells, 1928

allgemeinen Zukunft. Typischerweise sind die Schauplätze der meisten Werke «Nicht-Orte» (ou-topos) im eigentlichen Sinne. Die «neuen Gesellschaften» werden in nicht genauer lokalisierten fernen Welten, auf abgelegenen Inseln oder einfach überall und nirgendwo verortet. Einer ähnlichen Technik der Verschleierung bedienen sich neuere Zukunftsromane, deren Geschichten sich in zeitlichen oder räumlichen Parallelwelten entwickeln. Beschreibt die utopische Literatur bis Ende des 19. Jahrhunderts vorwiegend die harmonische Idealgesellschaft (Utopie), wird H. G. Wells mit *A Story of the Days to Come* (1899) → zu einem der ersten Vertreter der Anti-Utopie (Dystopie). Über die Darstellung endzeitlicher Schreckensherrschaften oder gesellschaftlicher Abwärtsspiralen versucht die Literatur des 20. Jahrhunderts die negativen Auswirkungen der industrialisierten Gesellschaft und die Erfahrungen mit Totalitarismus zu verarbeiten. «Eine Geschichte ist dann zu Ende gedacht, wenn sie ihre schlimmstmögliche Wendung genommen hat.»[2] Friedrich Dürrenmatts Dramentheorie «21 Punkte zu den Physikern» sucht das Groteske. Je paradoxer sich die Handlung entwickelt, umso mehr treten die Auswirkungen der Geschichte auf alle Menschen hervor, denn «im Paradoxen erscheint die Wirklichkeit». Instrumentiert der Autor bis zum Eintreten der Katastrophe den Zufall, um mit dramaturgischem Nervenkitzel den Zuschauer mit einer fiktiven Realität zu konfrontieren und zu stimulieren, setzen Architekten und Urbanisten in ihrem Entwurfsnarrativ alles daran, die Entwicklung zu einem zumindest intendierten positiven Ausgang zu bewegen. Die erhoffte utopische und die befürchtete dystopische Zukunftsfantasie arbeiten dabei Hand in Hand und treiben den kreativen Motor des «Zukunftsplaners» an.

Um die Wirkungsbereiche des Utopischen zu umreissen, unterscheidet die Literaturwissenschaftlerin Barbara Ventarola in der Einleitung zu ihrer Publikation *Literarische Stadtutopien zwischen totalitärer Gewalt und Ästhetisierung*[3] drei Bewusstseinsstufen, mit je unterscheidbaren Realitätsebenen, auf die sie Einfluss nehmen:

1   Das utopische Bewusstsein, das uns befähigt, Berührungspunkte zwischen Traum und Leben zu erkennen und unsere Fantasie über ein experimentelles, spielerisches Moment von der Pragmatik der Wirklichkeit abzugrenzen.

2   Die literarische Utopie, in der das utopische Bewusstsein in Worten materialisiert wird, ästhetische Form erhält und zu konkreten Entwürfen gerinnt, die von einem Publikum antizipiert werden wollen.

3   Die reale Utopie, die konkrete lebensweltliche Versuche der Umsetzung beinhaltet. Das Spektrum liegt hier zwischen Alternativvorschlägen für Lebensmodelle mit konstruktiver, zukunftsgestaltender Kraft und dem Umkippen in Vollkommenheitsideale mit totalitärer Tendenz.

remote islands, or instead simply everywhere or nowhere. A similar technique of masking is exploited by more recent futuristic novels, whose narratives unfold in worlds that are temporarily or spatially parallel to ours. Up until the late nineteenth century, utopian literature was devoted mainly to conjuring the harmonious ideal society. With his novel *A Story of the Days to Come* (1899) →, H. G. Wells became one of the first exponents of an anti-Utopia (dystopia). Through depictions of apocalyptic reigns of terror or spirals of societal decline, twentieth century literature works through the negative impact of industrial society and the experience of totalitarianism. "A history has been thought through to the end only when things have taken the worst possible turn,"[2] says Friedrich Dürrenmatt whose dramatic theory *21 Points to the Physicists* seeks out the grotesque. The more paradoxical the plot development, the more the impact of a story on all human individuals emerges, for "reality appears in paradoxes." If the author instrumentalizes chance up until the emergence of the catastrophe in order to confront the audience with, and to simulate a fictive reality through, dramaturgical thrills, then architects and urbanists exploit everything in their design narratives in order to propel a development toward an outcome that is at least positive in intent. The hoped for and feared fantasies of the future therefore work hand-in-hand, driving the creative motor of the "planners of the future."

In the introduction to her publication *Literarische Stadtutopien zwischen totalitärer Gewalt und Ästhetisierung* (Literary urban utopias between totalitarian violence and aestheticization),[3] Barbara Ventarola distinguishes three levels of consciousness in order to circumscribe the sphere of action of the utopian. Each level corresponds to a different level of reality on which it exercises influence:

1   Utopian consciousness, which allows us to recognize points of contact between dream and real life, and—via an experimental, playful moment—to delimit our fantasies from the pragmatism of reality.

2   Literary utopia, where the utopian consciousness is materialized in words; where it acquires aesthetic form and solidifies into concrete designs that will hopefully be anticipated by a public.

3   Real utopia, which involves concrete attempts at realization in actual lived-in environments. Here, the spectrum extends from alternative proposals for models of life having a constructive force that is capable of shaping the future, all the way to a tipping over toward ideals of perfectibility with totalitarian tendencies.

---

2   Friedrich Dürrenmatt, «21 Punkte zu den Physikern», in: ders., *Die Physiker*, Zürich 1962
3   Barbara Ventarola (Hrsg.), *Literarische Stadtutopien zwischen totalitärer Gewalt und Ästhetisierung*, München 2011

2   Friedrich Dürrenmatt, "21 Punkte zu den Physikern," idem, *Die Physiker*, Zurich 1962.
3   Barbara Ventarola (ed.), *Literarische Stadtutopien zwischen totalitärer Gewalt und Ästhetisierung*, Munich 2011.

In architecture, utopain consciousness corresponds to an earlier conceptual and design phase during which fantasies that are remote from reality maintain the upper hand, without these ever arriving in the public sphere. The second level, literary utopia, calls for the concretization of that which has been conceived, but also somewhat more pluckiness on the part of the author who now actively exposes himself and boldly attempts to persuade humanity of his ideas. The third level, real utopia, is the most strenuous. To realize models that transgress social conventions, forms of sponsorship that are both fearless and receptive to idealism are required. An early example of a utopian project that was formulated in words and drawings, and which attained at least partial realization, and which was effective on all three levels of reality, is the *phalanstère* → 3 of Charles Fourier (1772—1836). The design, reminiscent of the palace complex at Versailles, is well known to architects. Less present in our awareness is the socialist form of organization upon which it was based, along with Fourier's fantastical vision of the future.

The depicted architectural complex was meant to accommodate a so-called "phalanx," a community of 1,620 members. Through an elaborate form of social organization, the requirements of the residents would remain in balance with the available products and services. The required activities would be engaged in voluntarily. The striven-for harmony is attained via spontaneous self-organization. The individual does what he likes, therefore satisfying existing needs, which are complementary to what is on offer. Fourier's description represents a kind of machinery for fulfilling wishes, one that satisfies every conceivable desire. Tillmann Reitz, who composed the analysis cited here, arrived at the critical conclusion that contemporary consumer society, with all of its demands, comes alarmingly close to a Fourierian land of milk and honey.[4] Its inventor, on the other hand, conceived of a social development that would extend through eight world ages and would culminate in the complete reshaping of the Earth, and finally, in a departure for other planets. Through the implementation of his ideas, Fourier believed that humanity stood at the dawn of 40,000 years of life in perfect harmony. Only modified versions of the concept ultimately attained realization, for example the *familistère* in Guise → 4, created by the manufacturer and socialist Jean-Baptiste André Godin (1817—1888). This reality may seem modest when compared to a fantasized utopia; nonetheless, Fourier thereby initiated the first social housing developments.

[4] Tilman Reitz, "Utopie, Spiel, Menschenmaschine. Charles Fourier und die Avantgarden," *Kunst, Spektakel und Revolution* 2, Hamburg 2011.

The Utopian Hope of Modernism

During the twentieth century, the most heterogeneous movements invoked Fourier. From the avant-garde to the Situationists of the 1960s, the connection between art and life was celebrated based on the principle "that no form of life and no revolt that fails to make us happy in the here and now is acceptable."[5] Asserted again and again, however, has been a skepticism around the feasibility of particular architectural utopias, a skepticism that was in the end linked to the realization that not every formal language that appears progressive contains future-oriented content.

Lucius Burckhardt repeatedly criticized the "utopian" hope of modernism for the unfolding of socially transformative effects via design. In his essay *Städtebauliche Utopie — Was verhindert ihre Verwirklichung* (Urbanistic Utopias—What Prevents Their Realization) of 1970, he remarked that even in the best instances, extraordinary realizations are only avant-garde on the formal level, but can never be regarded as utopian projects in a social sense.[6] For Burckhardt, the 1960s—the decade of utopias—culminated in the realization that utopian designs have not failed as a result of their technological infeasibility, but instead following the incapability of government to make the necessary decisions. According to him, utopias are utopian because it is utopian to abstract from the mechanisms that are capable of decision-making. The complexity of the grievances that are to be combated compels the architect to adopt simplifying tactics in the search for solutions, hence arriving at projects that can be communicated publicly. Burckhardt describes the problematical constellation between architects, politicians, and voters within which projects are torn out of their context and become political models that are capable of being brought to successful—that is, speedy and economical—realization. In this situation, he perceives the reason why urbanistic utopias are virtually incapable of solving contemporary problems, and why for the most part such constructive measures do not eliminate grievances, but instead only displace them or even create new ones. Up until the present, this incisive critique has lost none of its relevance.

In an essay about the *Wert und Sinn städtebaulicher Utopien* (Value and Meaning of Urbanistic Utopias), Burkhardt also critiques the technocratic character of contemporary utopias, which he considers grounded in the functionalists' way of thinking of modernism.[7] A "clean solution" is always aimed for. This kind of approach, he argues, leads to isolated realizations that are sealed off from many influential factors. He closes with the assertion that utopias are not to be understood as appeals for implementation, but instead as cries of despair on the part of designers through

---

5 Ibid.
6 Lucius Burckhardt, "Städtebauliche Utopien - Was hindert ihre Verwirklichung?" ,1970, http://www.lucius-burckhardt.org/Deutsch/Texte/Lucius_Burckhardt.html
7 Lucius Burckhardt, "Wert und Sinn städtebaulicher Utopien," *Wer Plant die Planung? Architektur, Politik und Mensch*, Berlin 2004.

Following his diagnosis of this "failure of utopias," Burckhardt tends to establish an altered understanding of the distribution of roles between the architect and society. Under existing preconditions, he believes, we must attempt to begin an "unrestrained and open discussion involving all participants and all those affected."⁹

For Manfredo Tafuri as well, the history of architecture is an open arena for debate between practice and theory, ideology, and critique. He criticizes the rationalism of his contemporary Aldo Rossi, who opposed an architecture that exists on a purely morphological level to the "commercial demon" of modern development. Tafuri regards such a pedantic "utopia of form," which is expected to supersede a "utopia of politics," as mysticism.¹⁰ Equally harsh is his judgment of the representatives of the avant-garde, for whom the utopian substance of modernity still exists only as formalism, and is perpetuated on the surface, bereft of all content.

In his publication *Progetto e Utopia* (Project and Utopia, 1973), Tafuri investigates the loss of ideology in architecture.¹¹ While in the past architectural utopias played an important social role as mediators between economic development and society, today this territory is administered directly by capitalism. He refers to this condition as the "death of architecture." →⏎ His charge is that the debate is shaped by an unspoken acceptance of the situation, and by an insistence on rescuing the discipline by means of a retrograde perspective. Emerging in place of an "innovative ideological production" is a "fragmentary recuperation of history."¹² Tafuri takes a stand against an architecture that is devoid of political perspectives and without an ideological attitude. In opposition to this, he favors a "'self-liberation' through the private use of the imagination" of the kind he believes he has discovered in the visions of Archizoom and Gaetano Pesce.¹³

→⏎

---

8 Lucius Burckhardt, "Design Is Invisible" (2012), *Design Is Invisible: Planning, Education, and Society*, Berlin 2012.
9 Burkhardt 1970.
10 Ullrich Schwarz, "Warum so autoritär?," *Die Zeit*, 17/2014.
11 Manfredo Tafuri, *Architecture and Utopia*, London 1976.
12 Niklaus Kuhnert, Juan Rodrugues-Lores: "Bemerkungen zur deutschen Ausgabe von *Progetto e Utopia*," *ARCH+* 38, 1978.
13 Tafuri 1976.

Social Criticism and Ideology

With Hans Widmer, alias p.m.,[14] who became known in Switzerland for his anarchist and anticapitalist project for society, entitled "bolo'bolo"[15] and published in 1983, the aspects of the utopias which have been described above seem to have become united. That is, Fourier's global overthrow of the accepted order through a community that develops in an autarkic fashion; Burckhardt's skepticism with regard to consumption and technology; and Tafuri's conviction that a form of freedom capable of shaping the future could emerge through the conjunction of an ideological-political attitude and individual powers of imagination. Having emerged from the squatter scene of the 1980s and as a pioneer of the new forms of cooperative living in Zurich, p.m. was a co-author of the founding text of *KraftWerk 1*, a building and residential cooperative in Zurich which has initiated and realized building projects based on alternative living concepts, hence substantially influencing other developers, for the past twenty years.

Bolo'bolo offers a sketch of a world community composed of small, autonomous communities *(bolos)* consisting of a few hundred residents *(ibus)*, whose allegiance is defined via shared interests *(nima)*. The invented terms are part of a fictive planned language → 9 . Remote from the "machine mechanisms of money, large-scale industry, and the state," the autarkic "bolos" are based on small-scale production, a barter economy, corporations, and processes of direct democracy. In 1990, in the foreword to the fifth edition of his book, p.m. responded to the minimal impact of his text on immediate reality by posing the question of the social relevance of utopias:

"The idea of bolo'bolo has turned out to be ineffective, things have become even worse[…] [D]isenchanted, we must ask ourselves: Have conditions grown immune to fundamental change? Have utopias finally lost their practical impact? Have we become so reduced, satisfied, and apathetic that we can no longer strive for a different way of life? Are utopias simply a lie by which we live? Are they simply one pole in the spectrum of cynical reason, which informs us that we need utopias in order to better endure everyday life?"[16]

---

[14] Until his retirement, Zurich-born Hans Widmer worked as a teacher and journalist under the pseudonym, p.m., which stands fort the letters that appear most frequently in the Swiss telephone book.
[15] p.m., *bolo'bolo*, 7th. ed., Zurich 2015.
[16] p.m., foreword to the 5th ed. of *bolo'bolo*, http://www.geocities.ws/situ1968/bolo/bolobolo.html.

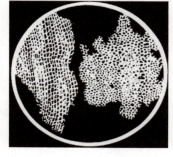

7   Aldo Rossi, L'architecture assassinée, 1974, in Manfredo Tafuri, *Progetto e Utopia*, Bari 1973
8   Gaetano Pesce, Church of Solitude Project, 1974–1977, Museum of Modern Art (MoMA), New York
9   p.m., urban "bolo"; in: p.m., *bolo'bolo*, Zürich 1983
10/11   Genossenschaft Kalkbreite, Müller Sigrist Architekten, Zürich, 2014; community in the interior courtyard and the entrance hall
12   Robert Hooke, *Micrographia*, London, 1665; Kisho Kurokawa, Nakagin Capsule Tower, Tokyo, 1972; Bertrand Goldberg, Marina City, Chicago/Illinois, 1964; in Peter Sloterdijk, "Architekturen des Schaums," in *ARCH+* 169/170, 2004
13   "Espress Yourself" ad campaign, Lavazza, 1994; in Peter Sloterdijk, "Architekturen des Schaums," in *ARCH+* 169/170, 2004

Utopias and Inventions

Das Grandhotel: Prototyp einer Kultur des Teilhabens

p.m.s Utopie will sich nicht als harmlose «Vorstellung eines fantastischen Schlaraffenlandes» verstanden wissen, die blosse Fluchtwelt ohne korrigierende Kraft ist. Sie bietet im Gegenteil «ein Inventar realer technischer, biologischer und sozialer Möglichkeiten. Fantasie und solide Dokumentation, Erfindungslust und praktischer Verstand sollen zusammenkommen und sich vermengen». Der selbstkritisch diagnostizierte Misserfolg hält p.m. jedoch nicht davon ab, die «lächelnde, unzufriedene Mehrheit», der scheinbar jede Sensibilität abtrainiert wurde, immer wieder in Versuchung zu führen.[17] Mit dem Essay «Die Grandhotel-Verschwörung von 2014»[18] veröffentlichte p.m. erneut einen Text, diesmal in der Form einer kurzen, humorvollen literarischen Utopie. Darin wird eine Gesellschaft skizziert, die in Grandhotels lebt. Die Bewohner sind sowohl Gäste des Hotels als auch Anbieter der Services, die ein Hotel im klassischen Sinn ausmachen. Mit «den Salons, Fumoirs, Bibliotheken, Billardzimmer, Ball- und Esssälen» steht dem Bewohner ein räumliches Angebot zur Verfügung, das weit über den gewohnten Komfort einer Standardwohnung hinausgeht. Auch ein Wechsel des Wohnorts ist kein Problem mehr. Die Summe aller Grandhotels erlaubt es der Menschen, von Ort zu Ort zu nomadisieren, ohne etwas mitzunehmen, denn in jedem Grandhotel gibt es schon alles: «Eine Ausleihgarderobe, Bettwäsche ist schon da, Schirme gibt's auch, Zahnbürste ebenfalls. Sogar Unterwäsche S, M, L, XL (nur in Schwarz).» Durch das Zusammendenken von gemeinsam genutzten Räumen wird der Flächenverbrauch pro Kopf von heute gegen 50 auf 22 Quadratmeter reduziert. Auch die Kosten sind niedrig und beinhalten alles, inklusive Reinigung und Unterhalt, die als aufgeteilte Hausarbeit von allen geleistet werden. Und dann sind natürlich auch ein paar Profis nötig, «sagen wir sechs: Köchin, Sommelière, Nanny, Sekretärin, Pianist, Lateinlehrer», die in den Nebenkosten eingerechnet sind. Alle Luxus- und Konsumgüter sind vorhanden. Von ihnen braucht man jedoch viel weniger, da jeder alles verwenden kann. Da die bestehende Infrastruktur genutzt wird, dauert der Umbau der Schweiz nur fünf Jahre. Danach lebt die ganze Bevölkerung in den 14 000 Grandhotels, niemand will mehr anders wohnen. Die Hotelformen sind den existierenden Bau- und Siedlungstypen angepasst: «Blockrandhotel, Hochhaushotel, diffuse Dorfhotels, mit Zwischenbauten verbundene Agglohotels usw. Einzig aus den Einfamilienhaussiedlungen liess sich nichts Vernünftiges machen: Sie wurden vom Zivilschutz abgerissen und wieder in stadtnahes Landwirtschaftsland zurückverwandelt.»

    p.m.s Beitrag schafft es mit einer überraschenden Frische, Gesellschaftskritik mit einem in die Zukunft projizierten Entwurf eines alternativen Zusammenlebens zu kombinieren. Die assoziative Verbindung zum Leben im Grandhotel lässt den Leser in nostalgischen

17 p.m., wie Anm. 16
18 Hans Widmer (alias p.m.), «Die Grandhotel-Verschwörung von 2014», in: *Das Magazin* 36/2014

Utopien und Erfindungen

The Grand Hotel: Prototype of a Sharing Culture

P.m.'s utopia does not want to be understood as a harmless "notion of a fantastical land of milk and honey," an escapist refuge without corrective force. He instead offers "an inventory of real technical, biological, and social possibilities. Fantasy and solid documentation, the delight in invention and practical reason should converge and mingle." This failure, diagnosed here so self-critically, did not, however, prevent p.m. from again and again attempting to lead into temptation the "smiling, dissatisfied majority," which had apparently been weaned from every sensibility.[17] With the essay "Die Grandhotel-Verschwörung von 2014" *(The Grand Hotel Conspiracy of 2014)* p.m. again published a text, this time in the form of a short, humorous literary utopia.[18] In it, he outlines a society that lives in grand hotels. The residents are both guests of the hotel as well as providers of the services which constitute a hotel in the classical sense. With its "salons, fumoirs, libraries, the billiard rooms, ballrooms, and dining rooms," it makes spatial amenities available to the occupants which goes far beyond the habitual comforts of a standard residence. Nor is a change of residence a problem any longer. The sum of all grand hotels allow people to move from place to place as nomads without taking anything with them, since every grand hotel already has everything: "A lending service for clothing, linens are already there, umbrellas too, along with toothbrushes. Even underwear, in S, M, L, XL (black only)." Through the consolidation of commonly used spaces, surface utilization per head can be reduced from the current 50 m² to just 22 m². Costs are minimal as well, since housework, including cleaning and maintenance, is shared by all. A few professionals are necessary as well, "Let's say six: cook, sommelièr, nanny, secretary, pianist, Latin instructor," all included in ancillary costs. All luxury and consumer goods are supplied. Far fewer such items are required, however, since everything can be used by anyone. Since the existing infrastructure can be used, the conversion of Switzerland would require only five years. Afterwards, the entire population will live in 14,000 grand hotels; no one will want to live any other way any longer. The forms of the hotels will be adapted to the existing building and settlement types: "Block perimeter hotel, high-rise hotel, diffuse village hotel, agglohotels linked via ancillary structures, and so forth. Only settlements of single-family houses cannot be used sensibly: they will be demolished by the civil defense and converted back into agricultural land in proximity to urban settlements."

    With its astonishing freshness, p.m.'s contribution succeeds in combining social critique with an alternative model of community that can be projected into the future. The associative connection to life in a grand hotel allows the reader to wallow in nostalgic film images while at the same time masking its

17 Ibid.
18 p.m., "Die Grandhotel-Verschwörung von 2014," *Das Magazin* 36, 2014.

Filmbildern schwelgen und kaschiert dabei gleichzeitig den fundamental disruptiven Inhalt. So unrealistisch der auf *bolo'bolo* basierende, von neuem umrissene Versuch eines gesellschaftsverändernden Lebensentwurfs anmuten mag, so überraschend sind bei genauerer Betrachtung die Parallelen zu zeitgleich realisierten Wohnbauten. Möglicherweise ist die assoziative Kraft, die in der Metapher Grandhotel steckt, als bildhafte und typologische Referenz, als Ideengeber stark genug, um vom Architekten in ein Bauwerk übersetzt und vom Nutzer ohne nähere Gebrauchsanweisung angenommen zu werden?

Der 2014 eröffnete, von Müller Sigrist Architekten über und um ein städtisches Tramdepot gebaute Wohnkomplex der Zürcher Baugenossenschaft Kalkbreite weist mit seinen durch «rues intérieurs» verbundenen Wohn- und Arbeitsräumen und einer Vielzahl begleitender Nutzungen und Serviceangebote, die den Bewohnern und dem Quartier zur Verfügung stehen, auffällige Ähnlichkeit mit einem solchen Grandhotel auf. Die Bewohner leben in minimalen Kleinwohnungen, die zu Clustern gruppiert sind, oder aber in Grosshaushalten. Ausserhalb der Wohnungen stehen Aufenthalts- und Arbeitsräume zur Verfügung, die Bedürfnisse abdecken, die in den Wohnungen keinen Platz finden. Die an einer ganztags besetzten Empfangstheke koordinierten Services sind hier nicht nur kommerziell, sondern basieren auf einer Sharing- und Beteiligungskultur. Läden, Kulturräume und Gastronomielokale verankern das Gebäude in der Stadt. Der im Sommer 2014 eingeweihte Bau wurde vom ersten Tag an von den Bewohnern des Quartiers angenommen und ist als lebendiger Beitrag in der Zürcher Stadtlandschaft seither ein Erfolg.
→ 10 11

Greifbare Visionen: zwischen Praxis und Theorie

Sind Utopien also doch realisierbar? Möglicherweise ja! Unter der Voraussetzung, dass eine kulturelle Praxis existiert, die zukunftsgerichtetes Fabulieren, das Was-wäre-wenn-Denken, mit einer realisierungsorientierten Pragmatik verbindet. Projekte wie die Kalkbreite in Zürich sind leider immer noch glückliche Ausnahmefälle, bei denen mutige Akteure zusammenfinden, um etwas bis anhin Utopisches zu realisieren. Im genannten Projekt war dies mit der Stadt Zürich eine Grundeigentümerin, die ein schwieriges, jedoch zentrales Grundstück zur Verfügung stellte; mit der Genossenschaft eine Trägerschaft, die in langwierigen und kräfteraubenden basisdemokratischen Prozessen ein Raum- und Betriebskonzept festschrieb; und schliesslich auch Planungsteams, die bereit waren, in einem Wettbewerb gegen 54 Konkurrenten anzutreten, die ausgetretenen Pfade des Gewohnten zu verlassen und sich auf ein Experiment mit unbekanntem Ausgang einzulassen. Gesucht sind also Gruppierungen, die aus gesellschaftskritischen, vernetzt denkenden, fachlich versierten und kreativen Personen bestehen, die

fundamentally disruptive contents. As unrealistic as this attempt, based on *bolo'bolo*, to sketch out a completely new, socially transformative way of life may be, a more precise consideration reveals astonishing parallels with residential buildings realized around the same time. Is it possible that the associative force offered by the metaphor of the grand hotel is powerful enough as a figurative and typological reference, as a generative idea, to be translated by architects into a building, and moreover to be adopted by users without more precise instructions for use?

With its residential and workspaces linked by "rues intérieurs," and a multiplicity of accompanying uses and service offerings which are made available to occupants and to the surrounding neighborhood, the residential complex, inaugurated in 2014, and built above and around an urban tram depot by Müller Sigrist Architekten for the Zurich housing cooperative Kalkbreite, displays striking affinities with such a grand hotel. The occupants occupy small, minimal residential units that are grouped in clusters, but also large households. Accessible outside of the apartments are leisure and workspaces which satisfy requirements that cannot be accommodated within residential units. Services, which are coordinated by a reception desk that is staffed full-time, are not exclusively commercial, but are also based on a cultural of sharing and participation. Shops, culture spaces, and restaurants anchor the building in the city. Inaugurated in the summer of 2014, the building was accepted by neighborhood residents from the very first day, and has been regarded as a lively contribution to Zurich's urban landscape ever since.
→ 10 11

Visions: Between Practice and Theory

Are utopias, then, actually realizable? Very possibly! Provided that cultural practices exist that are capable of conjuring future-oriented visions—of speculative or 'what if' thinking—and are capable of linking this to an implementation-oriented pragmatism. Unfortunately, projects such as the Kalkbreite in Zurich are happy exceptions through which courageous actors come together in order to realize something that incorporates the utopian. At Kalkbreite the city of Zurich was a vital actor as the landholder, which made available a difficult, but nonetheless central plot of land. Similarly, the building society, a trust which was successful as a result of protracted and exhausting direct democratic processes, codified a spatial and operational concept. And finally, planning teams were prepared to participate in a competition together with fifty-four others, and to deviate from the well-trodden path of the familiar to engage in experimentation with no certain outcome. Needed, then, are groups consisting of socially critical, technically adept, creative individuals who think in networks and who have the courage to go out on a limb, and at the same time allow their personal egos to retreat behind a common goal.

ausserdem den Mut haben, sich zu exponieren und die gleichzeitig ihr persönliches Ego hinter ein gemeinsames Ziel stellen.

Der gehorsame Auftragserfüller, der sich bloss an Mengengerüsten festhält, ist hier fehl am Platz. Wie Lucius Burckhardt schon bemerkte, fängt der Architekturentwurf bei der Festlegung der Aufgabenstellung an und nicht erst bei der Ausarbeitung eines konkreten Designs. Es braucht also eine Balance zwischen dem Expertentum des Architekten als Entwerfer und dem Generalisten, der das Wissen von Spezialisten verschiedener Fachrichtungen verbindet und mithilft, dieses in einem Zielbild festzuhalten. Fehlt dem Architekten dieses umfassende Rollenverständnis, kommen an seiner Stelle neue Akteure ins Spiel: Die Experten anderer Disziplinen springen in die entstandene Lücke. Verliert sich der Architekt hingegen im interdisziplinären Gerede, fehlt er als Entwerfer des Konkreten, was wiederum Gefahren birgt. Jesko Fezer, der deutsche Architekt und Grenzgänger zwischen den Disziplinen, reflektiert in «Deprofessionalisierungstendenzen»[19] anhand von Texten unterschiedlicher Autoren, wie sich der Rückzug des Architekten aus seiner Kernkompetenz als Entwerfer auf die Disziplin auswirkt. Er zitiert Tomás Maldonado, der das theoriebasierte, utopische Vorgehen, das Planen ohne Machen, einer entwurfsfeindlichen, protestierenden Gegenbewegung gegenüberstellt, die ein aktionistisches Spiel des Antiprofessionalismus, ein Machen ohne Plan betreibt.[20] Diese planungskritische Haltung sei eine subtile Form der Affirmation, denn ein projektloses Nein sei ein Nein mit leeren Händen und berge keine Gefahr für den Status quo. Maldonado kritisiert den utopischen Nihilismus seiner Zeit und plädiert für einen «konstruktiven Skeptizismus», der dafür sorgt, dass sich die Widersprüche der Umwelt nicht durch Tatenlosigkeit zu einer gesellschaftlichen Katastrophe verdichten. Die Lösung sieht er in einer Art Methodik, bei der sich der Planer auf das «Wie» der Planung, des Entwerfens und der Durchführung einlässt. Er fordert die technische Machbarkeit der Utopie, eine operable, in Handlung umsetzbare, kritische Theorie auf der einen Seite und gleichzeitig utopisch kritisches Denken, das sich an den Tatsächlichkeiten der Welt misst. Fezer bezeichnet Maldonados Ansatz als Kritik am selbstverliebten Expertentum der Architekten und Gestalter. Den falschen Alternativen des Professionalismus, der unglaubwürdigen Utopie, die jede Annäherung an eine Wirklichkeit scheut, und der rückhaltlosen Anbiederung an diese begegnet Maldonado mit einer «Allgemeinen Theorie der Entwurfspraxis».[21]

Sowohl p.m. wie Maldonado wollen utopisches Denken und das Handeln in einer realen, widersprüchlichen Welt zusammenbringen. Verfolgt p.m. einen bildhaft literarischen Ansatz und vertraut auf die gesellschaftsverändernde Kraft der Imagination, sucht Maldonado nach dem «Wie», nach einer Methode, die hilft, Vorstellung und Realität zu vereinen. Beide Haltungen gehen von einem Vorgehen aus, das die gesetzten Ziele Schritt für Schritt und mittels überschaubarer Einheiten zu erreichen versucht. p.m. liebäugelt

Here, the obedient implementer of tasks, who simply clings to project data, would be out of place. As Lucius Burckhardt remarks, architectural design begins with the definition of an assignment and not just with the elaboration of a concrete design. It therefore requires a balance between the expertise of the architect as designer and the generalist who brings together knowledge provided by specialists from various disciplines and who helps to contain it in a target vision. If the architect lacks this comprehensive understanding of the roles involved, then new actors will come into play to replace him or her: experts from other disciplines leap into the resultant gap. If, however, the architect becomes lost in interdisciplinary verbiage, then he becomes dangerously detached as a designer.

In *Tendencies Toward Deprofessionalization* Jesko Fezer, a German architect who crosses between disciplines, reflects on the retreat of the architect to his or her core competence as a designer.[19] He cites Tomás Maldonado, who contrasts a theory-based, utopian approach—a planning without doing—with a protest countermovement that is hostile to design and combines activist play with anti-professionalism—a doing without planning.[20] He argues that this latter attitude is in fact a subtle form of affirmation, rather than a radical critique, since a projectless 'no' is a 'no' with empty hands, and harbors no danger to the status quo. Maldonado criticizes the utopian nihilism of his time and argues for a "constructive skepticism" whose intent is to prevent inaction from allowing the contradictions of the environment to culminate in social catastrophe. In his view, the solution is a kind of methodology through which the planner is engaged with the "how" of planning, of the design, and of its implementation. He demands the technical feasibility of utopia and operational, practically realizable, critical theory alongside a utopian and critical thinking that is measured against objective reality. Fezer refers to Maldonado's approach as a critique of the narcissistic expert class of architects and designers. Maldonado counters the implausible utopia that shies away from every rapprochement with reality, or an unconditional accommodation with it, through a "general theory of design practice."[21]

Both p.m. and Maldonado strive to bring utopian thinking and action together in a real, contradictory world. While the first pursues a figurative, literary approach and relies upon the socially transformative power of the imagination, the second searches for the "how," for a method capable of uniting vision and reality. Both attitudes assume the necessity for approaching a set goal step-by-step and by means of manageable units. To be sure, p.m. flirts with an attitude that encompasses all of mankind on a global basis and aspires to alleviate problems such as migration and resource shortages, yet each one of his grand hotels is a manageable, realistic conglomerate. Maldonado's design methodology, which unites theory and practice, represents an attempt to effect concrete change and is not satisfied with a fantasized transformation of reality.

---

19 Jesko Fezer, «Deprofessionalisierungstendenzen (damals, in der Entwurfsmethodik)», in: *Disko 24*, 2011.
20 Tomás Maldonado, *Umwelt und Revolte. Zur Dialektik des Entwerfens im Spätkapitalismus*, Reinbek bei Hamburg 1972
21 Jesko Fezer, wie Anm. 19

19 Jesko Fezer, "Deprofessionalisierungstendenzen (damals, in der Entwurfsmethodik)," *Disko 24*, 2011.
20 Tomás Maldonado, *Umwelt und Revolte. Zur Dialektik des Entwerfens im Spätkapitalismus*, Reinbek bei Hamburg 1972.
21 Fezer 2011.
22 Harald Welzer, *Selbst denken. Eine Anleitung zum Widerstand*, Frankfurt am Main 2013.

zwar noch mit einer Grundhaltung, die von der gesamten Menschheit weltumspannend getragen wird und letztendlich auch globale Probleme wie Migration und Ressourcenknappheit abmildert, doch jedes einzelne seiner Grandhotels ist ein überschaubares, realitätsnahes Konglomerat. Auch Maldonados Theorie und Praxis verbindende Entwurfsmethodik stellt einen Versuch dar, eine tatsächliche und nicht bloss eine fantasierte Veränderung der Wirklichkeit zu erzielen.

Dies führt uns zum zeitgenössischen Soziologen und Sozialpsychologen Harald Welzer, der zukunftsfähige Denk- und Handlungsmodelle ergründet, die allmählich alternative Lebensstile und Wirtschaftsformen fördern sollen. In seinem Buch *Selbst denken — Eine Anleitung zum Widerstand*[22] vermeidet er es bewusst, ein präzises Zielbild zu formulieren. Seine gesellschaftskritischen Analysen sind als Anregung gedacht, die eigene Position zu reflektieren, und weisen auf die Gefahren einer vereinfachenden Sichtweise hin, die sich in jeder pointierten, noch so gut gemeinten Polemik verbirgt.

Welzer kritisiert die Geschichts- und Theorielosigkeit der aktuellen Ökobewegung und deren vermehrte Technikorientierung sowie das Favorisieren expertokratischer Strategien. Damit verbunden stellt er eine Utopieferne und einen eklatanten Mangel an Reflexivität fest.[23] Dem gegenüber ist der Kapitalismus geschmeidig genug, um für jede Bewegung und Gegenbewegung Teilmärkte zu schaffen und sich selbst dadurch ständig zu erneuern. Sein einziger Nachteil ist, dass er ohne Energiezufuhr von aussen nicht läuft. Wie Lucius Burkhardt beschreibt Welzer die Fähigkeit des Systems, für jedes Problem schnell technische Teillösungen bereitzustellen — Strategien, die aber nicht nachhaltig sein können. Aus Skepsis gegenüber Masterplänen, die sofortige und konsequente Massnahmen fordern, sieht er den Weg in einem langsameren Vorgehen.[24] Die Utopie, also die Imagination einer wünschenswerten Zukunft als Potenzial beschreibend, sieht Welzer den Status quo lediglich als eine Variante von vielen möglichen Wirklichkeiten. Die Zukunft wird dabei nicht als absolutes, zu erreichendes Ziel verstanden, sondern als Weg, den man zurückgelegt haben muss, um dorthin zu gelangen. Der Angst vor einer Totalitarismusgefahr grosser Masterplan-Utopien (20. Jahrhundert) wird ein schrittweises Vorgehen nach dem Trial-and-Error-Prinzip, bei dem das Ergebnis jeweils mit dem Gewünschten verglichen wird, entgegengesetzt: probieren, abbrechen, aufhören, innehalten, pausieren. Welzer spricht von sukzessiven und nicht von abrupten Veränderungen als wirkungsmächtige Strategien.[25]

Die Genossenschaften als Reanimationen einer tradierten Kulturtechnik basieren als gemeinschaftliche Wirtschaftsform auf der kooperativen Nutzung von Ressourcen. Genossenschaften existieren als landwirtschaftliche Gemeinschaften, handwerkliche Betriebe, Sparkassen, Einkaufs- und Handelsbetriebe sowie als Immobilienorganisationen seit langer Zeit. Für Welzer ist die Rückkehr der Genossenschaften ein wichtiger Schritt hin zu einer nachhaltigen Moderne. Dazu gehört auch das Tauschen von Eigenarbeitsleistungen neben

This leads us towards the contemporary sociologist and social psychologist Harald Welzer, who explores future-oriented models of thought and action that are expected to gradually foster alternative lifestyles and economic forms. In his book *Selbst denken — Eine Anleitung zum Widerstand* (Think for Yourself—A Manual of Resistance), he deliberately avoids formulating precise objectives.[22] His socially critical analyses are intended as a stimulus to reflect upon one's own position and he calls attention to the dangers of a simplified perspective of the kind that is harbored in every polemic, no matter how pointed or well-intended.

Welzer criticizes the lack of theoretical and historical awareness in the current ecological movement with its increasing technological orientation, as well as its preference for technocratic strategies. In conjunction with this stance, he identifies a striking absence of reflexivity that is remote from utopian thought.[23] In contrast, capitalism is flexible enough to create submarkets for every movement and countermovement, constantly renewing itself in the process. Its sole disadvantage is that it cannot function without inputs of energy from outside. Like Lucius Burkhardt, Welzer characterizes the capacity of the system to arrive quickly at partial technical solutions for every problem—strategies that may prove unsustainable. Impelled by a skepticism for masterplans that call for immediate and consequential measures, he sees the way forward in a slower approach.[24] Characterizing utopia as the potential inherent in a desirable imagined future, Welzer regards the status quo simply as a variant of many possible realities. The future, then, is understood not as an absolute goal to be reached, but instead as a path one must travel in order to arrive there. His anxiety in relation to the totalitarian threat of large-scale masterplanned utopias is opposed to a stepwise process that follows a trial and error principle. This involves a persistent comparison between results and what is ultimately desired: there is testing, interruption, termination, stopping, pausing. Welzer speaks of successive rather than abrupt changes as powerfully effective strategies.[25]

The cooperative is a reinvention of a traditional cultural technology, based—as a collective economic form—on the cooperative use of resources. Cooperatives have long existed in the form of agricultural collectives, artisanal enterprises, savings banks, purchasing and trading companies, as well as real estate organizations. For Welzer, the return to cooperatives is a key step toward a sustainable modernism. One part of this is the bartering of individual productivity alongside regular employment as a contribution to a macrosocial approach.[26]

Welzer demonstrates that as a consequence of the abandonment of claims to feasibility that encompass society as a whole, a vision becomes more graspable and—as many recent projects have shown—feasible on a smaller scale. In this way, utopia may perhaps be transferred into urban reality, its banishment to a remote island revoked. Such projects remain islands, each contextualized within its city and in communication with its occupants.

22 Harald Welzer, *Selbst denken. Eine Anleitung zum Widerstand*, Frankfurt am Main 2013
23 Ebd., Kapitel «Das Politische wird antiutopisch»
24 Ebd., Kapitel «Selbst denken»
25 Ebd., Kapitel «Utopien»

23 Ibid.
24 Ibid.
25 Ibid.
26 Ibid.

der regulären Erwerbstätigkeit als Beitrag in einer gesamtgesellschaftlichen Betrachtung.[26]

Harald Welzer zeigt, dass durch das Weglassen des Anspruchs einer auf die gesamte Gesellschaft bezogenen Realisierbarkeit die Vision greifbarer und, wie jüngere Projekte zeigen, auch im Kleinen umsetzbar wird. Die Utopie lässt sich auf diese Weise vielleicht doch aus ihrer Verbannung auf eine ferne Insel in eine urbane Realität transferieren. Dabei bleibt sie immer noch Insel, jedoch kontextualisiert in der Stadt und in Kommunikation mit deren Bewohnern.

Harald Welzers Ansatz setzt jedoch, was Gemeinschaftlichkeit und Beteiligungskultur anbelangt, eine grosse Freiwilligkeit voraus. Einen deutlich weniger idealistischen Ton schlägt der deutsche Philosoph Peter Sloterdijk in seiner Trilogie *Sphären*[27] an und holt uns damit nach den zuvor beschriebenen optimistisch-euphorischen Zukunftsvisionen wieder etwas auf den Boden der Realität zurück. Bedingt durch das im 20. Jahrhundert zunehmend sich artikulierende menschliche Bedürfnis nach Privatheit und Individualität, ist der Anspruch des Menschen auf ein eigenes Zimmer oder gar auf ein eigenes Apartment und sein Rückzug in eine selbstverwaltete und -gestaltete Egosphäre (Blase) das Gegenteil des seit der Moderne proklamierten, kollektivtauglichen «neuen Menschen». Die durch neue Technologien begünstigte serielle Fertigung von Zellen und deren Anordnung in (amorphen) Zellverbänden ermöglichte es den Architekten in den vergangenen hundert Jahren, mit grosser Gestaltungsfreiheit eine Vielzahl von Bauformen zu realisieren. Die Dichte der Zellstapelung und die physische Nähe ihrer Bewohner ist aber kaum Anlass für nachbarschaftlichen Austausch, sondern eher für einen Koexistenzstress, bei dem nur ein Minimum an Interaktion erwünscht ist. Der Kontakt des in diesen Raumzellen lebenden Menschen mit dem Kollektiv erfolgt vielmehr über technische Hilfsmittel wie Radio, TV und Social Media, die wie Prothesen die fehlende Aussenwelt zu ersetzen versuchen. Diese als Erweiterung des Selbst dienenden Technologien umreisst Sloterdijk mit dem Begriff «Egotechniken». Daraus entsteht ein Koexistieren des Individuums mit sich selbst, eine Selbstergänzung: Selbstpaarung, Selbstsorge, Selbstmodellierung. Das Apartment ist eine Miniaturisierung aller Funktionen zur routinemässigen Ausführung ritualisierter Tätigkeiten, damit man für sich selbst kochen, sich selber telekommunikativ unterhalten oder autodidaktisch weiterbilden, sich pflegen, die eigene Erscheinung justieren und sich selbst begehren kann. Sloterdijk beschreibt diese kulturelle und gesellschaftliche Entwicklung mit dem wertneutralen Auge des Beobachters. Er verbindet anthropologische Betrachtung mit dem dazu in Beziehung stehenden Raumverständnis der Städte des 20. Jahrhunderts. Gerade seine kritischen Analysen des Status quo können als Anlass und Motivation für neue Utopien verstanden werden.

→ 12 13

With regard to communality and a culture of participation, however, Welzer's approach presupposes a considerable degree of voluntary action. A far less idealistic tone is struck by Peter Sloterdijk in his *Sphere Trilogy*, in which we are pulled downward from Welzer's optimistic and euphoric visions of the future toward the ground of reality.[27] Conditioned by the human need—articulated to an increasing degree during the twentieth century—for privacy and individuality, the demand by the individual for a private room, even a private apartment, for a retreat into a self-governed and self-designed egosphere (bubble) is the counterpart to the "New Human," with his collectivist proclivities. The serial manufacture of cells and their arrangement into (amorphous) cellular agglomerations that has been facilitated by new technologies has enabled architects over the past century to realize a multiplicity of building forms with ever greater design freedom. But the density with which these cells are stacked and the physical proximity of their occupants hardly represents an opportunity for neighborly exchange. Instead it means a stressful coexistence since only a minimum of interaction is desirable. Contact between the people who occupy the spatial cells and the collective occurs via technical devices such as radio, television, and social media, which—like prostheses—attempt to replace the now absent external world. Sloterdijk describes these extensions of self-service technology with the term "egotechnologies." The result is the individual's coexistence with himself: a self-supplementation, self-pairing, self-care, self-modeling. The apartment is a miniaturization of all functions to the level of routinized execution of ritualized activities: the individual cooks for themselves, is entertained communicatively, or continues their education didactically, maintains themselves, adjusts their own appearance, satisfies their own desires. Sloterdijk describes this cultural and societal development with a value-neutral observer's eye. He links anthropological considerations with the relevant spatial understanding of the twentieth century city. Precisely his critical analysis of the status quo can be understood as a stimulus and a motivation for a new utopia.

→ 12 13

---

26 Ebd., Kapitel «Genossenschaften»
27 Peter Sloterdijk, «Architektur des Schaums», in: *ARCH+* 169/170, 2004, und Trilogie *Sphären: Sphären I – Blasen*, Frankfurt am Main 1998; *Sphären II – Globen*, Frankfurt am Main 1999; *Sphären III – Schäume*, Frankfurt am Main 2004

27 Peter Sloterdijk, "Architektur des Schaums," *ARCH+* 169/170, 2004; Peter Sloterdijk, *Bubbles: Microspherology*, London 2011; Peter Sloterdijk, *Globes*, London 2014; Peter Sloterdijk, *Foams*, London 2016.

14

16

15

17

18

19

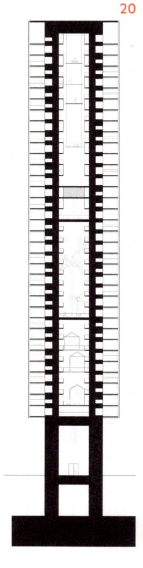

20

14/15 Walden 7, Ricardo Bofill, Sant Just Desvern bei Barcelona, 1975
16 Hugh Ferriss, *The Metropolis of Tomorrow*, 1929
17/18 Studierendenprojekt High Rise 01, Robert Bauer/Christa Elizabeth Beckmann, TU Berlin 2015/16; Wohncluster mit gemeinschaftlichen Terrassen
19/20 Studierendenprojekt High Rise 04, Merle Sudbrock/Roberta Zucchetti, TU Berlin 2015/16; raumhaltige Wand und kollektives Atrium

14/15 Walden 7, Ricardo Bofill, Sant Just Desvern near Barcelona, 1975
16 Hugh Ferriss, *The Metropolis of Tomorrow*, 1929
17/18 Student project, High Rise 01, Robert Bauer/Christa Elizabeth Beckmann, TU Berlin 2015/16; residential cluster with communal terraces
19/20 Student project, High Rise 04, Merle Sudbrock/Roberta Zucchetti, TU Berlin 2015/16; space-containing wall and collective atrium

The Order of Reality

To summarize: for architects, this *tour d'horizon* through a selection of visionary texts confronts us with a question of attitude. In particular as builders of homes, are we satisfied with realizing mere reflections of the status quo, thereby mirroring a fragmented society that is deeply insecure about its values? Or do we instead regard utopian thinking as the primary source for architecture and urban planning, mainly as an impetus to conceive of things in ways that go beyond the boundaries of present-day reality? As architects, we are in a perpetual struggle with the contradiction between the necessity for planning (residences must be built) for future occupants, and the impossibility of forseeing that same future. In conceptualizing structures for nameless occupants, we unavoidably enter the realm of the hypothetical. "Do architects inhabit not the reality, but the fiction of a society? Do they live in an anticipatory illusion? Or are they quite simply expressing what is already there?"[28] This question, posed by Jean Baudrillard in a lecture in 1999, goes to the heart of our insecurity. When we stand before a concrete building task, when we elaborate a spatial layout or architectural object for a competition program, the leeway for illusions is marginal. The designs for residential developments produced by our own architectural practice demonstrate that for most projects, the radius of action can be expanded only in the most subtle and subversive ways. These are expressed, for example, in spatial sequences that create a sense of identity, in intermediate spaces, in accesses, in expressive elements, but also in construction methods and the impact of materials. Overtly radical and challenging concepts are rarely encountered.

In teaching, of course, things are much simpler, and in selecting semester tasks at the Technical University Berlin we attempt to exploit this as far as possible. Here, the formulation of tasks involves exclusively complex spatial programs that are enriched by supplementary utilizations and spaces, as well as questions of the interaction between residents and the urban context. The elaboration of these tasks consistently leads toward large or very large residential conglomerates. Our practice has long been fascinated by extensive structures that belong to the city and which lead toward uncomfortable, yet powerful, communicable identities. By developing such building types, it becomes possible when working with students to explore the boundaries between utopia and dystopia, between the promising and failure. The semester assignments "High-Rise" →14—20 and "Grand Hotel" posed the question of how a building can be organized in such a way that it mediates between large and small scales and makes both conviviality and privacy possible. The Master's thesis project "Collective Courtyards" investigated the justification of the large-scale inner-city housing estates that were prevalent up until the mid-twentieth century in many European cities. "Urbanity to Production"

---

28 Jean Baudrillard, "Architecture: Truth or Radicality?," *The Baudrillard Reader*, New York 2008, p. 173.

Massstab zu vermitteln, Begegnung, aber auch Rückzug zu ermöglichen. In der freien Masterthesis-Arbeit «Kollektive Höfe» wurde schlicht nach der Berechtigung von innerstädtischen Grosssiedlungen gefragt, wie sie bis zur Mitte des 20. Jahrhunderts in vielen europäischen Städten die Regel waren. «Urbanity and Production» und «Supermärkte» waren Entwurfsaufgaben, die neben räumlicher Grösse auch die Frage nach der städtischen Versorgung mit Gütern und Arbeitsplätzen stellten. Im letzten Semester mit dem Titel «College» schliesslich wurde die Nachverdichtung eines bestehenden monofunktionalen Stadtteils, dem Areal der Technischen Universität Berlin, zu einem Wohn- und Arbeitsquartier untersucht, in dem wie in den angelsächsischen Vorbildern Lehre, Freizeit und Leben zu einer vibrierenden Urbanität zusammenkommen. In allen Semesteraufgaben waren keine abgehobenen utopistischen Architekturen, sondern über die Verbindung mit tradierten Gebäudetypen eine Anbindung an gewohnte, nahbare Bilder gesucht. Genau durch diese Kombination von Bekanntem und Gewagtem, im Schaffen einer spezifischen und aussagekräftigen Architektur, liegt das Potenzial, dass zwischen Mensch und Objekt eine Auseinandersetzung entsteht, die Bindung und Identifikation erzeugt. So gedacht, ergeben sich, um mit den Worten Baudrillards zu enden, Objekte, «welche die Ordnung der Umgebung herausfordern. Welche mit der Ordnung des Realen in einer dualen und eventuell konfliktbeladenen Beziehung stehen. In diesem Sinne könnte man statt von Wahrheit (der Objekte) von ihrer Radikalität sprechen. Sofern dieses Duell nicht stattfindet, wenn die Architektur nur die funktionelle und programmatische Transkription der Zwänge der sozialen und urbanen Ordnung sein soll, dann existiert sie als Architektur nicht mehr.» Ein gelungenes Objekt ist eines, das jenseits seiner eigenen Realität existiert und mit dem Benutzer in eine duale Beziehung tritt, die auch Fehlgebrauch (abus), Widerspruch und Destabilisierung zulässt. «Das Problem ist dasselbe beim Denken und beim Schreiben und im politischen und sozialen Feld. Überall, egal, was man tut, hat man nicht die Wahl des Ereignisses, sondern nur die Wahl des Konzepts. Diese Wahl aber muss man sich bewahren.» [29]

and "Supermarkets" were design assignments which posed questions around the provision of goods and jobs in urban contexts. Last semester, under the title "College," we explored the densification of an existing mono-functional urban district, namely the premises of the Technische Universität Berlin itself, and its conversion into a residential and commercial district where—as in Anglo-Saxon prototypes—teaching, leisure, and life would flow together to form a vibrant urbanity. Each of the semester assignments sought to find links to lived-in, approachable images via traditional building types as opposed to remote, utopian architecture. It is precisely through this combination of the familiar and the audacious, in the creation of a specific and profound architecture, that we discover the potential for instigating the kind of interaction between the human being and the object that engenders connection and identification. Conceived in this way, objects emerge which, to return to Baudrillard, "are a challenge to the surrounding order and stand in a dual—and potentially 'duelling'—relation with the order of reality. It is in this sense that we can speak not of their truth, but of their radicality. If this duel does not take place, if architecture has to be the functional and programmatic transcription of the constraints of the social and urban order, then it no longer exists as architecture." A successful object is one that exists beyond its own reality, and enters into a dual relationship with the user, one that also allows misuse, contradiction, and destabilization. "The problem is the same in the register of writing and in the political and social orders. Everywhere, whatever you do, you have no choice of events. You merely have a choice of concepts. But that choice is one we have to hold onto."[29]

---

29   Baudrillard, wie Anm. 28, S. 15

29   Ibid., p. 175.

←

Utopien
und Erfindungen

Utopias
and Inventions

pool Architekten:
Das charaktervolle
Haus in der Stadt.
Fotografien
realisierter Projekte

pool Architekten:
The Characterful
House in the City.
Photographs
of Realized Projects

→

← ← pool 0180; Frieden Alterswohnungen/Senior Housing Estate, Zürich-Affoltern, 2006–2013

↑ pool 0203; Dreifamilienhaus /Three-Family House, Im Dörfli, Oberrieden, 2007–2014
→ pool 0180; Frieden, Alterswohnungen/Senior Housing Estate, Zürich-Affoltern, 2006–2013

pool Architekten: The Characterful House in the City. Photographs of Realized Projects

← pool 0175; Wohn- und Geschäftshaus/Residential and Commercial Building, Am Bahnhof, Wohlen, 2006–2015

↑ pool 0203; Dreifamilienhaus/Three-Family House, Im Dörfli, Oberrieden, 2007–2014

pool Architekten: Das charaktervolle Haus in der Stadt.
Fotografien realisierter Projekte

← pool 0243; Genossenschaftliches Wohnhaus/Cooperative Apartment Building, «mehr als wohnen», Haus/Building L, Zürich-Leutschenbach, 2009–2015

↓ pool 0175; Wohn- und Geschäftshaus/Residential and Commercial Building, Am Bahnhof, Wohlen, 2006–2015

← pool 0229; Wohnhaus/Apartment Building, Laur-Park, Brugg, 2009–2012

↑ pool 0243; Genossenschaftliches Wohnhaus/Cooperative Apartment Building, «mehr als wohnen», Haus/Building L, Zürich-Leutschenbach, 2009–2015

pool Architekten: Das charaktervolle Haus in der Stadt.
Fotografien realisierter Projekte

↑ pool 0243; Genossenschaftliches Wohnhaus/Cooperative Apartment Building, «mehr als wohnen», Haus/Building J, Zürich-Leutschenbach, 2009–2015

→ pool 0243; Genossenschaftliches Wohnhaus/Cooperative Apartment Building, «mehr als wohnen», Häuser/Buildings G+J, Zürich-Leutschenbach, 2009–2015

pool Architekten: The Characterful House in the City.
Photographs of Realized Projects

← pool 0243; Genossenschaftliches Wohnhaus/Cooperative Apartment Building, «mehr als wohnen», Haus/Building J, Zürich-Leutschenbach, 2009–2015

↑ pool 0243; Genossenschaftliches Wohnhaus/Cooperative Apartment Building, «mehr als wohnen», Haus/Building G, Zürich-Leutschenbach, 2009–2015

pool Architekten: Das charaktervolle Haus in der Stadt.
Fotografien realisierter Projekte

← pool 0243; Genossenschaftliches Wohnhaus/Cooperative Apartment Building, «mehr als wohnen», Haus/Building J+G, Zürich-Leutschenbach, 2009–2015

↑ pool 0113; Wohnüberbauung/Residential Development, Aspholz Nord, Zürich-Affoltern, 2003–2007

pool Architekten: Das charaktervolle Haus in der Stadt. Fotografien realisierter Projekte

↑ pool 0113; Wohnüberbauung/Residential Development, Aspholz Nord, Zürich-Affoltern, 2003–2007

→ pool 0180; Frieden, Alterswohnen und Kindergarten/Senior Housing Estate and Kindergarten, Zürich-Affoltern, 2006–2013

pool Architekten: The Characterful House in the City. Photographs of Realized Projects

↑ pool 0176; Genossenschaftliches Wohn- und Geschäftshaus/Cooperative Residential and Commercial Building, Badenerstrasse, Zürich, 2006–2010

→ pool 0072; Genossenschaftssiedlung/Cooperative Housing Estate, Leimbachstrasse, Zürich-Leimbach, 2001–2005

pool Architekten: The Characterful House in the City. Photographs of Realized Projects

↑ pool 0229; Wohnhaus/Apartment Building, Laur-Park, Brugg, 2009–2012

→ pool 0254; Wohnhaus/Apartment Building, Limmattalstrasse, Zürich-Höngg, 2010–2013

pool Architekten: The Characterful House in the City. Photographs of Realized Projects

← pool 0219; Mehrfamilienhäuser/Multi-Family Dwellings, Loft/Split, Horgen, 2008–2012

↑ pool 0159; Wohnüberbauung/Residential Development, Im Blumenfeld, Zürich-Affoltern, 2005–2008

pool Architekten: Das charaktervolle Haus in der Stadt. Fotografien realisierter Projekte

↑ pool 0072; Genossenschaftssiedlung/Cooperative Housing Estate, Leimbachstrasse, Zürich-Leimbach, 2001–2005

→ pool 0132; Terrassenhäuser/Terraced Houses, Am Sonnenberg, Würenlingen, 2006–2008

pool Architekten: The Characterful House in the City. Photographs of Realized Projects

← pool 0177; Genossenschaftssiedlung/Cooperative Housing Estate, Im Sydefädeli, Häuser/Buildings X, Y, Z, Zürich-Wipkingen, 2006–2016

↑ pool 0177; Genossenschaftssiedlung/Cooperative Housing Estate, Im Sydefädeli, Häuser/Buildings A–G, Zürich-Wipkingen, 2006–2016

pool Architekten: Das charaktervolle Haus in der Stadt.
Fotografien realisierter Projekte

← pool 0199; Wohr- und Gewerbeüberbauung/ Residential and Commercial Development, Spätzstrasse, Horgen, 2007–2017

↑ pool 0177; Genossenschaftssiedlung/Cooperative Housing Estate, Im Sydefädeli, Häuser/ Buildings A–G, Zürich-Wipkingen, 2006–2016

pool Architekten: Das charaktervolle Haus in der Stadt. Fotografien realisierter Projekte

↑   pool 0180; Frieden Alterswohnungen/Senior Housing Estate, Zürich-Affoltern, 2006–2013
→   pool 0195; Reihenhäuser/Town Houses, Blue Notes, Richterswil, 2007–2010
→→ pool 0176; Genossenschaftliches Wohn- und Geschäftshaus/Cooperative Residential and Commercial Building, Badenerstrasse, Zürich, 2006–2010

pool Architekten: The Characterful House in the City. Photographs of Realized Projects

←

pool Architekten:
Das charaktervolle
Haus in der Stadt.
Fotografien
realisierter Projekte

pool Architekten:
The Characterful
House in the City.
Photographs
of Realized Projects

pool Architekten:
Vom Wohnen.
Möblierte Grundrisse
im Massstab 1:150

pool Architekten:
On Housing.
Furnished Floor Plans
on a Scale of 1:150

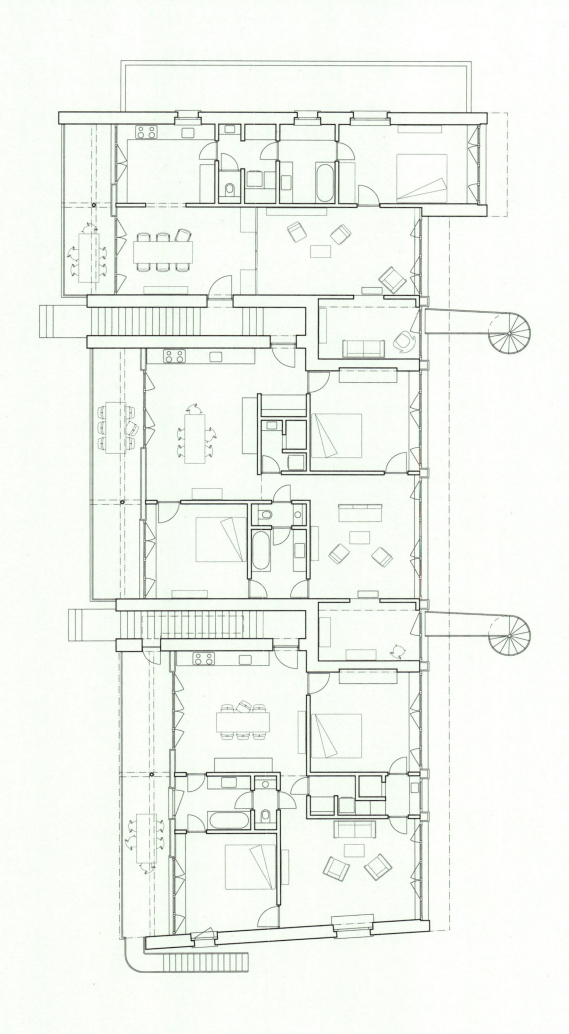

↑ pool 0351; Haus Mühlerain, Meilen, 2016–2019

pool Architekten: Vom Wohnen.
Möblierte Grundrisse im Massstab 1:150

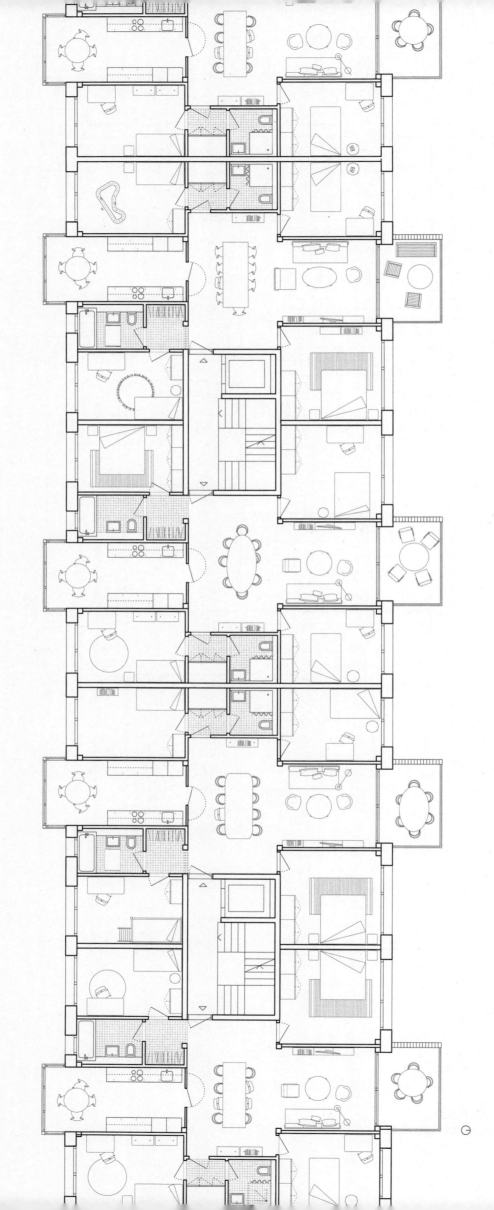

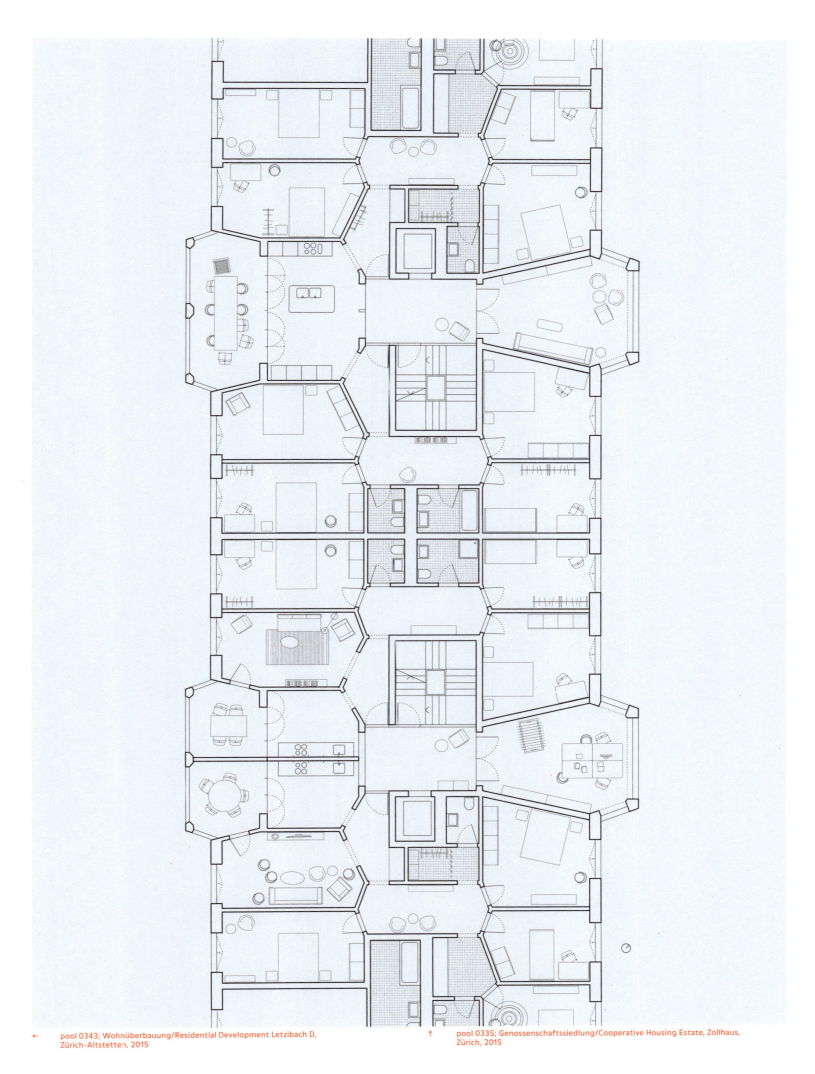

← pool 0343; Wohnüberbauung/Residential Development Letzibach D, Zürich-Altstetten, 2015

↑ pool 0335; Genossenschaftssiedlung/Cooperative Housing Estate, Zollhaus, Zürich, 2015

pool Architekten: Vom Wohnen.
Möblierte Grundrisse im Massstab 1:150

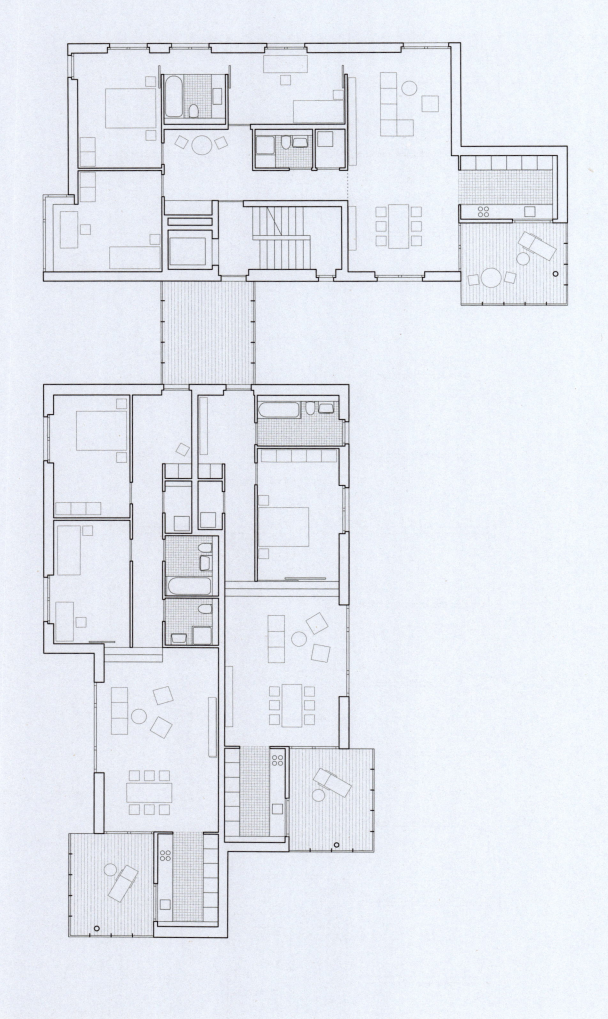

↑ pool 0229; Wohnhaus/Apartment Building, Laur-Park, Brugg, 2009–2012

→ pool 0195; Reihenhäuser/Town Houses, Blue Notes, Richterswil, 2007–2010

pool Architekten: On Housing.
Furnished Floor Plans on a Scale of 1:150

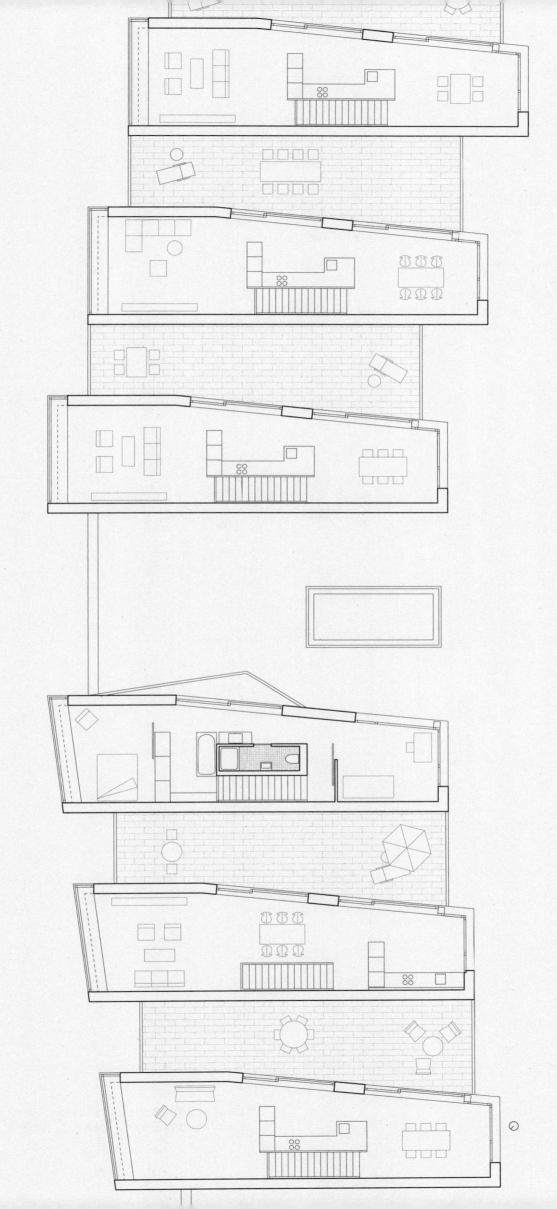

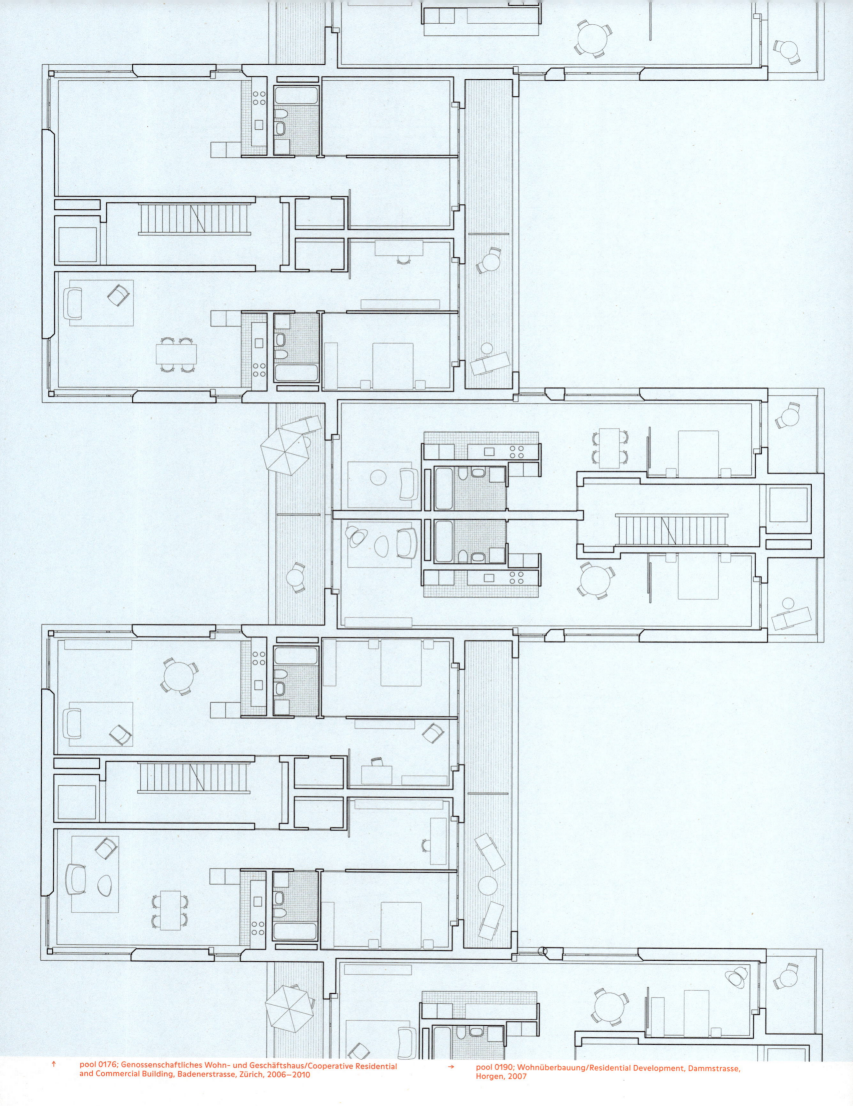

↑ pool 0176; Genossenschaftliches Wohn- und Geschäftshaus/Cooperative Residential and Commercial Building, Badenerstrasse, Zürich, 2006–2010

→ pool 0190; Wohnüberbauung/Residential Development, Dammstrasse, Horgen, 2007

pool Architekten: On Housing.
Furnished Floor Plans on a Scale of 1:150

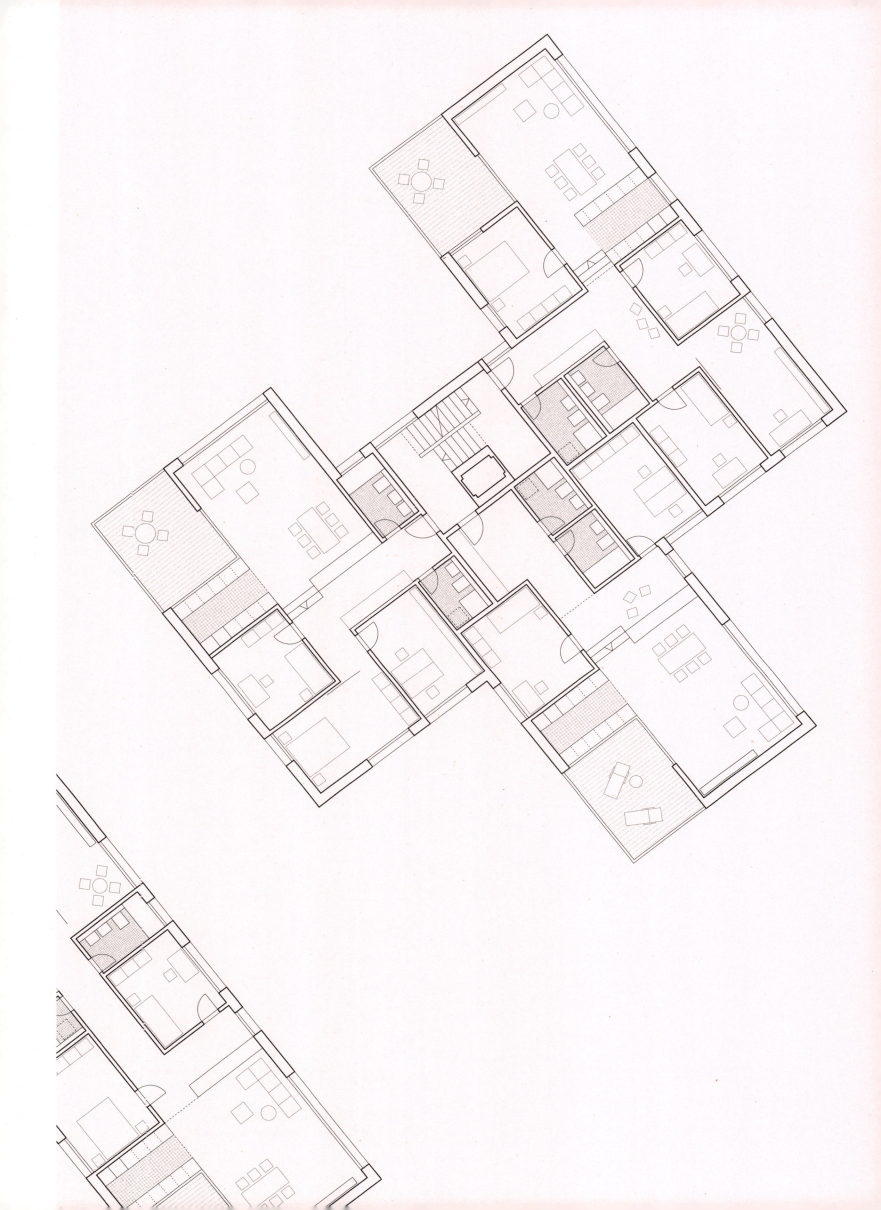

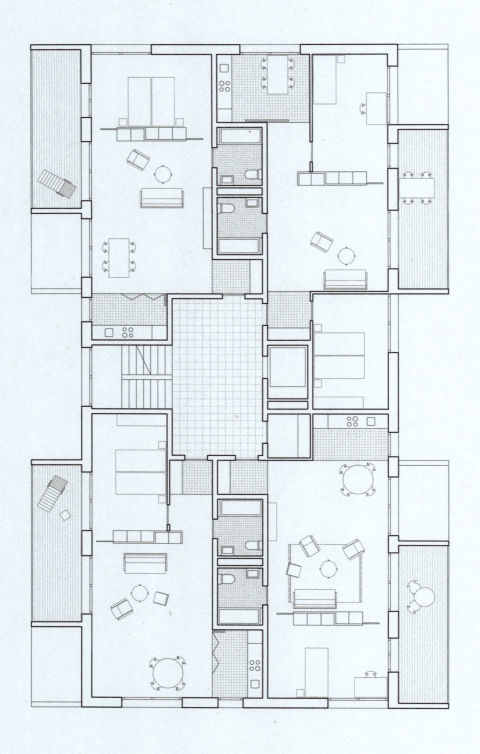

↑ pool 0180; Frieden Alterswohnungen/Senior Housing Estate, Zürich-Affoltern, 2006–2013

→ pool 0347; Genossenschaftssiedlung/Cooperative Housing, Hardturm-Areal, Zürich, 2016

pool Architekten: On Housing.
Furnished Floor Plans on a Scale of 1:150

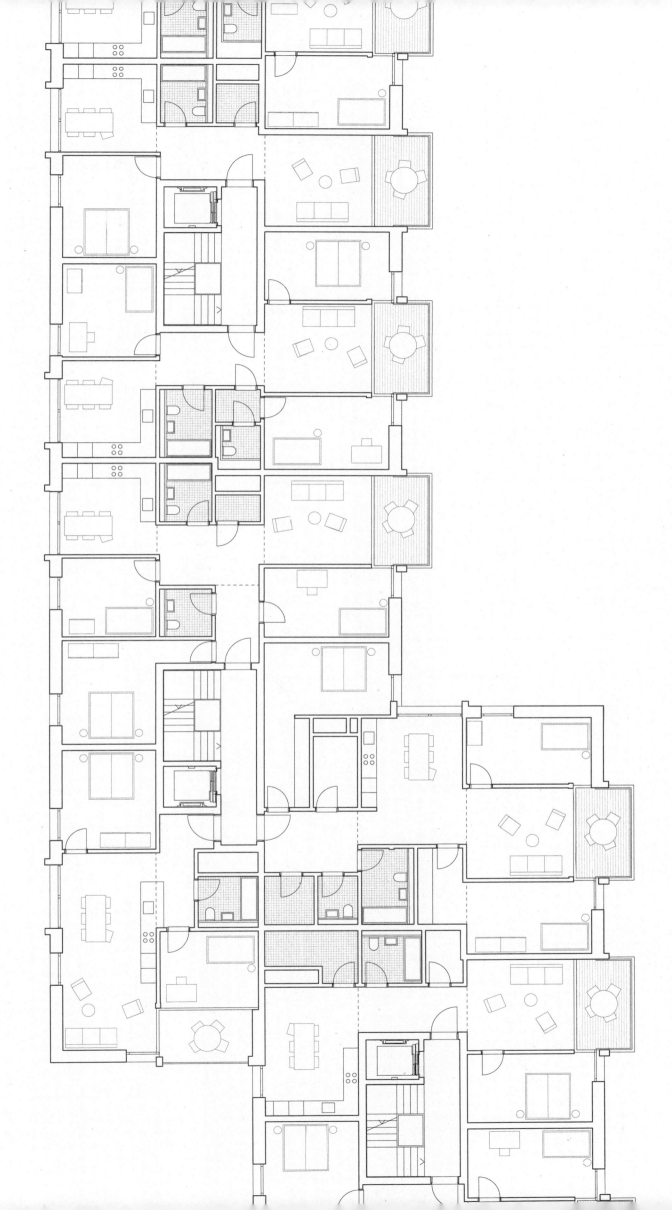

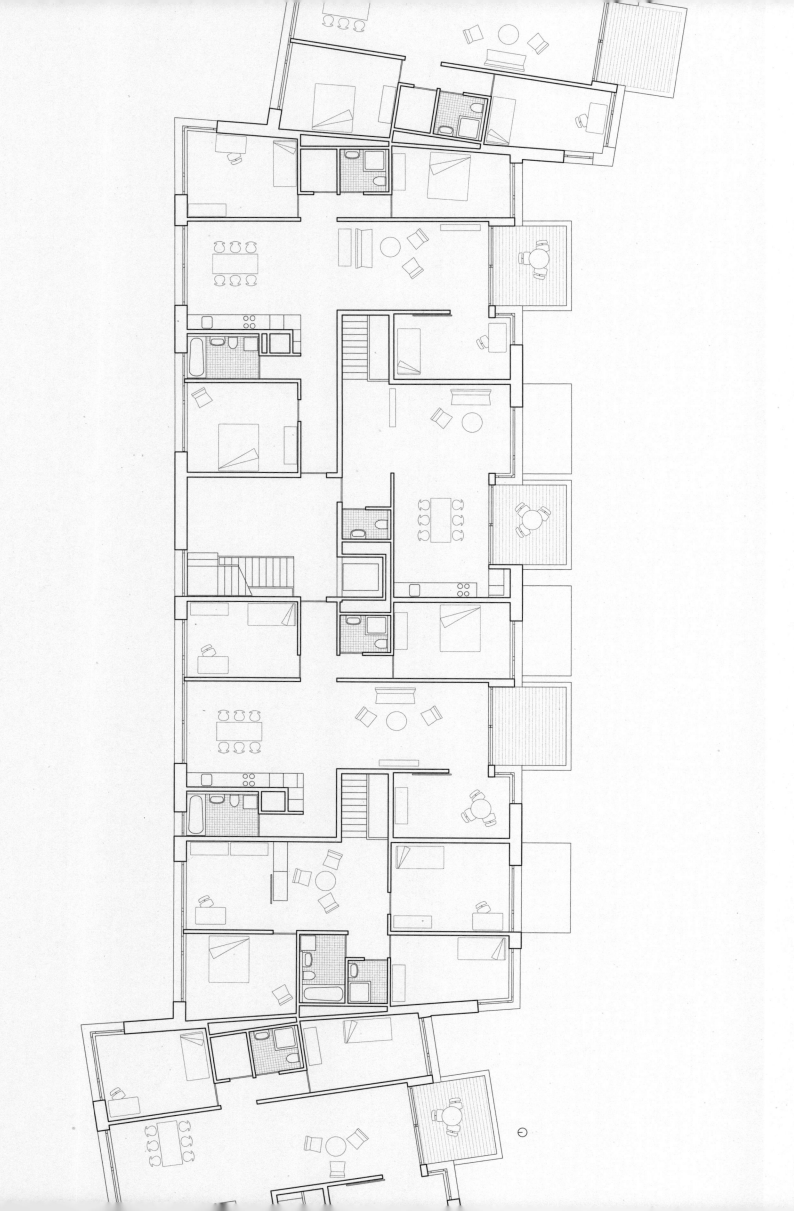

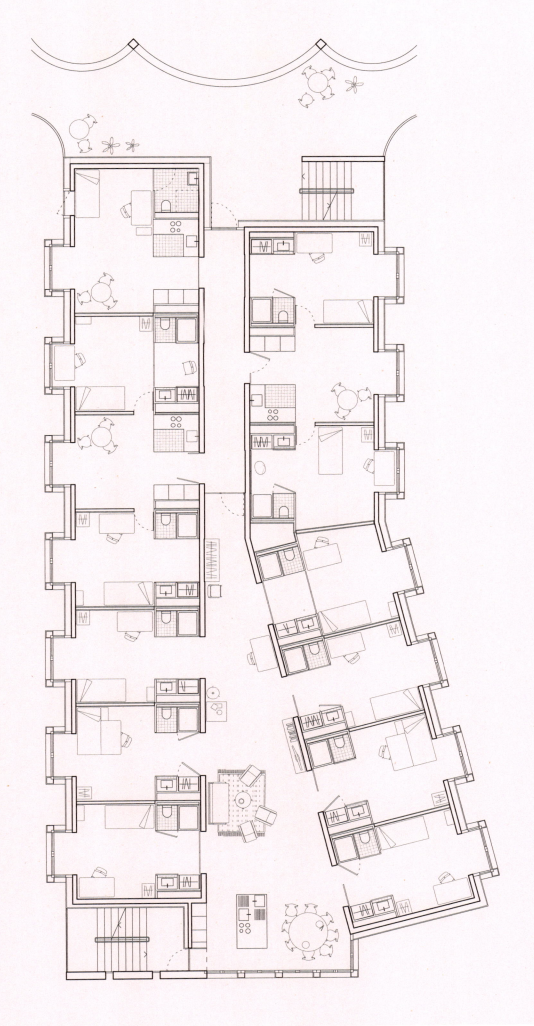

← pool 0072; Genossenschaftssiedlung/Cooperative Housing Estate, Leimbachstrasse, Zürich-Leimbach, 2001–2005

↑ pool 0291; Wohnsiedlung für Studierende/Housing Estate for Students, ETH, Zürich-Hönggerberg, 2012

pool Architekten: Vom Wohnen.
Möblierte Grundrisse im Massstab 1:150

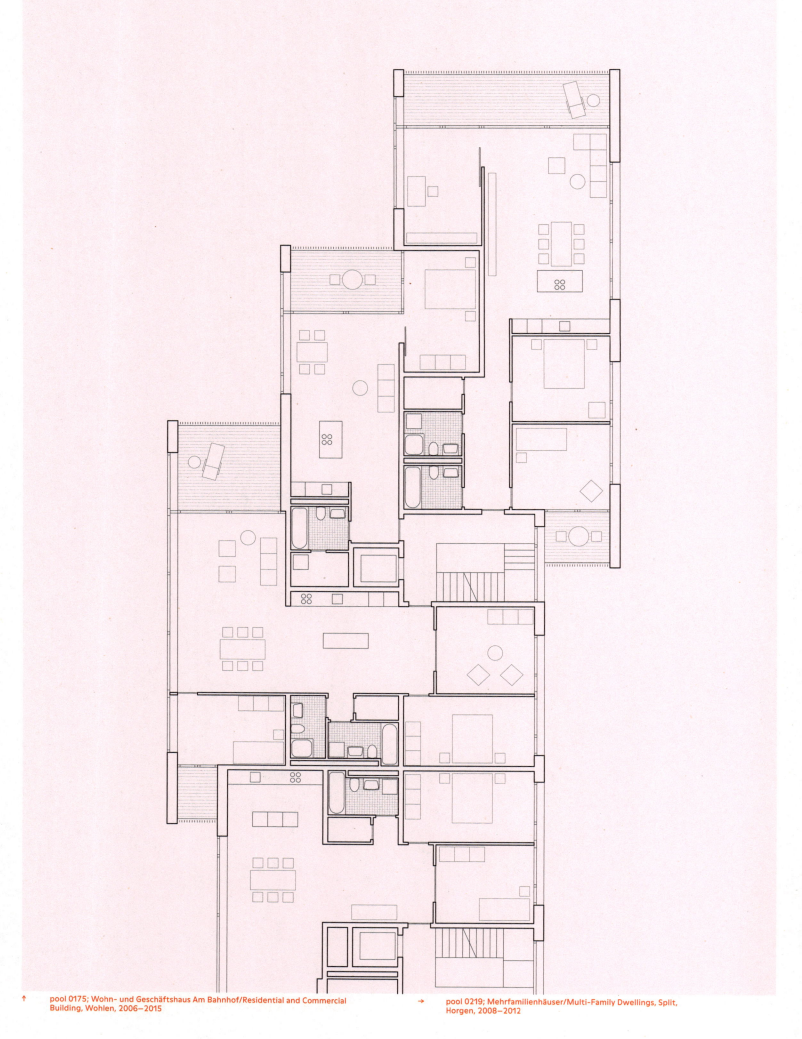

↑ pool 0175; Wohn- und Geschäftshaus Am Bahnhof/Residential and Commercial Building, Wohlen, 2006–2015

→ pool 0219; Mehrfamilienhäuser/Multi-Family Dwellings, Split, Horgen, 2008–2012

pool Architekten: On Housing.
Furnished Floor Plans on a Scale of 1:150

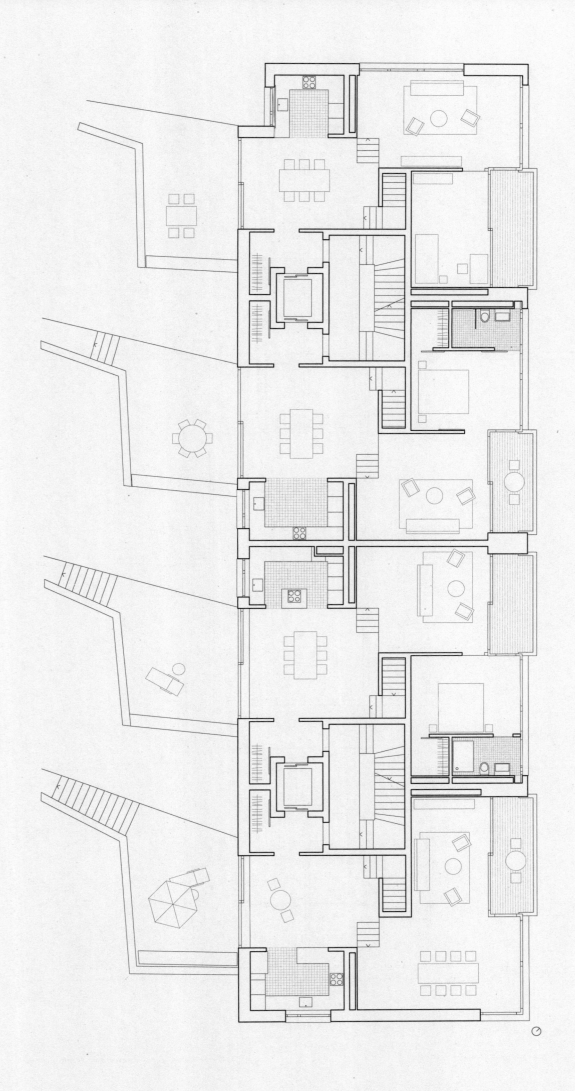

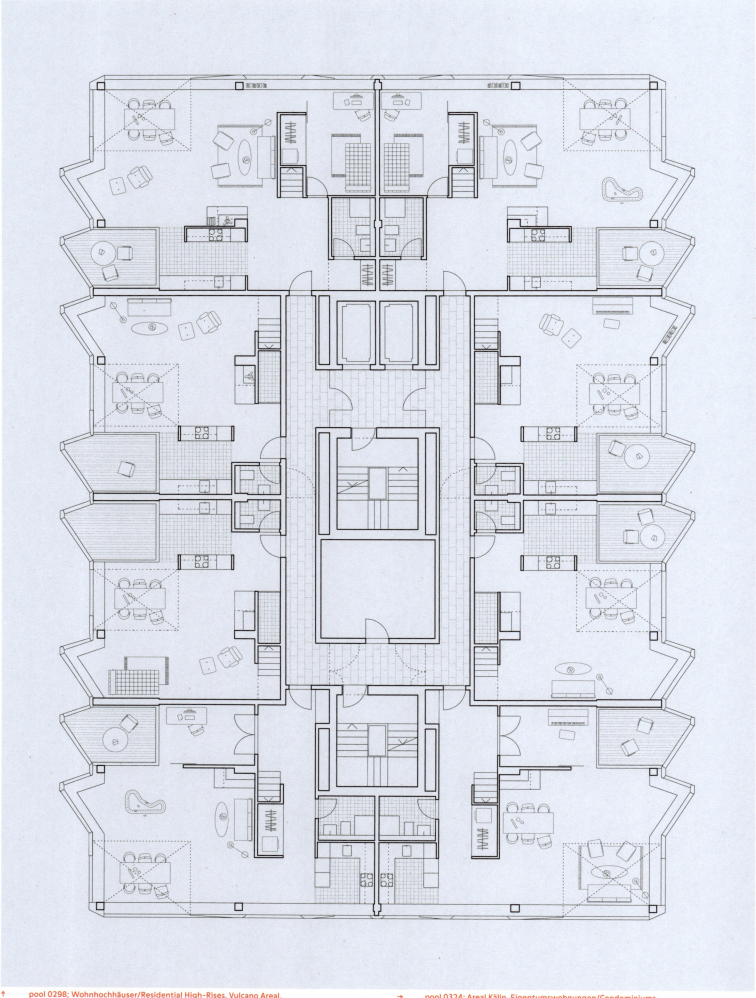

↑ pool 0298; Wohnhochhäuser/Residential High-Rises, Vulcano Areal, Zürich-Altstetten, 2012

→ pool 0324; Areal Kälin, Eigentumswohnungen/Condominiums, Oberwinterthur, 2014–2021

pool Architekten: On Housing.
Furnished Floor Plans on a Scale of 1:150

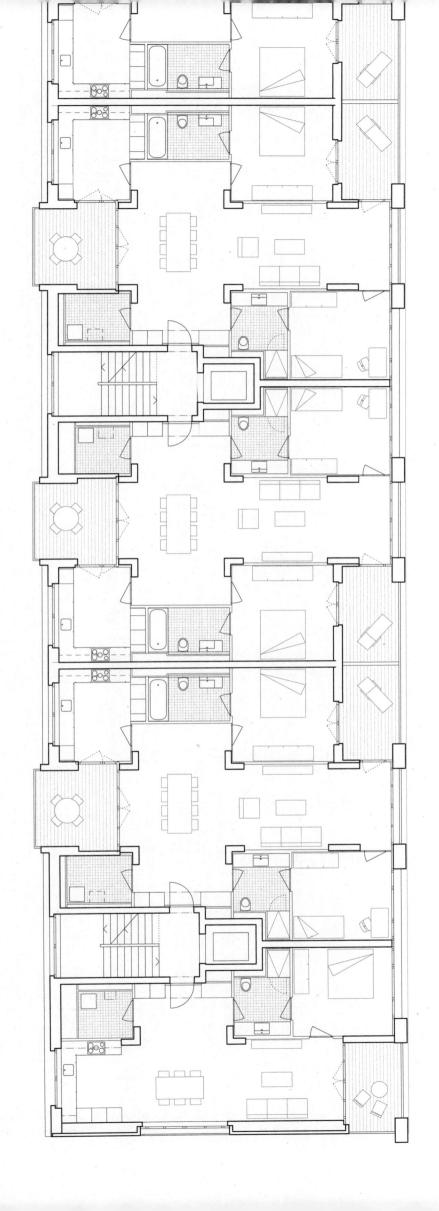

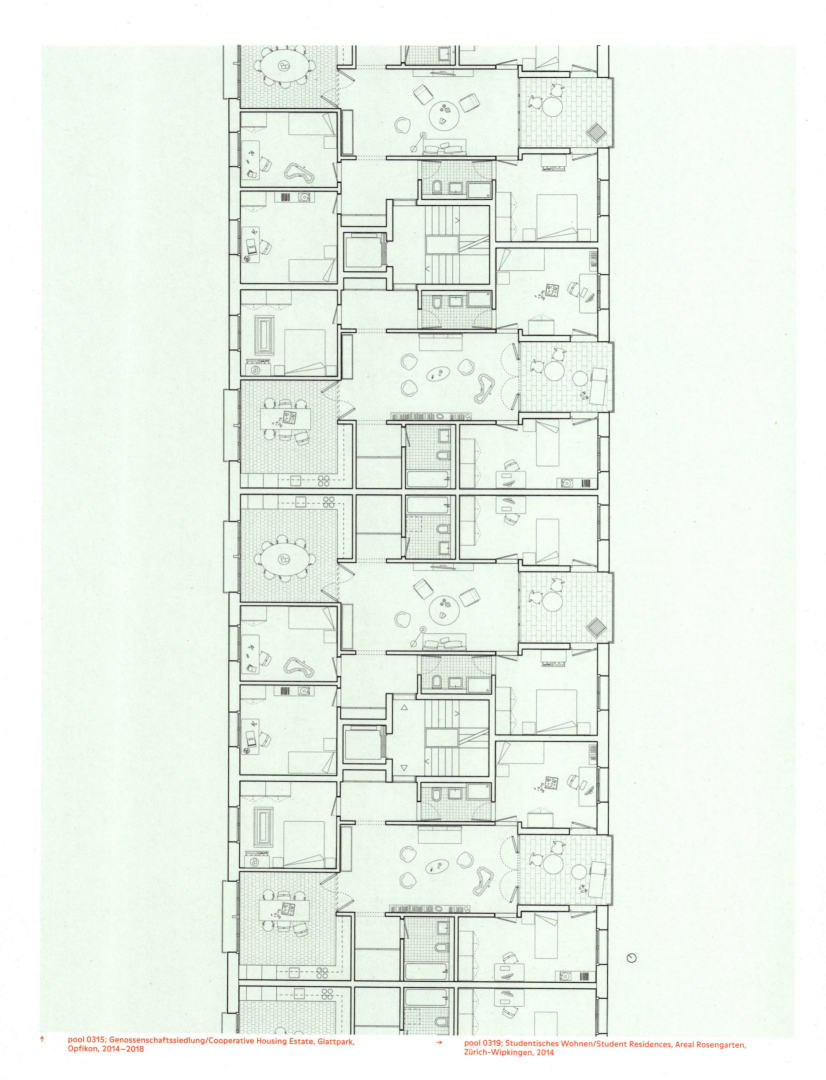

↑ pool 0315; Genossenschaftssiedlung/Cooperative Housing Estate, Glattpark, Opfikon, 2014–2018

→ pool 0319; Studentisches Wohnen/Student Residences, Areal Rosengarten, Zürich-Wipkingen, 2014

pool Architekten: On Housing.
Furnished Floor Plans on a Scale of 1:150

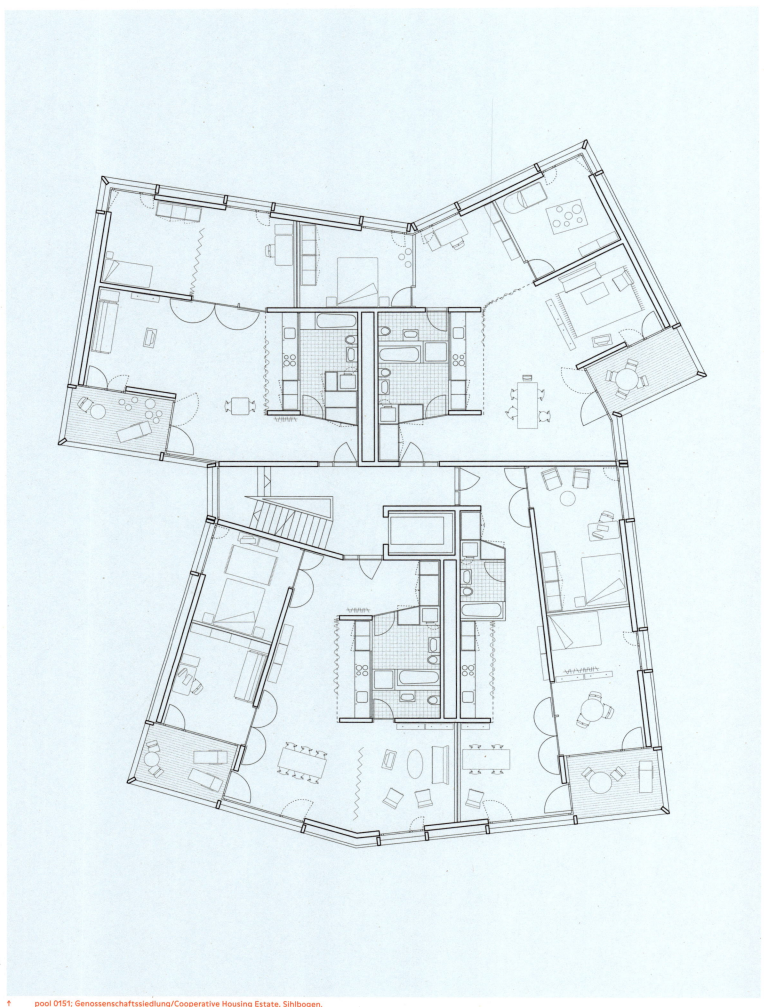

↑ pool 0151; Genossenschaftssiedlung/Cooperative Housing Estate, Sihlbogen, Zürich-Leimbach, 2005

pool Architekten: On Housing.
Furnished Floor Plans on a Scale of 1:150

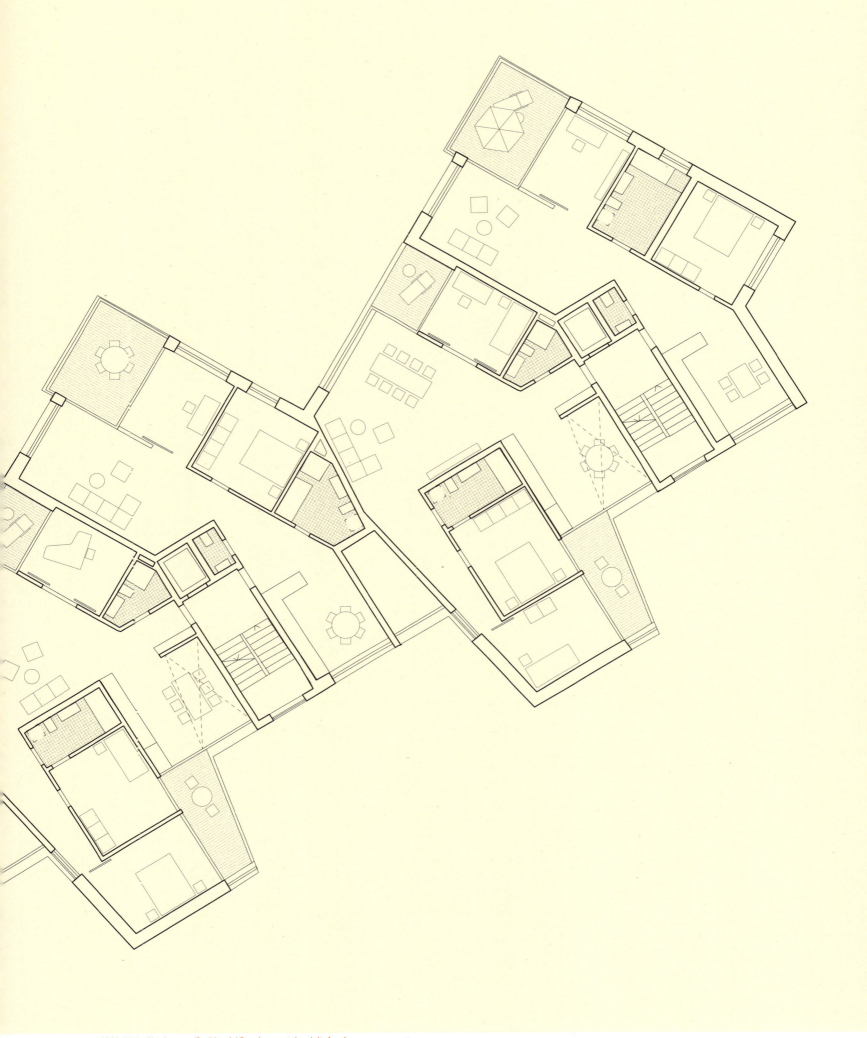

↑ pool 0282; Wohr überbauung/Residential Development, Landolt-Areal, Zürich, 2011

pool Architekten: Vom Wohnen.
Möblierte Grundrisse im Massstab 1:150

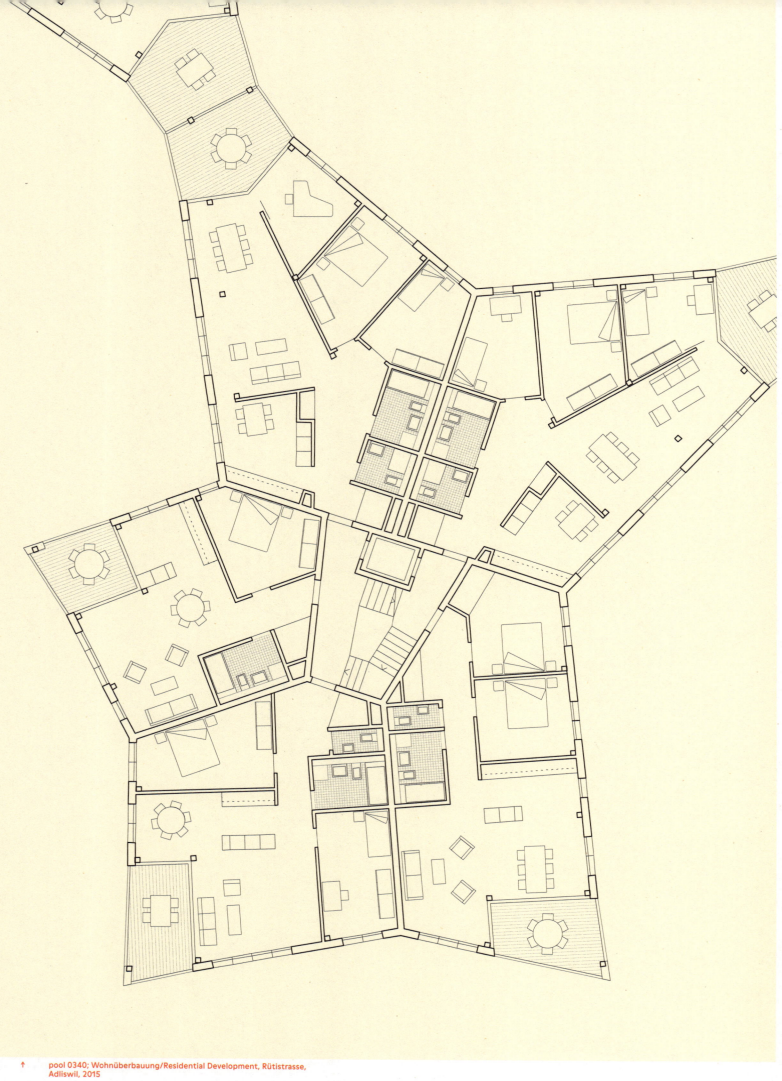

↑ pool 0340; Wohnüberbauung/Residential Development, Rütistrasse, Adliswil, 2015

↑ pool 0254; Wohnhaus/Apartment Building, Limmattalstrasse, Zürich-Höngg, 2010–2013

pool Architekten: Vom Wohnen.
Möblierte Grundrisse im Massstab 1:150

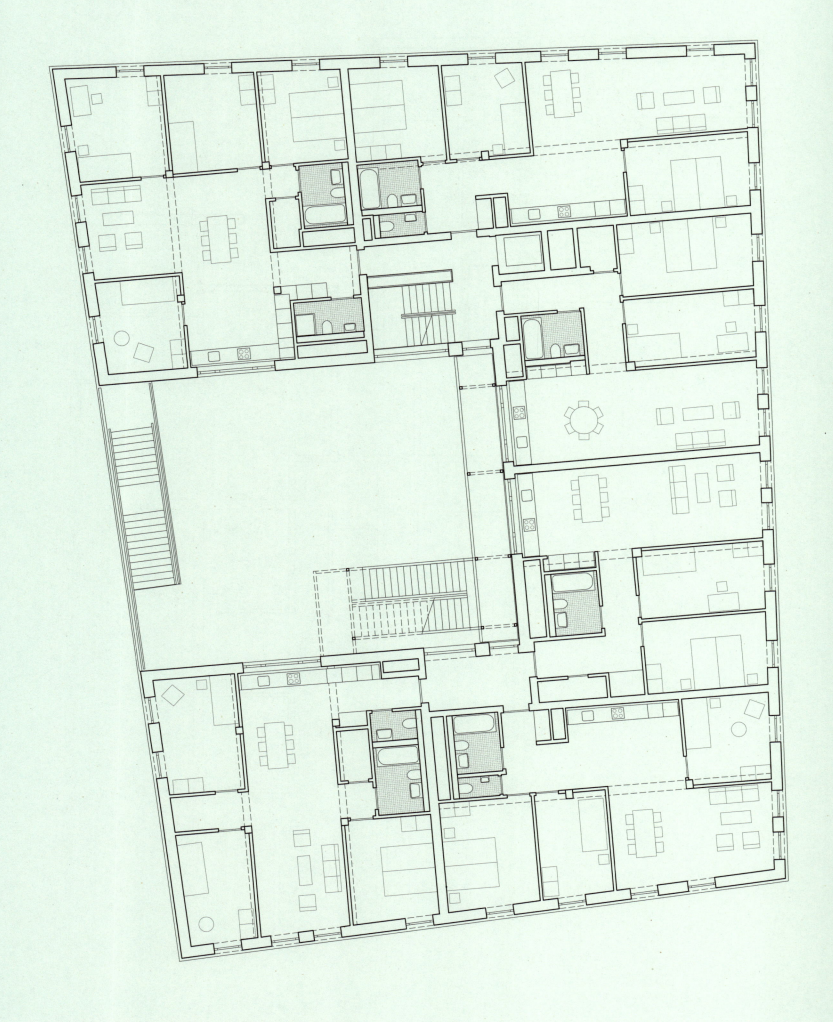

↑ pool 0243; Genossenschaftliches Wohnhaus/Cooperative Apartment Building, «mehr als wohnen», Haus/Building J, Zürich-Leutschenbach, 2009–2015

→ pool 0322; Genossenschaftliches Wohnhaus/Cooperative Apartment Building, Stadterle, Basel, 2014

pool Architekten: On Housing.
Furnished Floor Plans on a Scale of 1:150

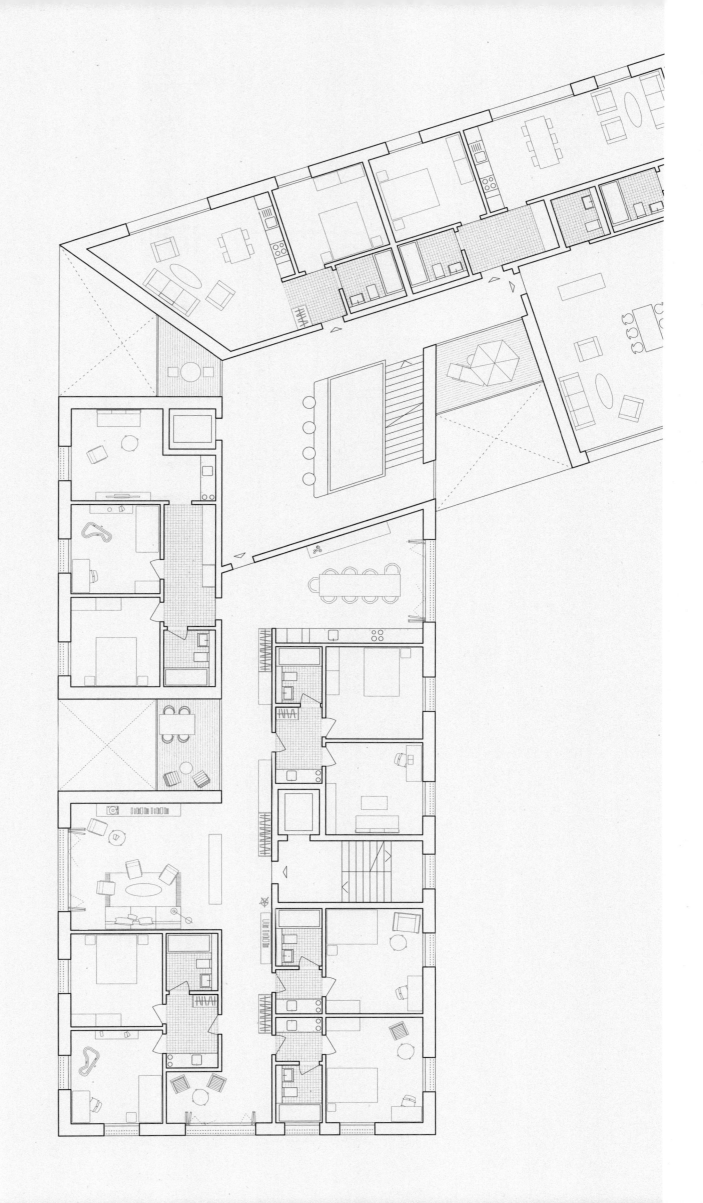

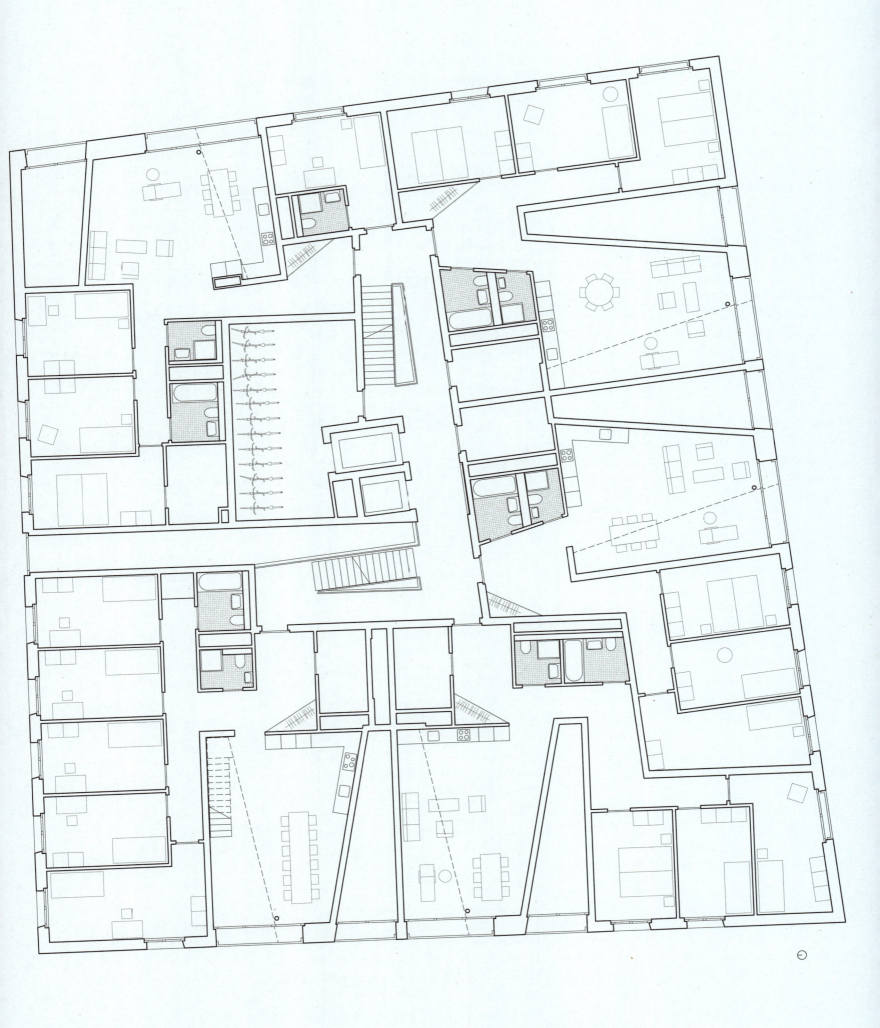

← pool 0113; Wohnüberbauung/Residential Development, Aspholz Nord, Zürich-Affoltern, 2003–2007

↑ pool 0243; Genossenschaftliches Wohnhaus/Cooperative Apartment Building, «mehr als wohnen», Haus/Building G, Zürich-Leutschenbach, 2009–2015

pool Architekten: Vom Wohnen.
Möblierte Grundrisse im Massstab 1:150

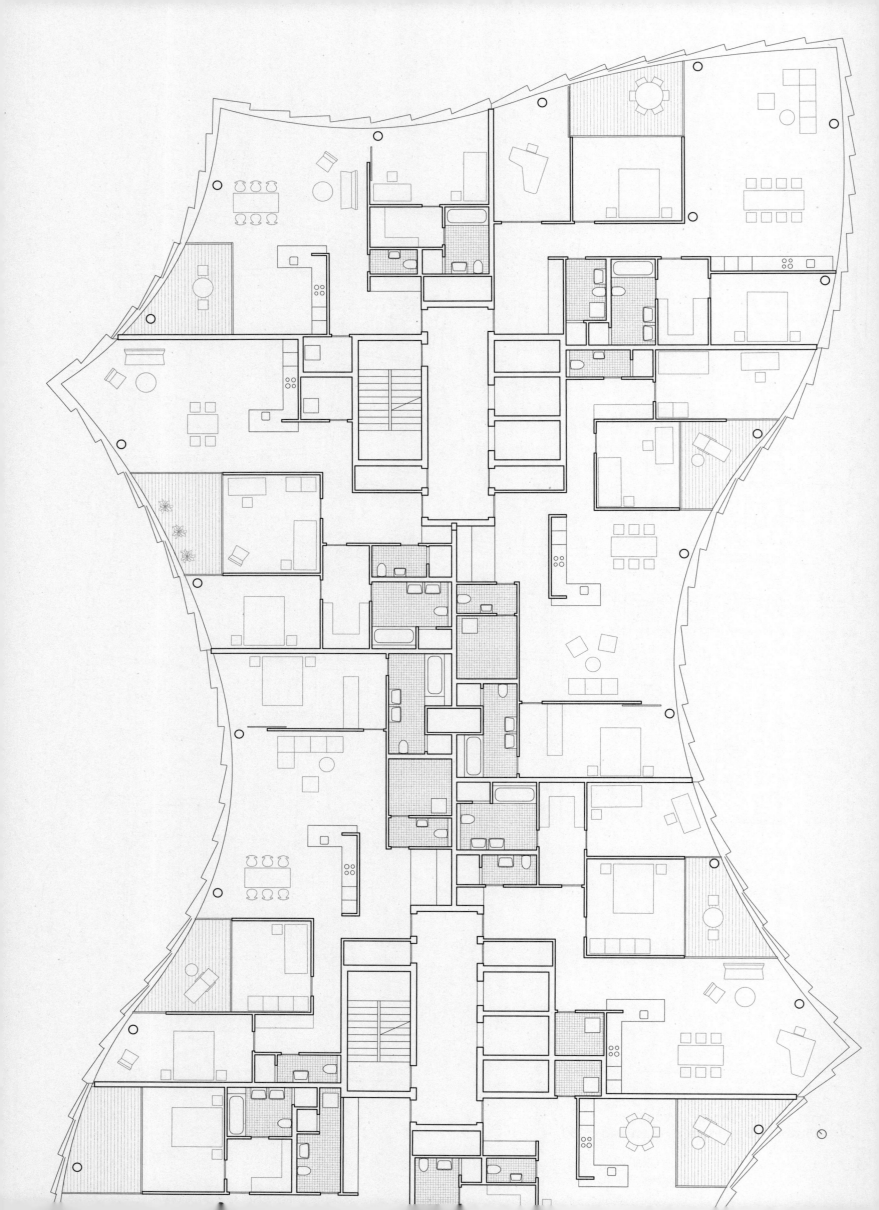

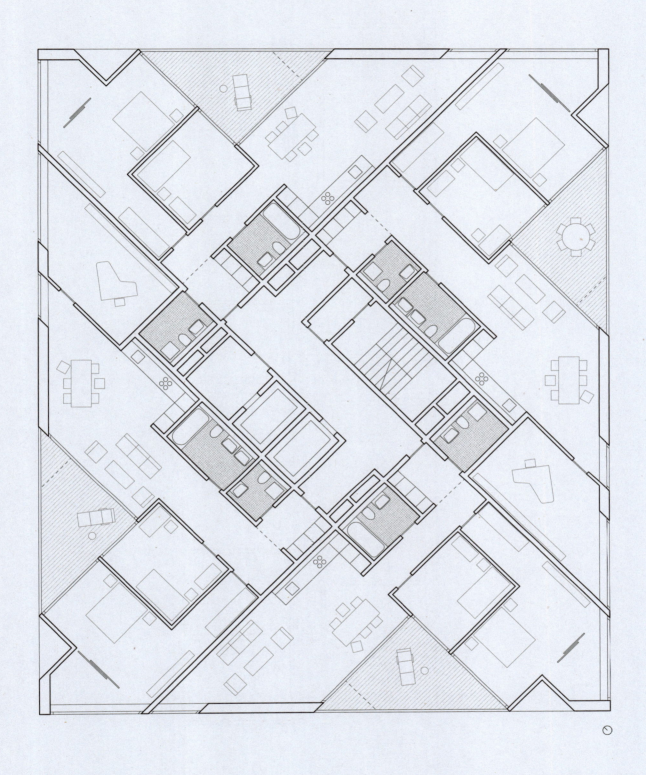

← pool 0200 Hochhaus/High-Rise, Hardturm-Areal, Zürich, 2007

↑ pool 0263; Wohnüberbauung/Residential Development, Zollfreilager, Zürich-Albisrieden, 2010

pool Architekten: Vom Wohnen.
Möblierte Grundrisse im Massstab 1:150

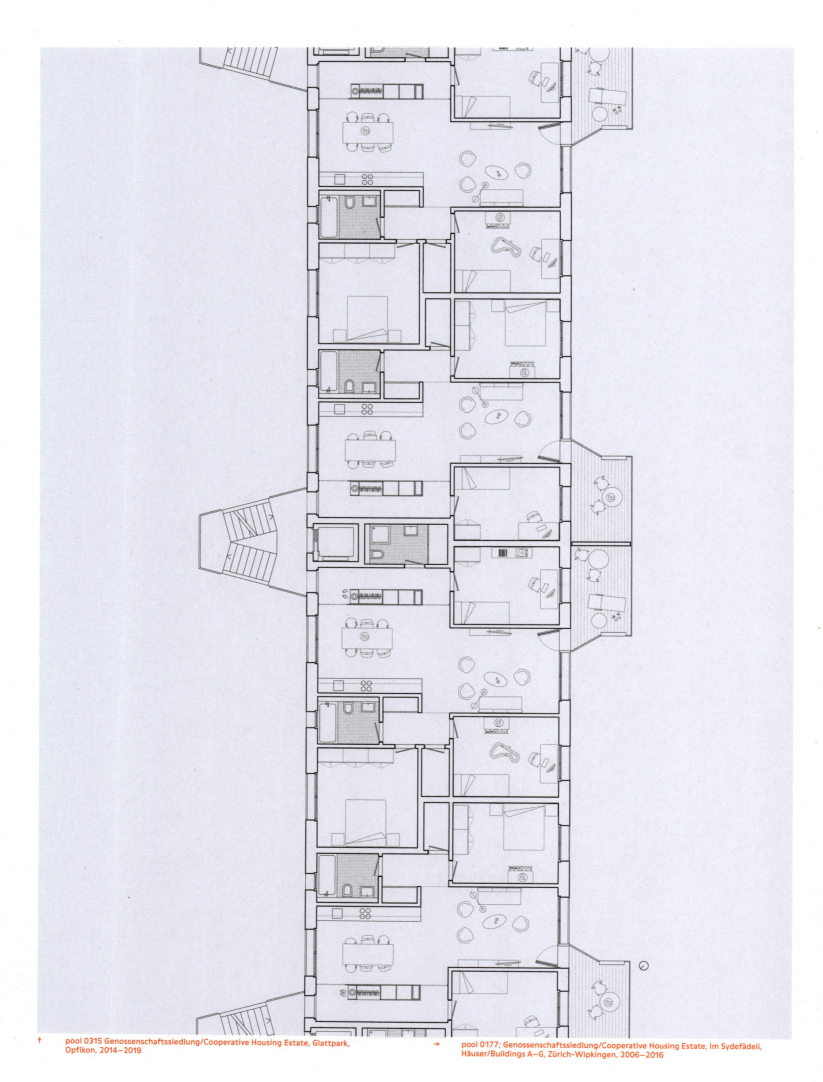

↑ pool 0315 Genossenschaftssiedlung/Cooperative Housing Estate, Glattpark, Opfikon, 2014–2019

→ pool 0177; Genossenschaftssiedlung/Cooperative Housing Estate, Im Sydefädeli, Häuser/Buildings A–G, Zürich-Wipkingen, 2006–2016

pool Architekten: On Housing.
Furnished Floor Plans on a Scale of 1:150

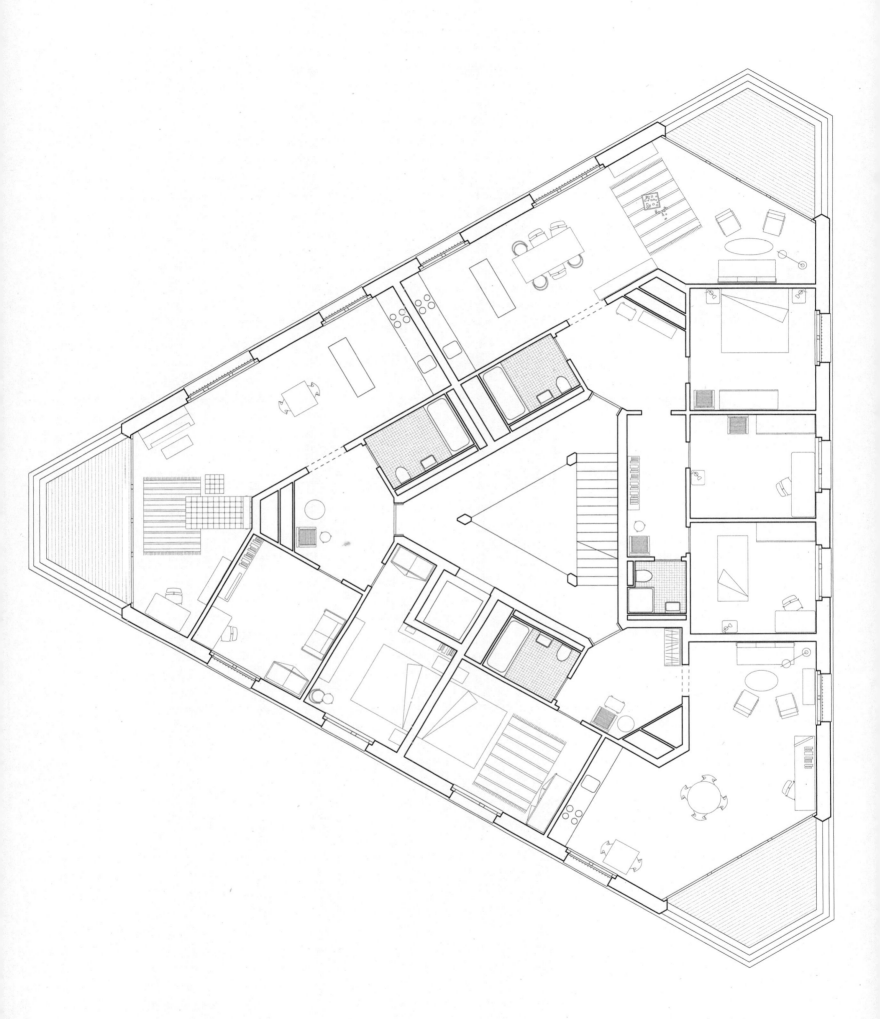

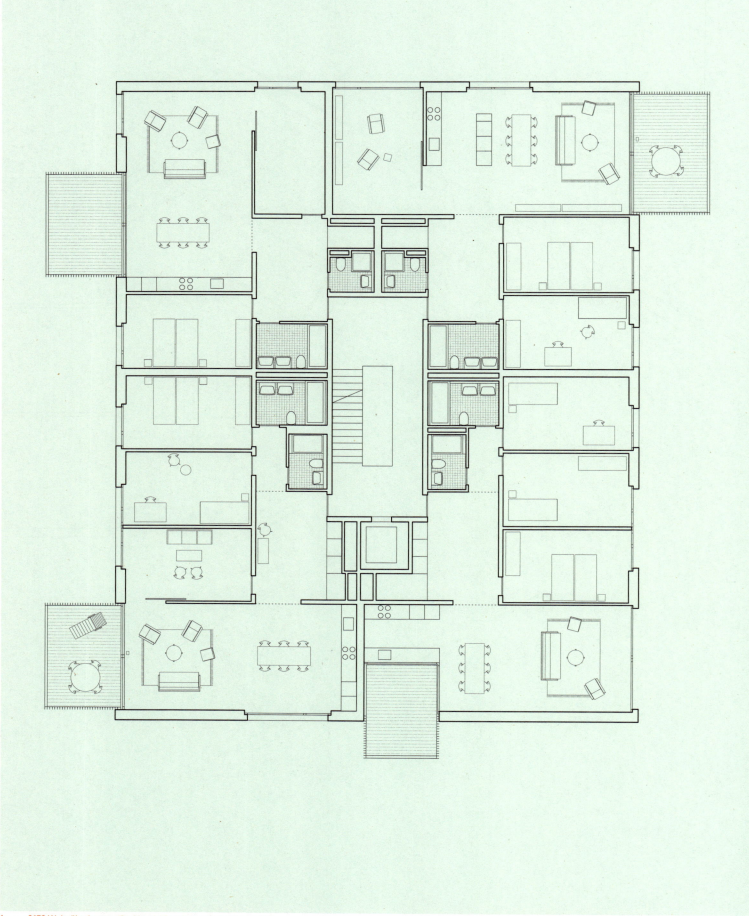

↑ 0159 Wohnüberbauung/Residential Development, Im Blumenfeld, Zürich-Affoltern, 2005–2008

→ pool 0280, Genossenschaftssiedlung/Cooperative Housing Estate, Am Glattbogen, Zürich-Schwamendingen, 2011–2019

pool Architekten: On Housing.
Furnished Floor Plans on a Scale of 1:150

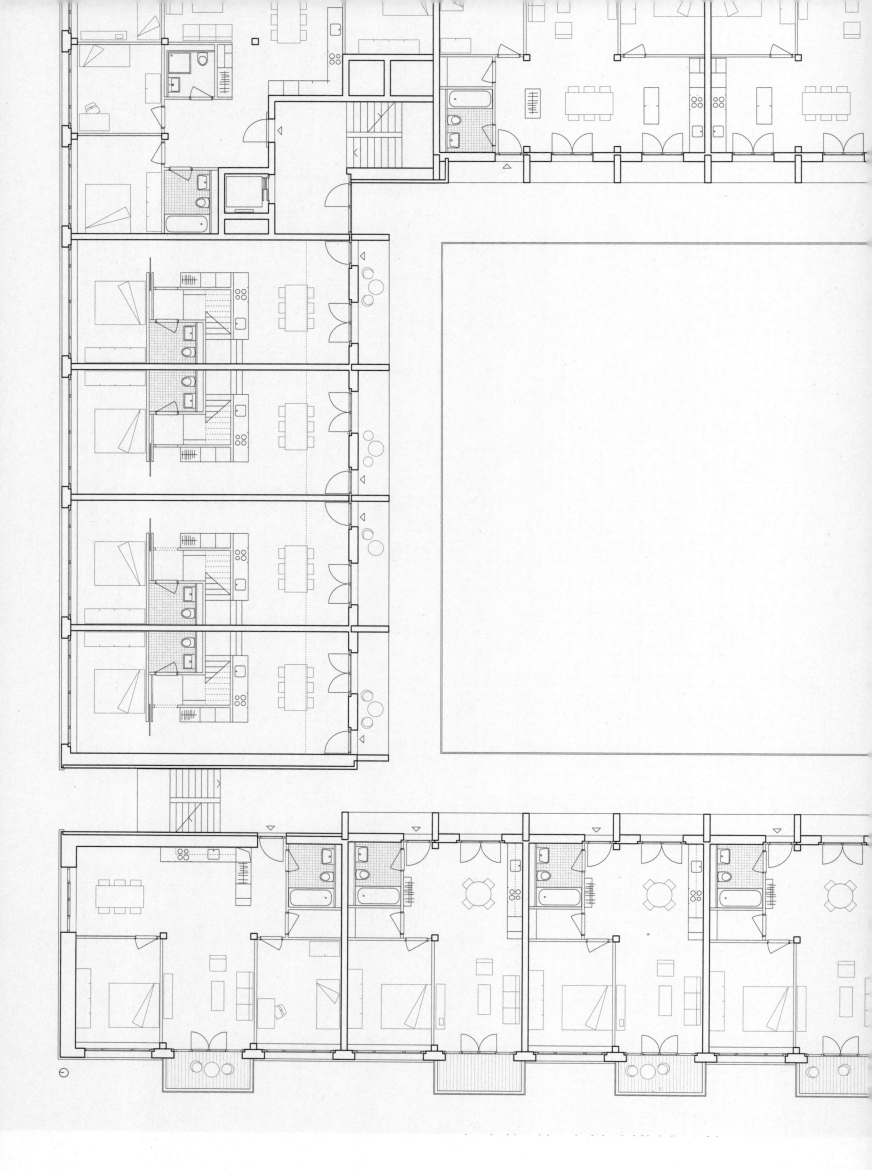

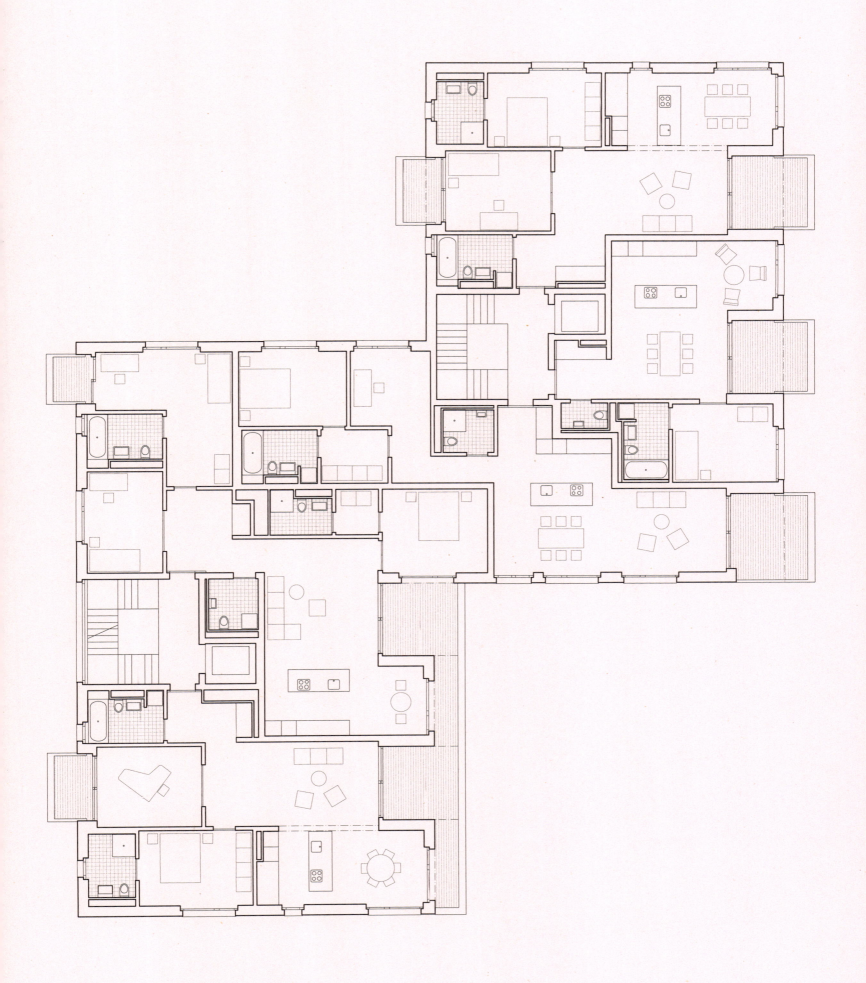

← pool 0324; Areal Kälin, Mietwohnungen/Rental Units, Oberwinterthur, 2014–2021   ↑ pool 0199; Wohn- und Gewerbeüberbauung/Residential and Commercial Development, Spätzstrasse, Horgen, 2007–2017

pool Architekten: Vom Wohnen.
Möblierte Grundrisse im Massstab 1:150

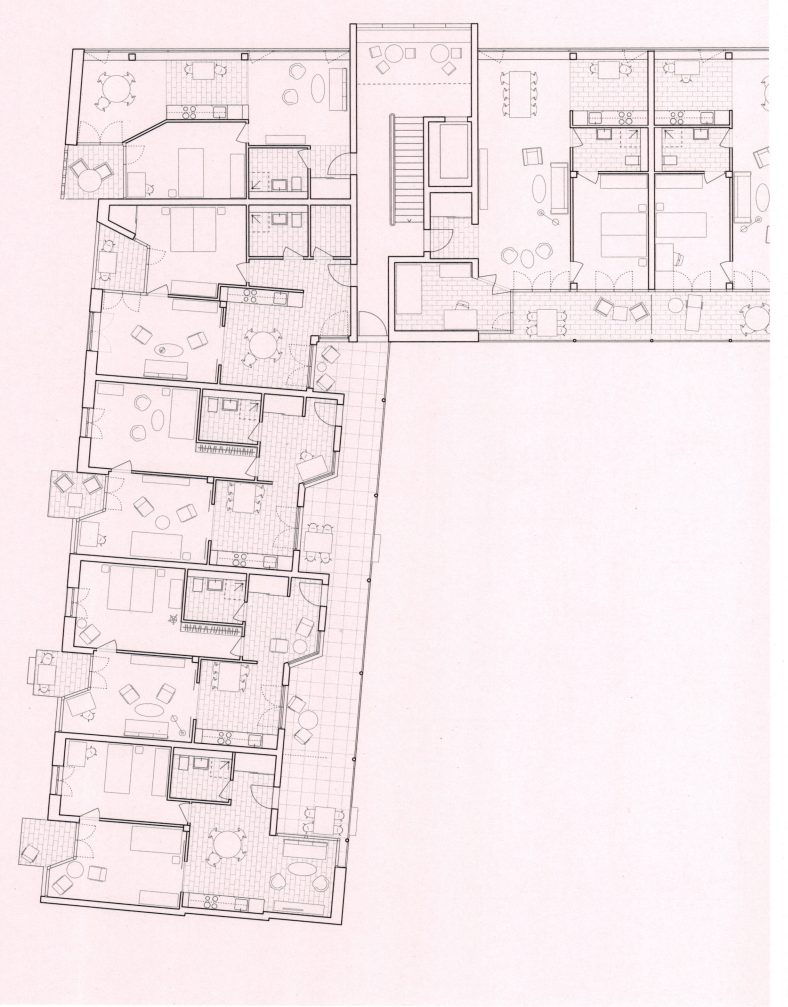

↑ pool 0323; Alterswohnen/Senior Housing, Erikastrasse, Zürich, 2014

pool Architekten: On Housing.
Furnished Floor Plans on a Scale of 1:150

←

pool Architekten:
Vom Wohnen.
Möblierte Grundrisse
im Massstab 1:150

pool Architekten:
On Housing.
Furnished Floor Plans
on a Scale of 1:150

pool Architekten:
Interieurs.
Das tägliche Leben

pool Architekten:
Interiors.
Daily Life

← ← pool 0254; Wohnhaus/Apartment Building, Limmattalstrasse, Zürich-Höngg, 2010–2013
← pool 0203; Dreifamilienhaus/Three-Family House, Im Dörfli, Oberrieden, 2007–2014
↑ pool 0276; Mehrfamilienhaus/Multifamily Dwelling, Kosakenweg, Zürich-Oerlikon, 2010–2014

pool Architekten: Interiors.
Das tägliche Leben

↑ pool 0243; Genossenschaftliches Wohnhaus/Cooperative Apartment Building, «Mehr als Wohnen», Haus/Building G, Zürich-Leutschenbach, 2009–2015

→ pool 0243; Genossenschaftliches Wohnhaus/Cooperative Apartment Building, «Mehr als Wohnen», Haus/Building G, Zürich-Leutschenbach, 2009–2015

pool Architekten: Interieurs.
Daily Life

← pool 0243; Genossenschaftliches Wohnhaus/Cooperative Apartment Building, «Mehr als Wohnen», Haus/Building G, Zürich-Leutschenbach, 2009–2015

↑ pool 0177; Genossenschaftssiedlung/Cooperative Housing Estate, Im Sydefädeli, Häuser/Buildings X, Y, Z, Zürich-Wipkingen, 2006–2016

pool Architekten: Interiors.
Das tägliche Leben

← ← pool 0201 Haus an der Bickelstrasse, Oberrieden, 2007–2009
← pool 0203 Dreifamilienhaus/Three-Family House, Im Dörfli, Oberrieden, 2007–2014
↑ pool 0176; Genossenschaftliches Wohn- und Geschäftshaus/Cooperative Residential and Commercial Building, Badenerstrasse, Zürich, 2006–2010
→ pool 0113; Wohnüberbauung/Residential Development, Aspholz Nord, Zürich-Affoltern, 2003

pool Architekten: Interieurs.
Daily Life

↑ pool 0072; Genossenschaftssiedlung/Cooperative Housing Estate, Leimbachstrasse, Zürich-Leimbach, 2001–2005

→ pool 0177; Genossenschaftssiedlung/Cooperative Housing Estate, Im Sydefädeli, Häuser/Buildings A–F, Zürich-Wipkingen, 2006–2016

pool Architekten: Interieurs.
Daily Life

↑ pool 0343; Wohnüberbauung/Residential Development, Letzibach D, Zürich-Altstetten, 2015
← pool 0079; Haus Buscaglia, Altendorf, 2001–2003
→ pool 0201; Haus an der Bickelstrasse, Oberrieden, 2007–2009
→→ pool 0315; Genossenschaftssiedlung/Cooperative Housing Estate, Glattpark, Opfikon, 2014–2019

pool Architekten: Interiors.
Das tägliche Leben

← pool 0243; Genossenschaftliches Wohnhaus/Cooperative Apartment Building, «Mehr als Wohnen», Haus/Building G, Zürich-Leutschenbach, 2009–2015

↑ pool 0354; Wohnüberbauung/Residential Development, Effretikon Illnau-Effretikon, 2017

pool Architekten: Interiors.
Das tägliche Leben

↑ pool 0195; Reihenhäuser/Town Houses, Blue Notes, Richterswil, 2007–2010   → pool 0203; Dreifamilienhaus/Three-Family House, Im Dörfli, Oberrieden, 2007–2014

pool Architekten: Interieurs.
Daily Life

← pool 0201; Haus an der Bickelstrasse, Oberrieden, 2007–2009   ↑ pool 0355; Wohnüberbauung/Residential Development, Manegg, Zürich-Manegg, 2017

← pool 0331; Wohnüberbauung/Residential Development, Eggbühl-Areal, Zürich-Seebach, 2014–2020

↑ pool 0177; Genossenschaftssiedlung/Cooperative Housing Estate, Im Sydefädeli, Häuser/Buildings X, Y, Z, Zürich-Wipkingen, 2006–2016

pool Architekten: Interiors. Das tägliche Leben

↑ pool 0176; Genossenschaftliches Wohn- und Geschäftshaus/Cooperative Residential and Commercial Building, Badenerstrasse, Zürich, 2006–2010

→ pool 0203; Dreifamilienhaus/Three-Family House, Im Dörfli, Oberrieden, 2007–2014

pool Architekten: Interieurs. Daily Life

↑ pool 0180; Alterswohnungen/Senior Housing Estate, Siedlung Frieden, Zürich-Affoltern, 2006–2013
← pool 0175; Wohn- und Geschäftshaus/Residential and Commercial Building, Am Bahnhof, Wohlen, 2006–2015
→ pool 0203; Dreifamilienhaus/Three-Family House, Im Dörfli, Oberrieden, 2007–2014
→→ pool 0176; Genossenschaftliches Wohn- und Geschäftshaus/Cooperative Residential and Commercial Building, Badenerstrasse, Zürich, 2006–2010

pool Architekten: Interiors.
Das tägliche Leben

↑ pool 0254; Wohnhaus/Apartment Building, Limmattalstrasse, Zürich-Höngg, 2010–2013

→ pool 0177; Genossenschaftssiedlung/Cooperative Housing Estate, Im Sydefädeli, Häuser/Buildings U–V, Zürich-Wipkingen, 2006–2016

pool Architekten: Interieurs.
Daily Life

↑ pool 0113; Wohnüberbauung/Residential Development, Aspholz Nord, Zürich-Affoltern, 2003–2007
← pool 0243; Genossenschaftliches Wohnhaus/Cooperative Apartment Building, «Mehr als Wohnen», Haus/Building L, Zürich-Leutschenbach, 2009–2015
→ pool 0229; Wohnhaus/Apartment Building, 2010–2013

pool Architekten: Interiors.
Das tägliche Leben

pool Architekten: pool Architekten:
Interieurs. Interiors.
Das tägliche Leben Daily Life

Der spezifische
Ausdruck
des Materials

The Specific
Expression
of the Materials

Mit der Suche nach dem Spezifischen in der Architektur rückt die Wesenhaftigkeit des Materials sowohl mit ihren optischen, haptischen, sinnlichen und atmosphärischen Qualitäten als auch mit ihren baukonstruktiven und physikalischen Eigenschaften wieder in den Vordergrund.

Homogene Konstruktionen aus Ziegel, Beton oder Holz, in denen das Material gleichzeitig trägt und dämmt, sowie materialspezifische Konstruktionen aus Stahl haben das Potenzial, eine Architektursprache zu entwickeln, die nicht mehr willkürlich und damit beliebig ist, sondern direkt an das gewählte Material und seine Füge- und Produktionstechniken, seine konstruktiven Besonderheiten sowie die statische Leistungsfähigkeit gebunden ist. Raumgrössen, Raumfolgen und Raumzusammenhänge, aber auch die Bauweise und der Ausdruck der Fassaden werden dann wieder vom Material bestimmt.

Ebenso wie sich standardisierte Grundrisse im Wohnungsbau durchgesetzt haben, sind Mischbauweisen als ökonomische Variante des Bauens der Standard geworden; mit Blick auf eine grösstmögliche Effizienz werden Stahlbetonkonstruktionen mit gedämmten Steinen, Gipskartonwänden oder Holzkonstruktionen gemischt. Meist geben die Tragwerksingenieure das Material den konstruktiven Eigenschaften entsprechend vor. Geputzte, weisse Oberflächen bringen wieder die gewünschte Einheitlichkeit und verbergen das «Dahinter» — eine Baumethode und Architekturauffassung, die bereits mit der Industrialisierung und dem starken Wachstum der Städte in der Gründerzeit des 19. Jahrhunderts zu finden war und sich in der Architektur des Neuen Bauens fortgesetzt hat.

Material versus Stil

Henry-Russell Hitchcock und Philip Johnson fassten 1932 in ihrer Architekturausstellung *Modern Architecture: International Exhibition* im Museum of Modern Art (MoMA) in New York die Prinzipien des International Style anhand der drei Prinzipien «Architektur als Volumen», «Regelmässigkeit» und «Verzicht auf jegliche applizierten Ornamente» zusammen und beschrieben das Verhältnis zum Material wie folgt: Nicht das Material an sich steht im Fokus der Betrachtungen, sondern die Ebenmässigkeit und Durchgängigkeit der Oberflächen, damit das Volumen und das Kubische in der Architektur zur Wirkung kommen kann.[1] Die gewünschte Einheitlichkeit und Ebenmässigkeit im Erscheinungsbild der Architektur und der Stadt werden hauptsächlich über

1 Henry Russell Hitchcock, Philip Johnson, *The International Style*. New York 1932, S. 64ff.

Der spezifische Ausdruck des Materials

Shifted into the foreground with the search for specificity in architecture are the essential properties of material; their optical, haptic, sensuous, and atmospheric qualities, together with their structural and physical characteristics.

A homogenous construction in brick, concrete, or wood, where the material simultaneously serves loadbearing and insulating functions, along with construction in steel, has the potential to develop an architectural language that is no longer haphazard, and hence arbitrary. Instead it is bound up directly with the chosen material and its assembly and production technologies, its constructive peculiarities, as well as its static performance capacities. Room sizes, sequences, and interrelationships, but also the construction and the expression of façades would be determined by the material.

Just as standardized floorplans have prevailed in housing development, composite construction—as an economical variant of building—has become the standard. With an eye toward maximal efficiency, reinforced concrete construction has been mixed with insulated brick, plasterboard, or wood. For the most part, the structural engineer specifies the material in conformity with constructive properties. White, plastered surfaces supply the desired uniformity while concealing what is "behind"; a building method and architectural conception that was present already with industrialization and the massive growth of the cities in the Wilhelminian era of the nineteenthth century, and which continued to assert itself in the architecture of the Neue Bauen.

Material versus Style

In the architectural exhibition they organized at MoMA in 1932, Hitchcock and Johnson summarized the tenets of the International Style with reference to the three principles of "composition in volume," "regularity," and "lack of ornament." They described the relationship to the material as follows: the material in and of itself is not the focus of consideration, but instead the evenness and consistency of the surfaces, which allows the volumes and the cubic qualities of the architecture to come into their own.[1] The desired uniformity and even appearance of the architecture and of the city were generated primarily through covering layers and cladding. In this context the atmospheric, sensual, and optical qualities of materials and construction were not integrated into the discussion. The extension of traditional building materials such as natural stone, brick,

1 Henry-Russel Hitchcock and Philip Johnson, *The International Style*, New York 1932, pp. 64ff.

Deckschichten und Bekleidungen hergestellt. Kulturelle Verankerung, atmosphärische, sinnliche und optische Qualitäten oder die architektonische und städtebauliche Ausdruckskraft des Materials und der Konstruktion sind in diesem Umfeld nicht Teil der architektonischen Auseinandersetzungen. Die Erweiterung der traditionellen Baumaterialien Naturstein, Ziegel und Holz um die modernen, neuen Baumaterialien wie Stahlbeton, Stahl oder Glas führt beim Bauen zu einer Materialvielfalt, die dem gewünschten Ausdruck widerspricht.

Auch wenn dieser Umgang mit dem Material im Wohnungsbau bis heute Gültigkeit hat, wird über das Verhältnis von Material und Architektur, man könnte auch sagen von Material und Form, seit mindestens zweihundert Jahren gestritten.

Form und Material im Dialog

Gottfried Semper setzte sich in seinen Schriften für den sogenannten Materialstil ein, bei dem jedes Material die jeweils zweckmässige Gestalt annehmen sollte. «Backsteine, Holz, besonders Eisen, Metall und Zink ersetzen die Stelle der Quadersteine und des Marmors. Es wäre unpassend, noch ferner mit falschem Scheine sie nachzuahmen. Es spreche das Material für sich und trete auf, unverhüllt, in der Gestalt, in den Verhältnissen, die als die zweckmässigsten für dasselbe durch Erfahrungen und Wissenschaften erprobt sind. Backstein erscheine als Backstein, Holz als Holz, Eisen als Eisen, ein jedes nach den ihm eigenen Gesetzen der Statik.»[2] An anderer Stelle beschreibt er die Formfindung als Resultat von Gebrauchszweck, verwendetem Material sowie der Herstellungsmethoden.[3] Damit adelte er das Material, das über Jahrhunderte dem Form- und Stilwillen der Architekten unterlag. Gleichzeitig lieferten die neuesten Entwicklungen in der Architektur der Markthallen, Gewächshäuser und Ausstellungsbauten aus filigranen Eisen-Glaskonstruktionen den praktischen Beweis zu Sempers Theorie und begründeten de facto einen neuen Baustil, bei dem nicht mehr die gestalterische Absicht, sondern das Material die Form und damit den Ausdruck der Architektur bestimmte. Architekten wie Otto Wagner, Adolf Loos oder Frank Lloyd Wright folgten Sempers Ausführungen, wenn sie sich für die «materialgerechte» Form einsetzten.

Während die Auseinandersetzung mit der Bedeutung des Materials in der Architektur des 19. und frühen 20. Jahrhunderts die «materialgerechte» Form fokussierte und deren Verfechter davon ausgingen, dass jedem Material eine ihm gerechte Form entspricht, löste sich dieses dualistische Material-Form-Prinzip ab Mitte der 1950er-Jahre auf. Es entstand ein komplexes Geflecht von Bedingungen und Abhängigkeiten, die das Material und die Form in der Architektur bestimmen. Unabhängig voneinander und dennoch immer wieder miteinander verwoben, folgen Form und Material ihren eigenen

and wood to include new, modern building materials such as reinforced concrete, steel, and glass led to a material diversity in building that contradicted the desired expressiveness.

Although this contention over materials in housing development retains its validity today, the relationship between material and architectural form has been an subject of dispute for at least 200 years.

Form and Material in Dialogue

In his writings, Gottfried Semper advocated the so-called material style in relation to which each respective material would assume its purposeful gestalt. "Brick, wood, iron, metal, and zinc in particular take the place of ashlars and marble. It would be inappropriate to continue imitating these last two—even more so to give the new materials a false appearance. Let the material speak for itself; let it step forth undisguised in the shape and proportions found most suitable by experience in science. Brick should appear as brick, wood as wood, iron as iron, each according to its own structural laws."[2] Elsewhere, he characterizes formal invention as a result of functional purpose, both regarding the material employed as well as the method of manufacture.[3] In this way, he ennobled material, which had been subjected for centuries to the formalistic and stylistic caprice of architects. Then recent developments in the architecture of market halls, greenhouses, and exhibition buildings based on filigree glass-and-iron construction supplied the practical confirmation of Semper's theory, de facto founding a new building style in which material determined the forms and hence the expression of the architecture rather than exclusively design intentions. Architects such as Otto Wagner, Adolf Loos, and Frank Lloyd Wright followed Semper's discussions, committing themselves to forms that were "appropriate to the materials."

While during the nineteenth and early twentieth centuries, discussions of the significance of material in architecture focused on forms that were "appropriate to the materials," and the advocates of this principle assumed that every material corresponded to a form that was adapted to it, this dualistic material/form principle began to dissolve in the mid-1950s as a complex network of conditions and dependencies emerged which came to determine material and form in architecture. Independent of one another and nonetheless repeatedly interwoven, form and material follow their own laws. The material is deployed in accordance with its "essence." This "essence" contains both its constructive actuality, with its static structural significance, and its sensuous actuality, with all of its optical, haptic, and atmospheric effects, as well as its symbolic meanings, which involve emotional values. Alvar Aalto was a determined advocate of this aspect

---

2   Gottfried Semper, «Über vielfarbige Architektur und Skulptur bei den Alten», 1834, in: Hans und Manfred Semper (Hrsg.), *Gottfried Semper. Kleine Schriften*, Mittenwald 1979, S. 219

3   «… und die keramischen Formen von einem andern Gesichtspunkt aus betrachten, indem wir ihre Formen und ihren Schmuck als Resultate: erstens ihrer wirklichen und fingierten Benutzung und Anwendung, zweitens der Materialien und Prozesse betrachten, welche bei ihrer Ausführung in Frage kommen.» (Ebd., «Keramisches», S. 24)

2   Gottfried Semper, "Preliminary Remarks on Polychrome Architecture and Sculpture in Antiquity", in *The Four Elements of Architecture and other Writings*, translated by Harry Francis Mallgrave and Wolfgang Herrmann, Cambridge 1989, p. 48.

3   "… and to consider the ceramic forms from a different point of view, by regarding their forms and their decoration as results: first, of their actual and simulated uses, second of the materials and processes that were involved in their execution." Gottfried Semper, "Keramisches," in *Kleine Schriften*, Mittenwald 1979, p. 24.

Gesetzen. Das Material wird seinem «Wesen» entsprechend eingesetzt; dieses beinhaltet sowohl die konstruktive Wirklichkeit in ihrer statischen und baukonstruktiven Bedeutung als auch die sinnliche Wirklichkeit mit der optischen, haptischen und atmosphärischen Wirkung und ihrer symbolischen Bedeutung, die emotionale Werte einbezieht. Alvar Aalto setzte sich dezidiert für diese Aspekte der Materialität in der Architektur ein. Jenseits von Schematismus, den die Massenproduktion von Wohnungen hervorgebracht hatte, und architektonischen Stilen vertrat er die Auffassung, dass jede Bauaufgabe nach einem adäquaten Material verlangt,[4] wobei die kulturelle Verankerung und emotionale Konnotation des Materials berücksichtigt werden sollte.

Damit rückten die Oberflächenqualität, die Textur oder die natürliche Farbigkeit der Materialien in das Blickfeld der Architekten. Diese Form der Annäherung führte in den 1990er-Jahren zu einem neuen Umgang mit dem Material, bei dem die Wirkung der Oberflächen im Vordergrund stand. Setzten Architekten wie Peter Zumthor und Tadao Ando neben dem Sinnlichen und Atmosphärischen noch auf die baukonstruktive Wesenhaftigkeit des Materials sowie kontextuelle und kulturelle Hintergründe, konterkarierten andere ganz bewusst eben diese Merkmale der Materialien; hauchdünn geschnittene Steinlagen auf ein Trägermaterial geklebt negieren die baurelevante Eigenschaft der Druckfestigkeit des Steins; herkömmliche Materialien werden verfremdet und in einen neuen Kontext gestellt, architekturfremde Materialien aus Raum- und Luftfahrt werden spielerisch in der Architektur eingesetzt und neue Materialien wie luminiszenter Beton und Kunststoffe oder Textilien, Metallgitter und -netze werden erprobt. Unabhängig von ihrem «Innenleben» behaupten gekrümmte und gefaltete Fassaden eine Eigenständigkeit, die die ästhetischen Effekte der Materialien nutzt.

Das architektonische Ergebnis ist häufig ein Konglomerat unterschiedlicher Methoden der Formfindung und Materialwahl. Letztendlich kann die Beziehung zwischen Form und Material als singuläres Ereignis beschrieben werden, das jeweils am konkreten Objekt grundsätzlich neu bestimmt wird.[5]

Material in der Architektur — eine Suchbewegung

Die Suche nach dem Spezifischen in der Architektur führt unweigerlich zu einer Auseinandersetzung mit der Architektursprache des Materials, die sich in der Einheitlichkeit und in dem Ineinandergreifen von Struktur und Ausdruck, von Grundriss, Interieur und Fassade darstellt. Damit rückt die Wesenhaftigkeit des Materials sowohl mit seinen sinnlichen und atmosphärischen Qualitäten als auch mit seinen baukonstruktiven und

of materiality in architecture. Beyond the schematism engendered by the mass production of housing, and beyond architectonic style, he represented the view that each building task called for an adequate material, and that at the same time, the cultural anchoring and emotional connotations of the material must be given their due.[4]

As a consequence, surface qualities, texture, and the natural coloration of materials shifted into focus for many architects. In the 1990s, this approach led to a new way of dealing with materials: standing in the foreground now were surface effects. If architects such as Peter Zumthor and Tadao Ando still relied on the structural traits of the materials alongside sensuous and atmospheric qualities and cultural contexts, others deliberately thwarted such material traits. For example, wafer-thin slices of stone glued onto the loadbearing material which negate the structurally relevant characteristics of the stone. Familiar materials become alien, positioned in new contexts, while materials from aeronautics and astronautics, intrinsically alien to architecture, are deployed playfully. Similar experimentation has been seen with materials such as luminescent concrete and plastic, textiles, or metal latticework and netting. Independently of "life in the interior," curvilinear or pleated façades assert their independence, exploiting the aesthetic effects of the materials.

Often, the architectonic result is a conglomerate of various methods of formal invention and material choices. Ultimately, the relationship between form and material can be characterized as a singular event that must be fundamentally redefined for each concrete object.[5]

Material in Architecture— an Exploratory Movement

The search for specificity in architecture leads unavoidably to a confrontation with the architectural language of materials, one that presents itself in the consistency and intertwining of structure and expression, of plan, interior, and façade. Shifted into the foreground once again is the essential nature of the material, with its sensuous and atmosphere qualities, but also its structural and physical potential. But neither the material nor the design concept determines the architecture: instead, they enter into a dialogue. The design concept leads toward an "appropriate" material, which in turn influences the design idea by virtue of its qualities and expressive possibilities. Concept and material influence one another reciprocally, forming an indissoluble unity in the final result.

---

4 «Die Architektur soll dem Menschen dienen. Das Material wird in diesem Zusammenhang zu einem humanistischen Element; humanistisch in dem Sinne, dass der Zweck des Gebäudes bei der Wahl des Materials eine Rolle spielt. Es gibt eine Beziehung zwischen den Menschen und dem Baumaterial. Das Material muss dem Menschen emotional entsprechen: er muss spüren, dass es ihm nicht feindlich gegenübersteht.» Alvar Aalto im Interview mit Göran Schildt, 1972, in: *Alvar Aalto, Bd. III Projekte und letzte Bauten*, Zürich 1978, S. 228
5 Sabine Kraft, «Werkstoffe. Eigenschaften als Variablen», in: *ARCH+* 172, 2004, S. 24–28

4 "… Architecture ought to serve man. In this connection, the material employed becomes a humanistic element. In this way, immemorial relationships with the material are appealed to. By humanistic I mean that the purpose of the building helps to determine the choice of materials. There does exist a relationship between man and any given building material. The material has to be emotionally attuned to the human being, who must sense that it is not hostile to him." Alvar Aalto in an interview with Göran Schildt, 1972, in *Alvar Aalto Vol. 3, Projects and Final Buildings*, Basel 1999, p. 232.
5 Sabine Kraft, "Werkstoffe— Eigenschaften als Variablen," in *ARCH+* 172, 2004, pp. 24–28.
6 In his treatise *Essai sur l'architecture*, published in 1753, Laugier propagates undecorated

physikalischen Eigenschaften wieder in den Vordergrund. Doch weder das Material noch die Entwurfsidee bestimmen die Architektur, sie treten vielmehr in einen Dialog. Der Entwurfsgedanke führt zu dem «passenden» Material, das wiederum mit seinen Qualitäten und Ausdrucksmöglichkeiten die Entwurfsidee beeinflusst. Gedanke und Material durchdringen und beeinflussen sich gegenseitig und bilden so als Resultat eine untrennbare Einheit.

Konstruktionen aus massiven Holzplatten folgen anderen Gesetzmässigkeiten und haben andere Spannweiten als Konstruktionen aus Beton, Stahl oder Ziegel. Nimmt man diesen Ansatz ernst, dann haben Ziegelbauten im Vergleich zu Stahlbetonbauten kleinere Räume und dickere Wände; gleichzeitig könnten Rund- und Segmentbögen sowie gewölbte Decken das Formenrepertoire in der Architektur bereichern und der Architektur eine Identität verleihen. Ein Wohnhaus, das aus Holzplatten gefügt wurde, weist ganz selbstverständlich andere Grundrisse und Fassaden auf als ein Wohnhaus, das in Stahlbeton- oder Stahlbauweise erstellt ist — Innenräume und Fassaden, die sich durch eine Komposition grossflächiger geschlossener und offener Wandflächen auszeichnen, stehen einer Architektur gegenüber, die von offenen Raumzusammenhängen und grossflächigen, durch Stützen rhythmisierten Fassadenöffnungen bestimmt ist.

Die studentischen Entwürfe und die Projekte von pool Architekten lassen sich als Suchbewegung betrachten, diese Zusammenhänge aufzuspüren und ihnen nachzugehen. Historische Referenzen geben oft Hinweise auf unterschiedliche Blickwinkel zu diesem Thema. Holz, Beton, Backstein und Stahl — Materialen, die seit jeher mit Stadtkultur verknüpft sind — sollen in den folgenden Kapiteln bezüglich ihrer Wesenhaftigkeit und ihres spezifischen Ausdrucks in der Architektur betrachtet werden.

Homogenous structures where the material serves loadbearing and insulating functions simultaneously have the potential to develop an architectural language that is no longer haphazard, and hence arbitrary, but is instead directly bound up with the chosen material and its assembly and production technologies, its constructive peculiarities, as well as its static performance capacities. Room sizes and sequences are again determined by the material—structures of massive panels follow different principles and have different spans from those in concrete or brick. If this approach is taken seriously, then brick buildings will have smaller rooms and thicker walls than those in reinforced concrete. At the same time, rounded and segmented arches as well as vaulted ceilings enrich the formal repertoire of the architecture, endowing it with a strong sense of identity. Self-evidently, a dwelling assembled from wooden paneling will display different floor plans and façades than one in reinforced concrete or steel construction. The former displays interior spaces and façades characterized by the composition of extensive closed or open wall surfaces. The latter is an architecture defined by open spatial configurations and extensive façade openings that are rhythmicized by supports.

The designs and projects of pool Architekten can be regarded as exploratory movements which attempt to track down these relationships and investigate them. In many cases, historical references supply a variety of perspectives onto this theme. In the following sections, wood, concrete, brick, and steel—materials long associated with urban culture—will be examined with regard to their essential nature and particular architectural expressiveness.

←

Der spezifische
Ausdruck
des Materials

The Specific
Expression
of the Materials

Holz — Stäbe und Platten

Wood — Posts and Panels

Wood is probably the oldest and most archaic building material, and some of the most important treatises in architectural theory base their conceptual edifices on the primordial character of timber building. Gottfried Semper's theory of cladding, for example, is inspired by the construction style of the "Caribbean hut," and Marc-Antoine Laugier's observations on architecture are based on the oft-cited primitive hut.[6]

Cities of Wood

As a renewable material that is simple to process and readily accessible, wood was predestined for the construction of houses. Settlements, villages, and entire towns and cities around the world are constructed in timber. Depending on the tradition and the region, wood has been combined with straw, clay, and stone, with wood used as a cladding material or for massive timber construction. Many towns in Russia, Turkey, the US, Asia, and Scandinavian countries in particular convey the richness, the potential, and expressive power of pure timber architecture in an urban context.

In the Ottoman Empire, building with wood was anchored in culture and religion. In contrast, using wood in southern and central Europe was seen to contradict the principal rules of the art of building since the days of Vitruvius, since such houses were "made to catch fire like torches."[7] While the more permanent stone architecture in the Ottoman Empire was reserved for mosques, dwellings were expected to express the finitude of human life. Consequently, the cityscape of Istanbul was characterized by multistory wood dwellings as late as the nineteenth century. Following this faith-based symbolism was not just the choice of materials, but also dwelling in all-purpose rooms that were reconfigured and refurbished depending on the time of day and the respective uses they served. The floorplan was configured through the sequencing of a multiplicity of all-purpose rooms having approximately the same sizes, which were assigned to women, men, or guests, and which followed the grid of the skeleton structure. As a rule, each of these rooms was supplemented by a bay window whose extensive window openings offered residents an overview of urban activity. The projecting bay window, with its bands, decorated wooden latticework or folding shutters and visible wooden supports, characterized this urban architecture. Equally characteristic were the recessions and projections of the façades, the expansive overhanging roofs, roofed terraces, balconies, and formal variety.

While the multistory, closed housing settlement of Istanbul corresponds to the urban character of the European city, the Japanese cities of the early twentieth century are characterized by two-story dwellings

---

6   beauty in architecture based on the principle of the primitive hut: four tree trunks arranged in a square like columns, which are then bound together at the top with rounded wooden beams, and which support a saddle-roof-style wooden structure.

7   Vitruvius, *The Ten Books of Architecture*, translated by Morris Hicky Morgan, New York 1960, p. 57.

8   In his book, *Das japanische Haus und sein Leben*, Bruno Taut refers to a Japanese cultural

in wood.[8] Various urban quarters are characterized by townhouses set-back and concealed behind tall fences or gable-topped houses which open themselves up toward the street space. This construction style, so reminiscent of village life, was conditioned by the historical emergence of cities in Japan, as well as with the nation's cultural peculiarities. The large town is distinguishable from the village solely through its denser development, the more extensive spread of shops, department stores, restaurants, and hotels.
→ 6

Japanese urban architecture is characterized by deeply projecting roofs, awnings running along entire façades, sliding doors and panels in the interior and on façades. The module of the Tatami mat, which determines the floorplan structure of all houses, is legible on façades as well, so that entire streets follow a unified rhythm. Façades are subdivided by rectangular fields which are provided with a multitude of filling types. Translucent wooden lattices and closed wooden surfaces alternate with glazed or paper-covered frames. These fields are subdivided by thin wooden slats into still smaller surfaces, which—through an interplay with the mobile or fixed façade elements—result in a multilayered system. → 7 Contrasts of planarity and plasticity, open and closed, panel and rod, transparent and opaque, are supplemented by the fine subdivisions of the elements and their varied surface treatment. Together these form a larger composition that emerges via chance. Hung before the façades are mats of straw or bamboo and these fragile façades are supplemented and protected by little fences, obliquely positioned "protective walls," or wooden latticework.

Textile properties are emphasized with the use of large sliding elements. Structural and space-delimiting elements reinforce one another, resulting in a unity. While the wafer-thin, shiftable façade layers are entirely detached from the supporting structure, a unity emerges through the technically adept transition between the art of building with timber and carpentry work.

The Renaissance of Solid Timber Construction

Both Ottoman and Japanese wooden architecture testify to the diversity of the material which already fascinated Frank Lloyd Wright. As timber construction or carpentry work, wood can be employed in interiors as paneling, as façade cladding, or as a construction material in the form of posts, ceilings, or roof beams. Slabs, rods, boards, and poles as elements of wooden architecture result in rhythmic variety and sculptural effects, while the grain of the wood heightens the aesthetic qualities of the material.[9]

peculiarity: the Japanese made no distinction between town and country, and a simple sequence of houses along the street was referred to as a town. The Japanese word for town, moreover, was identical with the word for street. This explains the identical manner of construction, independent of the size of the settlement. *Houses and People of Japan*, 2nd. ed., Tokyo 1958.
9   Frank Lloyd Wright, "Die Bedeutung der Materialien — Holz," *ARCH+* 193, 2009, p. 89.
10 Parallel to the development of new materials, fire protection regulations have been

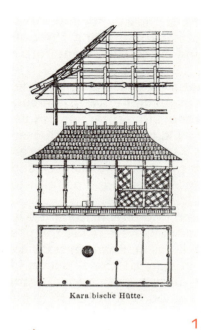
1

2

3

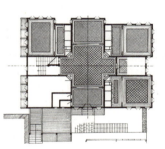

5

4

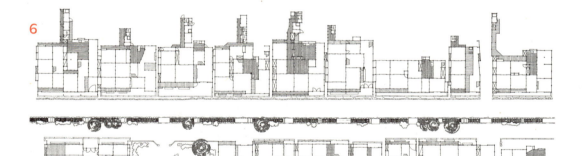
6

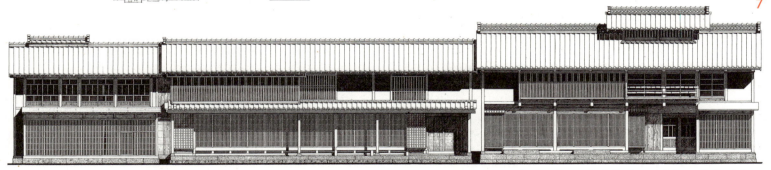
7

1　Karaibische Hütte, in: Gottfried Semper, *Der Stil in den technischen und tektonischen Künsten*, Bd. 2, München 1863, S. 263
2　Allegorische Darstellung der Vitruvianischen Urhütte von Charles Eisen, in: Marc-Antoine Laugier, *Essai sur l'architecture*, 1755
3/4　Holzarchitektur, Stadtansichten Istanbul
5　Grundriss historisches Wohnhaus aus Holz, Kavafyan Konagi, Istanbul, 1751
6/7　Grundriss und Fassaden aus dem japanischen Postenort Unno

1　Caribbean hut, in Gottfried Semper, *Der Stil in den technischen und tektonischen Künsten*, vol. 2, Munich 1863, p. 263
2　Allegorical depiction of the Vitruvian primitive hut by Charles Eisen, in Marc-Antoine Laugier, *Essai sur l'architecture*, 1755
3/4　Wooden architecture, cityscape, Istanbul
5　Floorplan, historic wooden residence, Kavafyan Konagi, Istanbul, 1751
6/7　Floorplan and façades from the Japanese post station at Unno

Holz — Stäbe und Platten

welche die charakteristischen Qualitäten des Materials wie die Holzmaserung und die Oberflächenbeschaffenheit noch verstärken.[9]

Das Tragwerk wird durch die Feinheit der konstruktiven Details zum sichtbaren Teil des Interieurs und bildet mit diesem durch Sprache, Feinheit (Massstab) und Ausdruck eine Einheit, die nur in Holz hergestellt werden kann.

Doch verheerende Brände, die ganze Stadtteile vernichteten, führten im 19. Jahrhundert zu einem Umdenken im Umgang mit Holz. Feuerschutzverordnungen verlangten nun für mehrgeschossige Gebäude Baukonstruktionen aus nicht brennbaren Materialien. Damit wurde die Holzarchitektur auf das Land verbannt und das urbane Holzhaus als Bautypus geriet in Vergessenheit.

Erst in den letzten Jahren wird der Holzbau aufgrund von Forschungen und Weiterentwicklungen des Materials und der Herstellungsmethoden für den mehrgeschossigen Wohnungsbau im urbanen Kontext wieder attraktiv und werden seine Vorteile evident. Unter den ökonomischen Aspekten der Vorfertigung, der Montagefreundlichkeit und der kurzen Bauzeiten betrachtet, ist Holz vielen anderen Baumaterialien überlegen. Ökologische Aspekte der Nachhaltigkeit, bauphysikalische Eigenschaften wie die Dämmfähigkeit und Hygroskopie (Aufnahme und Abgabe von Feuchtigkeit) sowie psychobiologische Aspekte, zu denen das Raumklima ebenso zählt wie optische und haptische Qualitäten, und nicht zuletzt das kulturelle Gedächtnis und die Traditionsverbundenheit heben es von allen anderen Materialien ab und prädestinieren es besonders für den Wohnungsbau.

Neue Holzwerkstoffe, wie zum Beispiel hochleistungsfähige Brettschichthölzer und Mehrschichtholzplatten, die auch im Verbund mit Beton eingesetzt werden können, lösen sowohl die Probleme des Brandschutzes[10] als auch die der Tragfähigkeit im mehrgeschossigen Wohnungsbau. Gleichzeitig findet im Holzbau eine epochale strukturelle Verschiebung statt — die Einführung strukturell wirksamer Holzplatten stellt einen Paradigmenwechsel vom stabförmigen Skelettbau zum plattenförmigen Massivbau dar, der die Möglichkeiten der Holzbauweise erweitert.

Zusätzlich erfahren Holzkonstruktionen durch die Digitalisierung von Entwurf und Produktion einen Innovationsschub, der sich durch eine Individualisierung der Standardisierung auszeichnet. Computergesteuerte Maschinen können nun komplexe geometrische Zusammenhänge erfassen und individuelle Geometrien fertigen. Im Gegensatz zu der Bauteilstandardisierung im 20. Jahrhundert, die auf gleichen Geometrien und Abmessungen beruhte, bedeutet die Herstellung von individuellen Geometrien heute keinen Mehraufwand mehr. Daher ist es möglich, jedes Bauteil wie bei der vorindustriellen, handwerklichen Bearbeitung als Unikat herzustellen, ohne wesentlich höhere Kosten zu verursachen. Das Ergebnis sind individuell zugeschnittene Wandscheiben, die mit beliebigen Ausschnitten versehen sowohl als tragende als auch nicht tragende Innen- oder Aussenwände eingesetzt werden können.

Through constructive details, the supporting structure becomes a visible part of the interior. Through language, finesse, scale, and expression, wood forms a unique unity.

In the nineteenth century, devastating fires destroyed entire city districts, leading toward a reconsideration of the use of wood. Fire protection regulations called for multistory buildings to be constructed in nonflammable materials. As a consequence, wooden architecture was banned throughout the country, and the urban wooden dwelling as a building type fell into oblivion.

In recent years, research into new material treatments and construction methods have made the use of wood for multistory dwellings in urban contexts appear attractive again. For residential construction in particular, wood has many unique advantages. From an economic perspective, wood is superior to many other construction materials as a result of its suitability for prefabrication, ease of assembly, and subsequent shortened building schedules. Wood also has ecological benefits. For example, its sustainability, structural properties such as insulation and hygroscopic characteristics (absorption and discharge of moisture). Similarly, wood has positive psychobiological traits. It contributes to the interior climate as well as optical and haptic qualities connecting to cultural memory and tradition.

New wood-based materials, among them high-performance, laminated timber and multilayer panels, which can also be used in combination with concrete, even resolve issues concerning fire protection, as well as the issue of loadbearing capacity for multistory residential buildings.[10] At the same time, an epochal structural shift is now occurring in timber construction. The introduction of structurally effective wooden paneling represents a paradigm change from bar-shaped skeleton construction to panel-based solid construction which further extends the possibilities of building in wood.

In addition, wooden construction is experiencing an innovation boost through digitalization of design and production that is characterized by the individualization of standardization. Today, computer-guided machines can process more complex geometric relationships and hence manufacture individual geometries. In contrast to the standardization of construction elements in the twentieth century, based on identical geometries and dimensions, the manufacture of individual geometries involves no additional expenditures. As a result, each construction element can be manufactured as an individual unit without requiring significantly higher costs, as with preindustrial, craft-based production. The results include individually customized wall panels in which any desired perforation can be applied, and which can be used as structural or nonstructural walls at the interior or exterior.

Building with wood in urban contexts calls for a rethinking and a redefinition of timber construction. While the latest efforts to build even high-rises in wood are primarily demonstrations of the material's

---

9   Frank Lloyd Wright, «Die Bedeutung der Materialien — Holz», in: *ARCH+* 193, 2009, S.89
10 Parallel zu den Neuentwicklungen der Holzwerkstoffe wurden die Brandschutzvorschriften etwas entschärft, sodass alternative Brandschutzkonzepte oder Ersatzmassnahmen wie Sprinkleranlagen und ausgelagerte Rettungswege anerkannt und genehmigt werden.

    tightened across Europe so that alternative fire safety concepts and alternative measures such as sprinkler systems or external escape routes are recognized and authorized.
11 The Top Wall system, developed by Hermann Blumer, consists of wooden planks

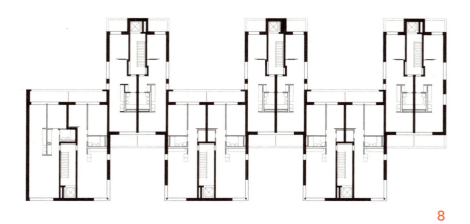

8

9

10

11

14

15

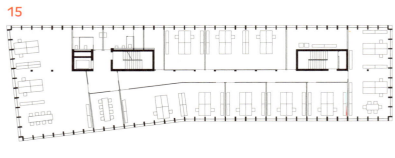

12

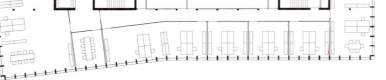

13

16

8–10 pool 0176 Wohn- und Geschäftshaus Badenerstrasse, Zürich, 2006–2010; Massivholzwände und Hohlkastendecken, Handmontage der Kanthölzer
11–13 pool 0243 «mehr als wohnen», Haus J, Zürich-Leutschenbach, 2009–2015; sichtbar bleibende, tragende Bauteile aus Massivholz
14–16 pool 0229 Wohnhaus Laur-Park, Brugg, 2009–2013; innen und aussen prägende Holzständer und Füllelemente

8–10 pool 0176 residential and commercial building on Badenerstrasse, Zürich, 2006–2010; solid wooden walls and hollow box ceiling, hand assembly of the square timbers
11–13 pool 0243 "more than housing," Haus J, Zürich-Leutschenbach, 2009–2015; permanently visible loadbearing construction parts in solid wood. Image: Niklaus Spoerri.
14–16 pool 0229 residential building, Laur-Park, Brugg, 2009–2013: wooden pillars and fill elements which characterize the interior and exterior.

Holz — Stäbe und Platten

17 18 19

20 21 22 23 24 25

17/18 Studierendenprojekt Urban Wood 07, Veronika Mosser/Nico Steinacker, TU Berlin 2013; kleinteilige Struktur, Minimalwohnungen mit zweigeschossiger Wohnloggia
19/20 Studierendenprojekt Urban Wood 16, Cem Baykal/Yuki Hanfeld, TU Berlin 2013; gestaffelte Raumelemente, Vielfalt bei geringer Wohnfläche
21/22 Studierendenprojekt Urban Wood 12, Marco Migliavacca/Friedrich Neukirchen, TU Berlin 2013; zweigeschossiger Gemeinschaftsbereich, Ständerbauweise
23–25 Studierendenprojekt Urban Wood 18, Timo Büscher/Olivier Laydevant, TU Berlin 2013; gestufte und zerklüftete Schottenstruktur

17/18 Student project Urban Wood 07, Veronika Mosser/Nico Steinacker, TU Berlin 2013; small-scale structure, minimal housing units with two-storied residential loggias
19/20 Student project, Urban Wood 16, Cem Baykal/Yuki Hanfeld, TU Berlin 2013; staggered spatial elements, multiplicity within a minimal residential area
21/22 Student project, Urban Wood 12, Marco Migliavacca/Friedrich Neukirchen, TU Berlin 2013; two-storied common area, timber frame construction
23–25 Student project, Urban Wood 18, Timo Büscher/Olivier Laydevant, TU Berlin 2013; stepped and indented bulkhead structure

Wood—Posts and Panels

Bauen mit Holz im urbanen Kontext erfordert ein Umdenken und eine Neudefinition des Holzbaus. Während die neuesten Bestrebungen, sogar Hochhäuser aus Holz zu bauen, vorrangig eine Demonstration der statischen Leistungsfähigkeit darstellen, gilt es, nach adäquaten, zeitgemässen Konzepten des Ausdrucks sowohl auf der Grundrissebene als auch im Stadtbild zu suchen — auch im Hinblick auf die strukturelle Verschiebung vom Skelettbau zum Massivbau. Ein Massivbau folgt anderen Gesetzmässigkeiten als ein Skelettbau, was sich in der Anordnung und Grösse der Wand- und Fassadenöffnungen, den Spannweiten und Auskragungen sowie der Ausrichtung der Struktur bemerkbar macht. Grundrisslayouts werden von Scheiben bestimmt, innenräumliche Zusammenhänge sind eindeutig gesetzt und müssen sich am «Widerstand» der Massivität reiben.

Die Ausbildung einer Schottenstruktur stellt nur eine der Möglichkeit im Umgang mit der neuen Holztektonik dar. Bei der siebengeschossigen Wohnbebauung der Baugenossenschaft Zurlinden an der Badenerstrasse in Zürich von pool Architekten lösen sich die Schotten aus Massivholz in Wandscheiben mit Öffnungen auf und setzen sich in den tragenden Fassaden fort. Zwischen den Schotten, die in einem Abstand von 4,70 bis 6,40 Metern angeordnet sind, entwickeln sich die einzelnen Wohneinheiten als offene Grundrisse. Statt aus komplett vorgefertigten Holzplatten setzen sich die tragenden Massivholzelemente aus geschosshohen Kanthölzern[11] zusammen, die vor Ort ohne maschinellen Einsatz von einer Person montiert und anhand weniger Dübel miteinander sowie mit der Bodenschwelle verankert werden. Wie bei der Bauweise mit Backstein geben die Abmessungen der Holzbohlen die Masse des Hauses, der Räume und Fensteröffnungen vor. In den Fassaden folgt der Holzbau einer Massivbauweise mit ihrem ausgewogenen Verhältnis von geschlossenen zu geöffneten Flächen und den eingeschnittenen Fenstern.

→ 8 9 10

Das Haus J, ebenfalls von pool Architekten, in der Siedlung auf dem Hunziker Areal hingegen «erzählt» von der massiven Holzkonstruktion aus raumhohen Kanthölzern, die sich in Form von geschosshohen Fassadenöffnungen abzeichnet. Im Gegensatz zu dem Projekt in der Badenerstrasse werden die tragenden, massiven Fassaden durch eine Skelettkonstruktion ergänzt. Die Anwendung unterschiedlicher Konstruktionsprinzipien zeigt sich in den Grundrissen als Mischung aus einer der Massivbauweise geschuldeten Raumnetzstruktur mit der stringenten Struktur einer Skelettbauweise. Statt eines rigiden Rasters folgt die Tragstruktur aus Holzstützen und -rippen den Raumgrössen und ist in unregelmässigen Abständen zwischen 3 und 6 Metern angeordnet. Das Prinzip der Tragstruktur wird durch die sichtbaren Holzoberflächen, die sich von den weissen Oberflächen der nicht tragenden Trennwände absetzen, nachvollziehbar und für den Bewohner erlebbar — und gleichzeitig Teil eines aussagekräftigen Interieurs.

→ 12 13

static performance capabilities, the task is to search for adequate, contemporary expressions both at the scale of the floorplan as well as at the urban scale. There is also a need to work with the structural shift from skeleton to solid construction. A solid construction follows different principles than a skeleton construction. This becomes noticeable in the arrangement and sizes of wall and façade openings, the widths of spans and overhangs, as well as the structure's orientation. Floor plan layouts are conditioned by slabs and interior interrelationships are fixed unambiguously, which generates a certain "resistance" against solidity.

The formation of a cross-wall structure represents just one possibility of applying new wood tectonics. At Haus J, a seven-story residential development realized by pool Architekten in Zurich, the solid wooden bulkheads are broken up into wall sections with openings and are continued in the supporting façades. Individual residential units are positioned as open floor plans between the bulkheads, which are arranged at intervals of between four and six meters. Instead of consisting completely of prefabricated wooden panels, the supporting solid wooden elements are assembled from one-story-high panels. These can be assembled on site by one worker without the application of machinery and anchored to one another as well as with the ground beam using just a few dowels[11]. As with brick construction, the sizes of the planks predetermine the dimensions of the building, the rooms, and window openings. In the façades, the timber construction adheres to a solid construction approach, with its balanced relationship between closed and open surfaces and the incised windows.

→ 8 9 10

The apartment building in the estate *Mehr als Wohnen* (More Than Housing), in contrast, utilizes solid wooden construction revealed by story-height windows and façade openings. With the project on Badenerstrasse, in contrast, load-bearing, solid façades are supplemented by a skeleton structure. The application of varying construction principles is evident in the floor plans. There exists a mixture of the spatial network structure—a function of solid construction—with the stringent structure of a skeleton construction approach. Rather than following a rigid grid, the supporting structure, consisting of wooden supports and ribs, follow the sizes of the rooms and is arranged at irregular intervals between three and six meters. The principle of the support structure is made comprehensible by the visible wooden surface, which is set off from the white surfaces of the non-loadbearing partition walls. It is experienced directly by inhabitants and is, at the same time, an element of the powerfully expressive interior.

→ 12 13

---

11 Das Wandsystem Top Wall, von Hermann Blumer entwickelt, besteht aus 20 Zentimeter breiten und 10 Zentimeter tiefen Holzbohlen, die auf einen Holzdorn in der Fussschwelle gesetzt und über ein Nut- und Federsystem und wenige Dübel zu einer massiven Holzwand gefügt werden. Durch die Kleinteiligkeit der Einzelelemente lassen sich die Wände von einer Person aufbauen.

measuring 20 cm in width and 10 cm in depth which are set onto a wooden mandrel in the inferior purlin and assembled on a solid wall via a tongue-and-groove system and a few dowels. Given the small sizes of the individual elements, the wall can be assembled by a single person.

Vom Kleinen und Grossen

Ebenso wie die oben beschriebenen Zürcher Projekte sind die neuen urbanen Holzbauten meist mit mineralischen Putzen oder Platten aus Beton, Metall oder Stein verkleidet und fügen sich so in das steinerne Stadtbild. Die historischen Referenzen im Blick, ist die Frage nach einem materialgerechten Ausdruck urbaner Holzarchitektur damit jedoch noch nicht beantwortet.

Beispielhaft für die Einheit von Konstruktion, Fassade, Grundriss und Interieur — und damit ein Anhaltspunkt für den adäquaten, zeitgemässen Umgang mit dem Material — ist das Büro- und Wohnhaus Laur-Park in Brugg von pool Architekten. Elementierte Holzfassaden in einem Raster von 1,35 Metern geben den Rhythmus des tragenden, schlanken Ständerwerks der dreigeschossigen Holzskelettkonstruktion vor. Als gestaltprägendes Element zeichnet die vertikale Tragstruktur das Gebäudevolumen des Baukörpers nach und setzt sich im Inneren in Form von Holzrippen fort. Die Kombination der sichtbaren Holzoberflächen der Rippen, Stützen, Decken und Fassaden mit Wänden aus transparentem Glas, grauem Sichtbeton oder weiss gestrichenem Gipskarton und dunklen Terrazzoböden kreiert ein charaktervolles Interieur, in dem sich die Grundrisse frei entwickeln können.

→ 14 15 16

Zusätzlich nutzten die Architekten die konstruktive Logik des Materials, um das Charaktervolle und Spezifische zu stärken: Unterschiedlich dimensionierte Holzunterzüge folgen der Statik, vertikal gekippte Fassadenelemente verhindern das Eindringen von Regenwasser und ausladende Dachüberstände sowie der massive Sockel schützen die Holzkonstruktion.

Auf der Suche nach einem adäquaten Ausdruck urbaner Holzarchitektur, nach einer materialspezifischen Logik sowie den architektonischen Möglichkeiten des Materials können die historischen Referenzen als Vorbild dienen. Auch wenn die Holzarchitektur — um die neue Bauweise der «Plattentektonik» erweitert — heute anderen Gesetzmässigkeiten folgt, haben die beschriebenen Aspekte der historischen Holzbauten dennoch Bestand. Holz ist das einzige Baumaterial, das von der grossformatigen Platte bis zum kleinen Holzstab eines Geländers oder Fensterladens sowohl im Inneren als auch im Aussen verwendbar ist. Dies führt zu einer Plastizität der Fassaden und einer Überlagerung von Tragstruktur und Interieur bis hin zum Mobiliar. Das Ineinandergreifen von Massiv- und Skelettbau und die daraus entstehenden Möglichkeiten sowohl auf der Grundrissebene als auch in den Fassaden ist ein weiterer Aspekt, der eine direkte Rückbindung an das Material beschreibt.

→ 17 18 19 20 21 22 23 24 25

Small and Large

Like the Zurich projects described above, most of the new urban wooden buildings are clad with mineral plaster, concrete, metal, or stone cladding, and hence blend well with an inorganic cityscape. With an eye toward historical references, it is clear that the question of an urban wooden architecture whose mode of expression would be appropriate to this material is yet to be resolved.

Exemplary of the unity of construction, façade, floorplan, and interior—and hence a reference point for the adequate, contemporary handling of the material—is the office and apartment building at Laur Park in Brugg, Switzerland. Wooden façades with elements in a repeated grid of 2.4 meters predetermine the rhythm of a supporting, slender framework of the three-story wooden skeleton construction. As a design-shaping element, the vertical support structure traces out the volumes of the building, and is continued within in the form of wooden ribs. The combination of the visible wooden surfaces (ribs, supports, ceiling, and façades) with transparent glass walls, grey exposed concrete, white painted plasterboard, and dark terrazzo flooring produces a characterful interior. Within this the floorplan is able to develop freely.

→ 14 15 16

Moreover, the architects exploited the constructive logic of the material in order to enhance the building's character and specificity. Various wooden beams follow the statics, vertically inclined façade elements impede the intrusion of rainwater, while the wooden construction is shielded by cantilevered overhangs and the building's massive base.

In the search for an adequate expression of urban wooden architecture, for a material-specific logic, as well as for the architectonic potentials of the material, historical references can serve as models. And although wooden architecture today—extended by means of new building methods involving "panel tectonics"—follows different principles to its precedents, the above-described aspects of historical wooden buildings are nonetheless pertinent. Wood is the only building material that can be applied all the way from extremely large panels to the small elements of a handrail or window shutters, and in a building's interior as well as on the exterior. This results in the plastic quality of the façade and a superimposition of loadbearing structure and interior, all the way down to items of furniture. The interlocking of solid and skeleton structures and the resultant possibilities, both at the level of the floorplan as well as of the façade, is an additional aspect that is directly dependent on the traits of the material.

→ 17 18 19 20 21 22 23 24 25

Holz — Stäbe und Platten

Wood — Posts and Panels

Backstein — vom
Weben und Fügen

Brick — of Weaving
and Joining

The small size of brick units, their solidity in construction, and diverse joining techniques shape the expressiveness of both façades and interiors. As a symbolic language, whether ornamental or applied in accordance with the distribution of forces, brick can be a constructive or textile material that forms the basis of diverse spatial qualities. Spatial network structures are a trademark of brick architecture, as are structurally articulated sequences of spaces. As primal forms of brick construction, the arch and the vault have their origins in the small unit sizes of this flexible material, and correspond at the level of the floorplan to sculptural or curvilinear forms.

Alongside wood, clay, and natural stone, brick is among the oldest building materials. Excavations of the earliest known residential buildings constructed from clay bricks in the Middle East date from circa 8300 B.C.E., while the first baked bricks were produced in Mesopotamia around 3000 B.C.E.[12] In subsequent millennia, brick was diffused throughout the Mediterranean region, and was finally perfected in ancient Rome. This building method experienced a revaluation through Vitruvius's treatise on architecture, which dates from circa 14 B.C.E.[13] As a hard, permanent material, brick or quarry stone is superior to wood and should be preferred to it, says Vitruvius.[14] This initial written assessment and description of the material continues to shape building in Europe's cities to this day.[15]

Roman brick architecture and Middle Eastern brick architecture which was disseminated throughout southern Europe with the arrival of the Moors in Spain and Sicily in the eighth century represent two fundamentally divergent approaches to exposed brickwork, which hence led to very different expressive forms in architecture.

In the nineteenth century, Gottfried Semper was the first to formulate this distinction, and to integrate it in his "theory of cladding." The Moorish style was oriented toward exposed brickwork, with its woven surface serving to delimit space and as a bearer of meaning. → 26 27 Roman brick architecture approached the material as a structural element that was defined instead through solidity and craftsmanship.[16] Gottfried Semper aligned this double identity of brickwork in relation to his concepts of textile weaving and stereometry respectively.[17]

Semper's theory was confirmed by excavations of sections of walls from the Assyrian capital Nineveh, where bricks had been joined together, painted, enameled, and baked before being assembled as walls. He interpreted the masonry walls of Syrian culture, with

---

12 Richard Weston, *Material, Form and Architecture*, London 2008, p. 16; Barbara Perlich, *Mittelalterlicher Backsteinbau in Europa. Zur Frage nach der Herkunft der Backsteintechnik*, Petersberg 2007, p. 24.
13 Vitruvis, *The Ten Books On Architecture*, Cambridge 2001.
14 Ibid.
15 Disseminated through the expansion of the Roman Empire was the art of baking bricks, and brick became increasingly dominant as a suitable building material in opposition to traditional wooden architecture.
16 Cf. Ákos Moravánszky, "The Pathos of Masonry," in Andrea Deplazes (ed.), *Constructing Architecture: Materials, Processes, Structures; a Handbook*, Basel 2008, pp. 23–32.
17 In the two volumes of his *Style in the Technical and Tectonic Arts or Practical Aesthetics*, Semper formulated four fundamental forms/primordial techniques of production: textiles, ceramics, tectonics (carpentry), and stereometry (masonry), which correspond to the four primary elements of architecture.

Identität des Mauerwerks, seinen Begriffen des «Textilwebens» und der «Stereotomie» zu.[17]

Ausgrabungen von Mauerteilen der assyrischen Hauptstadt Ninive, deren Steine auf dem Boden liegend zusammengefügt, bemalt, emailliert, gebrannt und erst dann als Mauer aufgestellt wurden, bestätigten seine Theorie. Die Mauerwerkswände der assyrischen Kultur mit ihren Terrakotta-Oberflächen, prächtigen Friesen und Skulpturen deutete er als eine Imitation der kunstvoll gewebten Teppiche, die in den Innenräumen als Wandbekleidung dienten.

Als Ursprung dieser Bauweise machte Semper die frühe chinesische Baukultur aus, deren Wandkonstruktionen aus Hohlziegeln wiederum eine Nachahmung der Mattengeflechte karibischer Hütten darstellten.[18] Dementsprechend bestimmte nicht die Fügetechnik das Erscheinungsbild, sondern das Erscheinungsbild des Mauerwerks, seine flechtwerkartige Oberfläche, bestimmte die Technik.

Ausgehend von der chinesischen Architektur mit dem Mauerwerk als textilem Gewebe entwickelte er eine Genealogie der Ziegelarchitektur, die in dem konstruktiven Stil der römischen Antike mündete. Erst die Römer waren die «Erfinder der wahren Steinkonstruktion»[19], die sich dadurch auszeichnete, dass die Steinwände in einem konstruktiven Verband hergestellt wurden und die Steingewölbe als adäquates Konstruktionsprinzip erstmalig in der Geschichte zur Anwendung kamen, so Semper.

Sempers Ausführungen sowie die im 19. Jahrhundert geführte Debatte über Materialgerechtigkeit und das «Wesen» des Materials in der Architektur führten zu einer Renaissance der Backsteinarchitektur und dem bewussten Einsatz des Ziegels als textiles oder konstruktives Material im Sinne eines orientalischen oder okzidentalen Stils.

their terracotta surfaces, splendid friezes, and sculptures, as imitations of the artfully woven carpets that served in the interior rooms as wall cladding.

Semper identified early Chinese building culture as the origin of this method of construction. Here, wall constructions in wooden bricks were, in turn, an imitation of the woven matting of the Caribbean hut.[18] Accordingly, its appearance was not determined by joining techniques. Instead, the technique of joining was shaped by the desired appearance of the masonry, its basketry-work-style surface.

With a point of departure in Chinese architecture, whose masonry work resembles textile weaving, Semper developed a genealogy of brick architecture that culminated in the constructive style of Roman antiquity. For him, the Romans were the true "inventors of genuine stone construction." This is because Roman stone walls were assembled into constructive masonry bonds and the stone vault, according to Semper, was applied by the Romans as an adequate constructive principle for the first time in history.[19] Semper's remarks, alongside nineteenth century debates on the relation between material and form, and the "essence" of material in architecture, led to a renaissance of brick architecture and to the deliberate deployment of brick as a textile or constructive material in the spirit of the Middle Eastern or Occidental styles respectively.

---

17 In den zwei Bänden *Der Stil in den technischen und tektonischen Künsten oder praktische Ästhetik* formuliert Semper vier grundsätzliche Formen bzw. Urtechniken der Herstellung: Textilweben, Töpfern, Tektonik (Holzkonstruktion) und Stereotomie (Steinkonstruktionen), die den vier Urelementen der Architektur entsprechen.
18 Hans und Manfred Semper (Hrsg.), *Gottfried Semper. Kleine Schriften,* 1884, Nachdruck Mittenwald 1979
19 Ebd., S. 394

18 Hans and Manfred Semper (eds), *Gottfried Semper. Kleine Schriften,* 1884, Mittenwald 1979.
19 Ibid, p. 394.

26

27

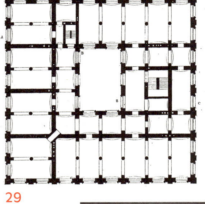

28

29

30

32

31

26/27   Ischtar-Tor, Babylon, 605–562 v. Chr.; Ziegelsteinreliefs
28–30   Bauakademie, Karl Friedrich Schinkel, Berlin, 1836; Pfeiler und Bögen
31/32   Chilehaus, Fritz Höger, Hamburg, 1924; ornamentale Fassadenreliefs

26/27   Ishtar Gate, Babylon, 605–562 B.C.E.: brick reliefs
28–30   Bauakademie (Building Academy), Karl Friedrich Schinkel, Berlin, 1836; pillars and arches
31/32   Chilehaus, Fritz Höger, Hamburg, 1924; ornamental facade reliefs

Backstein — vom Weben und Fügen

The Occidental Style— on Constructive Truth

Based on the constructive logic of brick, Karl Friedrich Schinkel's Bauakademie (Building Academy) is the first building to implement these theoretical considerations on a "material style" in actual practice.[20] Cruciform supporting shafts that are linked with one another above each story via segmented arches, project from the plane of the façade, creating a regular rhythm across the building. Prefabricated clay bricks and windows serve as non-supporting façade filling. In the interior, the space is spanned by a segmented barrel vault that rests upon transverse arches. This makes the supporting and non-supporting functions of the constructive elements, as well as the distribution of forces, legible.[21] At the same time, the construction of the arches, vaults, supports, and walls follow the laws of the material, determining both the building's axial dimension as well as the shaping of the details of the slightly projecting roof cornice.[22] In realizing the Bauakademie, Schinkel was able to demonstrate his essential architectural principles and to fulfill his architectural doctrine of material style.[23] For him, it was not just a question of choosing the material that corresponded to a given building task, but also to use the material in such a way that it would engender a formal language that was proper to it. That is, so it could not simply be replaced by a different material.[24] According to Semper, style in architecture is not a question of applied ornament, but instead of constructive laws of the material, which is "visibly characterized."[25]

Schinkel's handling of the material, which focused on the "constructive actuality" of brick, found its continuation in Fritz Schumacher's early twentieth century brick buildings. Wall thicknesses, projecting and receding elements, the shapes and dimensions of wall openings, as well as room sizes and subdivisions, follow the logic of the supporting, finely subdivided material. For Schumacher, the material becomes the "teacher" of the architectonic gestalt. It counteracts arbitrariness, redeeming the architect from his or her dematerialized, abstract preoccupation with line and proportion and reconnects him or her with the material and its handicraft qualities.[26] With brick, according to Schumacher, the correspondence between form and material is virtually compulsory. "That which presents itself to us as a

---

20 The Bauakademie, erected in 1836, was embedded in discussions taking place around 1800, which revolved around the 'correct' or 'appropriate' style, and the question of 'Kernform' (core form) and 'Kunstform' (art form). This pair of terms, introduced by Carl Bötticher, was intended to characterize the essence of architecture. The Kunstform, according to Bötticher, was the form through which the static and construction are "represented" in order to symbolize it in a characterful, "to make visible the concept of structure and space that in its purely structural state cannot be perceived." *In What Style Should We Build? The German Debate on Architectural Style,* translated and introduced by Wolfgang Hermann, Santa Monica CA 1992, pp. 147–168.
21 Goerd Peschken, *Karl Friedrich Schinkel. Lebenswerk. Das architektonische Lehrbuch,* Munich 1979, pp. 55–56.
22 Ibid., p. 7.
23 The Building Academy is an "architecture that emerges from construction in brick." Cf. Karl Friedrich Schinkel, "Die allgemeine Bau-Schule in Berlin," published in idem, *Sammlung Architektonischer Entwürfe,* Berlin 1858.
24 Peschken 1979, p. 115.
25 "Style in architecture is achieved when the construction of an entire building: 1) is visibly characterized in the most fitting and beautiful way by a single material, 2) when, in a construction consisting of a number of different materials, i.e. stone, wood, iron, brick, each is visibly characterized in a manner that is peculiar to it. And in such a way that, concerning the whole, difficulties are overcome and turmoil and a variegated impression are avoided." Ibid., p. 117.
26 Fritz Schumacher, *Das Wesen des Neuzeitlichen Backsteinbaues,* Munich 1985 (reprint), p. 5.

33

34

35

36

37

38

39

33–35 Indian Institute of Management, Louis I. Kahn, Ahmedabad, 1962–1974; Mauerwerksbögen in Varianten
36–39 Casa Dieste, Eladio Dieste, Montevideo, 1963; Gewölbeschale aus Ziegelsteinen

33–35 Indian Institute of Management, Louis I. Kahn, Ahmedabad, 1962–1974; masonry arches in variants
36–39 Casa Dieste, Eladio Dieste, Montevideo, 1963; brick shell vaulting

Backstein — vom Weben und Fügen

structure of forms and lines is indissolubly linked with the shaping material, which emerges and grows out of it, and in such a way that without this material, it could not be present at all, or at least not comprehensively."[27] The constructive character of Schinkel's *Bauakademie*, with its ambiguous support and load, becomes evident in the shaping and rhythmic realization of the façade and interior spaces. Schumacher's architecture, however, is characterized by planar, closed wall surfaces. By means of the formation of the joints, of the way in which the bricks are interwoven with one another, the structural functions of the material become visible in a far subtler fashion. "As a consequence, it becomes possible to allow the surfaces, without breaking through or even perforating them, to speak a lively language, which, so to speak, accompanies the principal stresses as an undertone."[28]

Fritz Höger's Chilehaus further illustrates Schumacher's exposition. The façade construction, with its arch-shaped openings, as well as the extensive wall pillars on the ground floor, are unambiguously indebted to brick construction. In contrast, the vertical, pilaster-style projections rhythmically define the façade and allude to the supporting function of the wall. Alongside the narrative aspect, Höger exploits the sculptural shaping of the receding and projecting brick as ornamentation on the façade. Weaving rhomboid patterns extend across the entire façade and floral ornamentation emphasizes the building's dramaturgical and functional peculiarities. And while narrative, ornamental, and constructive aspects are superimposed upon one another, the structural character of the brick is dominant.

→ 31 32

The particularity of brick, with its small individual units, as a material structural becomes evident as soon as openings or spaces are spanned. In contrast to concrete, timber, or steel, brick facilitates the realization of arches and vaults. And in the putative weakness of the material, architects such as Louis Kahn and Eladio Dieste have perceived an opportunity and a challenge, for it is precisely this feature that endows brick architecture with its unmistakable character.

→ 33 34 35

In a lecture at the Pratt Institute in 1973, Louis Kahn characterizes the search for the essential nature of the material in architecture as a dialogue in which he asks brick what it wants:

"You say to brick, 'What do you want, brick?' And brick says to you, 'I would like an arch.' And you say to brick, 'Look, I want one too, but arches are expensive and I can use a concrete lintel over you, over an opening.' And then you say, 'What do you think of that, brick?' Brick says 'I like an arch.'"[29]

In his Ahmedabad projects, the arches are the characteristic design elements. Hall-sized, arch-shaped, or rounded openings are opposed to the massive, closed architectural volumes, endowing the architecture with its identity.

---

27 Ibid., p. 13.
28 Ibid., p. 101.
29 David B. Brownlee, David G. DeLong, *Louis I. Kahn. In the Realm of Architecture,"* New York 2005 (reprint), p. 167.

Bei seinem Projekt in Ahmedabad wurde der Bogen zum gestaltprägenden Element — hallengrosse, bogenförmige oder runde Öffnungen stehen den massiven, geschlossenen Baukörpern aus Ziegel gegenüber und verleihen der Architektur ihre Identität.

Eladio Dieste ging in Uruguay noch einen Schritt weiter und entwickelte eine neuartige Bogenkonstruktion aus Ziegel.[30] Inspiriert von den dünnwandigen Betonschalenkonstruktionen Felix Candelas lotete er das Potenzial des Mauerwerks jenseits seiner üblichen Verwendung aus. Als Weiterentwicklung katalanischer Gewölbe bestehen seine Hybridkonstruktionen aus einem Verbund von Ziegel, Stahl und Beton[31] und bilden frei stehende, dünnwandige Ziegelgewölbe mit kettenlinienförmiger Mantellinie aus.[32] Die auf schmalen Stützen stehenden, gewölbten Dächer, die an den Enden über die Auflager hinaus auskragen, wirken wie leichte Zeltkonstruktionen und entbehren jeglicher «Schwere» der traditionellen, gemauerten Backsteinschalen. Ein Höhepunkt seiner Arbeit ist die Church of Christ the Worker in Atlantida. Die doppeltgekrümmten, vorgespannten Ziegelschalen der Dachkonstruktion, die auf sinusförmig gewellten Wänden auflagern, eröffnen ein neues architektonisches Feld im Mauerwerksbau — sein neues Vokabular der Strukturformen aus Backstein ist rational und ausdrucksstark zugleich.[33]

Anders als die technoid wirkenden Betonschalen kreieren die Ziegelschalen Raumatmosphären, die an Tradition und Handwerklichkeit gebunden sind — ein Aspekt, der sie auch für den Einsatz im Wohnungsbau geeignet macht. Bei seinem eigenen Wohnhaus in Montevideo wird jeder Raum von einem eigenen Schalendach überspannt. Die Gebäudestruktur, die sich entlang von Patios, Terrassen und Gärten entwickelt, folgt einer der Schalenkonstruktion geschuldeten, klaren linearen Gliederung und wird durch Höhenstaffelungen, die Differenzierung der Raumbreiten und die Kombination der Schalengewölbe mit Flachdecken hierarchisiert. Gleichzeitig nutzte Dieste die bis zu 50 Zentimeter starken Wandscheiben, um Nischen für Schränke, Betten, Sitz- oder Waschgelegenheiten auszubilden. Rohe und geschlämmte Ziegel, ebene und gekrümmte Flächen erzählen vom Material und seiner Konstruktion und verleihen den Räumen einen unverwechselbaren Charakter.

→ 36 37 38 39

In Uruguay, Eladio Dieste took things a step further, developing a novel type of arch construction in brick.[30] Inspired by the thin-walled, concrete shell constructions of Felix Candelas, he explored the potential of brick beyond its conventional utilization.

As a development of Catalan vaulting, his hybrid constructions consist of composites formed of brick, steel, and concrete. These form freestanding, thin-walled brick vaults with catenary surface lines.[31] These vaulted roofs, set on narrow supports, which project beyond the end of the supports, resemble lightweight tent structures and are devoid of the heaviness of traditional masonry shells in brick.[32] A highpoint of his work is the Church of Christ the Worker in Atlantida. The doubly curved, pre-stressed brick shell of the roof construction, which rests on sinusoidal, undulating walls, opened up a new architectural field in brick building. His vocabulary of structural forms in brick is simultaneously rational and powerfully expressive.[33]

Unlike concrete cells, which make such a technoid impression, brick shells generate spatial atmospheres that are bound up with tradition and handicraft production—an aspect that makes them particularly suitable for dwellings. In his own home in Montevideo, each room is spanned by its own shell roof. The building structure, which runs along patios, terraces, and gardens, follows a clear linear articulation that is indebted to shell construction, and to its hierarchy, realized via staggered heights, differentiated spatial breadths, and a combination of shell vaulting with flat roofs. At the same time, Dieste employs wall panels up to 50 cm thick, which allows him to form niches for cabinets, beds, window seats, or washing facilities. Untreated and whitewashed brick, planar and curving surfaces, are suggestive of the material in its construction, endowing the space with an unmistakable character.

→ 36 37 38 39

---

30 Eladio Dieste setzte erstmalig eine Ziegelschalenkonstruktionen als Gegenvorschlag zu der geplanten Betonschalenkonstruktion 1946 beim Haus Berlingieri in Punta Ballena ein, als er mit dem Architekten Antoni Bonet zusammenarbeitete.
31 Die Konstruktionen bestanden aus einer einlagigen, mit Stahl bewehrten Ziegelschicht im Verbund mit einer Deckschicht aus Betonmörtel.
32 Vorläufer und Vordenker dieser Konstruktion war Rafael Guastavino, der in den späten 1860er-Jahren eine Vielzahl grosser Industriegebäude in Barcelona entwarf und konstruierte, in denen er traditionelle katalanische Ziegelgewölbe für die Boden- und Dachkonstruktionen einsetzte.
33 Standford Anderson (Hrsg.), *Eladio Dieste. Innovation in Structural Art*, New York 2004, S. 72

30 In 1946, when collaborating with the architect Antoni Bonet, he became the first to introduce a brick shell construction as a counterproposal to the planned concrete shell construction of the Casa Berlingieri in Punta Ballena.
31 These constructions consist of single layers of brick reinforced with steel in conjunction with a surface layer of concrete mortar.
32 The precursor and pioneer of this construction is Rafael Gustavino, who designed and constructed a multitude of industrial buildings in Barcelona in the late 1860s, employing traditional Catalan brick vaulting for floor and roof structures.
33 Standford Anderson (ed.), *Eladio Dieste: Innovation in Structural Art*, New York 2004, p. 72.

40

41

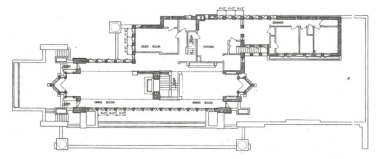

42

43

44

45

46

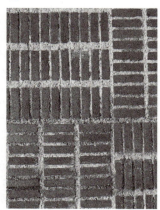

47

48

40 Henry Adams Building, Louis Sullivan, Algona/Iowa, 1912; ornamentales Gewebe	40 Henry Adams Building, Louis Sullivan, Algona/Iowa, 1912; ornamental texture
41/42 Robie House, Frank Lloyd Wright, Chicago/Illinois, 1909; Horizontale durch Mauerwerksfugen verstärkt	41/42 Robie House, Frank Lloyd Wright, Chicago/Illinois, 1909; horizontals strengthened by masonry joints
43/44 Studentenwohnheim Baker House am MIT, Alvar Aalto, Cambridge/Massachusetts, 1948; Plastizität durch fehlerhafte Steine	43/44 Baker House (student residence), MIT, Alvar Aalto, Cambridge/Massachusetts, 1948; plasticity achieved via imperfections in brick
45 Midway Gardens, Frank Lloyd Wright, Chicago/Illinois, 1914; ornamentierte Terracotta-Steine	45 Midway Gardens, Frank Lloyd Wright, Chicago/Illinois, 1914; ornamented terracotta bricks
46–48 Markuskyrkan, Björkhagen, und Sankt Petri Kyrka, Klippan, Sigurd Lewerentz, 1960/1966; Fugenbild	46–48 Markuskyrkan, Björkhagen, and Sankt Petri Kyrka, Klippan, Sigurd Lewerentz, 1960/1966; appearance of joints

Brick—of Weaving and Joining

The Oriental Style—The Poetics of Weaving

Emerging parallel to developments in constructive brick style, particularly in the US, were brick buildings that took the Oriental style as a model.

Louis Sullivan's and Frank Lloyd Wright's interest in the textile character of masonry led Kenneth Frampton to examine the influence of German architects working in Chicago and their links back to Gottfried Semper as well as to the resulting, widely-held preoccupation with Oriental architecture and Oriental mysticism.[34] In this context ornamentation was employed as a component of a powerful, magic symbolic meaning—the building's shell, with its tattoos or inscriptions, now becomes a kind of skin.[35]

It was in this spirit that Sullivan took the position that ornamentation should not be applied externally, but should emerge instead out of function and material in a quasi-vegetal process of growth.[36] His comparison between brickwork masonry and the weaving of Oriental carpets clarifies his attitude toward Oriental architecture, his own brick buildings leave little doubt of this.

In Oriental architecture, Frank Lloyd Wright—a student and colleague of Sullivan—recognized a universal writing of humanity that preceded Gutenberg's printing press.[37] In search of expressive forms suited to a modern American architecture, he adopted the principles of Asian and Oriental building culture and developed his so-called organic architecture, based among other things on the "plasticity" of materials. Plasticity in this context means the development of forms following from the material features. That is, exploiting the expressive force of a material for architecture. This may become manifest in the grain of the wood, for example, or in the configuration of style joints in brick masonry work.

The thematic concerns of Wright's work were conditioned by the textile character of architecture, as seen in the narrative and ornamental aspects of the Orient, as well as in the folding screens of Japanese architecture. At his Prairie Houses this theme is approached through the dissolution of walls, as well as through an emphasis on the horizontal. With the Robie House in Chicago, this effect is further strengthened by the use of brick and the horizontal configuration of the flat brick layers, so fundamental to the design. Midway Gardens, a beer and dance locale in Chicago, represents a variation on this theme. Here, he combines ornamented or symbolically charged terracotta bricks with harmonious brick masonry work. With the "textile block," the design intent of brick masonry work becomes explicit.

---

34 See Kenneth Frampton, *Studies in Tectonic Culture*, Cambridge: MIT Press, 2001.
35 "Thus a progressive pantheism came to be inscribed in everything they did, as a kind of cryptic language that invariably took the form of a petrified textile of which we may say that the walls were as much written as they were built." Ibid., p. 100.
36 Hanno-Walter Kruft, *History of Architectural Theory*, Munich 2017.
37 Edgar Kaufmann, Ben Raeburn (eds.), *Frank Lloyd Wright: Writings and Buildings*, New York 1960.

Gestaltungsabsicht des gewebten Mauerwerks wurde mit dem «textile block» explizit.

→ 41 42 45

Seit Mitte des 20. Jahrhundert wurde die von Semper beschriebene Dichotomie einer Backsteinarchitektur sublimiert und durch das Interesse an der Textur, der Handwerklichkeit, dem seriellen, zellenartigen Charakter und der atmosphärischen Wirkung des Materials ergänzt. Je nach Blickwinkel und Fokus zeigten die Backsteinbauten aber auch Kombinationen unterschiedlicher Haltungen auf.

Alvar Aalto verglich den standardisierten Ziegelstein als kleinsten Teil eines gebauten Organismus mit den «standardisierten» organischen Zellen der Natur, die aufgrund ihrer elastischen Verbindungen an keine Form gebunden sind.[38] Als elastische Verbindung einer Backsteinkonstruktion erfuhr die Fuge somit einen Bedeutungswandel und wurde zum wesentlichen Element seiner Architektur. Gleichzeitig etablierte Aalto als Kennzeichen eines «neuen Humanismus» emotionale oder atmosphärische Werte, zu denen optische und haptische Qualitäten sowie lokale Eingebundenheit gehörten. Die geschwungenen Wandflächen des Studentenwohnheims Baker House am MIT in Cambridge, Massachusetts, aus unregelmässig gebrannten Ziegeln und wertlosem Ausschussmaterial, die als Verformungen aus der Mauer hervortreten, sind das Ergebnis dieser Überlegungen. Das fehlerhafte Material wird zum Ornament einer plastischen Oberfläche und stellt gleichzeitig eine assoziative Verknüpfung zum Handwerklichen und Archaischen her.

→ 43 44

Die Verwendung ungeschnittener Steine in variierenden Grössen führte beim Bau der Kirche St. Peter in Klippan von Sigurd Lewerentz dazu, dass sich das Verhältnis von Stein zu Fuge umkehrt und das Fugenmaterial zum primären Wandmaterial wird. Fugenhöhen und -breiten passen sich den spezifischen Situationen an und ergeben ein lebendiges Wandmuster, in dem sich Ziegel verdichten oder entspannen. Gleichzeitig treten sie aus der Wandoberfläche hervor oder springen zurück, wodurch die Backsteinarchitektur den Charakter des Unfertigen, Improvisierten, Rauen und Handwerklichen erhält. Wandöffnungen vermitteln den Eindruck, als hätte man sie nachträglich in eine bestehende Wand geschnitten. Stehende und liegende Steinschichten, die einfach gestapelt wurden, verweisen auf den textilen Aspekt der Wand.

→ 46 47 48

Eine Fortsetzung dieses bildhaften Umgangs mit dem Material sind die Gewölbedecken im Inneren der Kirche. Obwohl Lewerentz Gewölbebögen als adäquates Konstruktionsprinzip einer Steinarchitektur ausbildete, konterkarierte er eben dieses, indem er die Backsteine längs zum Gewölbe ohne Verband einsetzte — das Gewölbe wird zum Symbol seiner eigenen Konstruktion.

Es ist der atmosphärische Ausdruck des Materials, der Lewerentz' Architektur bestimmt. Beim Betreten der Kirche tritt man in die ganz eigene Welt des Ziegels oder, wie Richard Weston es ausdrückt: «Lewerentz ist entschlossen, uns zu zeigen, was Backstein ist».[39]

Beginning in the mid-twentieth century, the dichotomy of brick architecture described by Semper has been sublimated and supplemented by an interest in texture, in handicraft, the atmospheric effects of the material and the serial, cell-style character of brick building. A particular strength of brick is its potential variety of uses that can respond to the particular attitude, focus, or perspective of the architect. Alvar Aalto compared the standardized brick as the smallest unit of a built organism with the "standardized" organic cell in nature which, by virtue of its elastic connective capacities, is not bound to any specific form.[38] As an elastic connection in brick construction, the joint hence experiences a shift of meaning, becoming an essential element of his architecture. Established by Aalto as the trademarks of a "new humanism," meanwhile, are emotional and atmospheric values which include optical and haptic qualities as well as the integration of local conditions. The curvilinear wall surfaces of his student residence in Cambridge Massachusetts, constructed using unevenly baked bricks and worthless scrap material that protrudes from the walls as deformations, resulted from these considerations. The defective material is used as ornamentation on a sculptural surface, while generating associations with handicraft values and archaism.

→ 43 44

At Sigurd Lewerentz' Church of St. Peter in Klippan, the use of untrimmed brick in various dimensions led to a reversal in the relationship between brick and joint, allowing the joint material itself to become the primary material of the wall. The heights and widths of the joints are adapted to specific situations and produce a lively wall pattern within which the bricks are arranged in denser or looser fashion. At the same time, they protrude from or recede into the wall surface, giving the brick architecture an unfinished, improvised, rough, and hand-made character.

Wall openings convey the impression that incisions were made subsequently in an existing wall, while upright and reclining layers, which are simply stacked up, allude to the textile aspect of the wall.

→ 46 47 48

A continuation of this picturesque treatment of brick as a material is found in the ceiling falls of the church interior. Although Lewerentz shapes the vaulted arches as an adequate construction principle for brick architecture, he contradicts it by positioning the bricks lengthwise in relation to the vault without joints—the vault becomes a symbol of its own construction.

It is the atmospheric expression of the materials that shapes his architecture. Upon entering the church, we encounter a fully autonomous world of brick or, as Richard Weston expressed it: "Gazing at, Lewerentz's brickwork [...], we may feel that we are being granted a privileged glance into the essence of the material."[39]

---

38 Alvar Aalto, *Synopsis: Malerei, Architektur, Skulptur*, Basel 1970
39 Richard Weston, *Material, Form und Architektur*, Stuttgart 2003, S. 96

38 Alvar Aalto, *Synopsis: Painting, Architecture, Sculpture*, Basel 1970.
39 Richard Weston, *Material, Form and Architecture*, New Haven CT 2003.

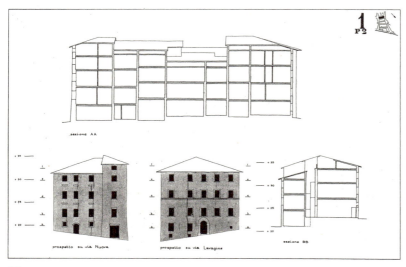

49

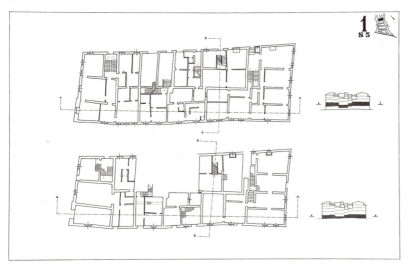

50

52

51

53

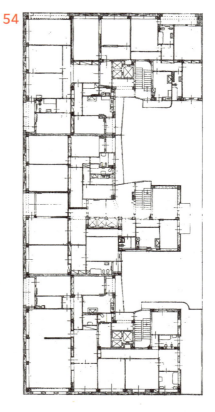

54

55

49/50　Auf- und Grundrisse eines Gebäudeblocks, Giancarlo De Carlo, Urbino, 1966; körperhafte Backsteinbauten und unregelmässiges Raumnetz
51/52　Stadtansicht von Urbino
53–55　Casa Bonaiti Malugani, Giovanni Muzio, Mailand, 1936; innere Pfeilerarchitektur wird an der Fassade abgebildet

49/50　Elevation and plan of a building, Giancarlo De Carlo, Urbino, 1966; corporeal presence of brick buildings and irregular spatial network
51/52　Urbino, cityscape
53–55　Casa Bonaiti Malugani, Giovanni Muzio, Milan, 1936; the interior pillar architecture is pictured on the façade

Backstein — vom Weben und Fügen

Of Spatial Networks, Spatial Niches, and Spatial Sequences

The multitude of expressive possibilities offered by brick are also reflected in layout design. Early brick buildings are a point of reference here and provide insights into the influence of the material on the design of floor plans in residential buildings. One such example is Urbino, which originated as a fortified town in the sixth century. The corporeal presence that is intrinsic to brick buildings also finds expression in floor plan structures. In contradiction to the clearly structured and delimited layouts of historic urban wooden architecture, or to settlements constructed in concrete, brick buildings tend to generate an irregular spatial network. Brick buildings display an interlocking pattern that extends beyond the limits of the individual buildings and along the entire length of the street. As components of this spatial network, niches as well as projections and setbacks from the wall, along with the floor plan, yield forms that seem to develop organically.

→ 49 50 51 52

For multistoried residential construction, the combination of brick construction with steel or reinforced concrete girders results in novel design possibilities at the level of the floor plan. Supporting structures taking the form of brick pillars dissolve the small-scale spatial network of the wall in favor of larger formations. Exemplary of this approach are the dwellings of Giovanni Muzio. The rationalistic yet multiform façade of the eleven story Casa Bonaiti e Malugani in Milan → 53 54 55 depicts the constructive character of the pillar in architecture. Projections and setbacks in the façade, but also the differentiated application of a variety of brick courses allude to the load-bearing or filling function of the wall. The prestigious rooms along the street front follow the structured rhythm of the pillars and are not distinguishable in their dimensions from those of historical brick buildings. Typical traits of pillar structures are enfilades or spatial relationships generated by large wall openings.

Frank Lloyd Wright's floor plans illustrate an additional aspect of brick building, and one that is related to the "woven" character of his architecture. Pillars and wall slabs are combined with one another and spatial effects deployed accordingly. The construction is defined by visual and spatial interrelationships, but also by the dramaturgy of the elements.

→ 45

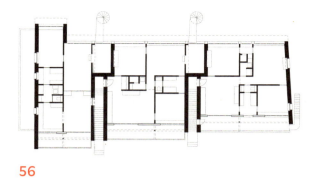

56

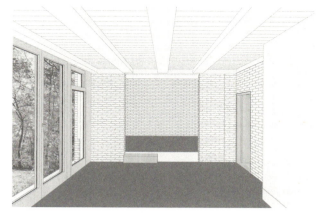

57

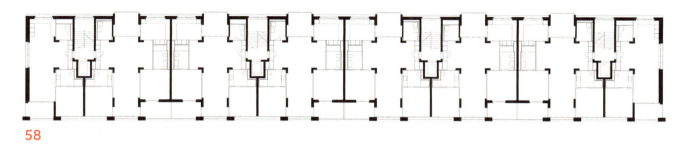

58

59

60

61

62

56/57 pool 0351 Haus Mühlerain, Meilen, 2016–2019; Körperhaft — Wandnischen, Vorzonen, Alkoven
58–60 pool 0324 Areal Kälin, Oberwinterthur, 2014–2020; Haus B: Zonierung des kreuzförmigen Hallengrundrisses durch Backsteinpfeiler
61/62 pool 0324 Areal Kälin, Oberwinterthur, 2014–2021; Haus A: Laubengang mit nischenbildenden Mauerscheiben

56/57 pool 0351 Haus Mühlerain, Meilen, 2016–2019; sculptural wall niches, front zones, alcoves
58–60 pool 0324 Kälin Areal, Oberwinterthur, 2014–2020; Haus B: zoning of the cruciform plan through brick pillars
61/62 pool 0324 Kälin Areal, Oberwinterthur, 2014–2021; Haus A: arcade with niche-forming wall slabs

Backstein — vom Weben und Fügen

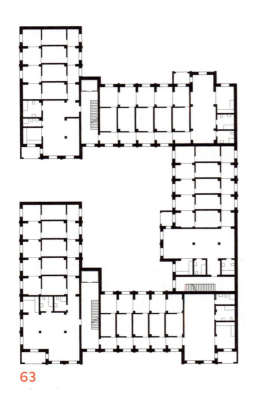

63

64

65

66

67

68

69

70

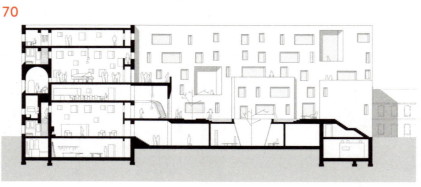

63 Studierendenprojekt Urban Brick 03, Anna Gert/Cemile Kolgu, TU Berlin 2014/15; Backsteinpfeiler strukturieren den Grundriss	63 Student project, Urban Brick 03, Anna Gert/Cemile Kolgu, TU Berlin 2014/15; brick pillars structure the ground plan
64/65 Studierendenprojekt Urban Brick 07, Luca Gericke/Franco Scheuplein/Carolin Trahorsch, TU Berlin 2014/15; archaische Massivität	64/65 Student project, Urban Brick 07, Luca Gericke/Franco Scheuplein/Carolin Trahorsch, TU Berlin 2014/15; archaic solidity
66 Studierendenprojekt Urban Brick, TU Berlin 2014/15; Ausschnitt aus dem Gesamtmodell	66 Student project, Urban Brick, TU Berlin 2014/15; section of the complete model
67 Studierendenprojekt Urban Brick 05, Vera Marie Glas/Rafael Lozykowski/Florian Rizek, TU Berlin 2014/15; Innenhof	67 Student project, Urban Brick 05, Vera Marie Glas/Rafael Lozykowski/Florian Rizek, TU Berlin 2014/15; inner courtyard
68 Studierendenprojekt Urban Brick 06, Larsen Berg/Harald Niessner, TU Berlin 2014/15; Industrie und Urbanität	68 Student project, Urban Brick 06, Larsen Berg/Harald Niessner, TU Berlin 2014/15; industry and urbanity
69/70 Studierendenprojekt Urban Brick 01, Julius Blencke/Caspar Kollmeyer/Jan Wind, TU Berlin 2014/15; raumhaltige Aussenwand	69/70 Student project, Urban Brick 01, Julius Blencke/Caspar Kollmeyer/Jan Wind, TU Berlin 2014/15; space-containing outer wall

Von Ausblicken und Eindrücken

Mit der Ölkrise in den 1970er-Jahren und der Einführung von Wärmeschutzverordnungen kamen tragende Wandkonstruktionen aus massivem Mauerwerk, die nicht den geforderten Dämmwerten entsprechen, in Europa als Fassadenkonstruktionen nicht mehr in Frage. Von nun an existierte Sichtmauerwerk nur noch als Bekleidung mehrschichtiger Fassadenkonstruktionen, ohne dies jedoch als architekturästhetischen oder gestalterischen Aspekt zu thematisieren; vielmehr führen die Bekleidungen eine «hohle» Existenz als Imitation massiver, strukturell wirksamer Wandkonstruktionen.

Seit der Jahrtausendwende, mit den Bestrebungen der Rückbindung der Architektur an das Material, entstehen auch aus Backstein wieder Gebäude mit monolithischen Wandkonstruktionen. Bis zu 60 Zentimeter starke Aussenwände, bei denen sich poröse, dämmende Ziegelsteine mit frost- und wasserbeständigen Backsteinen verzahnen, sind ein Ergebnis dieser jüngsten Auseinandersetzung.

Bei ihrem dreigeschossigen Wohnhaus in Meilen fokussieren pool Architekten grundrisstypologische und atmosphärische Aspekte der Ziegelbauweise, indem sie die massive Körperhaftigkeit des Ziegelsteins durch die Ausbildung raumhaltiger Wände verstärken. Wandnischen integrieren Schränke, Kamine, Fenster, Treppenstufen sowie die Ausstattung der Küchen oder Badezimmer und bilden kleine Vorzonen aus. Statt eines rationalen, festgelegten Standards folgt die Artikulation der Nischen, der Vor- und Rücksprünge und damit die Relation von Mobiliar zu Wand der konstruktiven Logik, sodass räumlich unterschiedlich spezifische Situationen entstehen. In einen grösseren Massstab übersetzt ergibt sich aus dem Thema der Nischenbildung ein alkovenartiger Raum, der über zwei Stufen mit dem Wohnzimmer verbunden ist und sich mit der benachbarten Wohneinheit verschränkt. Dem historischen Beispiel Urbinos ähnlich, scheint die Struktur organisch gewachsen statt am Reissbrett entworfen zu sein. Neben den räumlichen Themen des Ziegelbaus prägt das Fugenbild der geschlämmten, roh belassenen Ziegelsteine die Atmosphäre der Räume und wird zu einem wesentlichen Aspekt des Interieurs.

→ 56 57

Auf dem Areal Kälin in Oberwinterthur, einem ehemaligen Hobelwerk mit Industriebauten aus Ziegel, nutzten pool Architekten gelben Backstein als strukturelles Material für die tragenden Stützen ihrer mehrgeschossigen Wohnungsbauten. Dabei verfolgten sie zwei unterschiedliche Strategien: Die raumbildende Backsteinkonstruktion ist dem vierseitig angelegten, hofbildenden Gebäude als kreuzgangartige Laubengangerschliessung vorgelagert und wirkt vorrangig identitätsstiftend. Dagegen folgen die Grundrisse des lang gestreckten Wohnungsriegels der Logik einer Pfeilerkonstruktion und sind punktsymmetrisch — jedoch mit starken Verschiebungen — aufgebaut. Die Verschiebungen zeigen sich in den Differenzierungen der Stützenabstände, in der Aussermittigkeit der Stützenanordnung sowie in der Ausbildung der Stützenform.

Of Prospects and Impressions

With the oil crisis of the 1970s and the introduction of thermal insulation regulations in Europe, solid brickwork supporting walls, which failed to provide the required insulation values, fell out of demand for façade construction. From this point onward, exposed masonry existed only as cladding on multilayered façade constructions, albeit without highlighting these as aesthetic or design elements. Instead, the cladding led a "hollow" existence as an imitation of solid, structurally effective walls.

Since the turn of the twenty-first century, and with efforts to reconnect architecture with materials, we have seen a return of brick buildings featuring monolithic wall constructions. One result of recent investigations is the construction of external walls up to 60 cm thick, where porous, insulating brick is interlinked with frost and water-resistant brick.

In their three-story apartment building in Meilen, pool Architekten focused on the floor plan typologies and atmospheric aspects of this type of building, emphasizing the solidity and corporeality of brick by forming space-containing walls. Wall niches and integrated cabinets, fireplaces, windows, stairs, as well as kitchen and bathroom fittings form small liminal zones. In place of a rational, pre-established standard, this articulation of niches and projections, and hence the relationship between furnishings and walls, follows a constructive logic, giving rise to spatially diverse and individualized situations. Translated onto a larger scale, the theme of niche formation results in an alcove-style room that is linked to the living room via two steps, and is interlocked with neighboring residential units. Not unlike the historical example of Urbino, the structure seems to grow organically rather than having been designed at the drafting table. Alongside the spatial theme of brick building, the pattern created by the whitewashed bricks shapes the atmosphere of the rooms and becomes an essential aspect of the interior.

→ 56 57

On the Kälin areal site in northern Zürich, a former planing mill with brick industrial buildings, the architects are using yellow brick as a structural material for the supporting pillars of their multistoried apartment buildings. Here, they follow two different strategies. First, the brick of the residential building that forms the courtyard is set in front of the cloister-style access balcony and primarily serves to create a sense of visual identity. Second, the layouts of the elongated residential building follow the logic of pillar construction and are point-symmetrical—albeit with marked displacements. The displacements are displayed in the differentiated intervals between pillars, in the eccentric arrangement of the pillars, as well as in the formation of the pillars themselves. The center of each apartment is the living hall, which extends westward into a loggia-style outdoor space. In the four corners, the sleeping and utility rooms are shifted into the hall, resulting in an incisive, cruciform spatial structure. The space-containing brick pillars demarcate the

Zentrum der Wohnungen ist die Wohnhalle, die sich im Westen zu einem loggiaartigen Aussenraum erweitert. An ihren vier Ecken schieben sich die Schlaf- und Funktionsräume in die Halle, sodass eine prägnante, kreuzförmige Raumstruktur entsteht. Die raumhaltigen Backsteinpfeiler markieren den zentralen Raum und bilden je nach Position im Grundriss quadratische, winkel- oder linienförmige Wandstücke aus. Zur Verdeutlichung des strukturellen Prinzips setzen sich die nicht tragenden Raum- und Fassadenelemente durch den Wechsel im Material eindeutig von der Tragstruktur ab.

Die sichtbaren Backsteinpfeiler werden zu markanten raumbildenden Elementen, die als Interieur «Position beziehen», die Fassaden rhythmisieren und wesentlich den Ausdruck der Architektur bestimmen.

→ 58 59 60 61 62

central space and—depending on their position in the floor plan—give shape to rectangular, angular, or linear wall sections. In order to clarify the structural principle, non-supporting spatial and façade elements are set off clearly from the supporting structure via material contrasts.

The visible brick pillars become striking space-shaping elements, which "take a stance" in the interior, rhythmicize the façades, and shape the expressive character of this architecture in essential ways.

→ 58 59 60 61 62

←

Backstein — vom
Weben und Fügen

Brick—of Weaving
and Joining

Beton — vom Feinen im Rohen

Concrete — the Fine within the Rough

Bauen mit Beton ist gekennzeichnet durch die Gussform. Als vorgefertigte Bauteile von der raumgrossen Platte bis zu kleinteiligen Stäben oder als Ortbeton mit rauen oder glatten Oberflächen ausgebildet, lässt das Material unterschiedliche konstruktive oder räumliche Konzepte und Ausdrucksformen zu. Während das Fügen grossformatiger Platten die Komposition von Volumen und Raumzusammenhängen verlangt und präzise geformte, industriell gefertigte Elemente die Tektonik erweitern, wohnt dem Ortbeton die Erhabenheit des Archaischen inne, das sowohl in der Unebenheit der Oberflächen als auch in der monolithischen Grossform des Steins zum Ausdruck kommen kann.

Raummodule und befreite Grundrisse

Die Einführung des Eisenbetons in der Architektur inspirierte Anfang des 20. Jahrhunderts eine ganze Architektengeneration und initiierte einen neuen Architekturstil. Das neue Baumaterial war wie geschaffen für die architektonischen Themen der Zeit: die Skelettbauweise mit ihren «befreiten» Grundrissen und Fassaden, standardisierte und serielle Herstellung im Wohnungsbau, aber auch plastisch geformte Architektur konnten sich dank des Einsatzes von Eisenbeton durchsetzen.

Eine der Besonderheiten des Materials und ein Novum in der Architektur war die Möglichkeit der Vorfertigung grosser Bauelemente, die vor Ort nur noch gefügt werden müssen. Bereits im 19. Jahrhundert experimentierten Architekten und Ingenieure mit vorgefertigten, schweren Betonbauteilen — Häuser aus Betonblocksteinen, bewehrte Betonplatten oder vorfabrizierte Raumzellen bildeten das Spektrum dieser frühen Experimente [40] — und in den 1920er-Jahren wurde diese Bauweise zu einem Themenschwerpunkt in der Architektur.

Für die Architekten des Neuen Bauens, besonders im Bauhaus-Umfeld, war das Bauen mit vorgefertigten Betonelementen Ausdruck einer zeitgemässen, modernen Architektur, die auf einen Schlag die Wohnprobleme der damaligen Zeit lösen sollte: Durch die industrielle Vorfertigung der Häuser sollte sich fortan jeder «arbeitende Mensch eine gute, gesunde Wohnung» [41] leisten können. Ebenso wie die Bekleidung würde auch das Haus von der Stange die Bedürfnisse des modernen Menschen befriedigen. Auf der Grundlage von Festlegungen allgemeingültiger Wohnbedürfnisse sollten Typenhäuser mit einheitlichen Materialien und Grundrissen industriell gefertigt werden. Walter Gropius entwickelte 1923 ein Typenserienhaus aus genormten

Concrete building is characterized by the casting mold. As a prefabricated building element, ranging from room-sized panels to small-scale rods, or as site-poured concrete that is given rough or smooth surfaces, this material leads to the most diverse spatial conceptions and expressive forms. While joining large panels together requires the composition of volumes and spatial relationships and extends tectonics through precisely-shaped, industrially-manufactured elements, there is an archaic solidity inherent in concrete cast-in-place. The unevenness of the surfaces and the large, monolithic forms of the individual blocks contribute to this expression.

Space Module and Open Plans

In the early twentieth century, the introduction of reinforced concrete in architecture inspired an entire generation of architects and initiated a new style of building. The new building material was tailor-made for the architectonic themes of the time: the application of reinforced concrete made possible skeleton construction, with its "liberated" floor plans and façades, standardized and serial production in residential development, but also an amorphous architecture.

One of the peculiarities of the material and its novelty in the history of architecture is the possibility for prefabricated building elements to be assembled simply on site. Already in the nineteenth century, architects and engineers experimented with heavy, prefabricated concrete building elements. These early experiments encompass houses built from concrete blocks, reinforced concrete panels, and prefabricated spatial cells. In the 1920s, this style of building became a thematic focus in architecture.[40]

For the architecture of the Neue Bauen, particularly in the Bauhaus milieu, construction with prefabricated concrete elements was regarded as an expression of a modern architecture capable of solving the housing problems of the time in one fell swoop. From this point onward, it was believed that the industrial prefabrication of dwellings could provide every working person with "good, healthy housing."[41] Just as in the realm of fashion, off-the-rack housing would satisfy the requirements of the modern individual. Based on definitions of generally-understood residential needs, standard houses using uniform materials and floor plans would be industrially manufactured. In 1923, Walter Gropius developed a series of standard houses constructed from large, standardized concrete panels

---

[40] 1832 wurden in England Häuser aus Blocksteinen gebaut und um 1860 in Frankreich bewehrte und mit Tonzuschlägen versetzte Betonplatten für den Hausbau in den Kolonien hergestellt. Von dem französischen Ingenieur François Hennebique entwickelte Bahnwärterhäuschen wurden 1896 als eine der ersten vorfabrizierten Raumzellen per Eisenbahn transportiert und vor Ort installiert. Siehe: Daniel Spillmann, «Die gefügte Gussform», in: Arthur Rüegg, Reto Gadola, Daniel Spillmann, Michael Widrig (Hrsg.), *Die Unschuld des Betons*, Zürich 2004.

[41] Walter Gropius, *Ein Versuchshaus des Bauhauses in Weimar*, München 1923 (Reprint 1999), S. 6f.

[40] In 1832, houses were built in England using concrete blocks, and in France around 1860, reinforced concrete panels with clay additions were manufactured for housing construction in the colonies. In 1896, signalmen's houses developed by the French engineer Hennebique were among the first prefabricated room modules to be transported by rail and installed on-site. See Arthur Rüegg, Reto Gadola, Daniel Spillmann, Michael Widrig (eds.), *Die Unschuld des Betons: Wege zu einer materialspezifischen Architektur*, Zurich 2004.

[41] Walter Gropius, *Bauhausbücher 3: Ein Versuchshaus des Bauhauses in Weimar*, Munich 1923 (reprint 1999), pp. 6–7.

Betongrosstafeln, das sich nach dem Baukastenprinzip aus vielfältig kombinierbaren Raummodulen zusammensetzte. Trotz des Versuchs, diese Prinzipien im damaligen Siedlungsbau im grossen Massstab anzuwenden — die Siedlung in Dessau-Törten und die Weissenhofsiedlung in Stuttgart gingen aus diesen Überlegungen hervor[42] — wurden nur wenige Siedlungen tatsächlich aus Betontafeln erstellt.[43]

→ 71 72

Auch wenn sich die Betonsystembauweise in der damaligen Zeit aus unterschiedlichen Gründen nicht durchsetzte, so eröffneten die Entwürfe und Ideen, die hieraus hervorgingen, ein neues Gedankenfeld in der Architektur, das in der Baukasten- und Raummodulidee zum Ausdruck kam. Architektur wurde in Raumzusammenhängen und der Komposition von Volumen gedacht.

Gleichzeitig rangen die Architekten um einen adäquaten architektonischen Ausdruck des Betons. Besonders Auguste Perret oder Josef Plecnik loteten Anfang des 20. Jahrhunderts das ästhetische und strukturelle Potenzial und die Besonderheiten des neuen Materials aus. Traditioneller Holzbau, die klassische Antike, aber auch der zeitgenössische Brückenbau dienten ihnen als Analogie und führten zu einem neuen Ausdruck in der Architektur.

→ 73 74 77

Auguste Perret bewies das gestalterische oder ästhetische Potenzial des Eisenbetons nicht nur in den Details seiner Betonskelettbauten, sondern auch in den Grundrissen und den Fassaden. Die Rahmenbauweise als zeitgemässe Konstruktion war «rhythmisch, ausgeglichen und symmetrisch» und gleichzeitig flexibel in der Grundrissgestalt. Für Perret stellte sie die Muttersprache des Architekten dar.[44] Und mit dem Satz «Il n'y a pas de détail dans la construction»[45] brachte er seine Haltung zum Ausdruck, dass jedes Detail der Konstruktion inhärent ist, aus dieser quasi «erwächst».

Auch wenn die Fassaden seines Wohnhauses in der Rue Franklin mit ornamentierten Fliesen verkleidet waren, so war die Stahlbetonrahmenbauweise, die sich dahinter verbirgt, gestaltgebend. Peter Behrens, der mit seinen Bürobauten am Alexanderplatz Perrets rationalistischem Ansatz folgte, formulierte diese architektonische Haltung folgendermassen: «Die Kassettierung des Raster, die Doppelfenster und die Muschelkalkverkleidung sind Formentscheidungen, die eindeutig aus

which could be assembled according to a modular construction principle using a variety of spatial modules. Despite the attempt to apply these principles on a large scale in housing development at the time (the housing estate in Dessau-Törten and the Weissenhofsiedlung in Stuttgart emerged from such considerations),[42] only a few estates using concrete panels were actually built.[43]

→ 71 72

Although the concrete system of construction did not prevail at the time, the designs and ideas that emerged from it opened up new fields of thought in architecture. Architecture was conceived now in terms of spatial relationships and the composition of volumes.

At the same time, architects struggle toward an adequate architectonic expression of concrete. In the early twentieth century, Auguste Perret and Josef Plecnik in particular explored the aesthetic and structural potential and peculiar features of this new material. Traditional timber construction, classical antiquity, but also contemporary bridge-building, serve for them as analogies and led toward a new form of expression.

→ 73 74 77

Auguste Perret demonstrated the design and aesthetic potential of reinforced concrete, not just in the details of his concrete skeleton constructions but also in his floor plans and façades.

Frame construction, as a contemporary approach, is "rhythmic, balanced, and symmetrical," and at the same time flexible in the design of the floor plan. For Perret, construction is the "mother tongue" of the architect.[44] "Il n'y a pas de détail dans la construction," he says, suggesting the construction is inherent in each detail, and "grows" from it.[45]

Although the façades of his apartment building on Rue Franklin are clad in ornamental tiles, the reinforced concrete framework construction they conceal is nonetheless integral for the design. Peter Behrens, who follows Perret's rationalistic approach in his office buildings on Alexanderplatz, formulates this architectonic attitude as follows: "The coffering of the grid, the double windows, and the limestone cladding are decisions concerning form that are explicitly derived from the construction as the primary quality, but which do not leave it materially unchanged, but instead alter, circumscribe, and hence enhance it. [...] The natural stone cladding serves the grid structure, but

---

42 Vorerst scheiterte die Verwirklichung der Idee vom industriell gefertigten Montagehaus aus Betongrosstafeln an Herstellungs-, Transport- und Montageproblemen der schweren, raumhohen Elemente und die Architekten griffen vorwiegend auf Skelettkonstruktionen aus Eisen oder Eisenbeton zurück, die mit grossformatigen Bimsbeton- oder Schlackenbetonhohlblocksteinen ausgefacht wurden. 1927 stellte Ernst May sein Baukastensystem aus Betonplatten für ein tragendes Wandgefüge an der Stuttgarter Werkbund-Ausstellung vor. Siehe: Ute Hassler, Hartwig Schmidt (Hrsg.), *Häuser aus Beton*, Tübingen/Berlin 2004, S. 19

43 Durch die Anpassung der Grösse der Betontafeln an die Transport- und Montagemöglichkeiten gelang es Ernst May in Frankfurt in den Jahren 1926–1930 (Frankfurt-Praunheim mit 560 Wohnungen und das «Neue Frankfurt» mit 400 Wohnungen), erste Versuchssiedlungen aus vorfabrizierten Betonbauteilen zu verwirklichen. Sein Baukastensystem bestand aus 20 Zentimeter starken Bimsbetonplatten, deren Masse sich mit einer Länge von 3 Metern und einer Höhe von 1,10 bzw. 0,40 Metern an den Brüstungs- und Sturzhöhen des Gebäudes sowie an den Montagemöglichkeiten und der Tragfähigkeit des Turmdrehkrans orientierten. Für die Vorfertigung der Elemente wurde eigens eine Fabrik in der Nähe der Baugelände in Frankfurt errichtet.

Holländische Firmen, die sich auf die Vorfertigung von Betongrosstafeln spezialisiert hatten, entwickelten nach amerikanischem Vorbild Verfahren, um die raumgrossen, schweren Elemente vor Ort zu fabrizieren und zu montieren. Basierend auf dem Grossplattenverfahren Bron entstand in den Jahren 1923–1925 das sogenannte Betondorp nach Plänen von Dick Greiner in der Versuchssiedlung Amsterdam-Watergrafsmeer und wenige Jahre später in Berlin-Friedrichsfelde unter der Federführung Martin Wagners eine Siedlung mit 138 Zwei- bis Dreizimmerwohnungen für Kriegsopfer und Kriegshinterbliebene. Die überwiegend 7,5 × 3 Meter grossen Platten mit einem dreischichtigen Aufbau aus wetterbeständigem Kiesbeton, trockener Schlacke und porösem Schlackenbeton wurden inklusive Fenster- und Türrahmen und Aussenputz auf der Baustelle liegend vorgefertigt und mit einem elektrischen Portalkran aufgestellt.

44 Nach Kenneth Frampton, *Grundlagen der Architektur. Studien zur Kultur des Tektonischen*, München 1993, S. 168

45 Ebd., S. 31

42 Initially, the realization of industrially prefabricated buildings was hindered by problems relating to the manufacture, transport, and assembly of large, room-height elements. Instead architects worked with skeleton constructions of iron or reinforced concrete which could be filled in with large from pumice concrete or hollow slag concrete blocks. In 1927, Ernst May presented his modular construction system, consisting of concrete panels, for a loadbearing wall structure at the Stuttgart Exhibition. See Ute Hassler, Hartwig Schmidt (eds.), *Häuser aus Beton*, Tübingen/Berlin 2004, p. 19.

43 By customizing the sizes of the concrete panels according to the available transport and assembly possibilities, Ernst May succeeded in Frankfurt in the years 1926–1930 (Frankfurt-Praunheim, with 560 apartments, and the "New Frankfurt," with 400 units) in realizing the first experimental housing using prefabricated concrete construction elements. His modular construction system consisted of pumice concrete panels, 20 cm thick, 3 m long, and 1.10 m or. 0.4 m high. The panels were oriented towards the heights of building's railings and lintels as well as to the possibilities of assembly and the carrying capacity of a rotating tower crane. A factory in close proximity to the building site in Frankfurt was built especially for the prefabrication of the elements.

A Dutch firm specializing in the pre-allocation of large concrete panels developed procedures, borrowing from American models, for fabricating and assembling room-sized, heavy elements. Betondorp, an experimental housing estate Amsterdam-Watergrafsmeer was constructed between 1923–1925 based on the large panel procedures of Bron and according to plans by Dick Greiner. A few years later in Berlin-Friedrichsfelde under the supervision of Martin Wagner, a settlement with 138 two- to three-room apartments was constructed. The panels, for the most part measuring 7.5 × 3 m with a triple layered structure consisting of weather-resistant gravel concrete, dry slag, and porous slag concrete were prefabricated at the building site, including window and door frames and external plaster, and set into position using an electric gantry crane.

44 Cf. Kenneth Frampton, *Studies in Tectonic Culture*, Cambridge 1995, p. 153.

45 Ibid., p. 26.

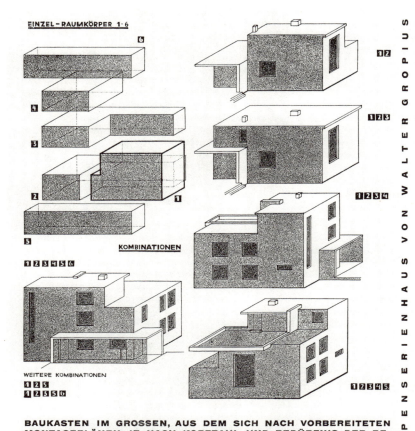

71 «Baukasten im Grossen» für das Versuchshaus in Weimar, Walter Gropius, 1923
72 Siedlung Praunheim im Bau, Ernst May, Frankfurt am Main, 1926
73/74 Palais d'Iéna, Auguste Perret, Paris, 1937; Säulen aus Beton
75/76 Wohnhaus in der Rue Franklin, Auguste Perret, Paris, 1905; Stahlbetonrahmenbauweise
77 Heilig-Geist-Kirche, Josef Plecnik, Wien, 1913; Stützenkopf

71 "Full-scale construction kit" for the experimental house in Weimar, Walter Gropius, 1923
72 Praunheim housing estate under construction, Ernst May, Frankfurt am Main, 1926
73/74 Palais d'Iéna, Auguste Perret, Paris, 1937; concrete pillars
75/76 Apartment building on Rue Franklin, Auguste Perret, Paris, 1905; reinforced concrete frame construction
77 Heilig-Geist-Kirche, Josef Plecnik, Vienna, 1913; column head

Beton — vom Feinen im Rohen

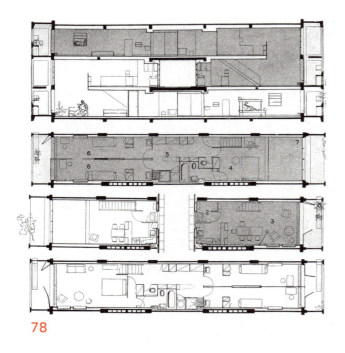

78

79

80

81

83

82

84

78–80 Unité d'Habitation, Le Corbusier, Marseille, 1952; Schönheit unterschiedlicher Oberflächentexturen des rohen Betons
81–84 Robin Hood Gardens, Peter und Alison Smithson, London, 1970; Synthese aus serieller Vorfertigung und unmittelbarer Betonästhetik

78–80 Unité d'Habitation, Le Corbusier, Marseille, 1952; the beauty of diverse surface textures in rough concrete
81–84 Robin Hood Gardens, Peter and Alison Smithson, London, 1970; synthesis of serial prefabrication and a palpable concrete aesthetic

Concrete—the Fine within the Rough

Der poetische Ausdruck des Betons

Dieses Ringen um einen adäquaten Ausdruck des Materials fand in Le Corbusiers Unité d'habitation in Marseille einen Höhepunkt. Er selbst brachte in seiner Beschreibung anlässlich der Übergabe des Bauwerks 1952 den Stellenwert der Unité zum Ausdruck: «Sie ist Ausdruck gesunder Kraft und offenbart eine ganz neuartige Schönheit, die des rohen Betons. [...] Der Bau der Unité von Marseille hat der neuen Architektur die Gewissheit gebracht, dass armierter Beton, als Rohmaterial verwendet, ebenso viel Schönheit besitzt wie Stein, Holz oder Backstein. [...] Es erscheint nunmehr möglich, den Beton wie Stein in seinem Rohzustand zu zeigen.»[47]

Um die Schönheit des rauen Betons zu behaupten, bediente er sich der Gegensätze von Rohheit und Feinheit, Mattem und Leuchtendem oder Präzision und Zufälligkeit. Er kombinierte Betonfertigteile mit Sichtbeton, das Serielle mit dem Individuellen. Die Schalungsbretter, die sich auf den Oberflächen der meist plastisch geformten Sichtbetonelemente abdrücken, werden zu Kanneluren oder zum Ornament und verleihen den Oberflächen eine Textur, die sowohl an die Unebenmässigkeit natürlicher Materialien als auch an die bearbeiteten Steine der Tempel in der griechischen Antike erinnert. Die seriell gefertigten Sichtbetonbrüstungen und -seitenwände mit ihren ebenmässigen, glatten Oberflächen hingegen werden als Sitz- und Fensterbänke zu einem Teil des Mobiliars. Mit der Unité gelang es Le Corbusier, das gesamte Spektrum und die Möglichkeiten des Betons zu demonstrieren oder, um es mit den Worten des britischen Architekturkritikers Reyner Banham auszudrücken: «Le Corbusier erfand den Beton beinahe als neuen Baustoff. [...] Marseille ist in der Tat der Ort, an dem das Versprechen des Buchtitels (Vers une Architecture) erfüllt wurde. [...] ‹L'Architecture, c'est avec des matières brutes établir des rapports émouvants.›»[48]

Diese «matières brutes» oder der «béton brut», den Le Corbusier mit der Unité einführte, wurden der Ausgangspunkt einer neuen Architekturrichtung, die sich in den 1950er-Jahren unter dem Begriff des Brutalismus formierte. «Die Schaffung erregender Zusammenhänge aus rauem Material sollte das zentrale Anliegen des Brutalismus werden», beschreibt Reyner Banham den Einfluss der Unité.

Alison und Peter Smithson, Hauptinitiatoren und Mitbegründer der Bewegung des Brutalismus,

The Poetic Expression of Concrete

The struggle for an adequate expression of material finds its highpoint in Le Corbusier's Unité d'habitation. On the occasion of the building's completion, the architect himself characterized the importance of the Unité as follows: "It has also the robustness which is inherent in modern technique, and it shows the new splendor of the bare concrete. [...] The realization of the Unité in Marseille has shown the splendor which is possible by the use of reinforced concrete as a natural material of the same rank as stone, wood, or brick. It seems to be really possible to consider concrete as a reconstructed stone, worthy of being exposed in its natural state."[47]

In order to assert the beauty of the concrete, Le Corbusier exploited the opposition between coarse and fine, mat and brilliant, precision and contingency. He combined precast concrete parts with exposed concrete, the serial with the individual. The shuttering boards that leave their imprint on the surfaces of most of the sculpturally-formed exposed concrete elements become fluting or ornamentation. This endows the surface with a texture that is reminiscent of the unevenness of natural materials, as well as of the worked stone of ancient Greek temples. As with benches and windowsills, the serially-manufactured exposed concrete railings and lateral walls, with their even, smooth surfaces, become elements of the furnishings. With the Unité, Le Corbusier succeeded in demonstrating the entire spectrum of possibilities through concrete and, as Reyner Banham put it: "Le Corbusier conjured concrete almost as a new material [...] Marseille is where the promise of that book's title *(Vers une Architecture)* is fulfilled [...] 'L'Architecture, c'est avec des matières brutes établir des rapports émouvants.'"[48]

This "matières brutes" or *béton brut,* introduced by Le Corbusier at the Unité, became the point of departure for a new architectural tendency that formed during the 1950s around the concept of Brutalism. Reyner Banham describes the influence of the Unité as follows: "To construct moving relationships out of brute materials was to be the central ambition of Brutalism." The Smithsons, primary initiators and co-founders of the Brutalist movement, referred to their architecture as "anti-architecture" or "l'art brut." Their work expresses itself through a "reverence for the materials" and through the correspondence between the building and the human individual. As with more traditional or rustic forms of dwelling, the architecture should be the immediate result of a way of life.[49]

---

46 Tilmann Buddensieg, «Der Weltstadtplatz. Peter Behrens und das ‹Neue Herz› Berlins am Alexanderplatz», in: Gisela Fiedler-Bender, Heinz Höfchen, *Peter Behrens. Berlin Alexanderplatz,* Kaiserslautern 1993
47 Le Corbusier, *Œuvre Complète 1946–1952,* Zürich 1966, S. 192–193
48 Reyner Banham, *Brutalismus in der Architektur. Ethik oder Ästhetik?,* Stuttgart/Bern 1966

46 Tilmann Buddensieg, "Der Weltstadtplatz. Peter Behrens und das 'Neue Herz' Berlins am Alexanderplatz," Gisela Fiedler-Bender, Heinz Höfchen, *Peter Behrens — Berlin Alexanderplatz,* Kaiserslautern 1993.
47 Le Corbusier, *Oeuvre Complete,* vol. London 1953, p. 191.
48 Reyner Banham, *The New Brutalism,* London 1966, p. 16.
49 Peter and Alison Smithson in *Architectural Design,* April 1957; cited in Banham, *The New Brutalism,* p. 47.

bezeichneten ihre Architektur als «Anti-Architektur» oder «L'art brut», die sich durch die «Ehrfurcht vor dem Material» und die Übereinstimmung zwischen Bauwerk und Mensch ausdrückte — wie bei den bäuerlichen Wohnformen sollte die Architektur zu einem unmittelbaren Ergebnis einer Lebensweise werden.[49] Der Brutalismus war für sie Synonym für die «wahre Architektur», die «die Wirklichkeit objektiv» betrachtete und einem ständigen Wandel unterlag. «Der Brutalismus versuchte, der Gesellschaft der Massenproduktion zu entsprechen und den verworrenen und starken Kräften, die am Werke sind, eine raue Poesie zu entreissen.»[50]

→ 81 82 83 84

Als Gegenposition zum funktionalistischen Ansatz des Rationalismus, «der in der Architektur zu einer Ausdruckslosigkeit führt», setzten die Architekten im Umfeld des Team X mit ihren Forderungen nach dem Individuellen als Teil eines Systems, nach Ausdruck, Ehrlichkeit, Materialgebundenheit sowie einer Rückbindung an Tradition oder archaische Formen neue Massstäbe. Auf der Suche nach Wahrheit in der Architektur und deren unmittelbarer Sprache spielte die Synthese der seriellen Vorfertigung und des ästhetischen Ausdrucks von Beton eine entscheidende Rolle. Unter diesen Prämissen entstanden innerhalb der Gruppe unterschiedliche Strömungen mit unterschiedlichen Schwerpunkten.

Von Prozessen und wachsenden Häusern

Eine dieser Strömungen repräsentierten die sogenannten Strukturalisten, die besonders in Holland stark vertreten waren.[51] Die Theorien von Claude Lévi-Strauss, Jacques Lacan und Roland Barthes, die sich mit den Phänomenen, Prinzipien und Strukturen von soziologischen und kulturell geprägten Systemen auseinandersetzten, beeinflussten den Strukturalismus.[52] Einer der Hauptgedanken des Strukturalismus war die Objektivierbarkeit der Welt. Auf die Architektur übertragen suchten die Strukturalisten nach netzartigen oder modularen (Bau-)Systemen, die variabel, flexibel und robust waren und sich erst durch die Aneignung der Bewohner vervollständigten. Den Fokus auf Beziehungsgeflechte, individuelle Selbstbestimmung, Wachstum und Wandel gerichtet, wurde die Form nicht mehr definiert, sondern sie entstand prozesshaft auf der Grundlage von Regeln. Die Entwurfsprozesse wurden objektiviert und die Architektur verwissenschaftlicht.

Moshe Safdies Komplex Habitat 67 in Montreal symbolisierte eine Architektur der automatischen, unbewussten Prozesse, die jenseits von Formvorstellungen entsteht.[53] Als konzeptionelle Mischung indigener Behausungen und industrieller Vorfertigung stapelte

For them, Brutalism was synonymous with "true architecture" which attempts to be "objective about 'reality'" that is subject to "constant change." They argued, "Brutalism tries to face up to a mass production society and drag a rough poetry out of the confused and powerful forces which are at work."[50]

→ 81 82 83 84

As a counterposition to the functionalist approach of rationalism, "which led toward expressionlessness in architecture," the architects of Team X set new standards with their demands for the individual as part of a system. They argued for expression, truthfulness, and connection to material, as well as recourse to tradition and archaic forms. Playing a decisive role in this search for truth in architecture and for immediacy of language was a synthesis of serial prefabrication with the material expression of concrete.

Out of Team X and this particular set of ideologies grew new sets of architectural styles and trends.

Of Processes and Growing Houses

Among these was so-called Structuralism, which grew with a particular interest in the Netherlands.[51] Structuralism was shaped by the theories of Claude Levi-Strauss, Jaques Lacan, and Roland Barthes, who were preoccupied with the phenomena, principles, and structures of sociological and culturally conditioned systems.[52] One of the key tenets of Structuralism is the objectification of the world. Transferred to architecture, the Structuralists sought network-style or modular (building) systems which were flexible and robust, and which attained completion only when appropriated by occupants. As a consequence of a focus on webs of relationships, individual self-determination, and growth, form was no longer defined but instead emerged gradually according to a set of rules. The design process became objectified, and architecture became an object of scientific research.

Moshe Safdie's Habitat 67 in Montreal symbolizes an architecture of automatized, unconscious processes which emerge beyond notions of form.[53] Creating a conceptual mixture of indigenous forms of dwelling and industrial prefabrication, he stacked 354 prefabricated concrete boxes to form a dense "vertical city" composed of 158 houses with gardens.

→ 85 86

---

49 Peter und Alison Smithson, «The Built World: Urban Reidentification», in: *Architectural Design* 06/1955, zitiert nach: Banham, wie Anm. 48, S. 45f.
50 Peter und Alison Smithson, «Thoughts in Progress», in: *Architectural Design* 04/1957
51 Der architektonische Strukturalismus war besonders in den Niederlanden stark verbreitet und wurde von Architekten wie Aldo van Eyck, Jacob Bakema und Johannes van den Broek, Piet Blom und Hermann Hertzberger vertreten.
52 Basierend auf Ferdinand de Saussures strukturalistischer Theorie zur Linguistik gründete Claude Lévi-Strauss in Frankreich den sogenannten kulturellen Strukturalismus.

50 Ibid., p. 66.
51 Architectural Structuralism was disseminated with particular strength in the Netherlands, and was advocated by architects such as Aldo van Eyck, Bakema and van den Broek, Piet Blom, and Hermann Hertzberger.
52 Claude Lévi-Strauss originated structural anthropology in France based on the structural linguistics of Ferdinand de Saussure.
53 Habitat 67, consisting of 158 houses assembled from 354 concrete modules, was assembled at the 1967 World's Fair in Montreal and was the result of many years of investigations into three-dimensional towns and habitats based on principles of modular housing, and ultimately on the idea of stacked casbah. The dense development, consisting of small prefabricated units, each having its own garden, facilitated the identification of inhabitants with their environment. The 13-story structure of the building results from the stacking of loadbearing, completely fabricated concrete boxes having sizes of 600 ft² (17.5 × 38.5 × 10.5 ft.).

Safdie 354 komplett vorgefertigte Betonboxen zu einer dichten «vertikalen Stadt» aus 158 Häusern mit Gärten.

Der niederländische Architekt Jacob B. Bakema forderte für die Architektur und den Städtebau partizipatorische Konzepte, in denen sich die zukünftigen Nutzer ausdrücken können.[54] Er gründete viele seiner Wohnungsbauprojekte auf der Idee des wachsenden Hauses, das ausgehend von einem in Serienproduktion geschaffenen, standardisierten Hauskern individuell erweitert werden kann.

Bei Aldo van Eyck führten die Untersuchungen vernakulärer Architektur archaischer Kulturen zu architektonischen Strukturen aus übergeordneten, modularen Systemen und kleinen, identischen Zellen.[55] Der übergeordneten Grossstruktur steht die Nische als Lebensraum, in dem sich der Mensch als Teil einer sozialen Gruppe entfaltet, gegenüber. Wie bei der musikalischen Fuge bei Bach wurde die Struktur bei ihm zur Basis für die vielfältige Variation zu einem Thema. Er kombinierte rohen Sichtbeton mit anderen, ebenfalls roh belassenen Materialien wie Stahl-Glaselementen, Glasbausteinen und Mauerwerk und entwickelte daraus eine Art Katalog. In der Anwendung entstanden unterschiedlich gestaltete Fassaden und Wandfüllungen sowie unterschiedliche räumliche Bezüge und Zusammenhänge. Dadurch würden Einheit und Verschiedenheit, gross und klein, viel und wenig, Einfachheit und Komplexität, das Konstante und das Veränderliche, Geschlossenheit und Offenheit, innen und aussen, Individualität und Gemeinschaft zu einem zusammenhängenden Phänomen, so Aldo van Eyck.[56]

Struktur, Charakter und Tradition

Im Gegensatz zu diesen objektivistischen Ansätzen, die eine neutrale Struktur für die Aneignung der Architektur durch den Bewohner nutzen, ist die japanische Architektur gekennzeichnet durch die charaktervolle Struktur. Die Verbindung des Seriellen, also Allgemeingültigen, mit dem Individuellen zeigt sich in der japanischen Architektur in der Ausformung der Details, dem differenzierten Umgang mit der Struktur und damit in der Architektursprache. Einfachheit, Leichtigkeit, Offenheit, das modulare Bauen mit vorgefertigten Elementen sowie die Anwendung unbearbeiteter Materialien sind traditionell in der japanischen Architektur verankert und der Schritt zu einer zeitgemässen Architektur ist in erster Linie eine Übersetzungsarbeit im Material — vom Holzbau zum Betonbau —, die sich vordergründig als Massstabssprung darstellt.

53 Das Habitat 67 mit 158 Häusern aus 354 Betonmodulen wurde zur Weltausstellung 1967 in Montreal errichtet, es war das Ergebnis jahrelanger Untersuchungen von dreidimensionalen Städten und Habitaten, die auf dem Prinzip des modularen Bauens basieren und letztendlich die Idee der gestapelten Kasbahs umsetzten. Die dichte Bebauung aus kleinen, vorgefertigten Einheiten mit eigenem Garten diente der Identifikation des Bewohners mit seinem Lebensraum. Die 13-geschossige Gebäudestruktur entstand durch die Stapelung der tragenden, komplett vorgefertigten Betonboxen mit den Massen 11,7 × 5,3 × 3 Meter
54 Jacob Berend Bakema, «Einige Bedingungen für die Architekturentwicklung heute», in: Bauen + wohnen 12/1975, S. 490
55 Aldo van Eycks Prinzip der Reziprozität zeigte sich auch in seiner Idee, das Haus als kleine Stadt und umgekehrt die Stadt als Haus zu betrachten, womit er sich sowohl auf Leon Battista Alberti (De Re Aedificatoria, I, IX, 4–5) als auch auf Andrea Palladio (Die vier Bücher zur Architektur, zweites Buch, Kap. XII) bezieht.
56 Francis Strauven, Aldo van Eyck. Relativiteit en verbeelding, Amsterdam 1994

Beton — vom Feinen im Rohen

Jacob B. Bakema demanded participatory concepts for architecture and urban planning through which future users could express themselves. He based many of his housing projects on the idea of the "growing house," a standardized, serially produced core that could be extended individually.[54]

In the case of Aldo van Eyck, research into vernacular architecture in different cultures led to architectonic structures consisting of modular systems with small, identical cells.[55] Standing opposed to the large structure is the "niche," a living space within which the individual can develop as part of a social group. For van Eyck, as in a fugue by Bach, the structure is the "basis" for multifarious variations on a theme. He combined untreated, exposed concrete with other untreated materials such as steel and glass, glass bricks, and masonry work, developing a catalog of sorts from them. In practice, the result was variously shaped façades and wall fillings as well as diverse spatial configurations and relationships. Through this approach, according to van Eyck, unity and variety, large and small, many and few, simplicity and complexity, the constant and the alterable, closeness and openness, inner and outer, individuality and community, come to form a larger, interrelated phenomenon.[56]

Structure, Character, and Tradition

In contrast to these objectivist approaches, deploying a neutral structure which allows the architecture to be appropriated by residents, Japanese architecture is highly distinctive in character. The connection between the serial—which is to say the generally valid—and the individual is manifested in Japanese architecture in the shaping of details, the treatment of the structure, and hence in the architectural language.

Simplicity, lightness, openness, modular building with prefabricated elements, and the application of untreated materials: all of these features are anchored in traditional Japanese architecture, and the step toward a contemporary architecture primarily involves a translation between different materials— for example, from timber to concrete construction—that is conspicuous, superficially at least, as a leap in scale.

Kunio Maekawa's Harumi Apartment Building in Tokyo is a striking instance of the interlocking of Japanese tradition and contemporary building in prefabricated concrete elements. Following the principles of traditional timber architecture, the ten-story apartment building consists of an overarching bar-shaped structure which dissolves into increasingly fine, ancillary structures, all the way down to the concrete rods of the railings.[57] Groups of six apartments are joined

54 Jacob Berend Bakema, "Einige Bedingungen für die Architekturentwicklung heute," Bauen + Wohnen, December 1975, p. 490.
55 Aldo van Eyck's principle of reciprocity is also manifested in his idea of regarding the house as a small town, and conversely the town as a house; here, he refers to Alberti (De Re Aedificatoria, I, IX, 4–5) as well as to Palladio (Book II, Chap. XII).
56 Francis Strauven, Aldo van Eyck. Relativiteit en verbeelding, Amsterdam 1994.
57 This residential high-rise contains 170 small apartments with living areas of either 32 m² or 42 m² which are accessed via access balconies and internal connecting staircases. Access balconies in the second, fifth, and eighth stories lead via connecting staircases to the apartments in the third, fourth, sixth, seventh, and ninth stories. Each unit has a living room and bedroom, the two connected via a sliding door, kitchen, bathroom, toilet, and storage room.

Kunio Maekawas Apartmenthaus Harumi in Tokio von zeigt eindrücklich das Ineinandergreifen von japanischer Tradition und zeitgenössischem Bauen mit vorgefertigten Betonelementen. Den Prinzipien der traditionellen Holzarchitektur folgend, besteht das zehngeschossige Wohnhaus[57] aus einer übergeordneten stabförmigen Struktur, die sich in immer feinere, untergeordnete Strukturen bis hin zu den Betonstäben der Brüstungen auflöst. Jeweils sechs Apartments werden in der Grossstruktur zu dreigeschossigen Häusern zusammengefasst — auskragende Loggien sind Reminiszenzen an die Gärten. Die Sekundärstruktur aus schlanken Stützen und Balken markiert die einzelnen Apartments und die Tertiärstruktur setzt sich im Inneren als Holzkonstruktion fort, um dort die einzelnen Raumbereiche zu definieren. Durch die Differenzierung der Struktur wird die architektonische Grossstruktur nicht nur auf einen «menschlichen Massstab» heruntergebrochen, sondern es entsteht eine plastisch gestaltete Fassade.

→ 90 91 92

Eine noch direktere Übersetzung vom Holzbau zum Betonbau lässt sich im Werk von Kenzo Tange entdecken. Die Betonbalken seiner Bauten sind nicht nur gefügt wie die Stäbe einer Holzkonstruktion, sondern entsprechen auch im Feinheitsgrad der Details den traditionellen Vorbildern. Die Nachahmung der strukturellen Prinzipien wurzelte bei Tange in der Suche nach der Schönheit in der Architektur, die in der Ausbildung von Typen zu finden ist — die traditionelle Bauweise in Japan und Westeuropa, die weder international-objektiv noch individualistisch war, steht Pate für diesen Ansatz. Architektur ist Ausdruck des Wesens menschlicher Tätigkeit und der Struktur, sie verbindet Tradition und zeitgemässe Technik.

→ 93 94

«Die mannigfaltigen Verkörperungen der Funktion im beständigen Wechsel und in der Vielfalt der Realität sind nicht schön an und für sich. Aber den Erscheinungsformen der Funktion, die den Grad der Typenbildung erreicht haben — mit anderen Worten, die eigentliche und entwickelte Funktion — wohnt die Möglichkeit inne, in ihrem Ausdruck Schönheit zu verkörpern.»[58]

Auch Angelo Mangiarotti in Italien ging es um die Ausbildung von Typen,[59] jedoch galt sein Fokus ganz besonders der allgemeingültigen Formensprache, denn die Sprache ist das «Medium der Entwurfsabsicht und Körperlichkeit des gestaltgebenden Instruments, welches durch das Projekt entsteht».[60] Die konstruktive Formensprache als Ausgangspunkt der Tätigkeit des Architekten sollte der Gegenwart verpflichtet und zugleich sozialbewusst sein.[61] Unter dieser Prämisse entwickelte er gemeinsam mit der Industrie präzise gestaltete Betonelemente für die serielle Fertigung. «Man muss im Grunde ein anderes Verhältnis zwischen der Produktion eines Mittels und seiner Verwendung

together within the larger structure to form three-story buildings, while cantilevered loggias are reminiscent of gardens. The secondary structure, consisting of slender supports and beams, marks out the individual apartments. The tertiary structure is continued on the inside as a wooden construction which defines individual spatial areas. Structural differentiation not only means that the larger architectonic whole is broken down to "human scale," it also produces a sculpturally shaped façade.

→ 90 91 92 93 94

An even more direct translation of timber into concrete construction can be found in the work of Kenzo Tange. The concrete beams of his buildings are not only joined together as in timber construction, but correspond, in the fineness of their details, to traditional prototypes.

For Tange, such an imitation of structural principles is rooted in the search for beauty in architecture, one that is found in the formation of types. The inspiration for this approach is an appreciation for traditional forms of building in Japan and Western Europe, which were neither universal nor individualistic. Architecture is an expression of the essence of human activity and its structures join together traditional and contemporary techniques.

→ 93 94

"The various manifestations of function in the flux and diversity of reality are not beautiful in themselves. Manifestation of function raised to the level of typology—in other words, essential and progressive function—holds the possibility of embodying beauty in expression."[58]

For Angelo Mangiarotti in Italy as well, it was a question of giving form to types, although he was very specifically focused on a universally valid formal language.[59] For Mangiarotti, language is the "medium of the design intention and the corporeality of the design-creating instrument through which the project emerges."[60] The constructive formal language as the point of departure for the architect's activity should be rooted in the present and be socially conscious.[61] Based on these premises he developed precisely designed concrete elements for serial manufacture in collaboration with industry. "Basically, one must establish a very different relationship between production of a resource and its application, a relationship that also respects the desires and expectations of later users. It is primarily a question of generating conditions that foster the creative activities of the architect rather than hindering them," he wrote in an article on his apartment building in Monza.[62]

→ 95 96 97

Correspondingly, the building systems[63] for his residential buildings consist of profiled concrete elements whose multiplicity and small dimensions allow

---

57   Das Wohnhochhaus enthält 170 Kleinwohnungen mit einer Wohnfläche von 32 bzw. 42 Quadratmetern, die über Laubengänge und interne Verbindungstreppen erschlossen werden. Laubengänge im zweiten, fünften und achten Obergeschoss führen über die Verbindungstreppen zu den Wohnungen des dritten, vierten, sechsten, siebten und neunten Obergeschosses. Jede Einheit hat einen Wohn- und einen Schlafraum, über eine Schiebetür miteinander verbunden, Küche und Bad, WC und Abstellraum.
58   Kenzo Tange, «Gestaltung in der Architektur der Gegenwart und die Tradition Japans», in: Robin Boyd, Kenzo Tange. Architekten von heute, Bd. 3, Ravensburg 1963
59   Ebenso wie die Antike in der Architektur allgemeingültige Prinzipen hervorgebracht hat, geht es Mangiarotti um Allgemeingültigkeit im Gegensatz zu der «individuellen Schöpfung», die «einer Formensprache kaum die nötige Dauerhaftigkeit verleihen [kann]», um ein für die Gemeinschaft verfügbares Gut zu werden».
60   Angelo Mangiarotti, «Architektur heute», in: Bausysteme von Angelo Mangiarotti, hrsg. von Thomas Herzog, Darmstadt 1998
61   Angelo Mangiarotti, «Struktur als Form», in: Bauen + Wohnen 12/1975, S. 504

58   Kenzo Tange, "Creation in present-day architecture and the Japanese tradition," in Robin Boyd, Kenzo Tange, New York 1963, p. 116.
59   Just as antiquity engendered universally valid principles in architecture, Mangiarotti is concerned primarily with general validity in contrast to "individual creation," which is hardly capable of "endowing a form language with the permanence that would allow it to become a generally available good for the community."
60   Angelo Mangiarotti, "Architektur heute," in Thomas Herzog (ed.), Bausysteme von Angelo Mangiarotti, Darmstadt 1998.
61   Mangiarotti, "Struktur als Form," Bauen + Wohnen, December 1975, p. 504.
62   Mangiarotti developed a multiplicity of systems in the years between 1957 and 1977.
63   Angelo Mangiarotti, "Industrialisiertes Bauen und Nutzerbeteiligung," Bauen + Wohnen, June 1977, p. 225.

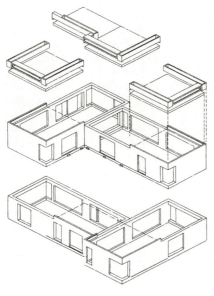

85

86

87

88

89

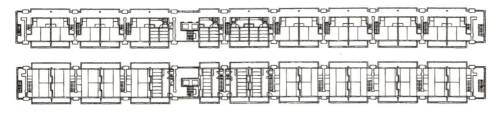

90

91

92

93 94

85/86   Habitat 67, Moshe Safdie, Montreal, 1967; vertikale Stadt aus vorgefertigten Betonboxen
87–89   Städtisches Waisenhaus, Aldo van Eyck, Amsterdam, 1960; modulare Systeme als Basis für Variationen
90–92   Apartmenthaus Harumi, Kunio Maekawa, Tokio, 1958; traditionelle und zeitgemässe Verbindung des Seriellen mit dem Individuellen
93/94   Rathaus, Kenzo Tange, Kurashiki, 1958–1960; Übersetzung vom Holzbau zum Betonbau

85/86   Habitat 67, Moshe Safdie, Montreal, 1967; vertical town of prefabricated concrete boxes
87–89   Municipal Orphanage, Aldo van Eyck, Amsterdam, 1960; modular systems as a basis for variation
90/92   Harumi apartment building, Kunio Maekawa, Tokyo, 1958; traditional and contemporary combination of the serial with the individual
92/93   Town Hall, Kenzo Tange, Kurashiki, 1958–1960; translation of timber building into concrete construction

Beton — vom Feinen im Rohen   271

95

96

98

99

97

100

101

102

103
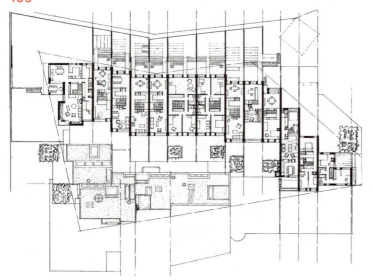

104

95–97 Residential building, Angelo Mangiarotti, Monza, 1972; industrially developed concrete elements for maximum design freedom
98/99 Node supporting structure, System FM, U 70, Briona 72, Angelo Mangiarotti, 1964–1972
100–102 Halen Housing Estate, Atelier 5, Herrenschwanden, 1955–1962; exposed concrete linking interior and exterior
103/104 Thalmatt Housing Estate 1, Atelier 5, Herrschwanden, 1974; immersion into the world of concrete

Concrete—the Fine within the Rough

herstellen, ein Verhältnis, das auch die Wünsche und Vorstellungen der späteren Nutzer berücksichtigt. Es geht in erster Linie aber darum, Bedingungen zu schaffen, welche die schöpferische Arbeit des Architekten fördern und nicht behindern»,[62] schrieb er in einem Artikel zu seinem Wohnhaus in Monza.

→ 95 96 97

Dementsprechend bestehen die Bausysteme[63] seiner Wohnungsbauten aus profilierten Betonelementen, deren Vielfalt und Kleinteiligkeit eine freie Gestaltung der Fassaden und Grundrisse erlaubt.[64] Vor- und Rücksprünge, horizontale Bänderungen sowie eine Diversität in der Anordnung der Fenster, Balkone und Loggien kennzeichnen die Fassaden. Mangiarotti bewies, dass Bauen mit Systemen mehr als nur eine Frage von Fugen und Knoten ist. Paradigmatisch zeigte er das Potenzial der Bauweise mit vorgefertigten Betonelementen auf, das in der Präzision der Profilierung, der Oberflächenqualität sowie in der Feingliedrigkeit der Details zu finden ist.

→ 98 99

Von Atmosphären und Stimmungen

Als Gegenposition zu den Strukturalisten ging es den Gründern von Atelier 5 bei dem Bau ihrer Siedlungen «um die ‹ideale› Lösung, das ‹Schönste› und ‹Beste› in diesem Moment und nicht darum, flexible Systeme zu schaffen, aus denen der Bewohner später selber macht, was er will».[65] Die traditionelle, gewachsene Dorfstruktur als Vorbild, wollten sie eine Stimmung, ein Milieu kreieren, das sich unter anderem in der Gestaltung der Aussenräume, der Verbindung der Häuser mit dem Aussenraum und als Fortsetzung in den fliessenden Übergängen der Innenräume ausdrückt. Farbigkeit, Alltagsleben, Lichtstimmungen, Proportionen, Relationen und ganz besonders die Materialität spielten dabei eine wesentliche Rolle.

Beton als zeitgemässes, lokales und universales Material, das sowohl innen als auch aussen, als Sockel, Dach, Decke, Loggia, Treppe, Brüstung, Stützmauer oder Sitzbankelement eingesetzt werden kann, kommt der Idee der fliessenden Übergänge und Aufhebung von Hierarchien entgegen. Ganz der Tradition Le Corbusiers verpflichtet, zeigte Atelier 5 den Sichtbeton in seiner Purheit und Rauheit und bewies die Ausdruckskraft und Schönheit des Materials an sich. Strukturierte Oberflächen aus Ortbeton kontrastieren die glatten Oberflächen von vorgefertigten Betonelementen und variieren das Thema einer Betonarchitektur. «Es gibt kein gutes oder schlechtes Material. Sondern es kommt darauf an, ob der Architekt es versteht, mit dem Material umzugehen.»[66]

---

62 Angelo Mangiarotti, «Industrialisiertes Bauen und Nutzerbeteiligung», in: *Bauen + Wohnen* 06/1977, S. 225
63 In den Jahren zwischen 1957 und 1977 entwickelte Mangiarotti eine Vielzahl von Systemen.
64 Die Fassaden seiner Wohnhäuser in Monza (1972) und Arosio (1977) setzen sich aus raumhohen, 95 Zentimeter breiten und 28 Zentimeter starken vorgefertigten Betonelementen mit einer Kerndämmung zusammen. Die Betonoberflächen sind durch ein feinkörniges Steingranulat strukturiert.
65 Anatole du Fresne, *Atelier 5. Siedlungen*, Zürich 1984.
66 Anatole de Fresne und Jacque Blumer (Atelier 5) in einem Dialog mit Giario Daghini, Balthasar Burkhard und Niele Toroni, in: *Das Seminar*, Zürich 1988

the free shaping of the façades and floor plans.[64] The façades are characterized by projections and setbacks, horizontal bands, and a varying arrangement of windows, balconies, and loggias. Mangiarotti demonstrates that building with systems is more than a question of joints and nodes. He demonstrates the potential of the building with prefabricated concrete elements, especially in the precision of profiling, in surface qualities, and the refinement of details.

→ 98 99

Of Atmospheres and Moods

In contrast to the Structuralists, the founders of Atelier 5 strive in their housing estates to arrive at "an 'ideal' solution, the most beautiful, the best, and at this moment, not to create flexible systems out of which residents can later make what they will."[65]

With the traditional, evolved village structure as a model, they seek to engender an atmosphere that is expressed amongst other things: in the shaping of exterior spaces; in connections between houses and outdoor spaces; and as a continuation of the flowing transitions within interior spaces. Playing essential roles here are color, everyday life, lighting moods, proportions, relationships, and, most importantly, materiality.

They see concrete as a contemporary, local, and universal material, which can be utilized in a plethora of ways: inside and outside, for pedestals, roofs, ceiling, loggias, staircases, railings, supporting walls, and seating elements. It also accommodates the idea of flowing transitions and the suspension of hierarchies. Entirely in the tradition of Le Corbusier, they display concrete as pure and rough, so demonstrating the intrinsic expressive power and beauty of the material. The surfaces of in-situ concrete contrast with prefabricated concrete elements, offering variations on the theme of concrete architecture. "There are no good or bad materials. It is a question of whether the architect understands how to handle the material."[66]

Thus although there is a considerable variety amongst Atelier 5's housing estates, they achieve unity through a consistent language and homogenous materiality.

In their estates, one is immersed in the world of concrete, with all of its beauty, roughness, and robustness. Rather than appearing as sheets of blank paper, their architecture constitutes a definite statement which residents must accept. Unsuprisingly, this can result in friction. Their projects demonstrate the potential and the expressive power of exposed concrete as a material and shapes a new understanding and handling of the material in the context of residential developments. Their experimental housing estates designed with a "new" architectural language combining the traditional idea of the village and new ideas

---

64 The façades of his apartment buildings in Monza (1972) and Arosio (1977) are composed of room-height, prefabricated concrete elements that are 95 cm in width and 28 cm in thickness, with insulating cores. The concrete surface is structured by means of a finely-grained mineral granulate.
65 Anatole du Fresne, *Atelier 5: Siedlungen*, Zürich 1984.
66 Anatole de Fresne and Jacque Blumer (Atelier 5) in a dialogue with Giario Daghini, Balthasar Burkhard, and Niele Toroni in *Das Seminar*, Zurich 1988.

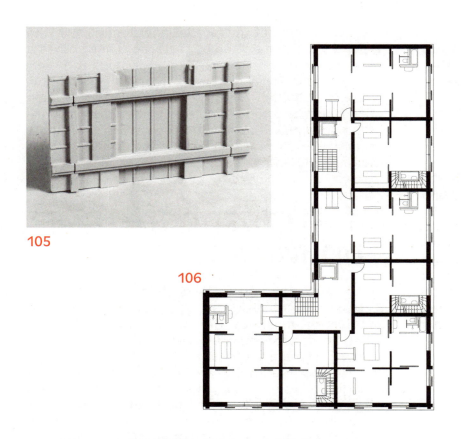

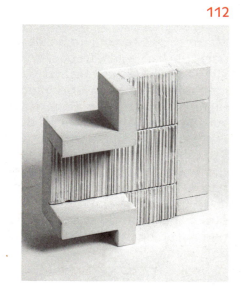

105–107 Studierendenprojekt Urban Concrete 20, Marlene Bühner/Cassandra Donath, TU Berlin 2013/14; Schichtung nach japanischem Vorbild
108 Studierendenprojekt Urban Concrete 16, Aydin Sunar/Tobias Wolski, TU Berlin 2013/14; Fassadenmodell Gips
109/110 Studierendenprojekt Urban Concrete 10, Marina Kolovou-Kouri/David Scharf, TU Berlin 2013/14; zelebrierte Fügung von Elementen
111 Studierendenprojekt Urban Concrete 18, Julia Schmidt/Sebastian Welzel, TU Berlin 2013/14; gestapelte Boxen
112 Studierendenprojekt Urban Concrete 08, Sophie Baum/Theresa Piechottka, TU Berlin 2013/14; Fassadenmodell Gips

105–107 Student project, Urban Concrete 20, Marlene Bühner/Cassandra Donath, TU Berlin 2013/14; layering according to Japanese models
108 Student project, Urban Concrete 16, Aydin Sunar/Tobias Wolski, TU Berlin 2013/14; façade model in plaster
109/110 Student project, Urban Concrete 10, Marina Kolovou-Kouri/David Scharf, TU Berlin 2013/14; celebrating the joining of elements
111 Student project, Urban Concrete 18, Julia Schmidt/Sebastian Welzel, TU Berlin 2013/14; stacked boxes
112 Student project, Urban Concrete 08, Sophie Baum/Theresa Piechottka, TU Berlin 2013/14; façade model in plaster

Auch wenn die Siedlungen von Atelier 5 sehr unterschiedlich und vielgestaltig sind, wird die Homogenität durch eine einheitliche Sprache und das einheitliche Material erreicht. In ihren Siedlungen taucht man quasi in die Welt des Betons ein, mit all seiner Schönheit, Rauheit, Robustheit. Statt eines leeren, unbeschriebenen Blattes ist ihre Architektur ein Statement, mit dem sich der Bewohner auseinandersetzen muss, an dem eine Reibung entsteht. Die Projekte zeigten das Potenzial und die Ausdruckskraft des sichtbaren Betonmaterials auf und prägten damit ein neues Verständnis von und im Umgang mit dem Material — die hohe Akzeptanz dieser in mehrerer Hinsicht experimentellen Siedlungen, die «neue» Architektursprache, die einherging mit der traditionellen Dorfidee, neuen Wohnkonzepten und dem Gemeinschaftsleben der Bewohner, führte nicht zuletzt zu einer positiven Konnotation des Materials im Wohnungsbau.

→ 100 101 102 103 104

Die dargestellten Projekte sind der Höhepunkt und gleichzeitig ein vorläufiger Endpunkt der ästhetischen und praktischen Auseinandersetzung mit Beton in der Architektur. In den 1970er-Jahren geriet das Material durch erste Bauschäden sowie den schlechten Alterungsprozess in Misskredit und Schreckensbilder von verwahrlosten Wohnhäusern und lebensfeindlichen Stadtteilen deformierten sein Image. Von nun an wurde der Beton als Konstruktionsmaterial im Inneren der Gebäude hinter Putz und Gipskartonverkleidungen versteckt.

Neue Herstellungsmethoden, eine hohe Oberflächen- und Ausführungsqualität und die Robustheit des Materials sind dafür verantwortlich, dass das Bauen mit vorgefertigten Betonelementen und Sichtbeton seit einigen Jahren vermehrt wieder in den Fokus der Architekten rückt. Betonplatten als vorgehängte Fassaden, aber auch Sichtbetonoberflächen im Inneren von Wohnungen sind vorsichtige Versuche, das Material für den Wohnungsbau neu zu etablieren.

Der Beton und das Spezifische

Anhand historischer Gedankenbilder und unterschiedlicher architektonischer Ansätze als Basis loten die studentischen Arbeiten, die im Rahmen des Entwurfsseminars «Urban Concrete» an der TU Berlin entstanden sind, die Möglichkeiten einer zeitgemässen Architektur aus vorgefertigten Betonelementen aus und kommen zu sehr unterschiedlichen Ergebnissen. Was die Entwürfe jedoch vereint, ist die Verbindung des Seriellen mit dem Spezifischen, die durch die Unterschiedlichkeit und Diversität der vorgefertigten Elemente zustande kommt. Sie zeigt sich in den Fassaden in rhythmischen Abfolgen, die einem Spannungsbogen folgen, sowie in der Plastizität, die durch Profilierungen oder räumliche Vor- und Rücksprünge entsteht. Betonformteile, die präzise bestimmte Geometrien und klare Kanten ausbilden, schaffen in den Fassaden räumlich komplexe loggienartige Zwischenräume und der Wechsel der Oberflächenqualitäten unterstützt die Gestaltungsabsicht. Im Interieur und auf der Grundrissebene

concerning residence and the communal all lead toward positive associations with concrete as a material for residential projects.

→ 100 101 102 103 104

The aforementioned projects represent a highpoint, and at the same time a provisional endpoint for the aesthetic and practical confrontation with concrete in architecture. During the 1970s building defects caused concrete to fall into disrepute. Appalling images of decaying apartment buildings and forbidding neighborhoods deformed its image. From this point onward, concrete as a construction material was concealed in the interiors of buildings behind stucco or plasterboard.

Yet in recent years there has been a renewed focus on exposed concrete in architecture, thanks to new production methods, high-quality surfaces and workmanship, and the persistent robustness of the material. For example, the use of concrete panels for non-loadbearing façades and exposed concrete surfaces in apartment interiors have begun to reestablish the material as suitable for residential development.

Concrete and Specificity

Using historical images and various architectonic approaches as a basis, students participating in the design seminar Urban Concrete explored the possibility of a contemporary architecture consisting of prefabricated concrete elements, and produced a wide variety of conclusions in the process.

What these designs share, however, is the connection between the serial and the specific which results from the heterogeneity and diversity of prefabricated elements. This connection is evident in the rhythmic sequencing of façades which follow an arc of tension, as well as in the plasticity that results from spatial projections and setbacks. On the façades, molded concrete parts give form to precisely determined geometries and clear edges result in spatially complex loggia-style interspaces. Transitions between surface qualities reinforce the design intention. Inside, and at the level of the floor plan, the designs take advantage of the cellular and serial character of this manner of building to generate unanticipated spatial relationships and diagonal connections, or to shape enfilades. Others exploit the structural elements of beams and supports as design-shaping elements or produce spatial variety by composing with panels.

→ 105 106 107 108 109 110 111 112

Rarely are the solutions and possibilities explored by student designs in laboratory conditions achieved in practice. Here, it is partly a question of discovering more pragmatic solutions. With Haus L, a seven-story apartment building in the housing estate Mehr als Wohnen (More than Housing), the project's materiality reflects that pragmatism. Here, exposed concrete and insulated brick were deployed to maximize the building's surface qualities, robustness, color, granularity, and functionality. As a robust material with a corporeal physicality, the prefabricated concrete elements

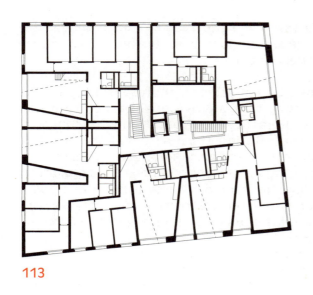

113

114

115

116

117

118

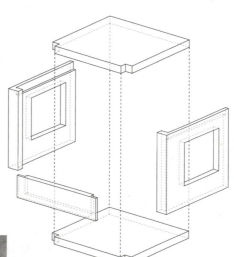

119

120

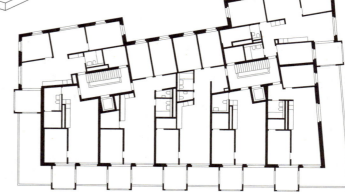

113–117 pool 0243 «mehr als wohnen», Haus G, Zürich-Leutschenbach, 2009–2015;
Dämmbetonhülle
118–120 pool 0243 «mehr als wohnen», Haus L, Zürich-Leutschenbach, 2009–2015;
gestapelte Loggien aus Betonelementen

113–117 pool 0243 "more than housing," Building G, Zürich-Leutschenbach, 2009–2015;
insulating concrete shell
118–120 pool 0243 "more than housing," Building L, Zürich-Leutschenbach, 2009–2015;
stacked loggias consisting of concrete elements

Concrete—the Fine within the Rough

bedienen sich die Entwürfe des zellulären oder seriellen Charakters der Bauweise, um unvorhergesehene räumliche Zusammenhänge und Diagonalbezüge in der Horizontalen oder in der Vertikalen zu schaffen oder um Enfiladen auszubilden. Andere nutzen die strukturellen Elemente der Balken und Stützen als gestaltprägendes Element des Interieurs oder bilden mit der Komposition der Platten eine räumliche Vielfalt.
→ 105 106 107 108 109 110 111 112

Die Lösungen und Möglichkeiten, die die studentischen Entwürfe unter Laborbedingungen aufzeigen, setzen sich in der Praxis selten in dieser Konsequenz durch. Hier gilt es teilweise pragmatischere Lösungen zu finden. Beim Haus L von pool Architekten, einem siebengeschossigen Wohnhaus in der Siedlung auf dem Hunziker Areal in Zürich, wurde dieser Pragmatismus zu einem Prinzip, das sich in der Materialität und im Umgang mit dem Material niederschlägt. Verputzter, gedämmter Ziegel und Sichtbeton wurden aufgrund ihrer Eigenschaften bezüglich Oberflächenqualitäten, Robustheit, Farbigkeit und Körnigkeit sowie ihrer Funktion gezielt eingesetzt. Die vorgefertigten Betonelemente der vorgelagerten, körperhaften Loggien oder des strassenseitigen, zweigeschossigen Sockels bilden als robustes Material einen Filter zwischen innen und aussen, zwischen weicher Haut und Umgebung. Auf diese Weise findet die Loggia als räumlicher und akustischer Filter eine Entsprechung im Material. Einerseits eine Zwischenzone, setzt die Loggia andererseits die innere Raumfolge der Wohnungen fort und behauptet sich als «Wohnraum» mit einem eigenständigen Charakter. Die Artikulation der Loggien — die Betonplatten sind mit fenstergroßen Öffnungen versehen — verweist auf diesen Ansatz.

Die Robustheit des Materials wird durch den feinen Detaillierungsgrad der Betonelemente veredelt. Präzise gesetzte, feine Fugen, akkurat gegratete Kanten sowie die Feinporigkeit und Ebenmässigkeit der Oberflächen verdeutlichen das Potenzial der Stahlbetonvorfertigung. Unterstützt wird diese Anmutung des Feinen oder Edlen durch das «verschachtelte» Ineinandergreifen der Elemente, die leichten Versprünge in den Ebenen und nicht zuletzt durch die Verwendung von Weisszement. Ganz im Gegensatz zu der archaisch anmutenden Betonarchitektur der Brutalisten, die das «Schwere» der Konstruktion besonders in der Ausführung der Knoten und Verbindungen zelebriert haben, sind die offenen Fugen und Auflagerpunkte eher beiläufig und zurückhaltend gestaltet.
→ 118 119 120

Folgt man tradierten Fügetechniken, dann führt das Fügen von vorgefertigten, platten- oder stabförmigen Betonelementen ganz selbstverständlich zu einer Orthogonalität der Struktur und damit auch der Räume und Öffnungen; die vor Ort gegossene Form hingegen ist frei von diesen Gesetzmässigkeiten.

Pool Architekten machen sich diese Freiheiten ebenso wie die monolithische Anmutung der Gussform zunutze und entwickeln für das Haus G — ebenfalls in der Siedlung Mehr als Wohnen — die Idee eines «Schwamms», man könnte auch sagen eines ausgehöhlten, porösen, monolithischen Steins. Dieser Idee folgend, wurde das Gebäude mit Ausnahme der Schlafraumwände komplett aus Beton erstellt: Die Hülle

of the loggias, positioned at the front, together with the street side, two-story base, form a filter between interior and exterior between the soft skin and the surroundings. In this way, the loggia as a spatial and acoustic filter finds it equivalent in the material. Functioning on the one hand as an intermediate zone, the loggia also continues the inner spatial sequence of the apartments and asserts itself as a "living space" with an independent character. This is expressed in the articulation of the loggias: the concrete panels are given window-sized openings.

The robustness of the material is ennobled by the fine attention to detail applied to the concrete elements. Precisely positioned fine joints, finely ridged edges, delicate porosity, and evenness of the surfaces all clarify the potential of reinforced and prefabricated concrete. This impression of refinement and nobility is reinforced by the intricate interlocking of the elements, the slight projections from the plane, and by the application of white cement. In strong contrast to the concrete architecture of the Brutalists, where the "heaviness" of the nodes and connections of buildings was celebrated, the open joints and support points of Haus L are instead shaped in an incidental and restrained manner.
→ 118 119 120

If traditional joining techniques are followed, then the joins of prefabricated, panel, or bar-shaped concrete elements lead quite self-evidently to an orthogonal structure, and hence of spaces and openings. In-situ forms, in contrast, are free from such constraints.

Pool Architekten takes full advantage of this freedom, along with the monolithic impression created by cast forms. They have developed the idea of the "sponge" for Haus G (also part of the housing estate *Mehr als Wohnen*). One could also speak of a hollowed-out, porous, monolithic rock. Consistent with this idea, the building was constructed entirely in concrete, with the exception of the bedroom walls. The shell, cast in in monolithic insulating concrete, was complemented by loadbearing interior walls in cast, untreated exposed concrete.

The outer edges of the structure follow the trapezoidal form of the plot, which continues into the interior as a "genetic code." Like the "voids" of a seven story monolith, the interior spaces form a network of angled, trapezoidal, and rectangular forms which vary in section as well. This unconventional floor plan, with its interlocking, richly varied spaces, can serve as a matrix for the mental states of inhabitants and has the potential, in the spirit of Bachelard's → p. 375, to mirror existential and spiritual states.

This archaic expression, which is linked with the mental image of an oversized, porous monolith, is present not just in the seamless and roughly structured façades, their window embrasures having depths of up to 80 centimeters, but characterizes the design of the interior as well.

This aspect of the concrete, solidified now to a kind of stone, becomes especially evident and even physically palpable in the exposed concrete walls of the multistory staircases and living spaces. In the rough, porous, and uneven surfaces of the material, residents encounter a surface of friction; one that provokes confrontation.

Beton — vom Feinen im Rohen

aus monolithischem Dämmbeton wird durch tragende Innenwände aus gegossenem, roh belassenem Sichtbeton ergänzt.

Die Aussenkanten des Baukörpers folgen der trapezoiden Form des Grundstücks, die sich dann als «genetischer Code» im Inneren fortsetzt. Wie die «Hohlräume» eines siebengeschossigen Monolithen bilden die Innenräume ein Raumgeflecht aus abgewinkelten, trapezoiden und rechteckigen Formen, die auch im Querschnitt variieren. Diese ungewöhnliche Grundrisstypologie mit ihren verschachtelten, variantenreichen Räumen kann für den Bewohner zu einer Matrix seiner inneren Befindlichkeiten werden und hat das Potenzial, ganz im Sinne Bachelards →S.375, die Seins- und Seelenzustände zu spiegeln.

Der Ausdruck des Archaischen, der per se mit dem Gedankenbild eines überdimensionierten, porösen Monolithen verknüpft ist, ist nicht nur in den fugenlosen, porösen und rau strukturierten Fassaden mit ihren bis zu 80 Zentimeter tiefen Fensterlaibungen präsent, sondern er prägt ebenso die Gestalt des Interieurs.

Besonders evident und physisch erfahrbar wird dieser Aspekt des zu Stein erstarrten Betons an den hohen Sichtbetonwänden der mehrgeschossigen Treppenhäuser und Wohnräume. In den rohen, porösen und unebenen Oberflächen des Materials findet die Bewohnerin eine Reibungsfläche, die zu einer Auseinandersetzung herausfordert.

Und genau hier offenbart sich die Innovationskraft, die das Durchdringen und gegenseitige Bedingen von Material, übergeordnetem architektonischen Konzept, Typologie und Interieur besitzt, was letztendlich zu einer Annäherung von Realität und Utopie führt.
→ 113 114 115 116 117

And revealing itself precisely here is the innovative energy inherent in this relationship between material, overarching architectonic concept, typology, and interior; one that leads, ultimately, toward a convergence of reality and utopia.
→ 113 114 115 116 117

←

Beton — vom Feinen im Rohen

Concrete—the Fine within the Rough

Stahl — der «unsicht-
bare» Stoff
der unbegrenzten
Möglichkeiten

Steel — the 'Invisible'
Material of Unlimited
Possibilities

Alongside its static performance efficiency and simple assembly, the intrinsic character of steel construction is grounded in the prefabrication of building elements and the neutrality of the structure. More than any other material, it demands a rigid grid that is derived from each element, down to the smallest. The grid, which in three dimensions forms a lattice, can be used first to create spatial relationships between identical cells, or to effect a "liberation" from the floor plans by creating an open, free floor plan design. This is equally true for the third dimension, for the spatial lattice in steel leads almost inescapably toward three-dimensional floor plan designs and toward thinking in terms of spatial relationships. This design freedom, which is the basis of construction, manifests itself in multifarious possibilities of stringing together or stacking identical spatial cells, or of open spatial structures which, by means of openings in walls or ceilings, give shape to highly specific spatial relationships—the specific and individual as filling stand opposed by the modular and serial.[67]

Ever since the use of iron for building began in the early nineteenth century there has been a struggle to find adequate forms of expression for the material. The filigree quality and minimal surface area of iron constructions made the material "invisible stuff" that evades the eye, as Semper wrote in 1849.[68]

It was precisely this trait of near invisibility that would engender a new aesthetic in architecture as seen with engineered buildings such as Joseph Paxton's Crystal Palace and Les Halles in Paris. As a counterposition to monumental stone architecture, they were objects of fascination by virtue of their sizes and spans, structural logic, fine details in construction, and the power of repetition. In this way, they established the themes that are essential for building with steel.

The ease of prefabrication and quick, simple assembly of the material led to the serial production of "iron cottages" in the 1850s. These were small mobile dwellings in iron and metal used for remote colonies and the military. Forty years later in North America these would lead to a new building type, the high-rise, which still characterizes the American landscape. But while the iron cottages, as functional buildings, displayed their steel members without disguise, high-rises are clad with stone and ceramic for purposes of insulation and fire safety, masking the structural material.[69]

→ 121 122 123 124

---

[67] In his investigation of steel construction in residential development, Christian Inderbitzin took up the idea of the "stacked villa" from Giuseppe De Finetti and used the spatial grid to create large, two-story spatial configurations.

[68] Gottfried Semper, *Kleine Schriften*, Mittenwald 1979, pp. 484ff (first published in: *Zeitschrift für praktische Baukunst*, 1849).

[69] As early as the 1850s, a number of firms manufactured so-called "portable cottages" and shipped them worldwide. British firms such as E.T. Bellhouse and Charles D. Young in particular specialized in the manufacture of "iron cottages"—small two-room houses in iron with metal façades that were shipped to Australia and California for use by immigrants and gold miners. Cf. Matthias Ludwig, *Mobile Architektur*, Stuttgart 1998.

Stahl unverhüllt zeigten, wurden die stählernen Hochhäuser aus Wärme- und Brandschutzgründen verkleidet und meist mit Stein- oder Keramikfassaden umhüllt, sodass das Material für den Betrachter nicht in Erscheinung trat.[69]

→ 121 122 123 124

In den europäischen Städten hingegen setzte sich der Stahlbau trotz seiner enormen Vorteile nicht durch und wurde stattdessen von Konstruktionen aus Stahlbeton abgelöst. Dies mag auch daran liegen, dass das ästhetische Potenzial einer Stahlarchitektur nicht ausgeschöpft wurde. Oder, um es mit den Worten des deutschen Kunstmäzens Karl Ernst Osthaus auszudrücken: «Aber man kann heute fast sagen, dass das Eisen eigentlich seinen Stil verpasst hat.»

Die Ästhetik des Stahlbaus

Dennoch entstanden seit dem frühen 20. Jahrhundert architektonische Ikonen, gewissermassen gebaute Manifeste, die das Potenzial von Stahlkonstruktionen auch im Wohnungsbau aufzeigten und bis heute einen Fluchtpunkt der Architektur darstellen. Der deutsche Pavillon in Barcelona und das Farnsworth House von Ludwig Mies van der Rohe wurden zum Symbol für eine entmaterialisierte und «entgrenzte» Architektur mit fliessenden Übergängen. Dennoch ging es Mies nicht vordergründig um die Verbindung von innen und aussen, sondern um die Einfachheit der Konstruktion, die Klarheit der tektonischen Mittel und die Reinheit des Materials, die bei Skelettbauten aus Eisenbeton oder Stahl nur in Verbindung mit Glas zum Ausdruck gebracht werden können.[70] Die Konstruktion war für ihn die Grundlage der Architektur, aus der heraus eine Erneuerung stattfindet, und Stahl als Material bindet die Architektur an die Zeit.[71] Fritz Neumeyer beschreibt Mies' Verhältnis zum Stahlbau folgendermassen: «Das Stahlskelett verkörperte und symbolisierte jene objektive Ordnung, durch welche die Baukunst der Zeit im erziehenden Hindurchschreiten zu sich selbst finden und die technische Ordnung sich zur Kultur verwandeln sollte.»[72] Letztendlich ging es Mies van der Rohe um das Suchen und Finden einer inneren Logik des Konstruktionssystems und des materialgerechten Verarbeitens und Fügens.

→ 125 126 127 128 129

Während er diesen konstruktiv-tektonischen Ansatz bei seinen eingeschossigen, pavillonartigen Bauten eins zu eins umsetzen konnte, bediente er sich bei seinen 26-geschossigen Apartmenthäusern am Lake Shore Drive in Chicago eines Kunstgriffs: Die vorgehängten, sichtbaren Fassadenstützen aus Doppel-T-Profilen sind quasi die Kunstform, die von den aus Brandschutzgründen ummantelten tragenden Stahlstützen erzählt.

69 Bereits in den 1850er-Jahren gab es einige Firmen, die die sogenannten portable cottages herstellten und weltweit versandten. Besonders britische Firmen wie E. T. Bellhouse und Charles D. Young hatten sich auf «Iron Cottages» — kleine Zweizimmerhäuser aus einer Eisenkonstruktion mit Metallfassaden — spezialisiert, die für Emigranten oder Goldsucher nach Australien oder Kalifornien verfrachtet wurden. Siehe hierzu: Matthias Ludwig, *Mobile Architektur*, Stuttgart 1998
70 Karl Ernst Osthaus, «Material und Stil» in: *Jahrbuch des Deutschen Werkbundes*, Bd.1, Jena 1912 S. 23–29
71 Vgl. Fritz Neumeyer, *Mies van der Rohe. Das kunstlose Wort*, Berlin 1986, S. 298/378
72 Ebd., S. 391: «Ein Rückblick auf die Zeit macht es deutlich, dass alle Versuche, die Baukunst von der Form her zu erneuern, misslangen […] das ist wohl der Grund für die Überzeugung, dass die Konstruktion die Grundlage der Baukunst zu sein hat.»

Despite its enormous advantages, construction in steel never established itself in European cities and was superseded by construction in reinforced concrete. This is arguably because the aesthetic potentials of steel architecture was not exploited. Or, to cite the words of Karl Ernst Osthaus: "[…] one could almost say that iron actually failed to find its own style."

The Aesthetic of Steel Construction

Nonetheless, the early twentieth century saw the creation of architectural icons, of built manifestos, which demonstrated the potential of steel construction for residential development and which remain crucial points of reference for architecture up to the present. The German Pavilion in Barcelona and the Farnsworth House by Mies van der Rohe became symbols of dematerialization and an unbounded architecture with flowing transitions between interior and exterior. Mies was not, however, simply concerned with the integration of interior and exterior, but also with simplicity of construction, clarity of tectonic resources, and the purity of material which, in the case of skeleton structures in reinforced concrete or steel, could only be brought to full expression in conjunction with glass.[70] For him, construction was the foundation of architecture and steel was the material that bound architecture to its own time.[71] Fritz Neumeyer characterizes Mies' relationship to steel construction as follows: "The steel skeleton embodies and symbolizes that objective by means of which the building art of this period should come to discover itself and transform technical order into culture."[72] Ultimately for him, it was a question of searching for an inner logic to the construction system and of processing and joining the elements in a way that is appropriate to the materials.

→ 125 126 127 128 129

While in his single-story, pavilion buildings he was able to implement this constructive-tectonic approach one-to-one, his 26-story apartment buildings on Lake Shore Drive in Chicago employed some artifice. The visible supports of the curtain wall, consisting of double-T profiles, "narrate" the loadbearing steel supports that are covered in order to satisfy fire safety requirements.

Mies' steel architecture is characterized by open floor plans, walls freely positioned and detached from the façades, visible construction elements fitted together in an extraordinarily "careful" manner, and expansive glazing.[73] These are the result of the search for the architectonic possibilities of steel building, for truth in architecture. These factors are interlocked with one another, forming a congruent structure that allows "beauty as the splendor of the true" to show itself.[74] A beauty that leads toward a new aesthetic for architecture,

70 Karl Ernst Osthaus, "Material und Stil," *Jahrbuch des Deutschen Werkbundes*, vol. 1, Jena 1912, pp. 23–29.
71 Cf. Fritz Neumeyer, *The Artless Word: Mies Van Der Rohe on the Art of Building*, translated by Mark Jarzombek, Cambridge 1991, p. 314.
72 Ibid., p. 327: "In retrospect, it becomes clear that all attempts to renew the art of building from the formal direction have failed […] This is doubtless the reason for the conviction by construction has to be the basis of the art of building."
73 Ibid., p. 224.
74 "The art of building begins with the careful fitting together of two bricks," Ludwig Mies van der Rohe in an interview with Christian Norberg-Schulz, cf. ibid., p. 338.

121

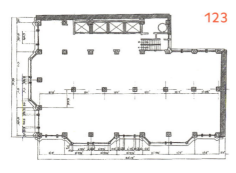

123

122

124

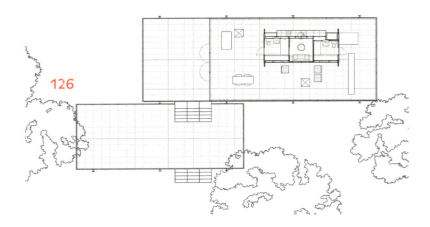

125

126

127

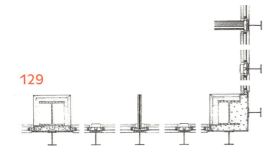

128

129

121	Iron Cottages for Emigrants, E. T. Bellhouse (Hersteller), 1851; kleine mobile Wohnhäuser
122–124	Reliance Building, Burnham Company, Chicago/Illinois, 1894; verhüllte Stahlstruktur
125–127	Farnsworth House, Ludwig Mies van der Rohe, Plano/Illinois, 1951
128/129	Lake Shore Drive Apartments, Ludwig Mies van der Rohe, Chicago/Illinois, 1951; vorgehängte Fassadenstützen als Kunstform

121	Iron Cottages for Emigrants, E. T. Bellhouse (manufacturer), 1851; small, mobile homes
122–124	Reliance Building, Burnham Company, Chicago/Illinois, 1894; cloaked steel structure
125–127	Farnsworth House, Ludwig Mies van der Rohe, Plano/Illinois, 1951
128/129	Lake Shore Drive Apartments, Ludwig Mies van der Rohe, Chicago/Illinois, 1951; curtain-style façade supports as ornament

Stahl — der «unsichtbare» Stoff der unbegrenzten …

130

131

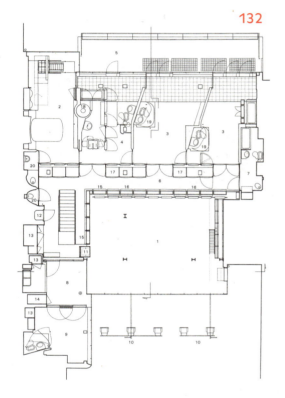

132

133

134

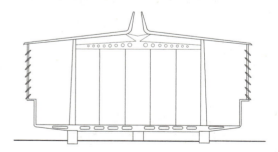

135

136

130   Eames House, Ray und Charles Eames, Los Angeles/Kalifornien, 1949; sichtbare Bauteile
131/132   Maison de Verre, Pierre Chareau, Paris, 1932; haptische Stahlarchitektur – handwerklich und industriell
133   Stahlhaus, Georg Muche und Richard Paulick, Dessau, 1926; zweckmässige Minimalbehausung
134/135   La Maison Tropicale, Jean Prouvé, Niamey/Niger, 1949; klimaoptimierte Konstruktion
136   Fassade der Residence Square Mozart, Jean Prouvé, Paris, 1954; Inspiration aus dem Fahrzeugbau

130   Eames House, Ray and Charles Eames, Los Angeles/California, 1949; exposed structural components
131/132   Maison de Verre, Pierre Chareau, Paris, 1932; haptic steel architecture; artistanal and industrial
133   Steel House, Georg Muche and Richard Paulick, Dessau, 1926; functional minimal dwelling
134/135   La Maison Tropical, Jean Prouvé, Niamey/Niger, 1949; climate-optimized construction
136   Façade, residence, Square Mozart, Jean Prouvé, Paris, 1954; inspired by motor vehicle manufacturing

Steel—the 'Invisible' Material of Unlimited Possibilities

Die Elemente seiner Stahlarchitektur — der offene Grundriss mit im Raum frei platzierten Wänden, die sich von den Fassaden lösen, die sichtbaren konstruktiven Elemente, die auf eine «sorgfältige» Weise gefügt sind[73], und die grossflächigen Verglasungen — sind das Ergebnis des Durchdringens und Suchens nach den architektonischen Möglichkeiten des Stahlbaus, nach der Wahrheit in der Architektur. Sie greifen ineinander und bilden ein in sich kongruentes Gefüge, sodass sich «das Schöne als Glanz des Wahren»[74] zeigen kann. Eine Schönheit, die eine neue Ästhetik in der Architektur einführte und die die nächste Architektengeneration aufgriff und unter den Vorzeichen des kostengünstigen Bauens und des Seriellen weiterentwickelte. Die Case Study Houses → [130] mit ihren sichtbaren Stahlkonstruktionen, weit ausladenden Dächern und grossflächigen Verglasungen sind nur ein Beispiel unter vielen.[75]

Etwa zeitgleich mit dem Pavillon in Barcelona baute Pierre Chareau in Paris das Maison de Verre.[76] Während die Ästhetik der Mies'schen Stahlarchitektur auf allgemeingültigen Prinzipien beruhte und in einer «Entkörperung» oder Auflösung des architektonischen Körpers mündete, bezeugte das Maison de Verre → [131] [132] den individuellen Charakter einer Stahlarchitektur, der sich in einer Art Verdichtung oder Verkörperung artikulierte.[77] Chareau näherte sich dem Wesen einer Architektur aus Stahl über die optischen und haptischen Qualitäten des Materials, seiner Vielfalt der Formen, Oberflächen, Farben, Verbindungen und Halbzeuge.

Unter ein bestehendes Geschoss eines Gründerzeithauses gebaut, folgt das dreigeschossige Stahltragwerk der Tragstruktur des Bestands. Das somit vorgegebene Volumen und die Struktur sind der Ausgangspunkt für eine dreidimensionale Raumkomposition aus Stahl und Glas, in der das Interieur und die Architektur untrennbar zu einer Einheit verschmelzen — Möbel werden zu Wänden und Wände werden zu Räumen oder Möbeln. Jede Stütze, jede Wand, jede Treppe, jedes Möbel ist ein Unikat, das dennoch durch eine einheitliche Sprache, die sich in der roh belassenen Oberflächenqualität sowie in der Textur der handwerklich bearbeiteten Stahl- und Metallelemente zeigt, in das Ganze eingebunden ist. Genietete Stahlverbindungen, Schiebewände aus Lochblech, handpolierte oder gehämmerte Stahloberflächen und schmucklose Stahltreppen verbinden sich mit Glasbausteinen, strukturiertem, milchigem oder transparentem Glas zu einem surrealistisch anmutenden Innenraum, in dem einerseits der von Semper beschriebene Charakter des «Nichtmateriellen» oder «Unsichtbaren» des Materials eine Vielschichtigkeit, Durchlässigkeit und Diffusität kreiert und der andererseits eine Ästhetik, die an den Maschinenraum von Ozeandampfern erinnert, für den Wohnungsbau

73 Neumeyer, wie Anm. 71, S. 282
74 «Baukunst fängt mit dem sorgfältigen Zusammenfügen zweier Ziegelsteine an.» Ludwig Mies van der Rohe in Interview mit Christian Norberg-Schulz, vgl. ebd., S. 404
75 «Das Schöne als Glanz des Wahren», ein Zitat von St. Augustin, findet sich in zahlreichen Vorträgen und Veröffentlichungen von Mies van der Rohe.
76 Auf der Suche nach einer zeitgemässen Architektur als Spiegelbild einer neuen Welt initiierte der Herausgeber einer avantgardistischen amerikanischen Kunstzeitschrift das Case-Study-House-Programm und beauftragt unter anderem die Architekten Charles und Ray Eames, Craig Ellwood, Pierre Koenig und Raphael Soriano mit dem Entwurf von experimentellen, kostengünstigen Wohnhäusern — der Einsatz neuer Materialien und Konstruktionstechniken, wie zum Beispiel neuer Bausysteme, war eine Prämisse für die Beauftragung.
77 Pierre Chareau, der als Innenarchitekt bis dato hauptsächlich Möbel entworfen hatte, arbeitete eng mit dem Schmied Louis Dalbet und dem holländischen Architekten Bernard Bijvoet zusammen. Das Maison de Verre wurde 1932 für die Familie des Arztes und Kunstförderers De sace in der Rue St. Guillaume in Paris fertiggestellt. Als Hinterhaus in dem Pariser Wohnviertel ersetzte es ein bestehendes dreigeschossiges Wohnhaus aus dem 18. Jahrhundert.

and one that was taken up by subsequent generations of architects and developed further as cost-effective, system building. The Case Study Houses, → [130] with their visible steel constructions, deep projecting roofs, and expansive glazing are just one example among many.[75]

Roughly contemporary with the Barcelona Pavilion is the Maison de Verre of Pierre Chareau.[76] While the Miesian aesthetic by steel architecture rests on generally valid principles and culminates in the "decorporealization" or dissolution of the architectonic members, the Maison de Verre → [131] [132] testifies to the individual character of a steel architecture that is articulated through a kind of "densification" or materialization.[77] Chareau approaches the essence of architecture in steel via its optic and haptic qualities, its multiplicity of forms, surfaces, colors, connections, and unfinished state.

Constructed beneath a pre-existing nineteenth-century building, the three-story steel supporting structure follows the loadbearing structure of the original building. The volumes and structure that were predetermined in this fashion formed the point of departure for a three-dimensional spatial composition in steel and glass in which the interior and the architecture are fused into an indissoluble unity—items of furniture become walls, and walls become rooms or items of furniture. Every support, every wall, every stair, every piece of furniture is a unique object integrated via a unified language. The untreated surface qualities and the texture of the handcrafted steel and metal elements are similarly incorporated into the whole. Riveted steel connections, sliding walls in perforated sheet-metal, hand-polished or hammered steel surfaces, and undecorated steel staircases are combined with glass bricks to form an interior with an almost surrealist atmosphere. It is reminiscent of engine rooms and ocean liners yet simultaneously has a complex, permeable ethereality thanks to the "nonmaterial" or "invisible" character of the material, as Semper puts it. In this way, the handcrafted and the industrial are united with atmospheric qualities.

In the architecture of Jean Prouvé and Buckminster Fuller, the industrial aesthetic becomes a mechanical aesthetic which is expressed in the specific instead of the universal. Minimal housing that is manufactured by industrial forces and assembled on site became the point of departure for their activities.

While the prefabricated steel houses of Georg Muche, → [133] for example, as well as the mass-produced military barracks of Prouvé himself, possess a purely functional character, Prouvé demonstrated the aesthetic possibilities of industrially prefabricated steel architecture with his Maison Tropique, → [134] [135] assembled for the first time in the Republic of Niger in 1949.[78]

Both the construction and design of this building owe much to the demands of the tropical climate, as

75 "The beauty as the splendor of the true," a citation from St. Augustine, appears in many lectures and publications by Mies van der Rohe.
76 In search of a contemporary architecture that would reflect a new world, the editor of an avant-garde American art magazine initiated the Case Study House Program, commissioning the architects Charles and Ray Eames, Craig Ellwood, Pierre Koenig, and Raphael Soriano to design experimental, cost-effective dwellings using new materials and construction techniques, for example new building systems.
77 Chareau, who—as an interior architect—had mainly designed furniture up to that point, worked closely with the blacksmith Louis Dalbet and the Dutch architect Bernard Bijvoet. The Maison de Verre was completed in 1932 for the family of the physician and patron of the arts Delsace on the Rue St. Germain (Rue St. Guillaume) in Paris. As a rear building in a Parisian residential district, it replaced an existing three-story dwelling from the 18th century.

etabliert. Auf diese Weise vereinen sich das Handwerkliche und das Industrielle im Atmosphärischen.

Die Ästhetik des Industriellen, die bei Chareau noch eine handwerkliche war, wurde in der Architektur von Jean Prouvé oder Richard Buckminster Fuller zu einer maschinellen Industrieästhetik, die sich im Spezifischen statt in einer Monotonie des Allgemeingültigen ausdrückte. Minimalbehausungen, die von der Industrie gefertigt und vor Ort montiert werden, waren als einer der thematischen Schwerpunkte des Stahlbaus der Ausgangspunkt ihrer Auseinandersetzungen.

Während die Montagehäuser aus Stahl, wie zum Beispiel von Georg Muche →133, aber auch die massenproduzierten Soldatenunterkünfte von Prouvé selbst einen reinen Zweckbaucharakter hatten, zeigte Prouvé[78] mit dem Maison Tropique →134 135, das erstmals 1949 in der Republik Niger aufgebaut wurde, die ästhetischen Möglichkeiten einer industriell vorgefertigten Stahlarchitektur auf.

Sowohl die Konstruktion als auch die Gestalt des Hauses sind den Anforderungen des tropischen Klimas sowie der Logik der Stahlbautechnik geschuldet: Die Stahlelemente für das zweischalige Dach, der Lüftungskamin, die doppelschalige Fassade oder die umlaufende, überdachte Veranda sind divers und ihren Funktionen entsprechend spezifisch; horizontale Lüftungslamellen, gelochte Schiebepaneele, profilierte oder glatte Metallplatten sind nach Bedarf gekantet und greifen ineinander. Das Spezifische der Elemente, aber auch die Präzision der Kantungen, Lochungen, Verbindungen und Oberflächen der Stahlelemente sprechen die Sprache der maschinellen Fertigung.

Wenige Jahre später, beim Bau des Maison du Peuple in Clichy[79], führte Prouvé dieses Prinzip zur Blüte. Als Volkshaus und Markthalle konzipiert, schöpft das flexibel nutzbare Gebäude mit seinen beweglichen Geschossdecken, Trennwänden und Glasüberdachungen die Möglichkeiten einer leichten Stahlbauweise aus, die konisch oder spitz geformten Profile der Fassadenstützen und auskragenden Vordächer oder die gewölbten Aufkantungen der Fassadenpaneele erinnern an die Flügel eines Flugzeuges oder das Fahrgestell eines Automobils →136. Die Forderung Le Corbusiers nach «Häusern, die Maschinen oder Flugzeugen gleichen», fand in den Entwürfen von Prouvé und Buckminster Fuller eine buchstäbliche Entsprechung und mündete in einer «Poetik des technischen Objekts».[80]

Vom Seriellen zum Raumgitter

→137 138 139

Le Corbusier fokussierte bei seinen Bauten aus Stahl weniger die ästhetischen Aspekte des Materials als die technischen Möglichkeiten der industriellen Fertigung,

well as to the logic of building with steel. The elements for the double-shell roof, the ventilation shaft, the double-layered façade, and the wrap-around, roofed veranda are varied and, in accordance with their functions, specific: horizontal ventilation lamellar, perforated sliding panels, profiled or smooth metal panels are canted as needed and interlock with one another. The specificity of the elements, but also the precision of the edges, perforations, connections, and surfaces of the steel elements speak the language of mechanical production.

With the construction of the Maison du Peuple just a few years later, Prouvé brought this principle to its peak.[79] Conceived as a community center and market hall, this flexible building with its movable floor slabs, partition walls, and glass roof elements, exploits the possibilities of a lightweight steel construction. The conical or pointed profiles of the façades and projecting marquees, as well as the projecting profiles of the façade panels, are reminiscent of the wings of an airplane or the chassis of an automobile. →136 In the designs of Prouvé and Fuller, Le Corbusier's notion that buildings "resemble machines or airplanes" finds a literal correspondence, culminating in a "poetics of the technical object."[80]

Of Seriality and Spatial Lattices

→137 138 139

In his steel buildings Le Corbusier focused less on the aesthetic aspects of the material and instead on the technical potential of industrial manufacturing. This is displayed in the precision and repeatable character of construction elements. For Le Corbusier, steel buildings testify to the "revolution of architecture" through which industrial production supersedes handicraft production.[81]

The nine-story Immeuble 'Clarté', →140 141 142 constructed in Geneva in the early 1930s, was factory-made in sections and assembled on location. Although both the supporting steel structure and the façades follow a rigid basic module, he exploited the possibilities of steel skeleton construction in order to configure the layouts freely. The internal partition walls are detached from the loadbearing structure and make possible individually shaped apartment layouts in various sizes. The spectrum of units extends from studios to two-story maisonette apartments with seven rooms. The grid of the façade, and hence the character of its production, is legible only in the widths of the rooms, which are oriented toward the dimensions of the façade fields. In section, the particular features of steel architecture become evident: the lightweight steel façades are staggered back upward through a number of stories

---

78 Jean Prouvé, der als Schmied ausgebildet wurde, gründete eine blechverarbeitende Firma, in der er gemeinsam mit Architekten seine Trennwand- und Fassadensysteme aus Blech entwickelte. Er arbeitete schon früh mit Architekten wie Eugène Beaudouin und Marcel Lods, Tony Garnier, Pierre Jeanneret, Le Corbusier und später seinem Bruder Henri Prouvé zusammen. Siehe: Peter Sulzer, «Jean Prouvé — ein Seminarbericht», *Schriftenreihe Baukonstruktion*, Heft 25, Universität Stuttgart, 1990; Peter Sulzer, *Jean Prouvé, Oeuvre complète*, Basel 2000
79 Prouvé entwarf das Volkshaus gemeinsam mit den Architekten Beaudouin und Lods sowie Vladimir Bodiansky als Ingenieur.
80 Buchtitel einer Veröffentlichung von Alexander von Vegesack über Jean Prouvé (Weil am Rhein 2006)

78 Prouvé, who was a trained blacksmith, founded a sheet-metal-working company through which he collaborated with architects to develop his partition walls and façade systems in sheet metal. Early on, he worked with architects such as Eugène Beaudouin and Marcel Lods, Tony Garnier, Pierre Jeanneret, Le Corbusier, and later with his brother Henri Prouvé. Peter Sulzer, "Jean Prouvé — ein Seminarbericht," *Schriftenreihe Baukonstruktion*, vol. 25, Stuttgart 1990.
79 Designed with the architects Beaudoin and Lods, as well as engineer Vladimir Bodiansky.
80 This is also the title of a book on Jean Prouvé by Alexander von Vegesack (Weil am Rhein 2006).
81 *Le Corbusier. Oeuvre Complete*, vol. 2, Zurich 1964, p. 20.

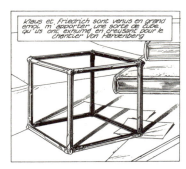

137

138

140

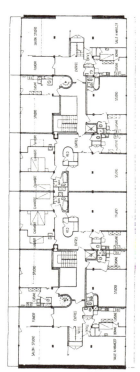

141

139

142

143

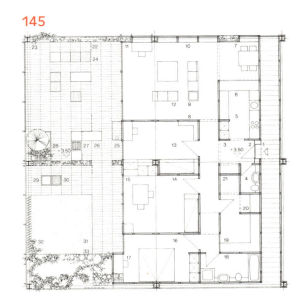

144

145

137–139 *La Fièvre d'Urbicande*, Graphic Novel von François Schuiten und Benoît Peeters, Casterman, Tournai 1985; Modul — Raumgitter — Megastruktur
140–142 Immeuble Clarté, Le Corbusier, Genf, 1932; Innenwände lösen sich vom Tragwerk
143–145 Versuchshaus aus Stahl, Jochen Brandi und Partner, Berlin, 1976; Flexibilität und Variabilität

137–139 *La Fièvre d'Urbicande*, comic by François Schuiten and Benoît Peeters, Casterman, Tournai 1985; module — spatial lattice — megastructure
140–142 Immeuble Clarté, Le Corbusier, Geneva, 1932; interior walls are detached from the supporting structure
143–145 Steel experimental building, Jochen Brandi und Partner, Berlin, 1976; flexibility and variability

Stahl — der «unsichtbare» Stoff der unbegrenzten …

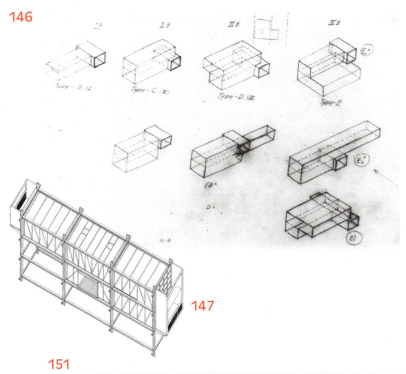

146

148

147

149

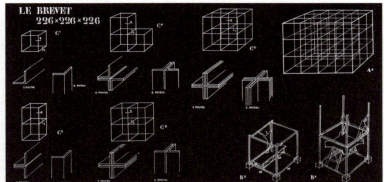

151

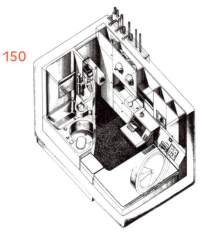

150

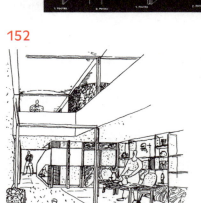

152

153

154

146/147 Unité d'Habitation, Le Corbusier, Meaux, 1957; Studie zur Verknüpfung von Raummodulen in einer Stahlstruktur
148 Ville Spatiale, Yona Friedman, 1959; Raumgitter als Megastruktur
149/150 Nakagin Capsule Tower, Kisho Kurokawa, Tokio, 1972; Minimalbehausung in Raumzelle
151 Stahlrahmensystem Bervet 226×226×226, Le Corbusier
152/153 Heidi-Weber-Haus, Le Corbusier, Zürich, 1967; offener Grundriss in rigider Struktur
154 Modell zum Metastadt-Konzept, Richard J. Dietrich und Bernd Steigerwald 1975; Grossstruktur wird zur dreidimensionalen Stadt

146/147 Unité d'Habitation, Le Corbusier, Meaux, 1957; study for linking modules into a steel structure
148 Ville Spatiale, Yona Friedman, 1959; spatial lattice as megastructure
149/150 Nakagin Capsule Tower, Kisho Kurokawa, Tokyo, 1972; minimal housing in spatial cells
151 Bervet steel frame system 226×226×226, Le Corbusier
151–153 Heidi Weber Haus, Le Corbusier, Zürich, 1967; open plan within a rigid structure
154 Model for the Metastadt concept, Richard J. Dietrich and Bernd Steigerwald 1975; large-scale structure becomes three-dimensional town

die sich in der Präzision, aber auch im seriellen Charakter der Bauteile zeigte — Häuser aus Stahl sind für Le Corbusier Zeugnisse der «Revolution der Architektur», in der die Industrie das Handwerk ablöst.[81]

Das neungeschossige Immeuble Clarté, → [140] [141] [142] das er Anfang der 1930er-Jahre in Genf baute, wurde in Serie in der Fabrik gefertigt und vor Ort nur noch montiert. Obwohl sowohl das Stahltragwerk als auch die Fassade einem rigiden Grundmodul folgen, nutzte er die Möglichkeiten der Stahlskelettbauweise, um die Grundrisse frei zu gestalten. Die Innentrennwände lösen sich vom Tragwerk und bilden individuell gestaltete, unterschiedlich grosse Wohnungsgrundrisse aus — das Spektrum der Wohnungen umfasst kleine Einzimmer-Studios bis zu zweigeschossigen Maisonettewohnungen mit sieben Zimmern. Nur an den Raumbreiten, die sich an den Massen der Fassadenfelder orientieren, wird das Raster der Fassade und damit der Charakter des Seriellen ablesbar. Im Schnitt werden die Besonderheiten einer Stahlarchitektur besonders deutlich: Die «leichten» Stahlfassaden staffeln sich über mehrere Geschosse bis zum schmalsten Obergeschoss zurück. Als raumhohe Verglasungen ausgebildet, erweitert sich der Wohnraum auf die vorgelagerten Balkone und es entsteht ein neues Wohngefühl.

Die Faszination für die technologischen Entwicklungen, die Industrialisierung und serielle Fertigung in der Architektur erfuhr in den Nachkriegsjahren mit den Themen Mitbestimmung und Selbstbauweise eine neue Richtung. Es entstand eine Vielzahl standardisierter Bausysteme aus Stahl, die sich flexibel den Bedürfnissen der Bewohner anpassen liessen und innerhalb kürzester Zeit vor Ort montierbar waren. Das Spektrum umfasste Lowtech-Systeme, die das Thema der Selbstmontage fokussieren, bis zu hochkomplexen, ausgefeilten Bausystemen, bei denen sowohl die Medieninstallation als auch die Fassaden, Decken, Böden und Innenwände mitgeliefert wurden.

In den 1960er-Jahren erschöpfte sich dieser architektonische Ansatz in Bausystemtheorien, die sich durch die intellektuelle Auseinandersetzung mit Knotentheorien, Flexibilität und Polyvalenz von Teilen auszeichneten und erreichte damit seinen Höhepunkt.

Exemplarisch für diese Art der Architektur ist das Versuchswohnhaus aus Stahl → [143] [144] [145] in Berlin.[82] Um eine grösstmögliche Flexibilität und Variabilität in der Gestaltung der Grundrisse zu erreichen, sind die Trag- und Fassadenstruktur sowie der Ausbau voneinander entkoppelt. Basierend auf einem quadratischen Raster von 7,50 Metern bildet das Stahltragwerk gemeinsam mit den horizontalen Deckenscheiben das Grundgerüst, in dem sich die Grundrisse und Fassaden beliebig entwickeln können. Der Systembaukasten 2010 integriert unterschiedliche Systemelemente für die Fassade sowie die Innenwände, die die Bewohner ihren Bedürfnissen entsprechend entlang der deckenintegrierten Schienen einsetzen und jederzeit verändern können. Allein die Abstände der Schienen von 30 Zentimetern sowie das Elementmodul mit 1,20 Metern bestimmen die Regeln der Grundrissgestaltung sowie den

toward the narrowest and uppermost story. The living space, which is given room-height glazing, is extended via balconies set in front.

In the postwar years, industrialization and system building in architecture experienced a new turn. This resulted in a range of standardized building systems using steel which could be assembled on site and in short periods of time. Their flexibility made them readily adaptable to the needs of residents. The spectrum extends from "low-tech" systems that focus on the theme of self-assembly, all the way to elaborate, highly-complex systems which involved the delivery of media installations along with façades, ceilings, floors, and internal walls.

In the 1960s, this approach exhausted itself in theories of building systems which were characterized by an intellectual preoccupation with nodes and the flexibility of their parts. Exemplary of attempts to think about architecture in this way is an experimental residential building in steel → [143] [144] [145] in Berlin.[82] To achieve the greatest possible flexibility and variability in the design of the floor plan, the supporting, interior, and façade structures are decoupled from one another. Based on a square grid measuring 7.5 meters, the steel structural frame, together with the horizontal ceiling plates, forms the basic framework within which the floor plan and façades can be developed as desired. The Systembaukasten 2010 integrates various system elements for the façade and interior walls, which inhabitants can manipulate using tracks that are integrated into the ceiling to reconfigure the floor plan at any time. Only the 30 cm intervals between the tracks and the elementary module, which measures 1.2 meters, determine the rules governing the shape of the floor plans. By decoupling the systems and the minimal sizes of the elements, standardization becomes compatible with individual customization.

The formation of spatial lattices is another important theme in steel construction. Internationally oriented architectural collectives like Archigram, GIAP (Groupe International d'Architecture Prospective), and the Japanese Metabolists, who were preoccupied with megastructures and standardized spatial cells, crystallized the architectonic possibilities of this building method. In the early 1960s, responding to the problem of overpopulation and referring to the modern, flexible, self-determined human individual in a fully automatized, technified world, Yona Friedman designed the Ville Spatiale → [148] and the Ville Pont. These were urban megastructures consisting of three-dimensional, multistory, supporting structures in steel that would be set on pillars 12 meters above ground level. Based on a 5 m grid, this structural framework could be fitted with spatial cells of 25 m² each as desired. The conventional apartment is superseded by an agglomeration of spaces made up of monolithic cells which are assigned to individual family members, and can be adapted to a range of uses.[83]

While this idea, proposed by Yona Friedman, maintains a high degree of abstraction, Le Corbusier was

---

81 Le Corbusier. Œuvre Complete, Bd. 2, Zürich 1964, S. 20
82 Der Systembaukasten 2010 von Jochen Brandi und Stefan Polónyi als Tragwerksplaner ging aus einem internationalen Wettbewerb zur «Entwicklung industriell gefertigter Wohnungseinheiten» hervor, der Mitte der 1960er-Jahre ausgelobt wurde. Das Gebäude wurde als sogenannte EGKS-Versuchsstation (Europäische Gemeinschaft für Kohle und Stahl) in den Jahren 1974–1977 gebaut.

82 The Systembaukasten (system construction kit) 2010 by Jochen Brandi and Stefan Polónyi as structural engineer emerged from the international competition for the "development of industrially prefabricated residential units," announced in the mid-1960s. The building was constructed in the years 1973–75? as the so-called EGKS-Versuchsstation (experiment station) (European Coal and Steel Community).
83 Yona Friedman, L'architecture mobile, Brussels 1968, pp. 20–21.

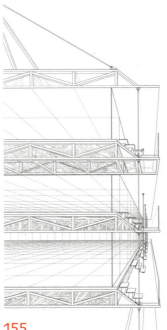

155

156

157

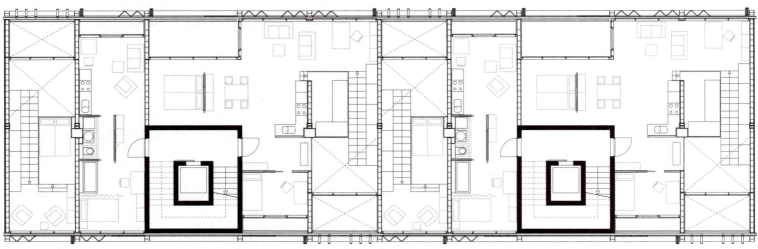

158

159

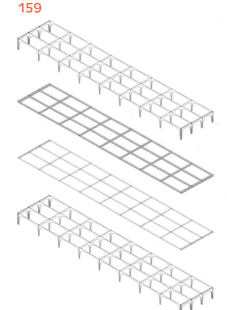

160

161

155–157   Studierendenprojekt Urban Steel 05, Felix Bardou/Carlo Fischer, TU Berlin 2014; Fachwerkstruktur und hängende Plattformen
158   Studierendenprojekt Urban Steel 11, Jialiang Cui/Liane Rosenthal, TU Berlin 2014; DDR-Plattenbau übersetzt in Stahlbau — gleiches Masssystem, andere Wohnform
159–161   Studierendenprojekt Urban Steel 02, Patryk Kujawa/Martyna Aleksandra Wojnarowska, TU Berlin 2014; steife Tische aus gekreuzten Stahlblechen

155–157   Student project, Urban Steel 05, Felix Bardou/Carlo Fischer, TU Berlin 2014; half-timbered structure and hanging platforms
158   Student project, Urban Steel 11, Jialiang Cui/Liane Rosenthal, TU Berlin 2014; DDR prefab high-rise translated into steel building; identical system of units, different housing type
159–161   Student project, Urban Steel 02, Patryk Kujawa/Martyna Aleksandra Wojnarowska, TU Berlin 2014; stiffened boards formed from intersecting sheet steel

Steel—the 'Invisible' Material of Unlimited Possibilities

Rhythmus der Fassaden. Durch die Entkopplung der Systeme und die Kleinteiligkeit der Elemente kann sich das Serielle mit dem Individuellen verbinden.

Ein weiteres Thema des Stahlbaus, das den seriellen Charakter der Struktur mit einbeziehen, war das Bilden von Raumgittern. International ausgerichtete Architektengruppen wie Archigram, GIAP (Groupe International d'Architecture Prospective) und die japanischen Metabolisten, die sich in experimentellen und utopischen Entwurfsansätzen mit Megastrukturen und standardisierten Raumzellen auseinandersetzten, brachten die architektonischen Möglichkeiten dieser Bauweise auf den Punkt. Auf der Suche nach Lösungen für die prognostizierte Überbevölkerung und mit dem «modernen» flexiblen und selbstbestimmten Menschen in einer vollautomatisierten, technisierten Welt im Blick, entwarf Yona Friedman Anfang der 1960er-Jahre die Ville Spatiale → [148] und die Ville pont — städtebauliche Megastrukturen aus einem dreidimensionalen, mehrgeschossigen Raumtragwerk aus Stahl, das 12 Meter über dem Erdboden auf Stützen lagert. Basierend auf einem Fünf-Meter-Raster kann das Tragwerk beliebig mit Raumzellen von je 25 Quadratmetern bestückt werden. Die konventionelle Wohnung wird abgelöst von einer Ansammlung von Räumen aus monolithischen Zellen, die sich den einzelnen Familienmitgliedern zuordnen und den jeweiligen Nutzungen anpassen lassen.[83]

Während diese Idee bei Yona Friedman in einem hohen Abstraktionsgrad verharrte, setzte sich Le Corbusier in einem kleineren Massstab mit deren Realisierung auseinander. In seinen Studien zur Unité in Meaux[84] → [146] [147] zeigte er auf, wie sich die in ein übergeordnetes Stahltragwerk eingesetzten Raummodule[85] zu diversen Wohneinheiten verknüpfen lassen. Aufgrund der unterschiedlichen räumlichen Konstellationen von horizontalen und vertikalen Verknüpfungen entstehen sechs übergeordnete Typen mit diversen Untertypen.

Mit dem Nakagin Capsule Tower → [149] [150] zeigte Kisho Kurokawa die Möglichkeiten, aber gleichzeitig auch die Grenzen dieser Idee auf[86]. Seine Raumzellen aus Stahl wurden mit der kompletten Ausstattung vorfabriziert und in eine Tragstruktur eingehängt. Als Minimalbehausung mit Bad, Schrank, Kochnische, Schreibplatz und Bett ausgestattet, lassen sie den Bewohnern metaphorisch und buchstäblich wenig Raum und dienen ausschliesslich dem temporären Wohnen.

Eine Lösung zu diesem Problem stellte das 1949 entworfene Stahlrahmensystem Brevet 226 × 226 × 226 von Le Corbusier dar → [151]. Das Raumgitter aus verschraubbaren Winkelprofilen, die in einem Raster von 2,26 Metern zu beliebigen Volumenkonfigurationen zusammengefügt werden können, bildet das Grundgerüst für Decken, Wände und Fassaden, die die räumliche Würfelstruktur beliebig ausfüllen.

83 Yona Friedman, *L'architecture mobile*, Brüssel 1968, S. 20f.
84 Das Projekt, eine städtebauliche Studie aus lang gestreckten Unités und runden Turmhäusern für 35 000 Einwohner, wurde nie realisiert. Zeichnungen und Skizzen in: H. Allen Brooks (Hrsg.), *The Le Corbusier Archive*, Bd. 29, Fondation Le Corbusier, New York/London 1984
85 Bereits bei der Unité in Marseille sollten vorgefertigte Raumzellen in die Tragstruktur aus Eisenbeton eingesetzt werden. Le Corbusier arbeitete gemeinsam mit Jean Prouvé an einer Lösung zu seiner Idee der «Flaschen im Regal», die jedoch zu keinem Ergebnis führte, sodass der Ausbau konventionell mit Gipskarton- und Holzplatten erfolgte. Siehe: Alexander von Vegesack (Hrsg.), *Jean Prouvé. Die Poetik des technischen Objekts*, Weil am Rhein 2015
86 Das 1970 fertiggestellte Projekt in Tokio besteht aus 140 komplett ausgestatteten Raumzellen, die in einen Betonkern eingehängt wurden. Das als Stahlfachwerk ausgebildete Tragwerk der Raumzellen wurde mit einer Aussenhaut aus galvanisierten, 1,6 Millimeter starken Blechpaneelen versehen, die jeweils die Grösse der gesamten Wandfläche abdecken. Siehe: Arthur Rüegg, Bruno Krucker, *Konstruktive Konzepte der Moderne*, Zürich 2001

Stahl — der «unsichtbare» Stoff der unbegrenzten ...

involved in a practical realization on a far smaller scale. In his studies on the Unité in Meaux,[84] → [146] [147] he shows how a special module, which is inserted into a steel supporting framework can be linked with diverse residential units.[85] Emerging as a result of various spatial constellations formed by horizontal and vertical linkages are six overarching types with diverse subtypes.

With the Nakagin Capsule Tower, → [149] [150] Kisho Kurokawa demonstrates the potential of this idea, but also its limitations.[86] His steel cells were prefabricated, complete with interior fittings, and suspended in a supporting framework. As minimal housing units equipped with a bathroom, closet, cooking area, desk area, and bed, they provide residents very little space, and serve as exclusively temporary dwellings.

One path toward solving this problem is presented by the steel frame system Brevet 226 × 226 × 226 developed by Le Corbusier in 1949. → [151] A spatial grid, composed of screw-mounted, profiles which can be assembled into configurations of volume as desired within a grid of 2.26 meters, forms the basic structure for ceilings, walls, and façades and fills in the spatial cube structure as needed.

This prototype, conceived as a studio/dwelling and realized during the 1960s, was formed by two cubes with edge lengths of 5.52 meters. → [152] [153] These were staggered in relation to one another. The rigid structure of the spatial lattice was opposed by the open, flowing layout, which took the form of a two-story structure and was separated into functional spaces such as the kitchen, covered spaces, and bathroom. The façade, conceived by Jean Prouvé, consisted of colored enameled sheet metal panels or Neoprene-framed glass.[87]

The meta-city in Wulfen, → [154] a design by Richard J. Dietrich and Bernd Steigerwald, was one of the few major projects through which the idea of a spatial lattice in steel was realized. The fundamental themes of the design were multifunctionality, the three-dimensional organization of units, high density, as well as flexibility and an ability to adapt to changing requirements. The intention was to develop a three-dimensional city containing "houses" set on semipublic routes and squares at various elevations by means of a large pile or tower-like structure. This was characterized by setbacks, terraces, and in-between spaces, and was based on the model of the cube.

Ultimately 102 apartments were constructed around an L-shaped structure ranging from 6–9 stories in height also including a kindergarten and shopping arcade. Single-story 3–5 room apartments accessed via balconies, terraces, or internal corridors are based around the steel Vierendeel girder grillage

84 The project, and urbanistic study for 35,000 residents consisting of elongated Unités and round tower houses, was never realized. For drawings and sketches, see H. Allen Brooks (ed.), *The Le Corbusier Archive*, vol. 29, New York/ London 1984.
85 Already the Unité in Marseille was to have had prefabricated special cells set into a living structure consisting of reinforced concrete—Le Corbusier worked together with Jean Prouvé on a solution to the idea of the "bottle in a rack," which however led to no results, so that the construction proceeded conventionally with plasterboard and wooden paneling. (Alexander von Vegesack (ed.), *Jean Prouvé: The Poetics of the Technical Object*, Weil am Rhein 2013.)
86 This project, completed in Tokyo in 1970, consists of 140 cells that are suspended on a concrete core. The steel supporting structure, formed from a steel truss framework of the spatial cells, was furnished with an outer shell consisting of galvanized, 1.6 mm-thick metal panels, each of which covers an entire wall surface. The completely prefabricated cells were delivered to the building site and mounted to the concrete core at just four points—the lower mounts plug into place, while the upper ones are bolted. Arthur Rüegg, Bruno Krucker, *Konstruktive Konzepte der Moderne*, Zurich 2001.
87 The steel frame system was employed for the first time in for the Heidi Weber-Haus, an exhibition pavilion in Zürich. The filigree steel construction, consisting of steel brackets with lengths of 55 mm, is positioned beneath a self-supporting roof structure. In 1949/1964?, Le Corbusier patented the system under the name "Brevet 226 × 226 × 226." Ibid.

Der in den 1960er-Jahren realisierte und als Atelier- und Wohnhaus konzipierte Prototyp formt zwei zueinander versetzte Würfel mit einer Kantenlänge von 5,52 Metern aus, die über eine Zwischenzone miteinander verbunden sind →152 153. Der rigiden Struktur des Raumgitters steht der offene, fliessende Grundriss gegenüber, der sich in einem zweigeschossigen Raumgefüge entwickelt und ausschliesslich durch frei platzierte Funktionsräume wie Küche, Schrankräume oder Bad in Zonen gegliedert wird. Die von Jean Prouvé konzipierten Fassaden bestanden aus farbig emaillierten Blechpaneelen oder aus mit Neopren-Dichtungen gehaltenen Gläsern.[87]

Die Metastadt in Wulfen →154, ein Entwurf von Richard J. Dietrich und Bernd Steigerwald, war eines der wenigen Grossprojekte, bei dem die Idee des Raumgitters aus Stahl realisiert wurde. Multifunktionalität, die dreidimensionale Organisation der Einheiten, eine hohe Dichte sowie Flexibilität und Anpassungsfähigkeit an sich ändernde Bedürfnisse waren die grundlegenden Themen des Entwurfs. In einer haufen- oder turmartigen Grossstruktur, geprägt von Rücksprüngen, Terrassierungen und Zwischenräumen und basierend auf dem Würfelmodul sollte sich eine «dreidimensionale Stadt» mit «Häusern» an halböffentlichen Wegen oder Plätzen auf unterschiedlichen Niveaus entwickeln.[88]

Die historischen Referenzen mit den stahlspezifischen Themen des Raumgitters, der Modularität, der Vorfertigung, der Raumzellen, der fliessenden Grundrisse und Raumzusammenhänge, der grossflächigen Öffnungen, der Durchlässigkeit, Vielschichtigkeit und Leichtigkeit wurden von den Studierenden an der TU Berlin in dem Seminar Urban Steel aufgegriffen und in zeitgemässe Raum- und Wohnkonzepte sowie in eine zeitgemässe Architektursprache übersetzt.

Eines der Projekte nutzt das rigide Raster der Stahlkonstruktion, um charaktervolle Stahlrahmen als raumbildende und raumgliedernde Elemente einzusetzen; innerhalb dieser Rahmenstruktur entwickeln sich offene Grundrisse, die vorwiegend durch möbelartige Einbauten unterteilt werden. →159 160 161 Andere entwarfen Raumgitterträger, die als Decken von den Treppentürmen abgehängt werden, um im Inneren stützenfreie Räume zu schaffen, die aneinandergereihte Raumschichten mit Enfiladen ausbilden. Umlaufende Balkone sowie raumhohe Verglasungen verstärken den Eindruck des stützenfreien Raumes. →155 156 157 Wohneinheiten, die sich als eine Verknüpfung von Raumnischen und Räumen über mehrere Ebenen in einem mehrgeschossigen Volumen formulieren, sind ebenso Thema der Projekte wie eine differenzierte Formulierung des Verhältnisses von innen und aussen. Mehrschichtige Fassaden, die jahreszeitliche, klimatische Zwischenräume ausbilden, verknüpfen sich mit Grundrissen, die durch ein vielschichtiges, offenes Raumnetz gekennzeichnet sind.

Die Ungerichtetheit oder auch Neutralität des Systems führt in der Grundriss- und Raumgestalt eben genau zum Spezifischen und Individuellen. Das Denken und Entwerfen in Rasterstrukturen und Raumgittern ist Korsett und Freiheit, Starrheit und Flexibilität zugleich.

[87] Das Stahlrahmensystem kam erst 1964 für das Heidi-Weber-Haus, einen Ausstellungspavillon in Zürich, zur Anwendung. Siehe: ebd.
[88] Abweichend von dem Entwurf wurden letztendlich 102 Wohnungen mit Kindergarten und Ladenpassage in einer L-förmigen sechs- bis neungeschossigen Gebäudestruktur untergebracht.

bolted together [88] to form a grid of 4.2 meters. System façades trace out the modular grid of the spatial lattice, giving form to a sculptural play of abstract steel cubes.

Historic and steel-specific themes such as the spatial lattice, modularity, prefabrication, the spatial cell, flowing layouts and spatial relationships, expansive openings, permeability, intricacy, and lightness were taken up by students in the seminar "Urban Steel" and translated into contemporary spatial and residential concepts.

One of these projects employed a rigid steel grid as a space-shaping and space-articulating element. Developed within this frame structure were open layouts subdivided by installations reminiscent of furniture. →159 160 161 Others designed spatial lattices that could be suspended, ceiling-like, from stair towers in order to create support-free rooms strung-together as an enfilade. Strengthening the impression of a support-free space are circumferential balconies supported by the bottom chord of the ceiling construction. These produce a change of elevation in relation to the apartments and room-height glazing. →155 156 157 Residential units that form links between spatial niches and rooms across multiple levels in multistory volumes constitute a theme for these projects, along with the differentiated formulation of the relationship between interior and exterior. Multilayered façades that form seasonal, climatic interspaces are linked with floor plans that are characterized by polyvalent, open spatial networks.

In the shaping of the floor plan and the space, it is precisely the non-directionality and neutrality of the system that leads toward the specific, the individual. Thinking and designing in grid structures and spatial lattices simultaneously represents constraint and freedom, rigidity, and flexibility.

[88] Independently of the supporting structure, there was a development grid whose smallest measurement unit was 60 centimeters, which made possible the modification of the elementized partition walls. In the end, for cost reasons, the partition walls were constructed only on a commercial scale, and the publicly subsidized apartments were provided with plasterboard walls leading the entire system toward absurdity. In 1988, the entire complex was dismantled. That the system failed to become established is can be attributed to the altered architectural themes which focused more on the reconstruction of existing urban structures, but also on elevated costs, considered undesirable for subsidized housing development. The idea of establishing a system for various uses is only possible provided the entire system is conceived in terms of the maximum case. In other words, the maximal load capacity at every point within the structure, maximal cable routing, etc.—all of which would in turn drive costs skyward. Cf. *Bauwelt* vol. 33, 1976, pp. 1004–1013.

←

Stahl — der «unsicht-
bare» Stoff
der unbegrenzten
Möglichkeiten

Steel — the 'Invisible'
Material of Unlimited
Possibilities

Studierende
der TU Berlin:
Eine Typensammlung.
Regelgeschosse
im Massstab 1:500

Students from
the TU Berlin:
A Type Collection.
Standard Floors
on a Scale of 1:500

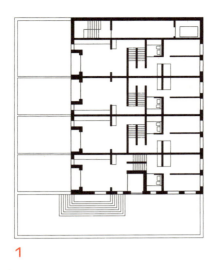

1

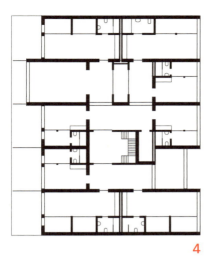

4

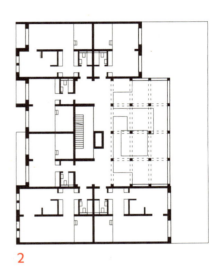

2

5

3   6

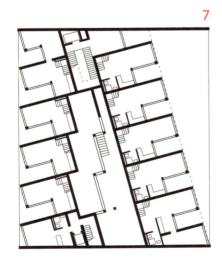

7

1   Wood 01; Lisa Hannes, Alexander Markau
2   Wood 14; Carolin Lehnerer, Aydin Sunar; Raumgitter im Atrium/lattice in atrium
3   Wood 03; Tatjana Anic, Timo Lück
4   Wood 04; Debora Mendler, Nicole Redmer
5   Wood 15; Yvonne Fissel, Katharina Woicke
6   Wood 09; Mathias Lehmann, Torbjørn Våge; Wohnlandschaft/landscaped interior
7   Wood 13; Jannes Beulting, Dominik Schad; Wellness im Zentrum/wellness center

Studierende der TU Berlin: Eine Typensammlung.
Regelgeschosse im Massstab 1:500

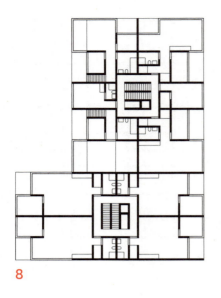

8

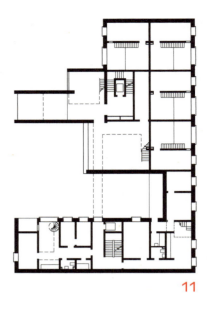

11

9

10

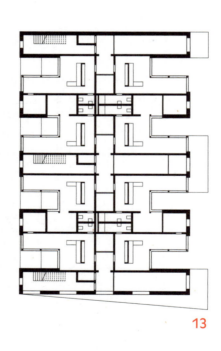

13

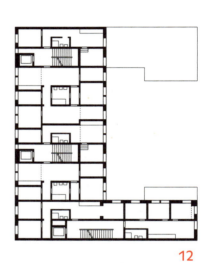

12

14

8   Wood 11; Jan Blifernez
9   Wood 17; Murat Erman Aksoy, Jana Wecker; Clusterwohnen/residential clusters
10 Wood 06; Christina Höller, Jakob Kress
11 Wood 10; Christobal Lambertini Herrera, Miguel Angel Reyes Benz, Jiajun Tan
12 Wood 16; Cem Baykal, Yuki Hanfeld; gestaffelte Raumelemente/staggered spatial elements
13 Wood 18; Timo Büscher, Olivier Laydevant; gestufte und zerklüftete Schottenstruktur/stepped, indented bulkhead structure
14 Wood 07; Veronika Mosser, Nico Steinacker; geteilte Wohnloggien/subdivided residential loggias

Students from the TU Berlin: A Type Collection.
Standard Floors on a Scale of 1:500

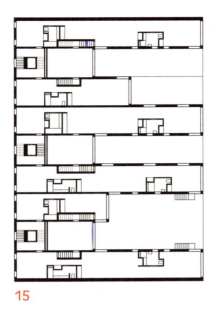
15

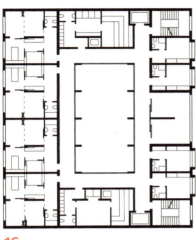
16

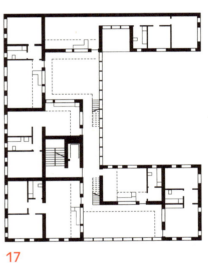
17

18

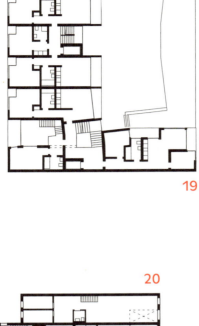
19

20

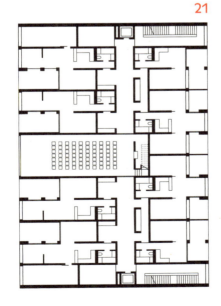
21

15 Wood 20; Evelyn Gröger, Darina Palazova; dazwischen Gemeinschaftsküchen/communal kitchens in between
16 Wood 05; Elisabeth Bork, Kerstin Krüger; Wohnen um Sporthallen/residence in sports hall
17 Wood 12; Marco Migliavacca, Friedrich Neukirchen; Ständerbauweise/timber frame construction
18 Wood 02; Pia Malina Kettler, Julia Schmidt
19 Wood 21; Philipp Steinmetz, Andreas Woyke
20 Wood 19; Daniela Knappe, Yasha Anil Kuhn
21 Wood 08; Katja Heieis, Lydia Kittelmann

Studierende der TU Berlin: Eine Typensammlung.
Regelgeschosse im Massstab 1:500

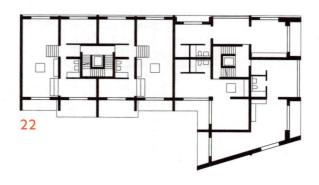

22

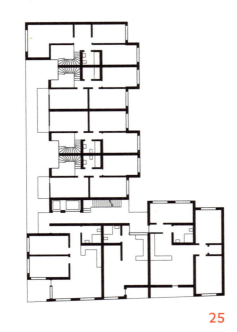

25

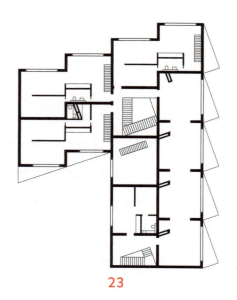

23

26

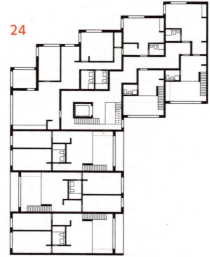

24

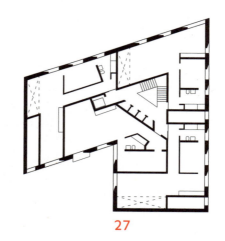

27

28

22	Concrete 12;	Johanna Backhaus, Tetyana Nesterenko
23	Concrete 18;	Julia Schmidt, Sebastian Welzel; gestapelte Boxen/stacked boxes
24	Concrete 17;	Mikal Skodjereite, Jakob Ulbrych
25	Concrete 04;	Cyrell Boehm, Kamila Marta Kojder
26	Concrete 11;	Rusi Ichev, Darina Palazova
27	Concrete 14;	Tatjana Anic, Timo Lück
28	Concrete 08;	Sophie Baum, Theresa Piechottka

Students from the TU Berlin: A Type Collection.
Standard Floors on a Scale of 1:500

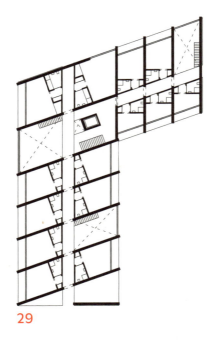

29

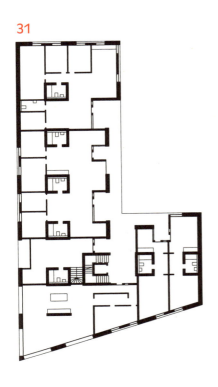

31

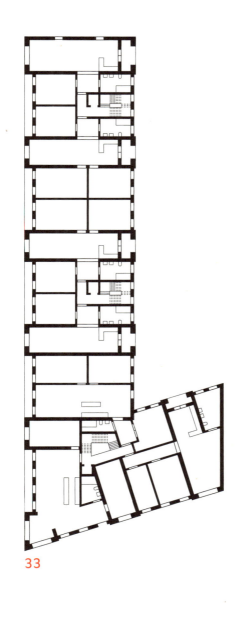

33

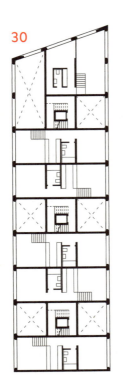

30

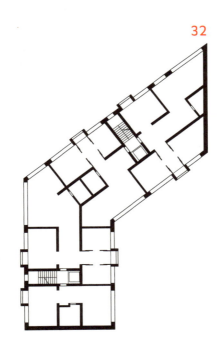

32

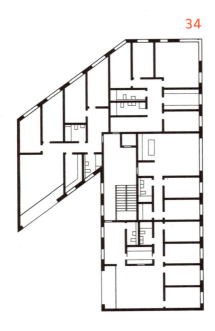

34

29 Concrete 13; Christopher Sitzler, Kristina Szeifert; Apartmenthaus/apartment building
30 Concrete 21; Sebastian Blatter, Zaneta Choroba
31 Concrete 10; Marina Kolovou-Kouri, David Scharf
32 Concrete 02; Julia Domanska, Mariana Ferreira
33 Concrete 07; Apostolos Klontzaris, Anja Kokott
34 Concrete 03; Evamaria Christel, Marta Salomó Coll

Studierende der TU Berlin: Eine Typensammlung.
Regelgeschosse im Massstab 1:500

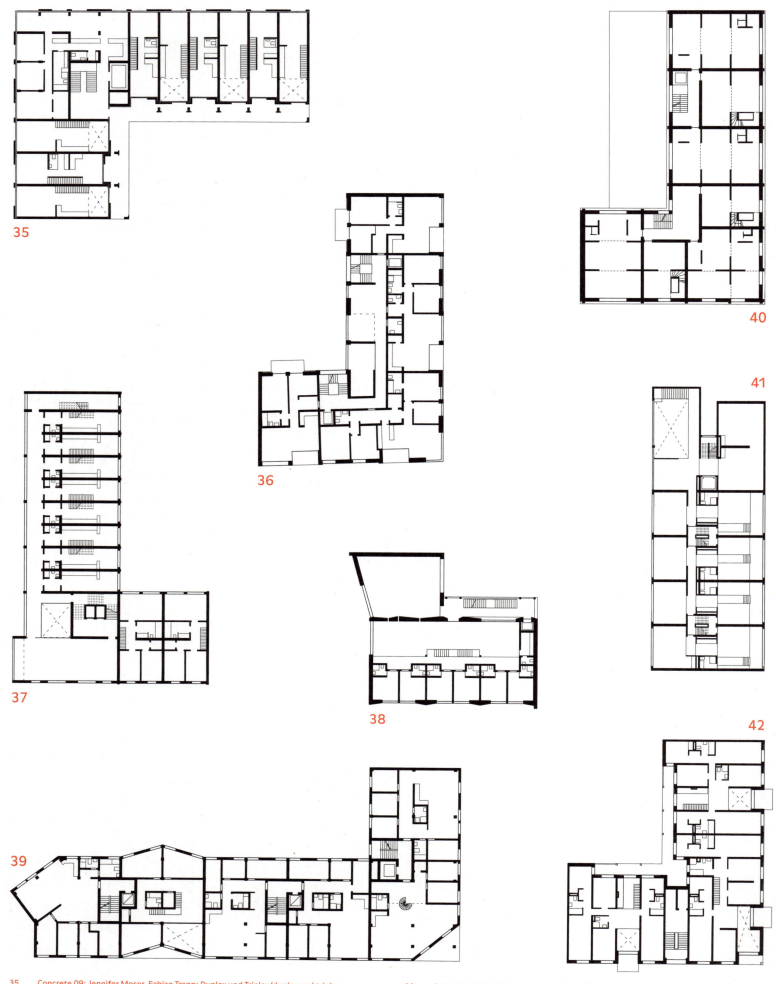

35 Concrete 09; Jennifer Moser, Fabian Trapp; Duplex und Triplex/duplex and triplex
36 Concrete 05; Ahmed Michael Abd Alla, Eva-Maria Thinius
37 Concrete 19; Sebastian Genzel, Christobal Lambertini Herrera; Wohnen und Co-Working/residence and co-working space
38 Concrete 15; Nicole Redmer, Claudia Schwiethale; Co-Living und Fablab/co-living and fab lab
39 Concrete 01; Jinglin Cai, Xiangyue Guan, Hang Yuan
40 Concrete 20; Marlene Bühner, Cassandra Donath; Raumschichten japanisch/japanese spatial layering
41 Concrete 06; Christobal Lambertini Herrera, Miquel Angel Reyes Benz; Atelierhaus/studio house
42 Concrete 16; Aydin Sunar, Tobias Wolski

Students from the TU Berlin: A Type Collection.
Standard Floors on a Scale of 1:500

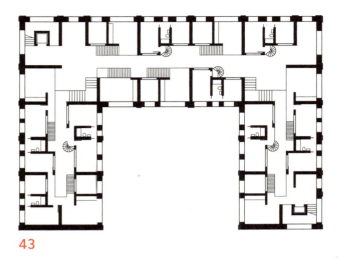

43

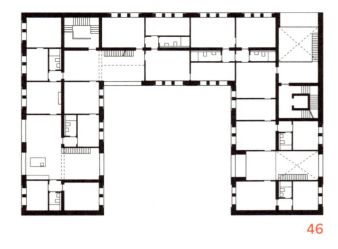

46

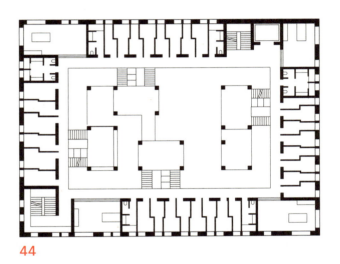

44

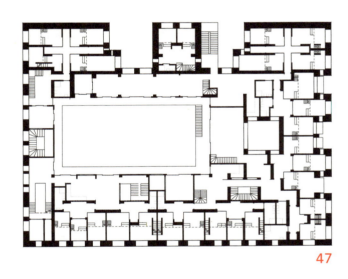

47

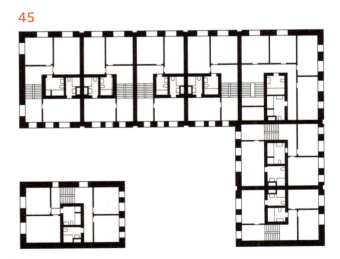

45

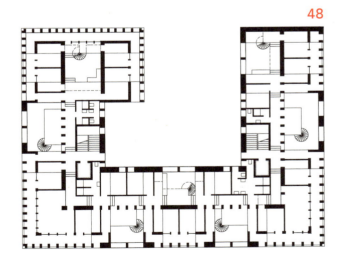

48

43   Brick B06; Mona Hartmann, Lukas Kesler; Studentenwohnen; Rue intérieure/student residence, rue intérieure
44   Brick B03; Judith Bartsch, Alexandr Minkin; Studentenwohnen; Terrassen im Atrium/student residence, terraces in atrium
45   Brick B05; Cansu Cantas, Sebastian Henschke; Studentenwohnen/student residence

46   Brick 08; Jessica Ganghofer, Anne-Katrin Schulz, Sarah Stein
47   Brick B01; Catherine Folawiyo, Gesa Holzbrecher; Studentenwohnen nach afghanischem Klanhaus/student residence based on Afghani clan house
48   Brick B02; Stefan File, Anne Kummetz; Studentenwohnen; potenzierter Raumplan/student residence, exponentiated spatial plan

Studierende der TU Berlin: Eine Typensammlung.
Regelgeschosse im Massstab 1:500

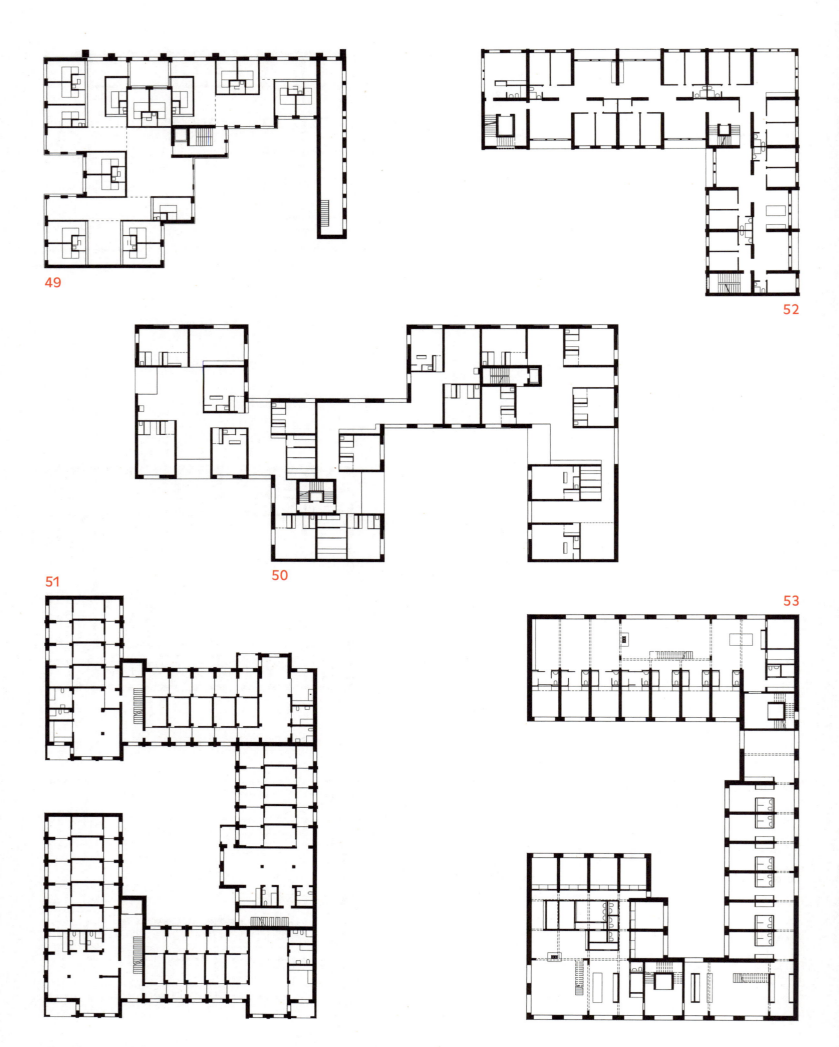

49 Brick B04; Christa Elizabeth Beckmann Zambrana; Studentenwohnen/student residence
50 Brick 04; Franziska Polleter, Simone Prill
51 Brick 03; Anna Gert, Cemile Kolgu; strukturierende Pfeiler/structuring pillars
52 Brick 14; Theodora Constantin, Vanessa Vogel; Künstlerhaus/artist's house
53 Brick 10; Marlene Bühner, Cassandra Donath

Students from the TU Berlin: A Type Collection.
Standard Floors on a Scale of 1:500

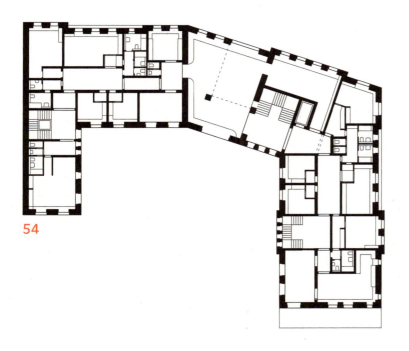
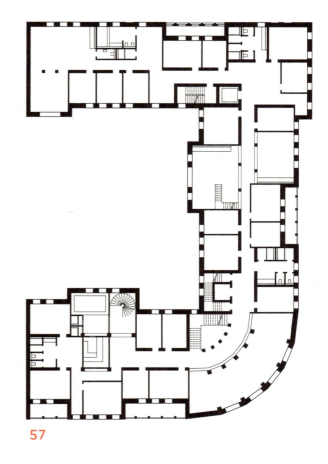
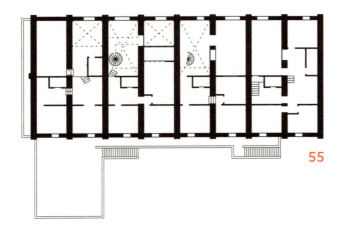
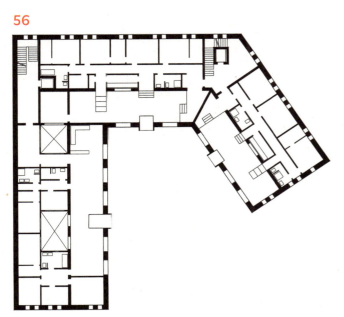
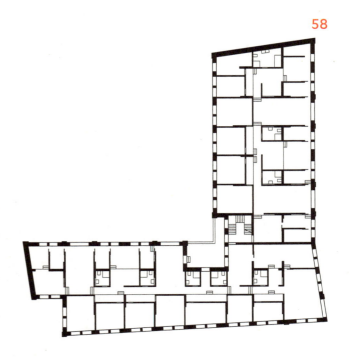

54 Brick 06; Larsen Berg, Harald Niessner; Hausgemeinschaft in Stadtpalais/ housing community in the Stadtpalais
55 Brick 07; Luca Gericke, Franco Scheuplein, Carolin Trahorsch; archaische Massivität/ archaic solidity
56 Brick 17; Josephine Brillowski, Alisa Joseph, Jana Morgenstern
57 Brick 11; Anika Weidlich, Franziska Wich
58 Brick 15; Sandra Schenavsky, Franziska Rüss

Studierende der TU Berlin: Eine Typensammlung.
Regelgeschosse im Massstab 1:500

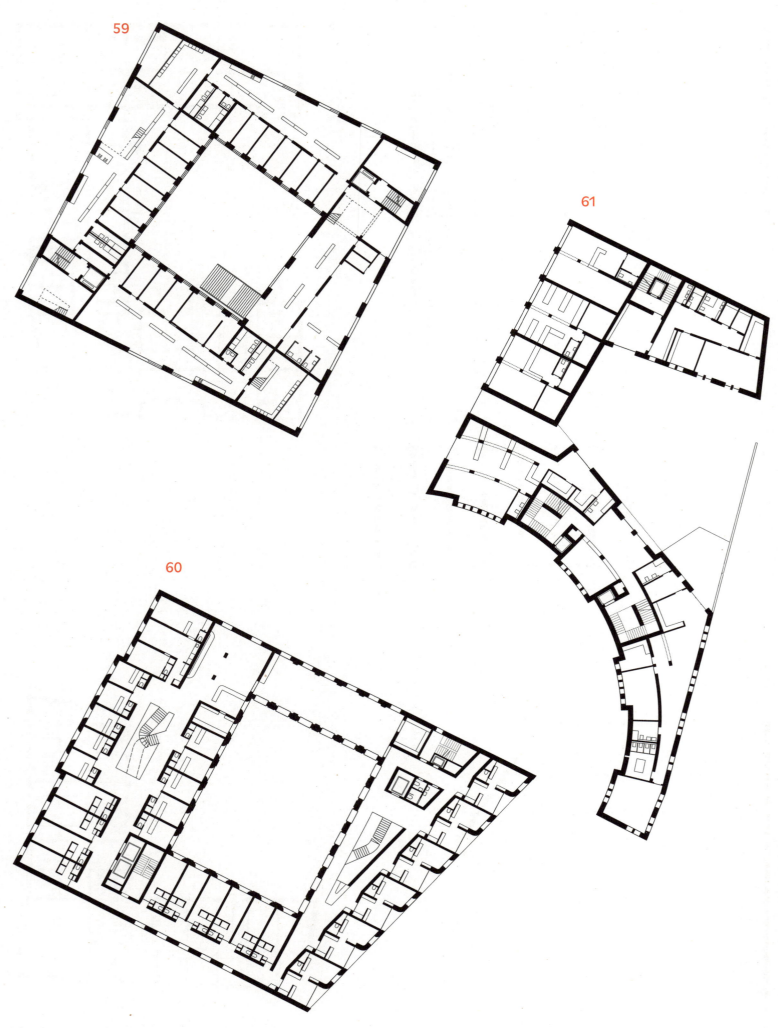

59 Brick 09; Kays Elbeyli, Arthur Schmock, Marc Wendland
60 Brick 13; Oskar Ellwanger, Ewa Kostecka, Judith Schiebel; Hotelresidenz/hotel residence
61 Brick 16; Simon Kiefer, Shaghayegh Moghaddasi Sikaroudi, Elena Wickenhöfer; Am Gasometer

Students from the TU Berlin: A Type Collection.
Standard Floors on a Scale of 1:500

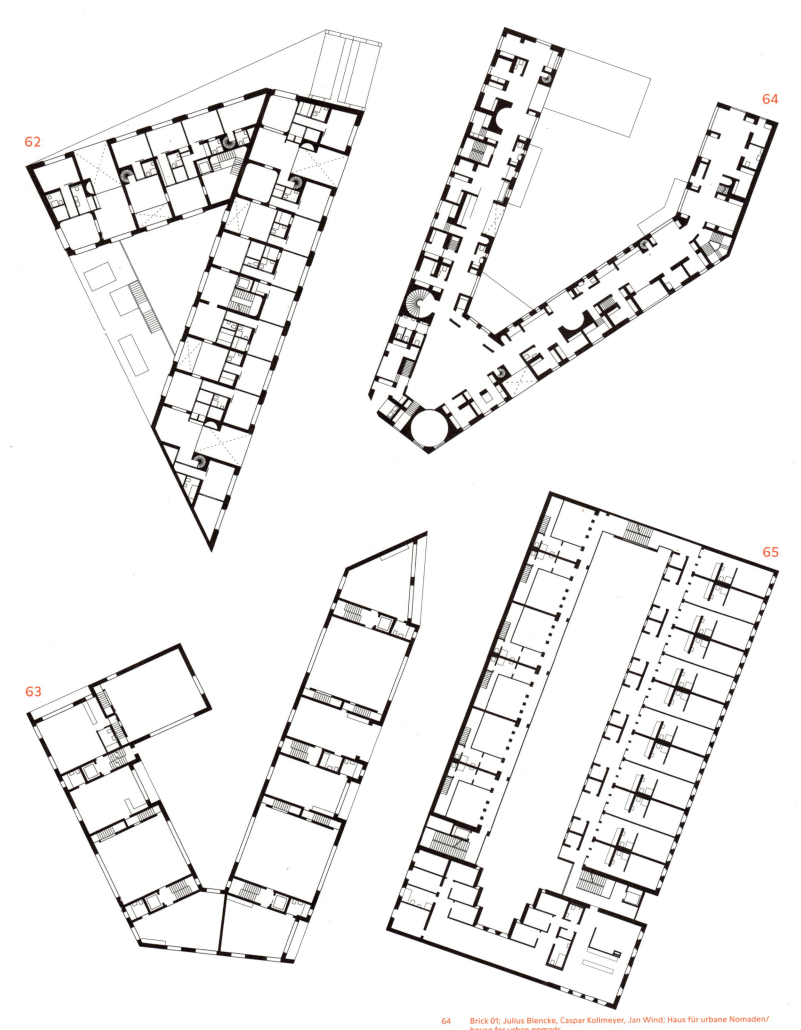

64 Brick 01; Julius Blencke, Caspar Kollmeyer, Jan Wind; Haus für urbane Nomaden/house for urban nomads
65 Brick 05; Vera Marie Glas, Rafael Lozykowski, Florian Rizek; Wohnen und Arbeiten/home and work
63 Brick 02; Kai Hikmet Canver, Sina Pauline Riedlinger
62 Brick 12; Véronique Baustert, Elena Petkova; Atelierwohnen/studio living

Studierende der TU Berlin: Eine Typensammlung.
Regelgeschosse im Massstab 1:500

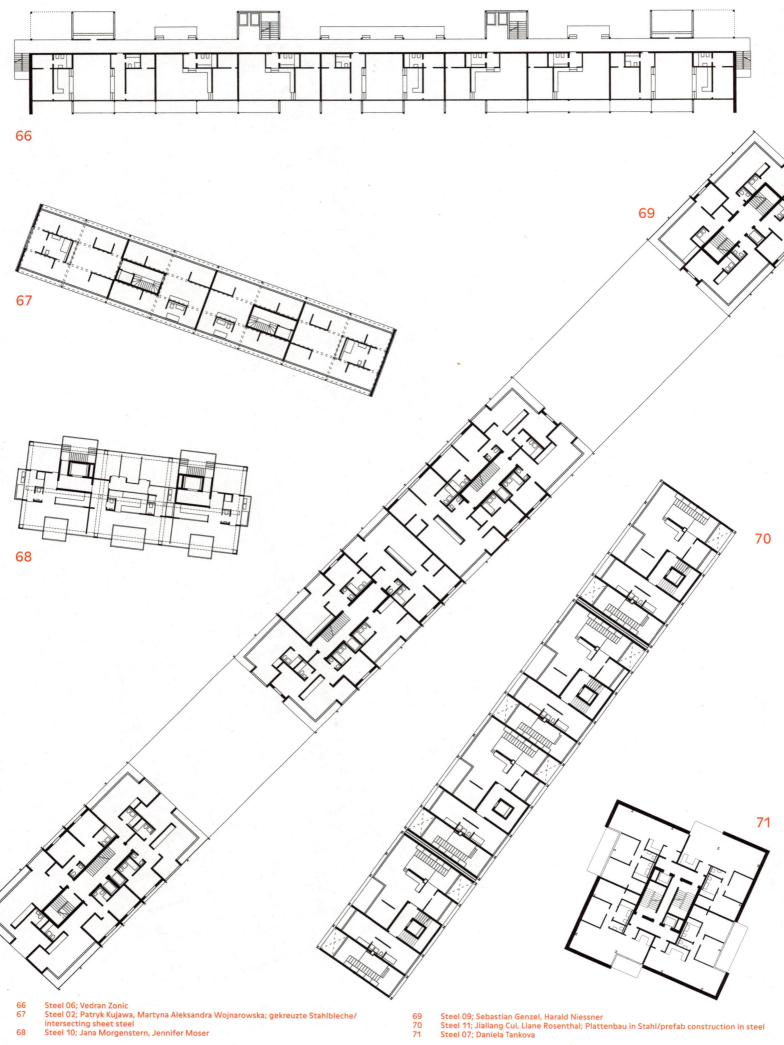

66 Steel 06; Vedran Zonic
67 Steel 02; Patryk Kujawa, Martyna Aleksandra Wojnarowska; gekreuzte Stahlbleche/ intersecting sheet steel
68 Steel 10; Jana Morgenstern, Jennifer Moser
69 Steel 09; Sebastian Genzel, Harald Niessner
70 Steel 11; Jialiang Cui, Liane Rosenthal; Plattenbau in Stahl/prefab construction in steel
71 Steel 07; Daniela Tankova

Students from the TU Berlin: A Type Collection.
Standard Floors on a Scale of 1:500

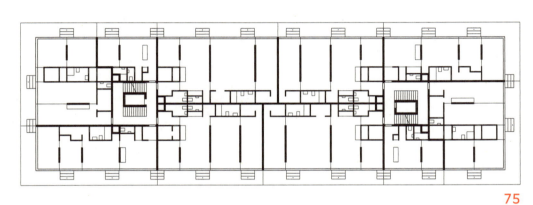
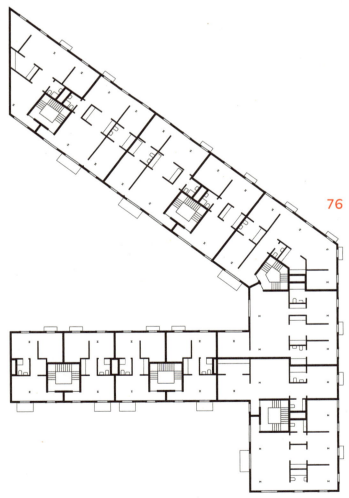

72 Steel 04; Thomas Pracht, Guang Xue
73 Steel 08; Myungjir Choi, Elena Schneider; Rahmenbauweise/frame construction
74 Steel 01; Ignasi Querol Diez, Ana Garcia Gasquet
75 Steel 05; Felix Bardou, Carlo Fischer; hängende Plattformen/hanging platforms
76 Steel 03; Hanna Grabmaier, Julia Naomi Henning, Lisa Nagy

Studierende der TU Berlin: Eine Typensammlung.
Regelgeschosse im Massstab 1:500

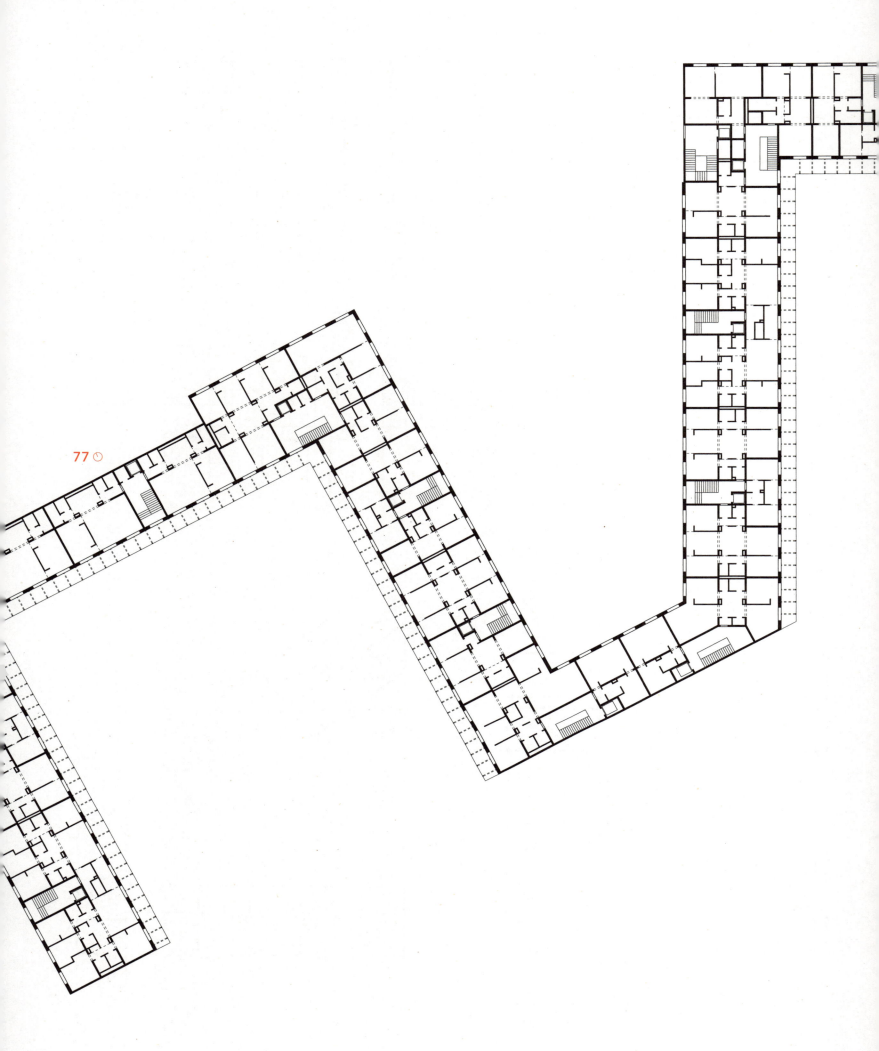

77 Kollektive Höfe M11; Timo Büscher; innerstädtische Grosssiedlung/
Large-scale Inner-city Housing Estate

Students from the TU Berlin: A Type Collection.
Standard Floors on a Scale of 1:500

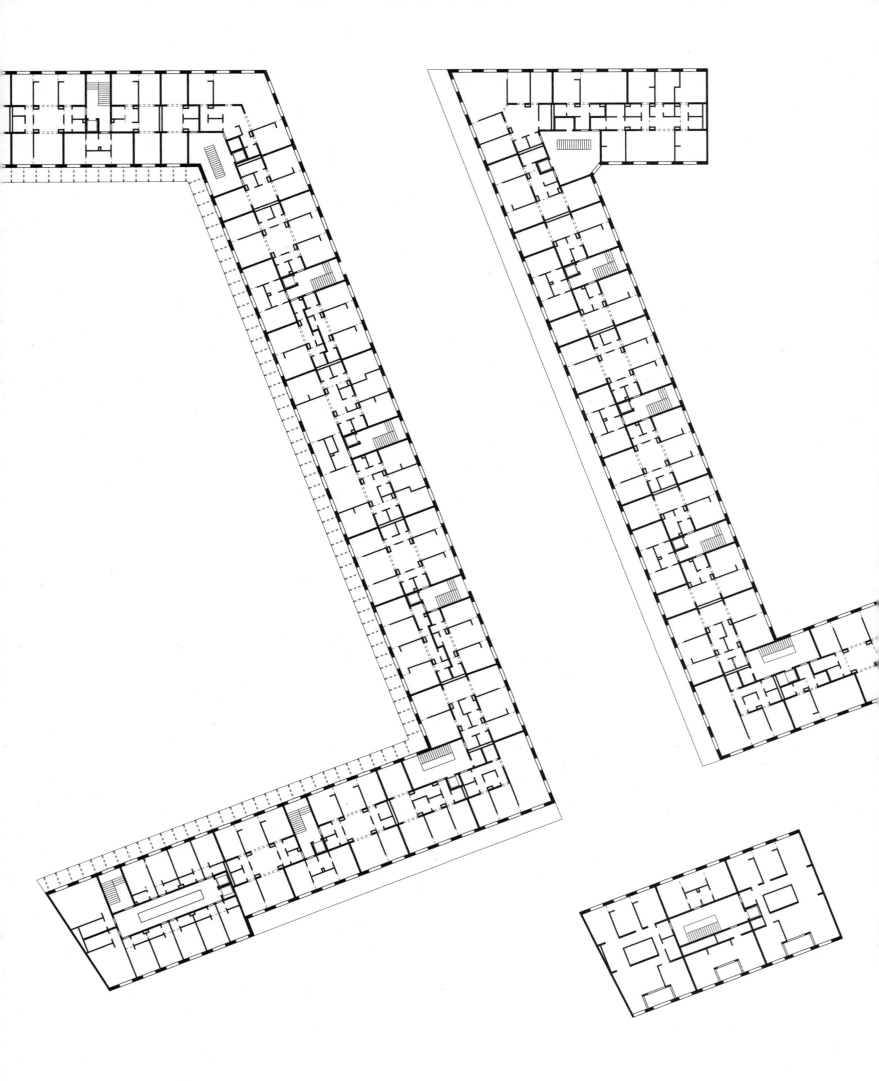

Studierende der TU Berlin: Eine Typensammlung.
Regelgeschosse im Massstab 1:500

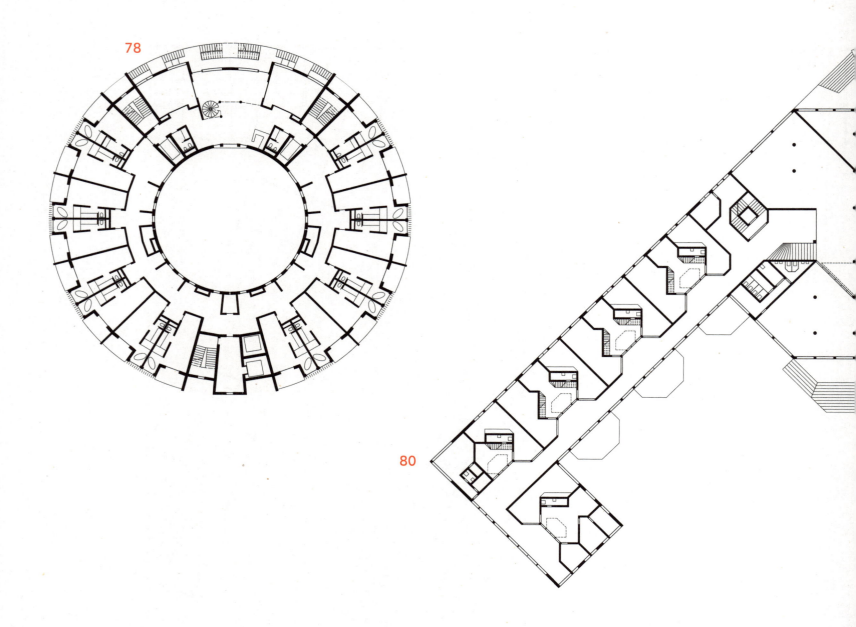

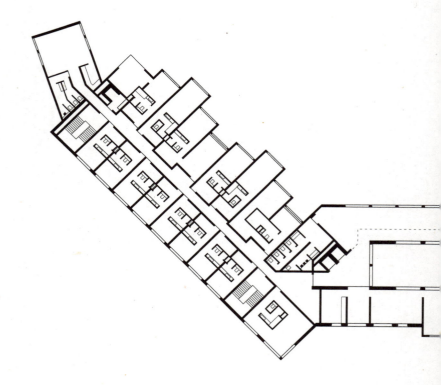

78 Grandhotel M02; Aydin Sunar; Hotel für urbane Nomaden/hotel for urban nomads
79 Grandhotel 04; Robert Essen

80 Grandhotel 07; Jakob Pawlowski; Strandhotel/seaside hotel

Students from the TU Berlin: A Type Collection.
Standard Floors on a Scale of 1:500

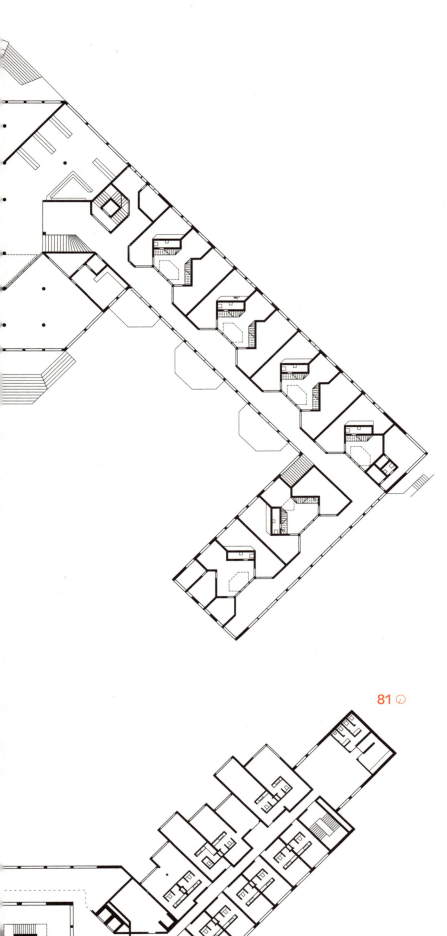
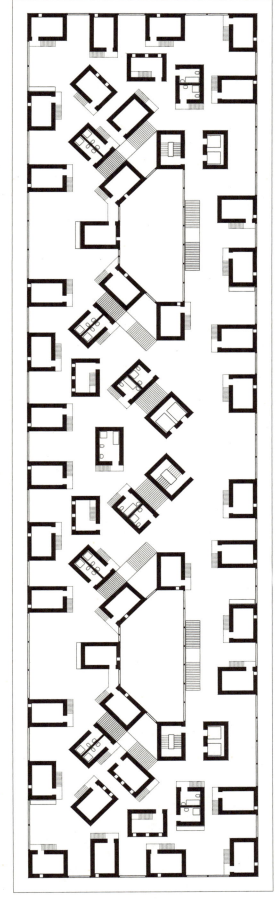

81 Grandhotel M01; Jennifer Moser

82 Grandhotel 08; Paul Achter; Kollektiv versus Rückzug/collective versus individual

Studierende der TU Berlin: Eine Typensammlung.
Regelgeschosse im Massstab 1:500

311

83

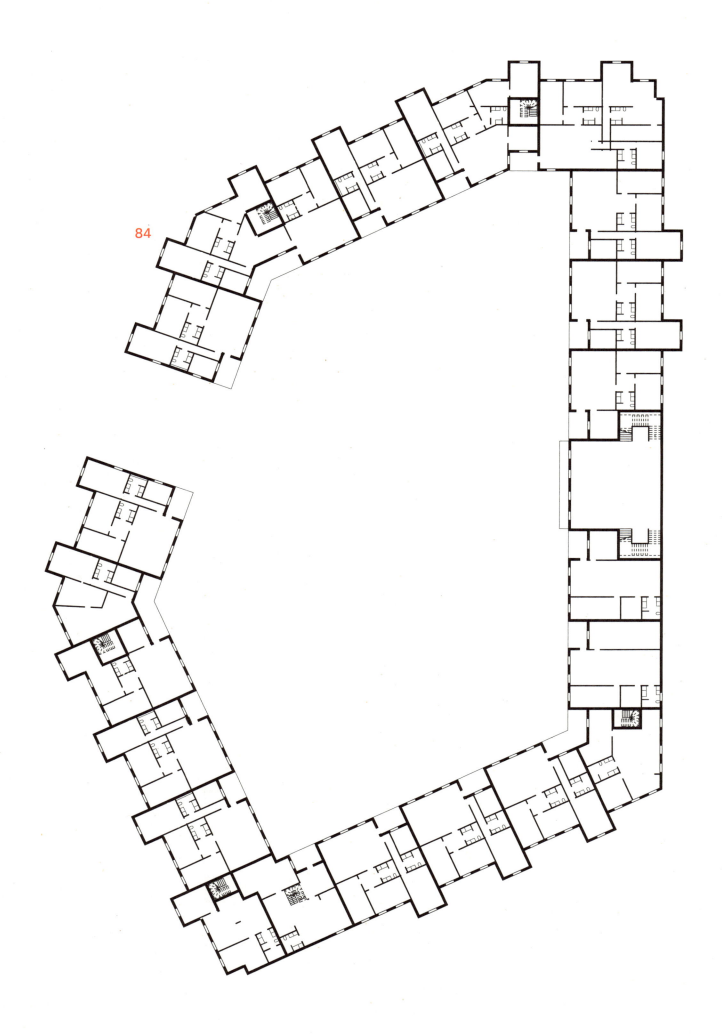

83 Grandhotel 03; Hanna Rohst; Künstlerkolonie/artist's colony
84 Grandhotel 05; Siemen Andreas Aas

**Studierende der TU Berlin: Eine Typensammlung.
Regelgeschosse im Massstab 1:500**

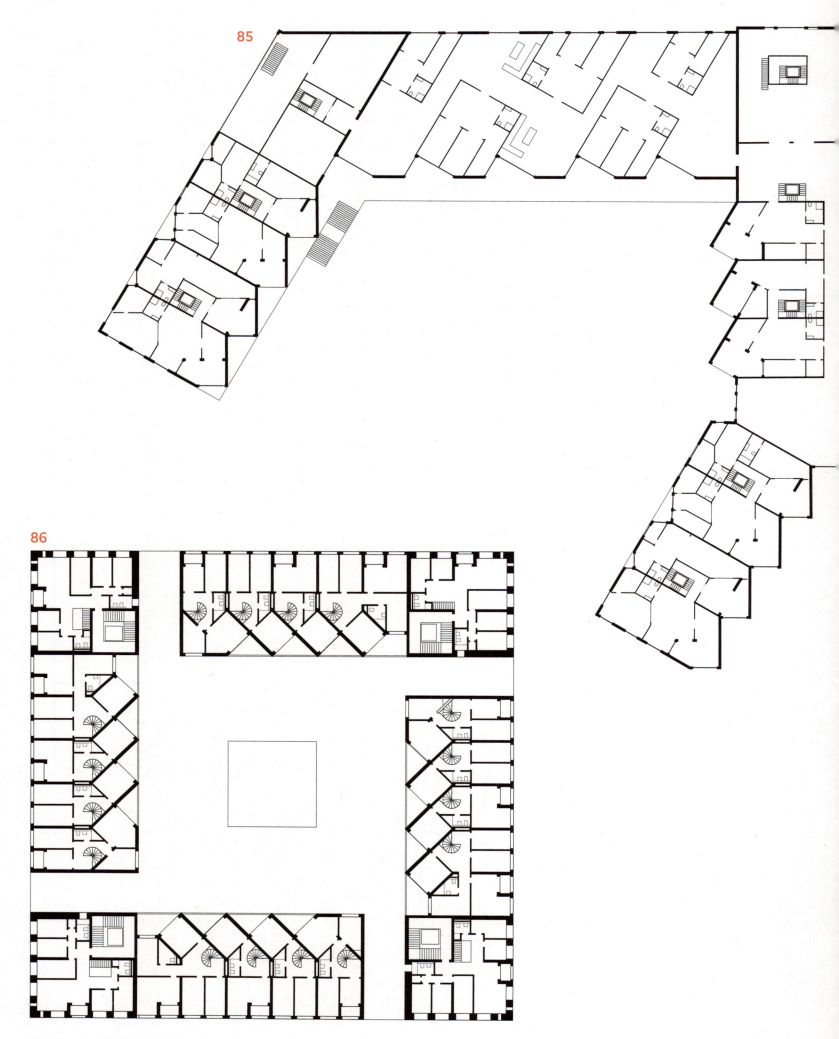

85 Grandhotel 06; Julia Rathmann Löcker
86 Supermärkte M09; Felix Bardou; Wohnen über Markthalle/residence above market hall

Students from the TU Berlin: A Type Collection.
Standard Floors on a Scale of 1:500

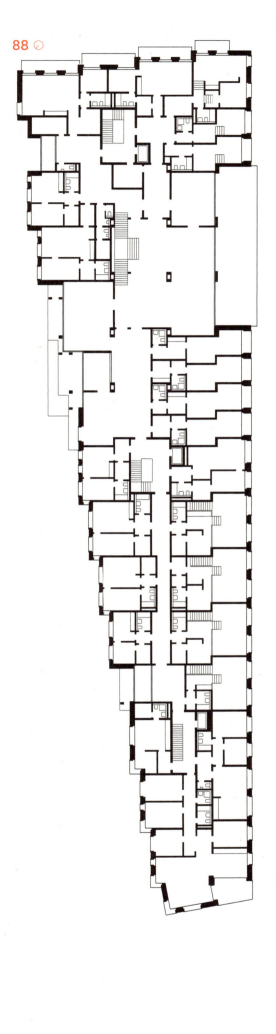
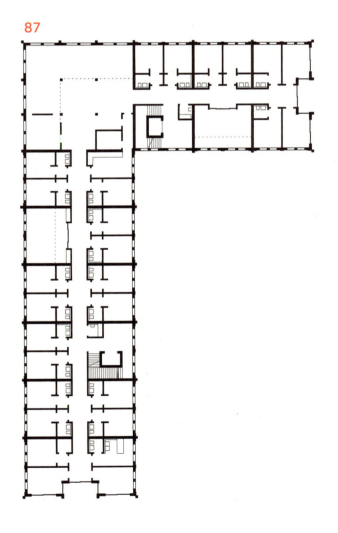
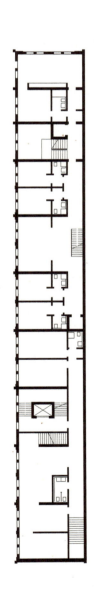

87 Supermärkte M10 Sebastian Genzel; Altersresidenz und Quartierversorgung/
senior residence and neighborhood provisions
88 Supermärkte M08 Harald Niessner; ein Stück soziale Stadt/A piece of the social city

**Studierende der TU Berlin: Eine Typensammlung.
Regelgeschosse im Massstab 1:500**

89 Urbanity and Production M05; Jana Morgenstern; Wohnen im Gewächshaus/residence in a greenhouse
90 Urbanity and Production M06; Robert Essen; Wohnen über Industriehalle/residence above factory building
91 Urbanity and Production M03; Tobias Wolski; Gewerbehof/business park

Students from the TU Berlin: A Type Collection.
Standard Floors on a Scale of 1:500

92 Urbanity and Production M07; Fidias Curiel Casteson; über der Fahrradfabrik/ above the bicycle factory

93 Urbanity and Production M04; Julia Rathmann Löcker; Musikerhaus und Gitarrenfabrik/ musician's house and guitar factory

Studierende der TU Berlin: Eine Typensammlung.
Regelgeschosse im Massstab 1:500

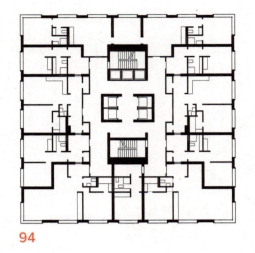

94

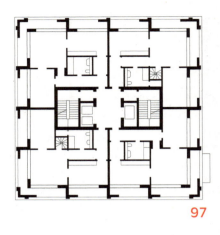

97

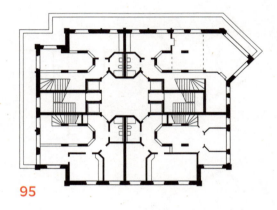

95

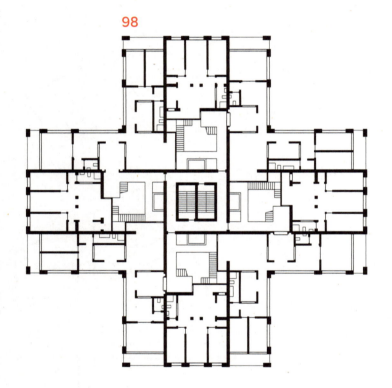

98

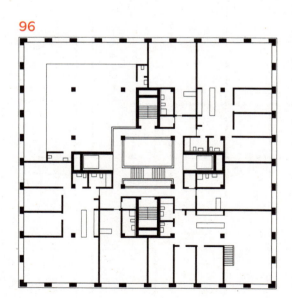

96

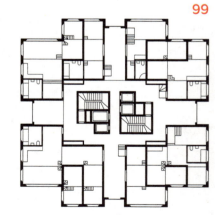

99

94 High Rise 03; Niki Apostolopoulou, Fidias Curiel Casteson, Bernhard Weikert
95 High Rise 12; Kristine Kazelnika, Maximilian Vesely
96 High Rise 15; Cansu Cantas, Elina Kolarova

97 High Rise 09; James Horkulak, Marko Shllaku
98 High Rise 05; Catherine Folawiyo, Clara Jereczek; römisches Hofhaus vertikal/ Roman courtyard house, vertical
99 High Rise 11; Annett Donat, Jakob Pawlowski; dreidimensionales Tetris/ three-dimensional tetris

Students from the TU Berlin: A Type Collection.
Standard Floors on a Scale of 1:500

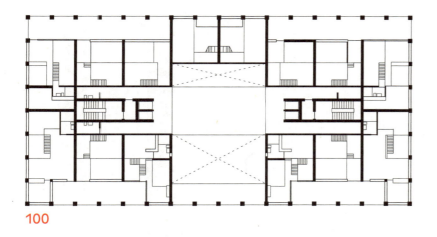

100

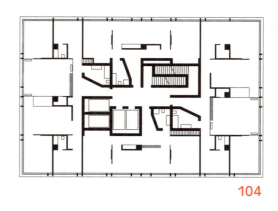

104

101

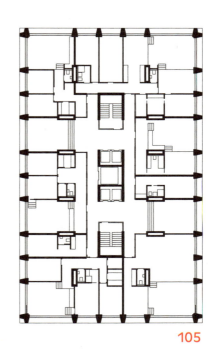

105

102

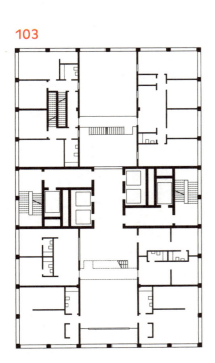

103

106

100 High Rise 01; Robert Bauer, Christa Elizabeth Beckmann
101 High Rise 17; Sarah Meier, Maximilian Quick; Rue intérieure/rue intérieure
102 High Rise 06; Tina Krause, Denitsa Todorova
103 High Rise 18; Tobias Bräunig, Tobias Scholz

104 High Rise 08; Julien Engelhardt, Simon Lehmann
105 High Rise 13; Maija Gavare, Johanna Sieberer
106 High Rise 02; Amélie Barande, Qin Qian

**Studierende der TU Berlin: Eine Typensammlung.
Regelgeschosse im Massstab 1:500**

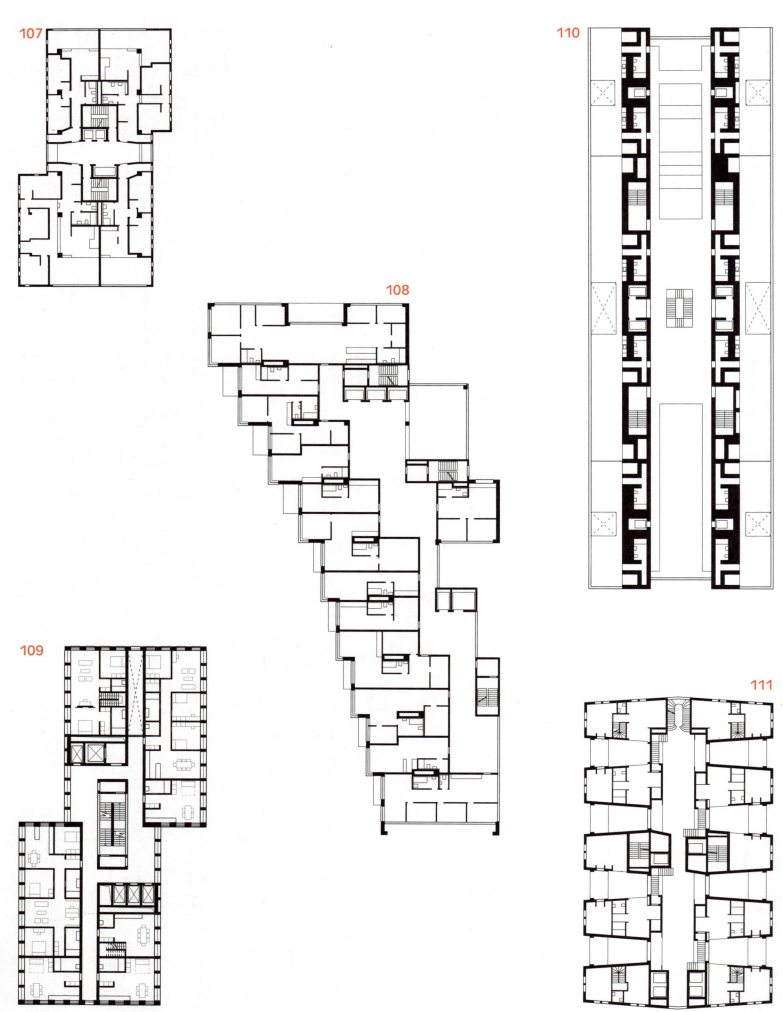

107 High Rise 07; Azad Saleem, Martin Ulitzka, Olivia Valenzuela
108 High Rise 10; Paul Achter, Lorenz Preußer, Ivan Zilic; Wohnen mit Zusatznutzungen/ residence with additional uses
109 High Rise 16; Lisa Beyer, Justus Preyer, Max Werner
110 High Rise 04; Merle Sudbrock, Roberta Zucchetti; befreite Wohn- und Kollektivräume/ residential and collective spaces
111 High Rise 14; Franziska Käuferle, Louisa Wahler; Häuser an Rue intérieure/ houses along a rue intérieure

Students from the TU Berlin: A Type Collection.
Standard Floors on a Scale of 1:500

112

115

113

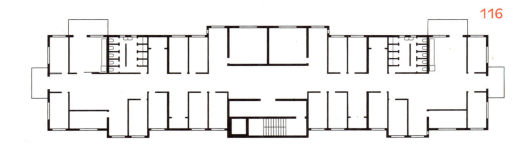

116

114

117

112 College 05; Isabel de Palacios, Julia Ratsch, Florian Tudzierz; Wohnlandschaft/ landscaped interior
113 College 01; Leonardo Jochim, Lukas Stadelmann, Samuel Yeboa; strassenabgewandt/ facing away from the street
114 College 03; Tan Phong Nguyen, Mai Tran

115 College 07; Paulina Grabowska, Luciana Lagoa de Nobile, Dilara Uzgeldi
116 College 02; Tycho Brand, Viktor Parijer, Felix Rottka
117 College 04; Marie-Louise Leeck, Lisa Thürer; Minimalboxen um Wohnhalle/ minimal boxes around a living area

Studierende der TU Berlin: Eine Typensammlung.
Regelgeschosse im Massstab 1:500

118

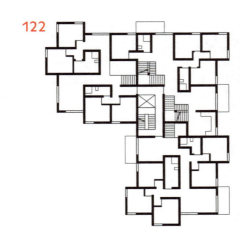

122

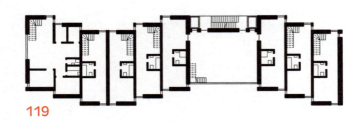

119

120

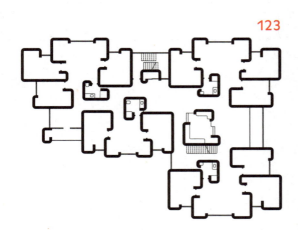

123

124

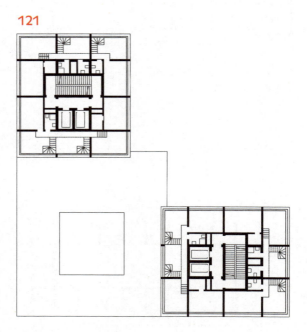

121

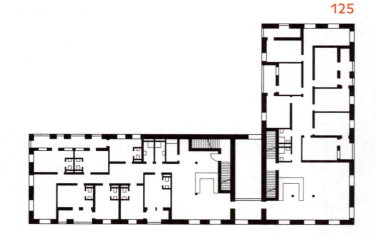

125

118 College 12; Daniel Dieren, Helena Reischel, Ann-Kathrin Salich; variabel durch Schiebewände/variation through sliding walls
119 College 10; Lysann Geller, Monika Pawlak, Kassandra Sarantis
120 College 09; Christine Feistl, Ellinor Förster
121 College 14; Paul Harries, Ana Richter de Arce, Florian Tropp; Raumkaskade im Turm/spatial cascade in tower

122 College 06; Vadim Below, Timo Strauch, Katharina Zull; Hommage an Mangiarottis Casa a Monza/homage to Mangiarotti's Casa a Monza
123 College 11; Amer Eid, Michael Roth; Hommage an Johansens Labyrinth House/homage to Johansen's Labyrinth House
124 College 08; Diana Aleksova, Tsvetomila Neshtereva, Nikoleta Nikolova
125 College 13; Antoan Antonov, Jakob Fischer, Maurice Luft

Students from the TU Berlin: A Type Collection.
Standard Floors on a Scale of 1:500

←

Studierende
der TU Berlin:
Eine Typensammlung.
Regelgeschosse
im Massstab 1:500

Students from
the TU Berlin:
A Type Collection.
Standard Floors
on a Scale of 1:500

Studierende der
TU Berlin:
Vom Wohnen.
Möblierte Grundrisse
im Massstab 1:150

Students from
the TU Berlin:
On Housing.
Furnished Floor Plans
on a Scale of 1:150

Studierende der
TU Berlin:
Vom Wohnen.
Möblierte Grundrisse
im Massstab 1:150

Students from
the TU Berlin:
On Housing.
Furnished Floor Plans
on a Scale of 1:150

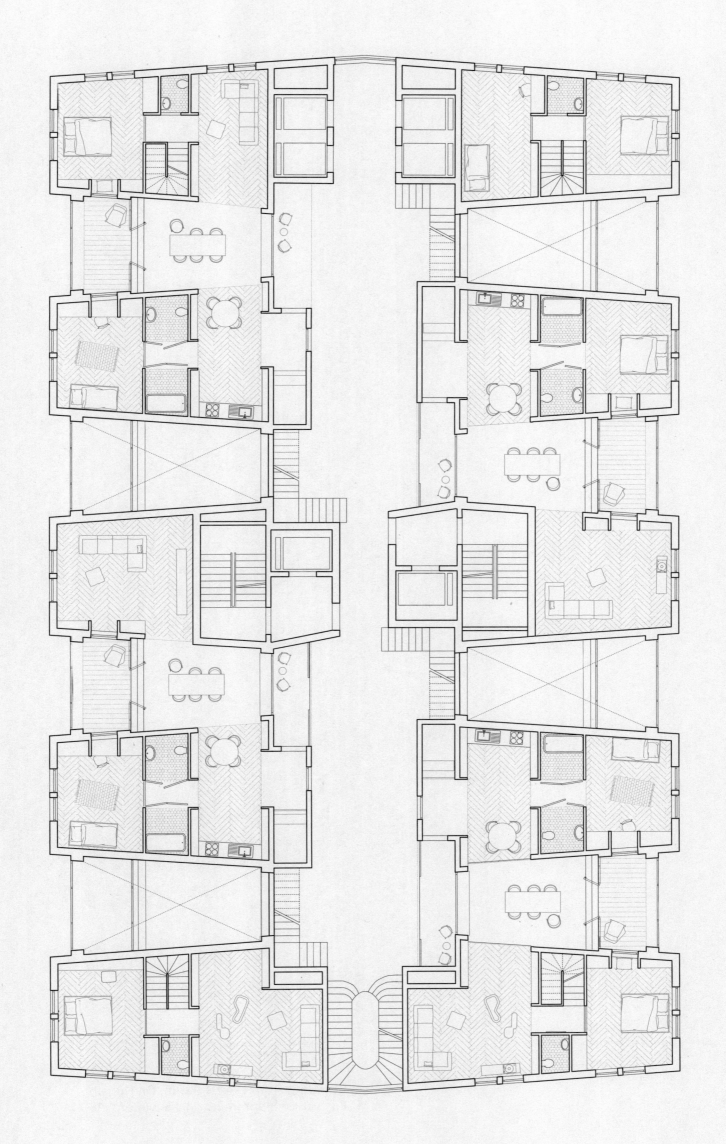

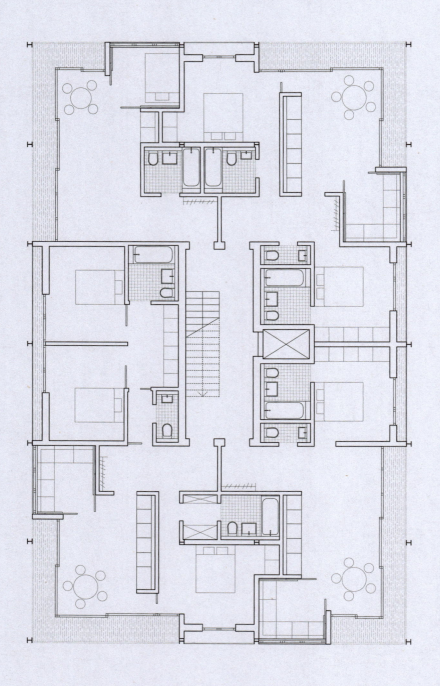

←← High Rise 14; Franziska Käuferle, Louisa Wahler

↑ Steel 09; Sebastian Genzel, Harald Niessner
→ Urbanity and Production M02; Julia Rathmann Löcker

Students from the TU Berlin: On Housing.
Furnished Floor Plans on a Scale of 1:150

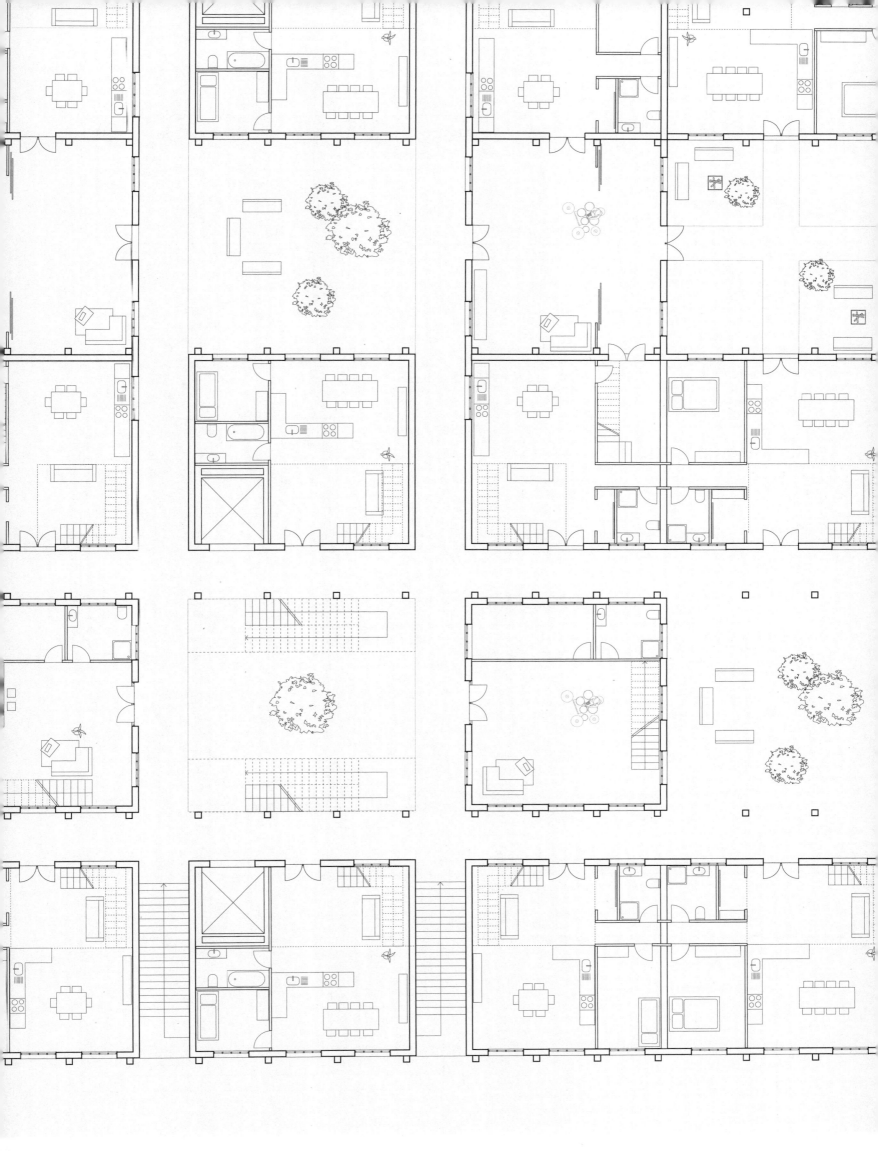

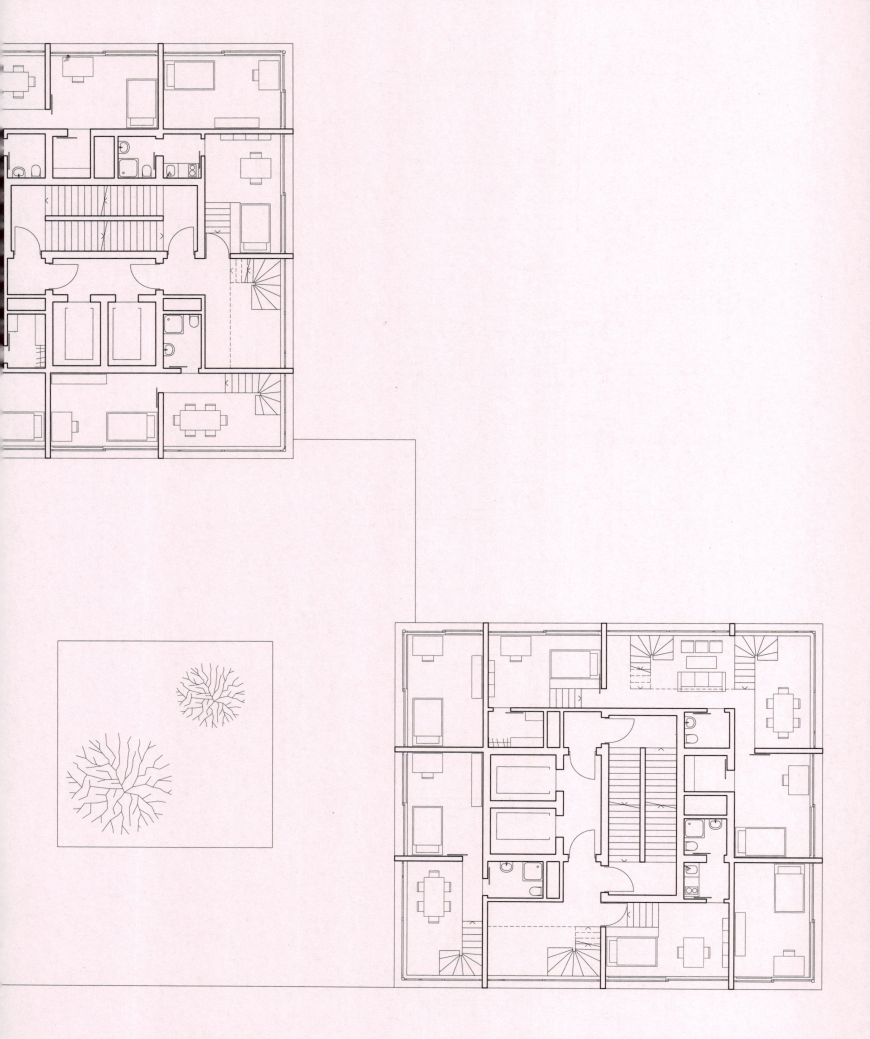

← Brick 14; Theodora Constantin, Vanessa Vogel
↙ Brick 08; Jessica Ganghofer, Anne-Katrin Schulz, Sarah Stein
↑ College 14; Paul Harries, Ana Richter de Arce, Florian Tropp
→ Concrete 20; Marlene Bühner, Cassandra Donath

Students from the TU Berlin: On Housing.
Furnished Floor Plans on a Scale of 1:150

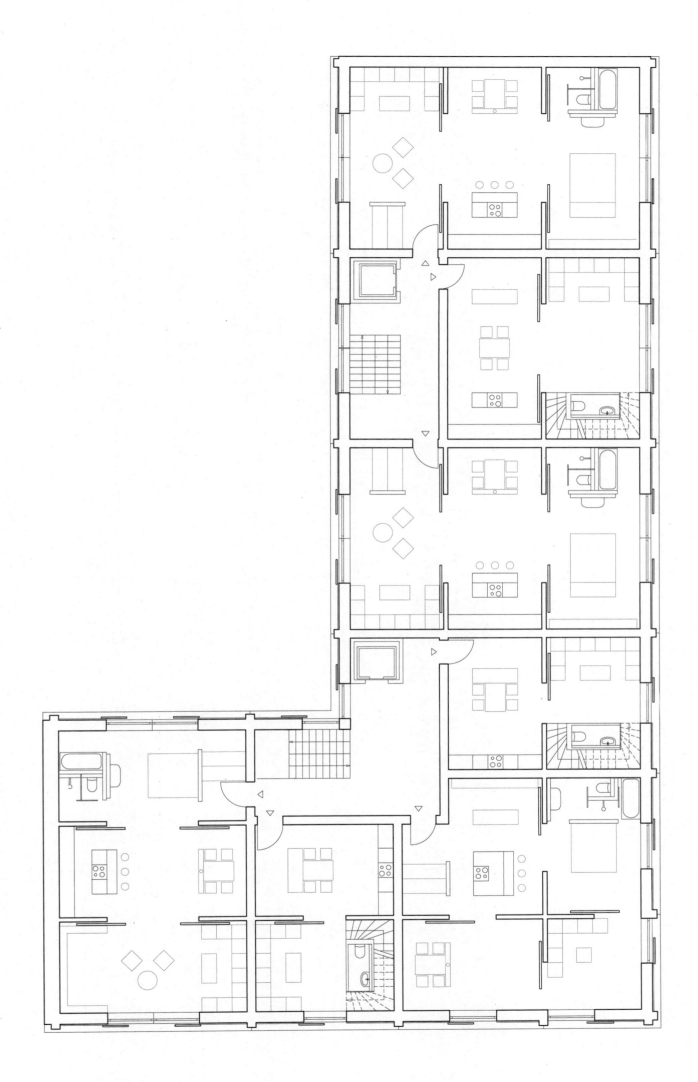

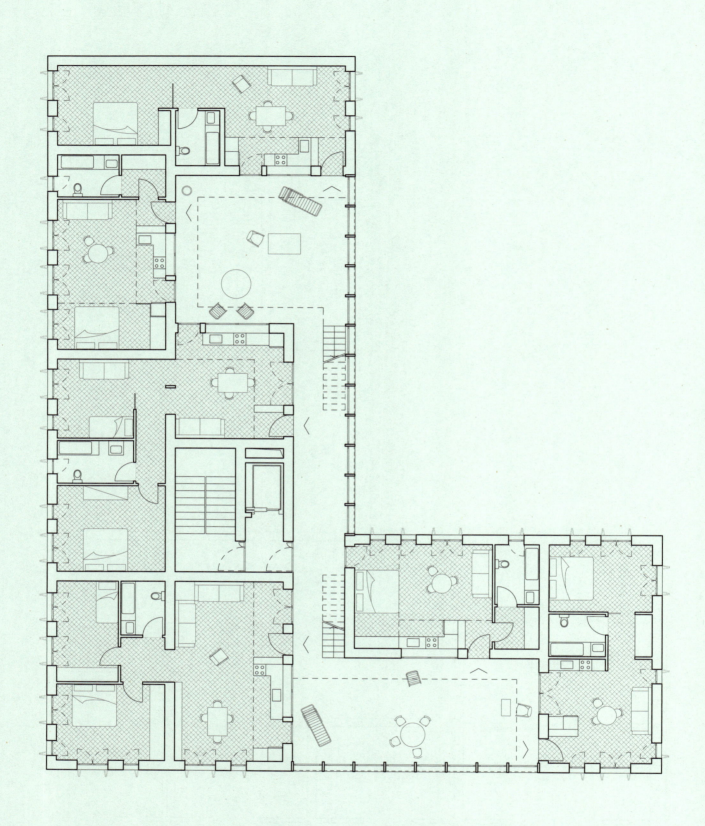

↑ Wood 12; Marco Migliavacca, Friedrich Neukirchen → Brick B06; Mona Hartmann, Lukas Kesler

Students from the TU Berlin: On Housing.
Furnished Floor Plans on a Scale of 1:150

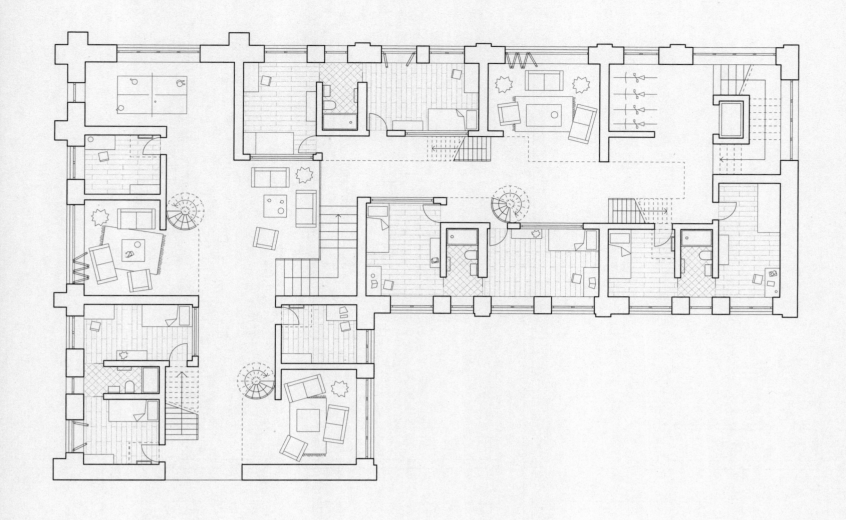
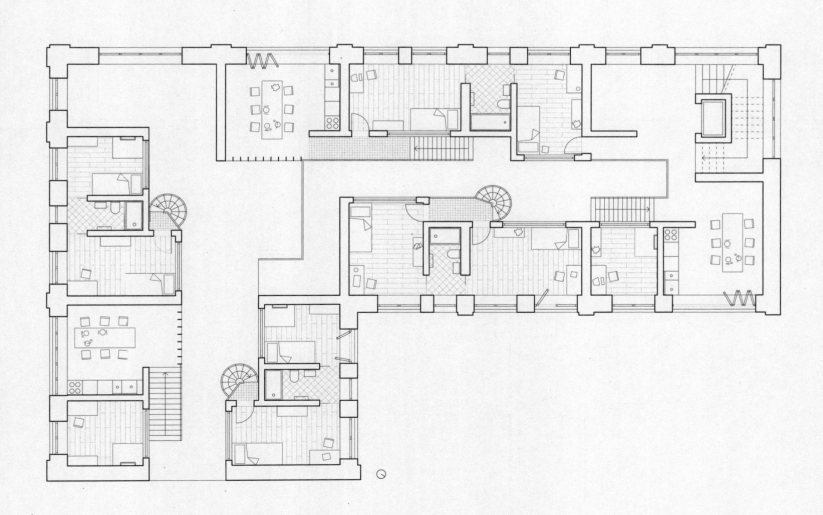

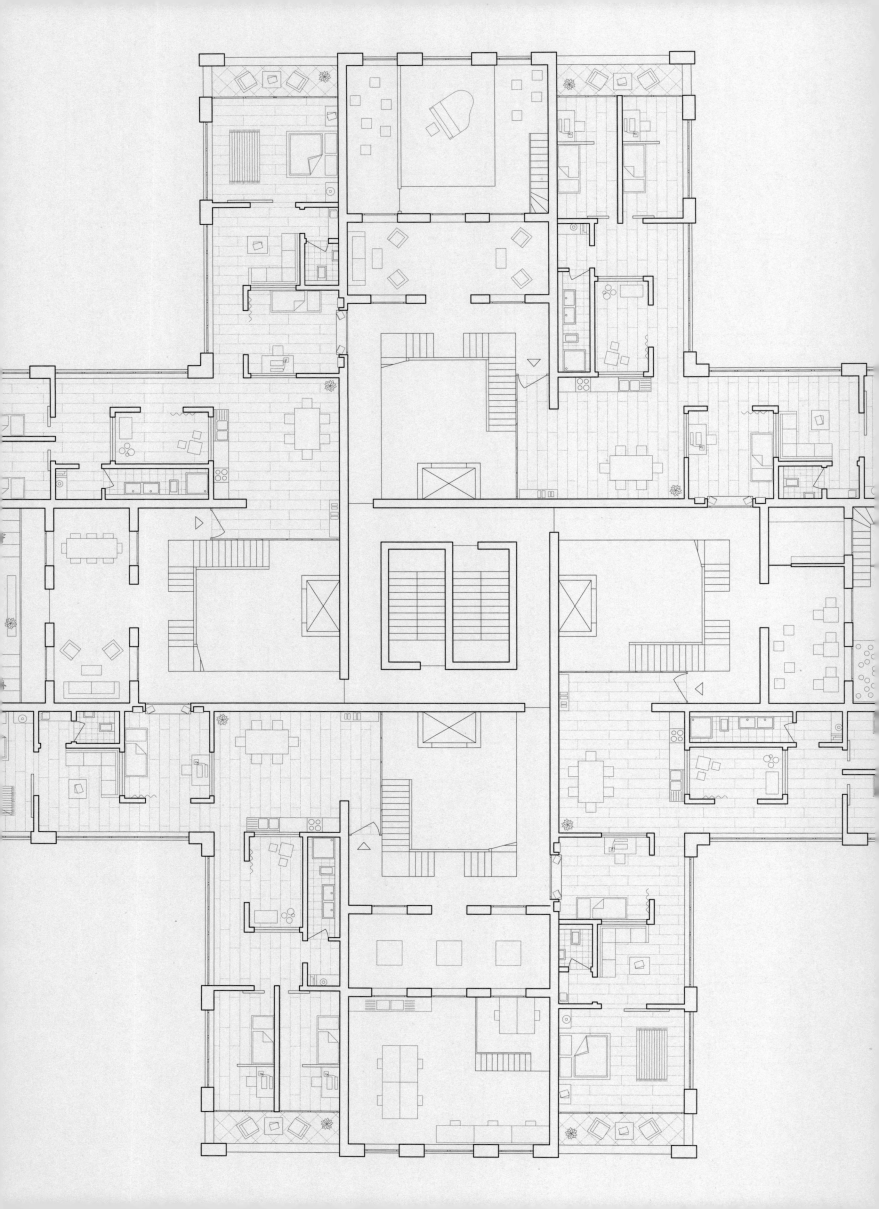

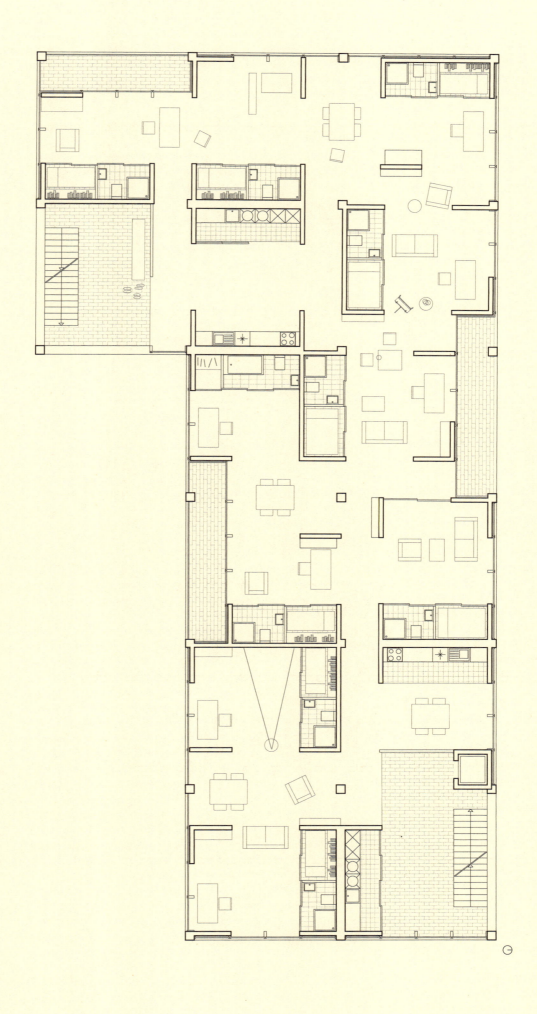

← High Rise 05; Catherine Folawiyo, Clara Jereczek ↑ College 12; Daniel Dieren, Helena Reischel, Ann-Kathrin Salich

**Studierende der TU Berlin: Vom Wohnen.
Möblierte Grundrisse im Massstab 1:150**

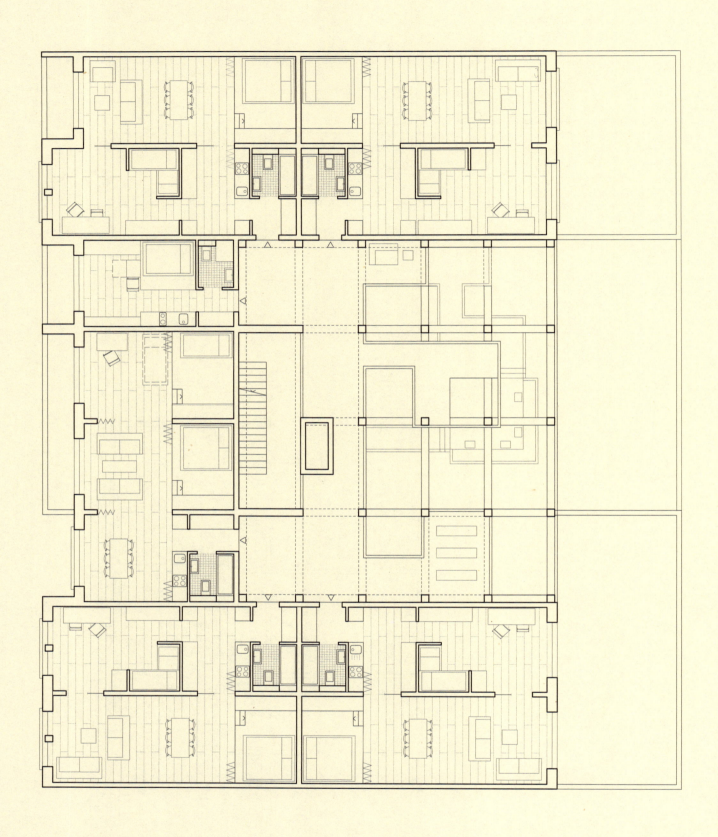

↑ Wood 14; Carolin Lehnerer, Aydin Sunar

Students from the TU Berlin: On Housing.
Furnished Floor Plans on a Scale of 1:150

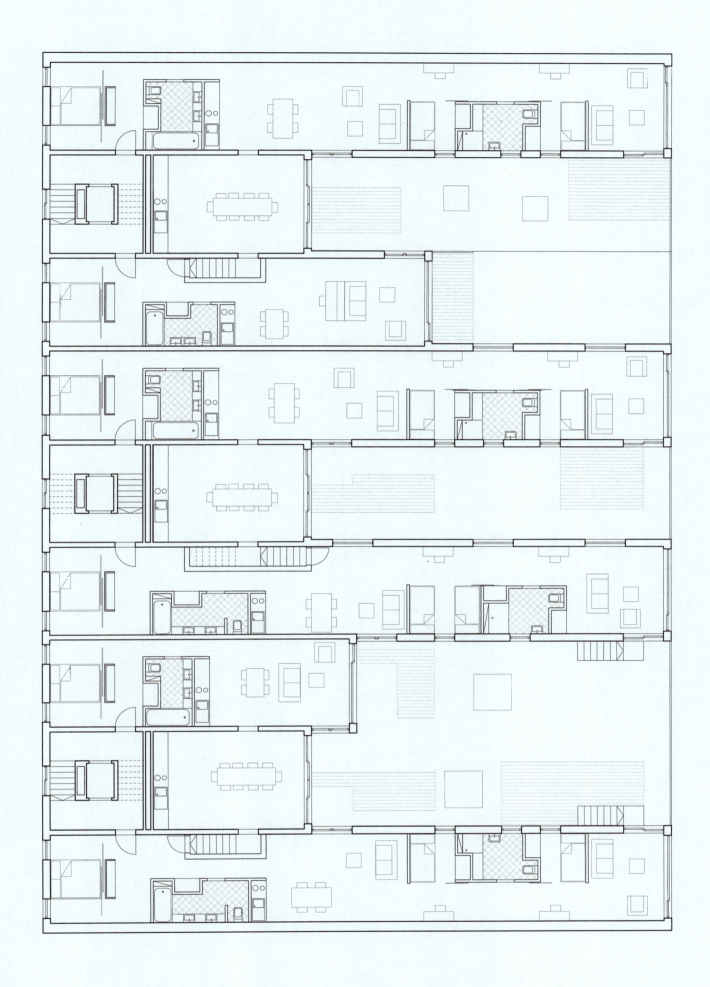

↑ Wood 20; Evelyn Gröger, Darina Palazova

Studierende der TU Berlin: Vom Wohnen.
Möblierte Grundrisse im Massstab 1:150

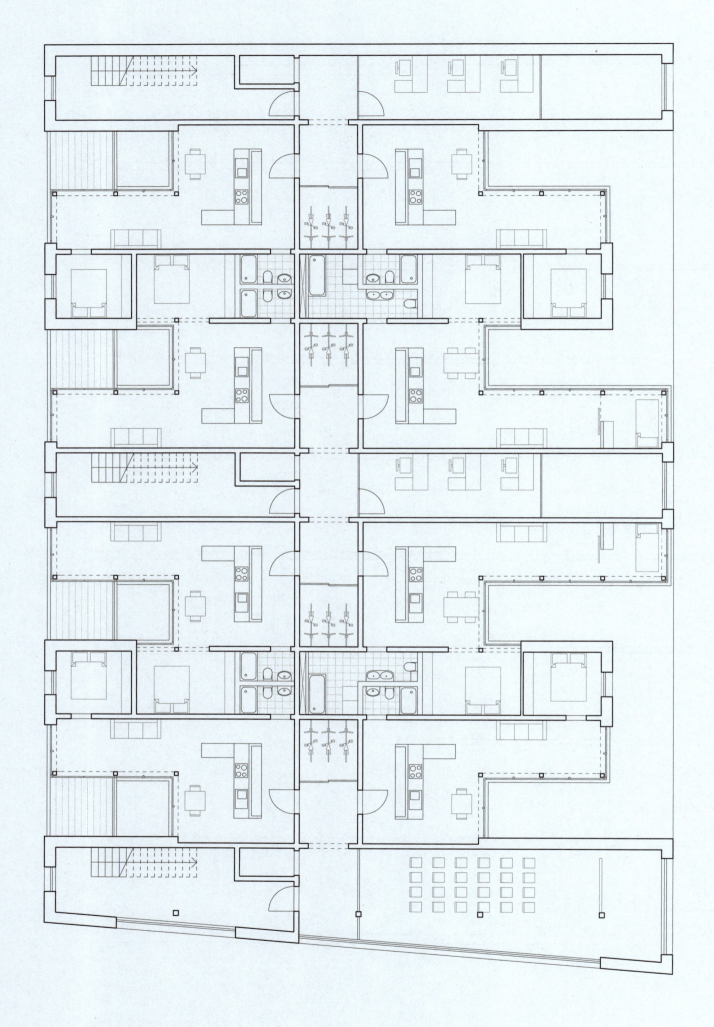

↑ Wood 18; Timo Büscher, Olivier Laydevant

Students from the TU Berlin: On Housing.
Furnished Floor Plans on a Scale of 1:150

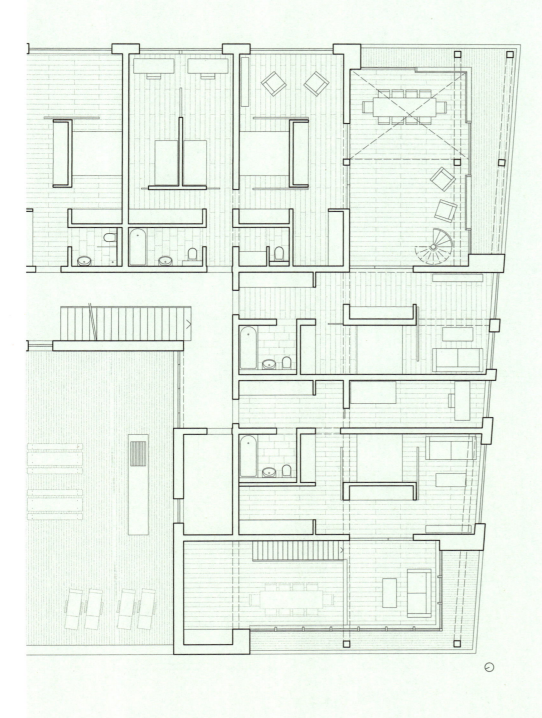

↑ Wood 07; Veronika Mosser, Nico Steinacker

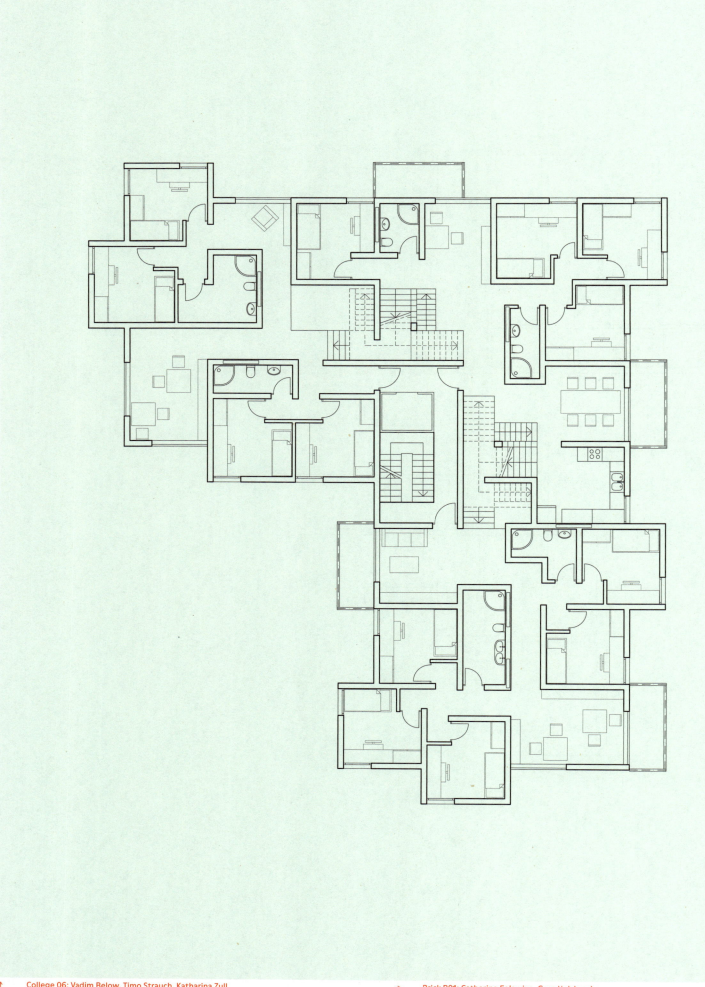

↑ College 06; Vadim Below, Timo Strauch, Katharina Zull   → Brick B01; Catherine Folawiyo, Gesa Holzbrecher

340

Students from the TU Berlin: On Housing.
Furnished Floor Plans on a Scale of 1:150

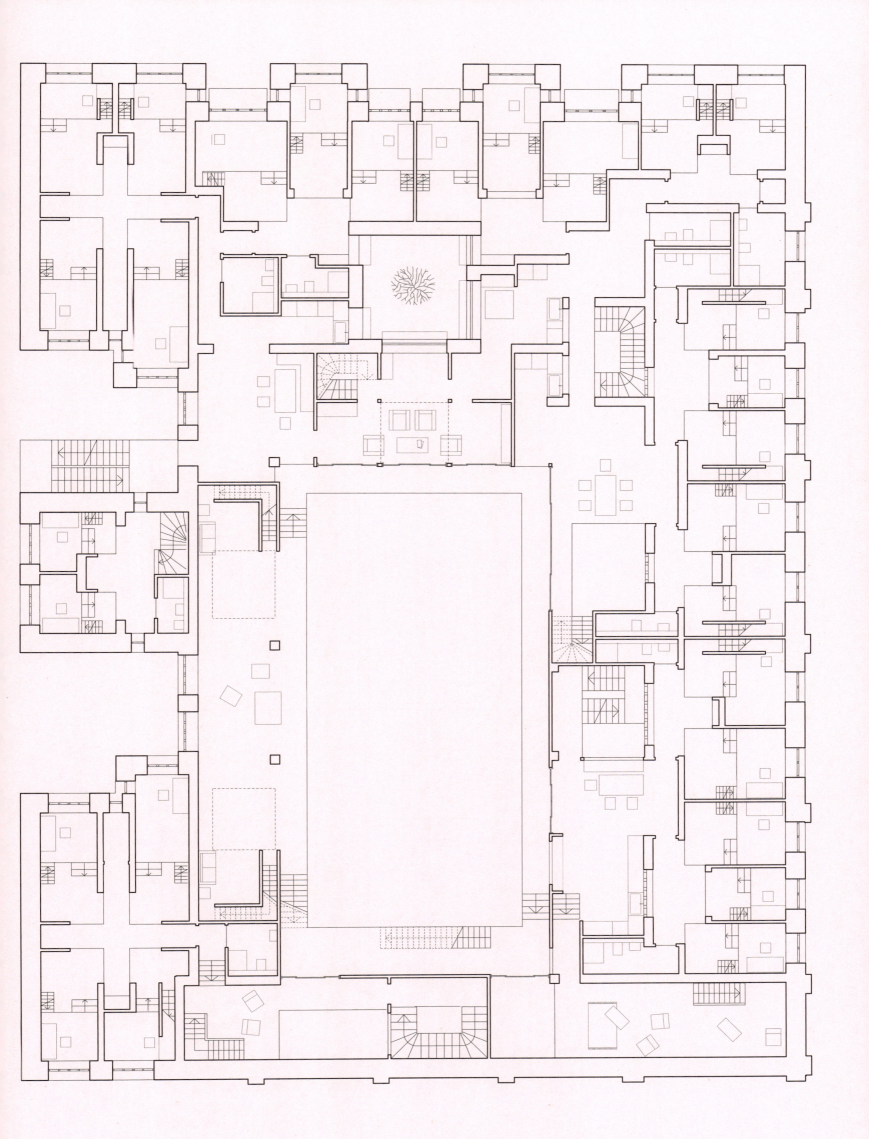

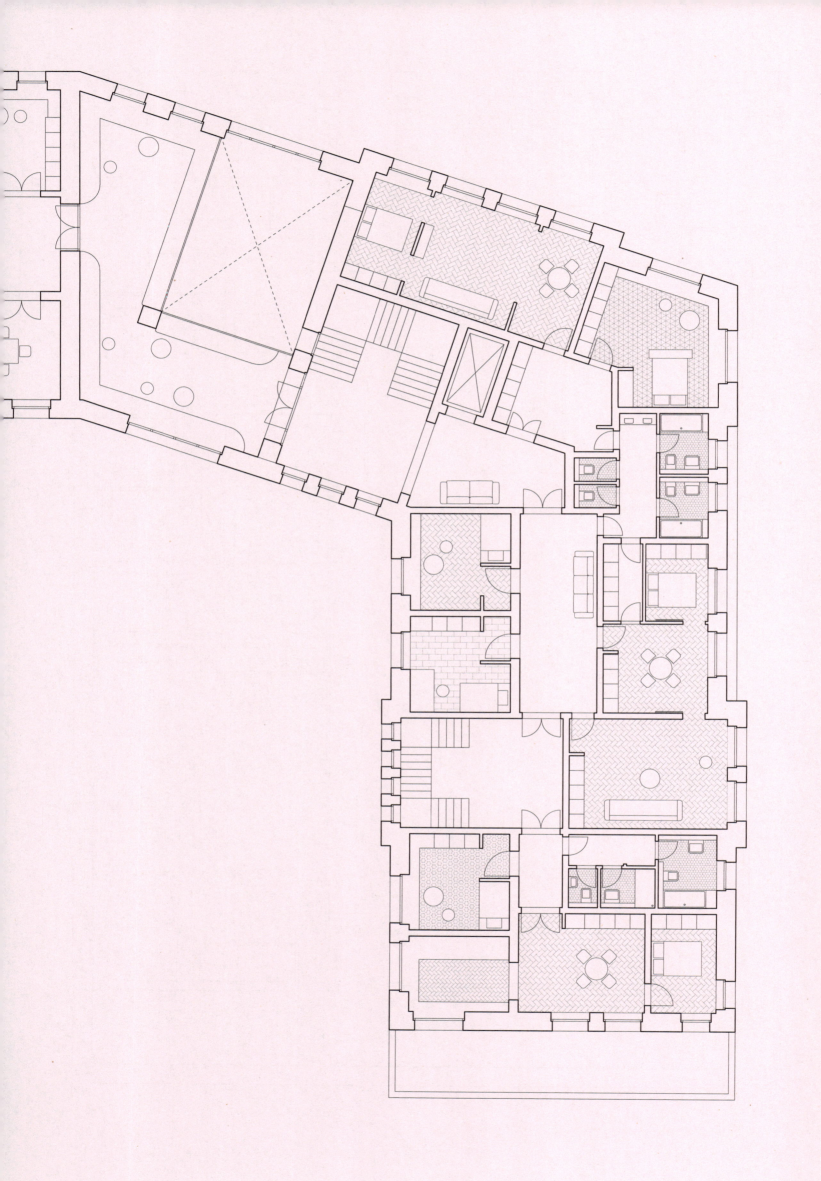

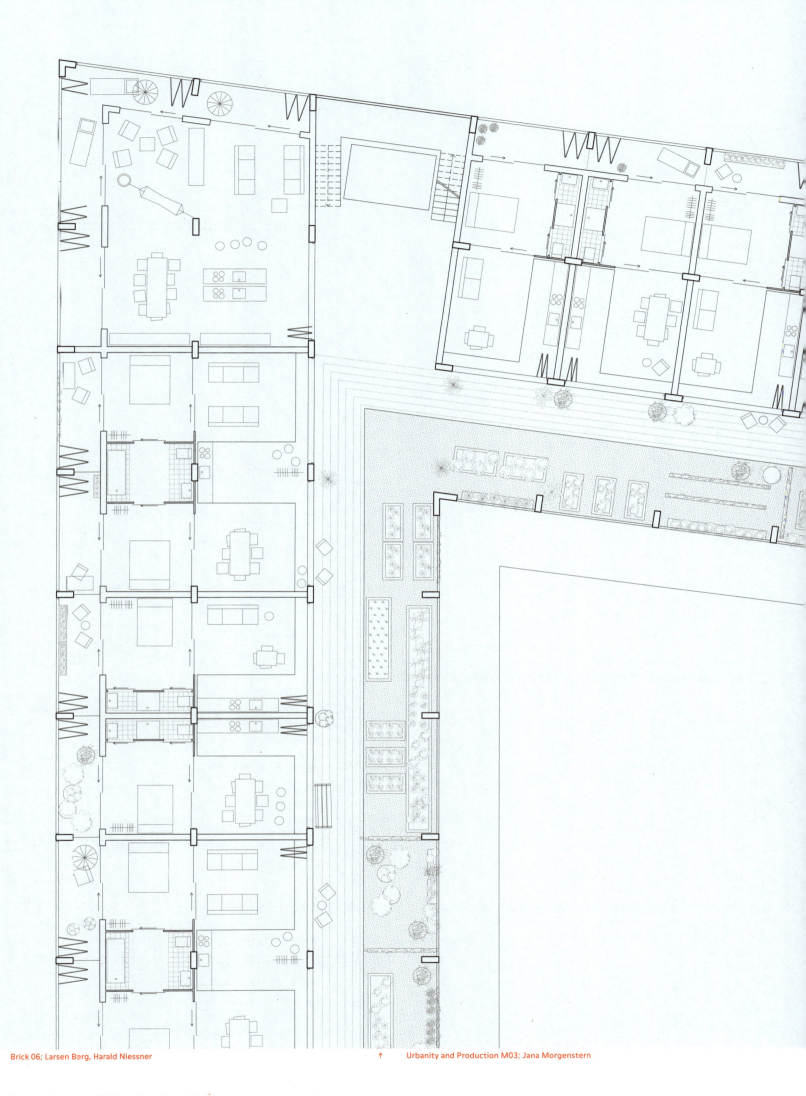

← Brick 06; Larsen Berg, Harald Niessner ↑ Urbanity and Production M03; Jana Morgenstern

Studierende der TU Berlin: Vom Wohnen.
Möblierte Grundrisse im Massstab 1:150

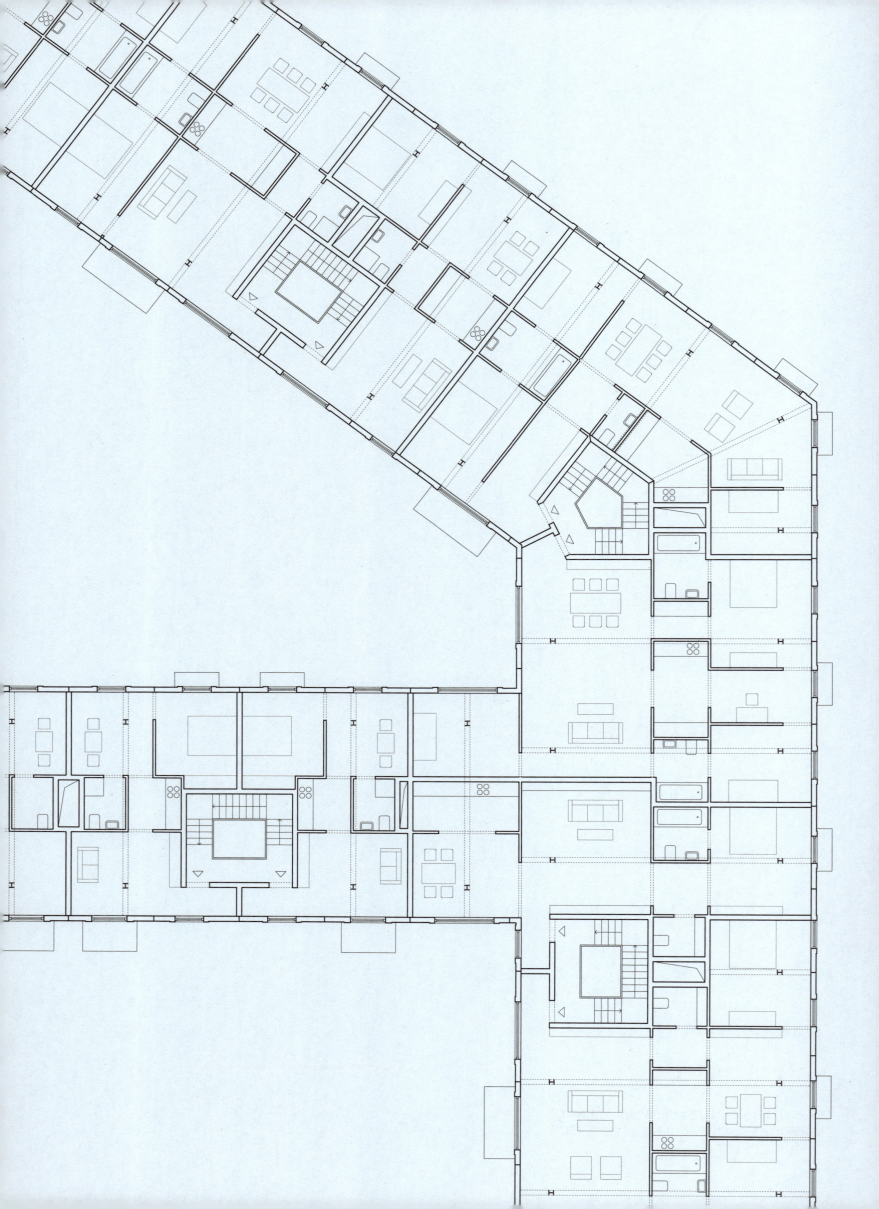

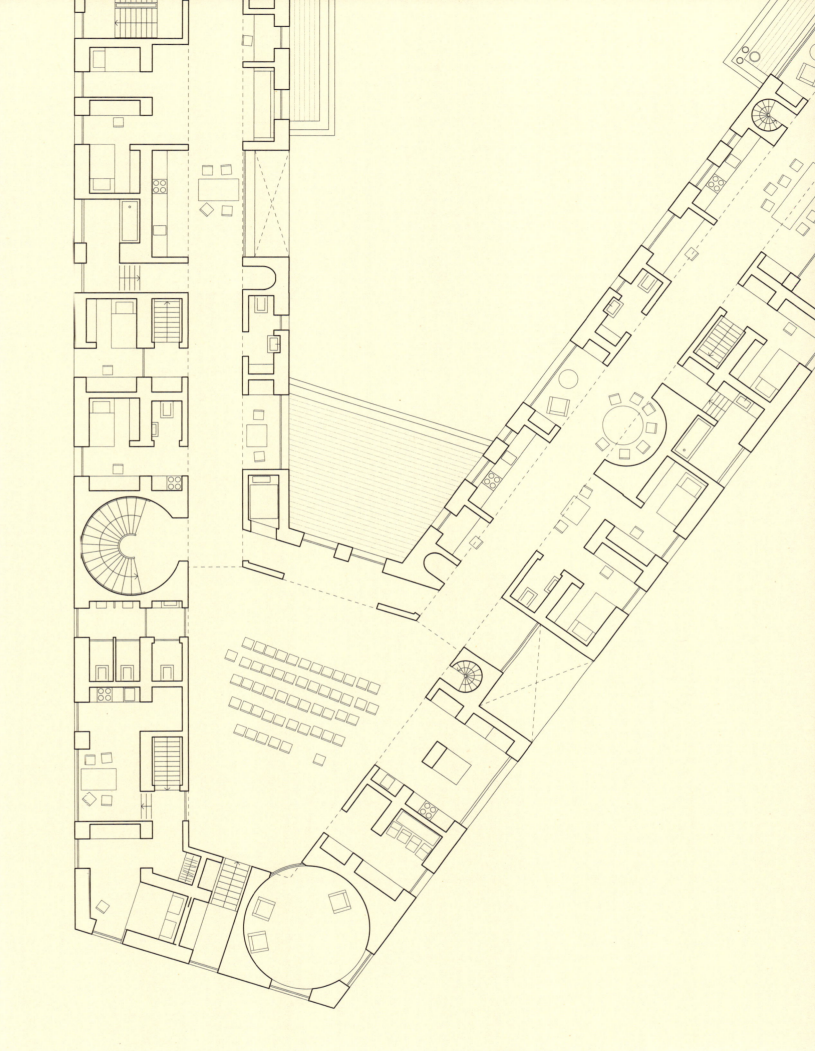

← Steel 03; Hanna Grabmaier, Julia Naomi Henning, Lisa Nagy   ↑ Brick 01; Julius Blencke, Caspar Kollmeyer, Jan Wind

Studierende der TU Berlin: Vom Wohnen.
Möblierte Grundrisse im Massstab 1:150

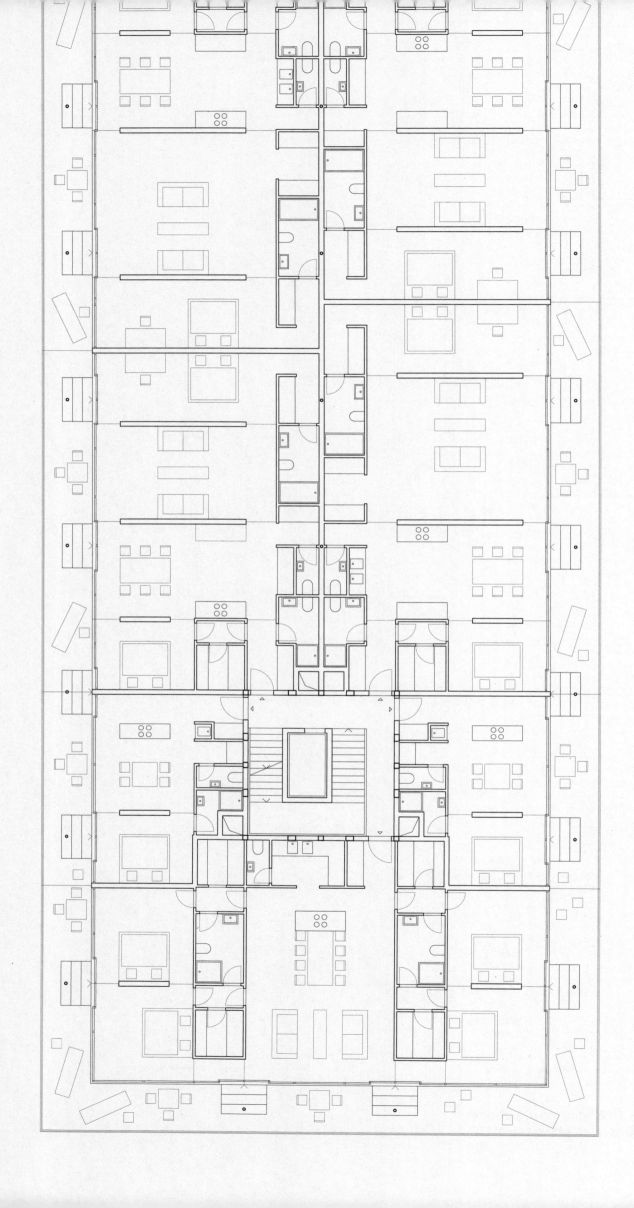

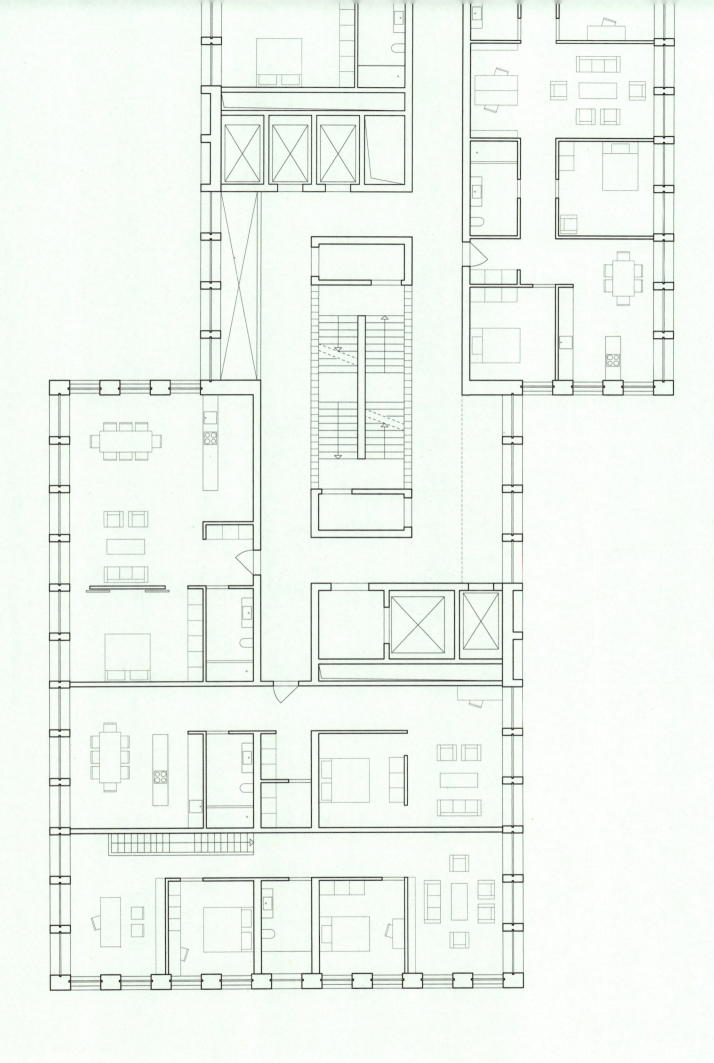

← Steel 05; Felix Bardou, Carlo Fischer   ↑ High Rise 16; Lisa Beyer, Justus Preyer, Max Werner

Studierende der TU Berlin: Vom Wohnen.
Möblierte Grundrisse im Massstab 1:150

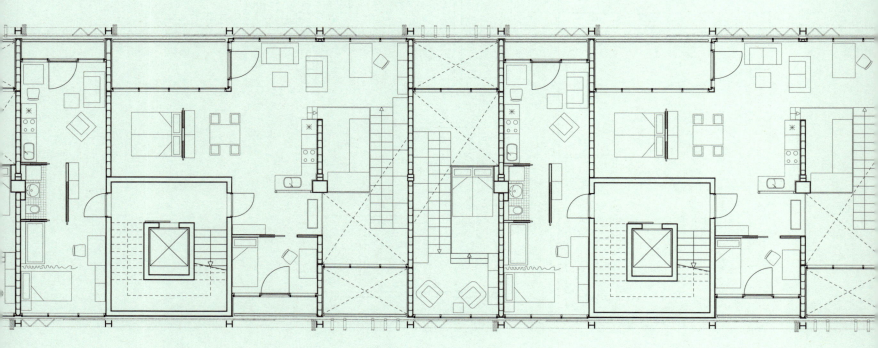

↑ Steel 11; Jialiang Cui, Liane Rosenthal

Students from the TU Berlin: On Housing.
Furnished Floor Plans on a Scale of 1:150

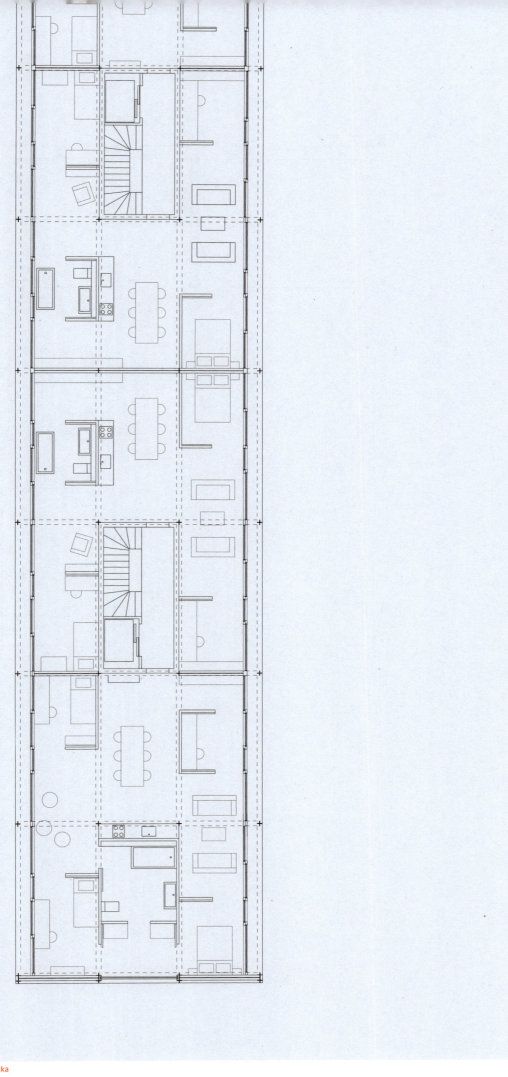

↑ Steel 02; Patryk Kujawa, Martyna Aleksandra Wojnarowska

Studierende der TU Berlin: Vom Wohnen.
Möblierte Grundrisse im Massstab 1:150

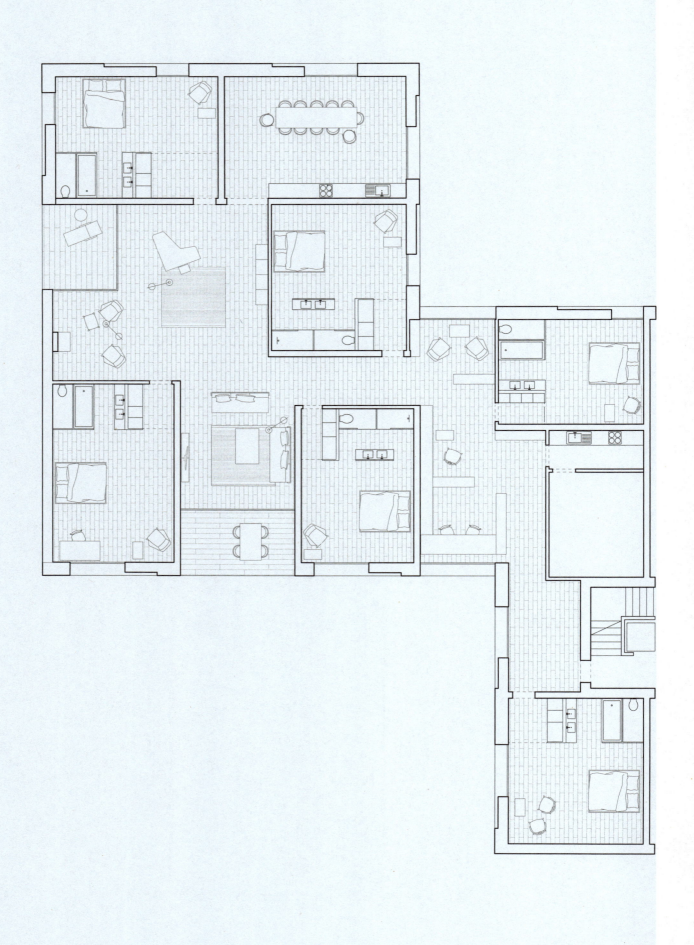

↑ Brick 04; Franziska Polleter, Simone Prill → High Rise 04; Merle Sudbrock, Roberta Zucchetti

Students from the TU Berlin: On Housing.
Furnished Floor Plans on a Scale of 1:150

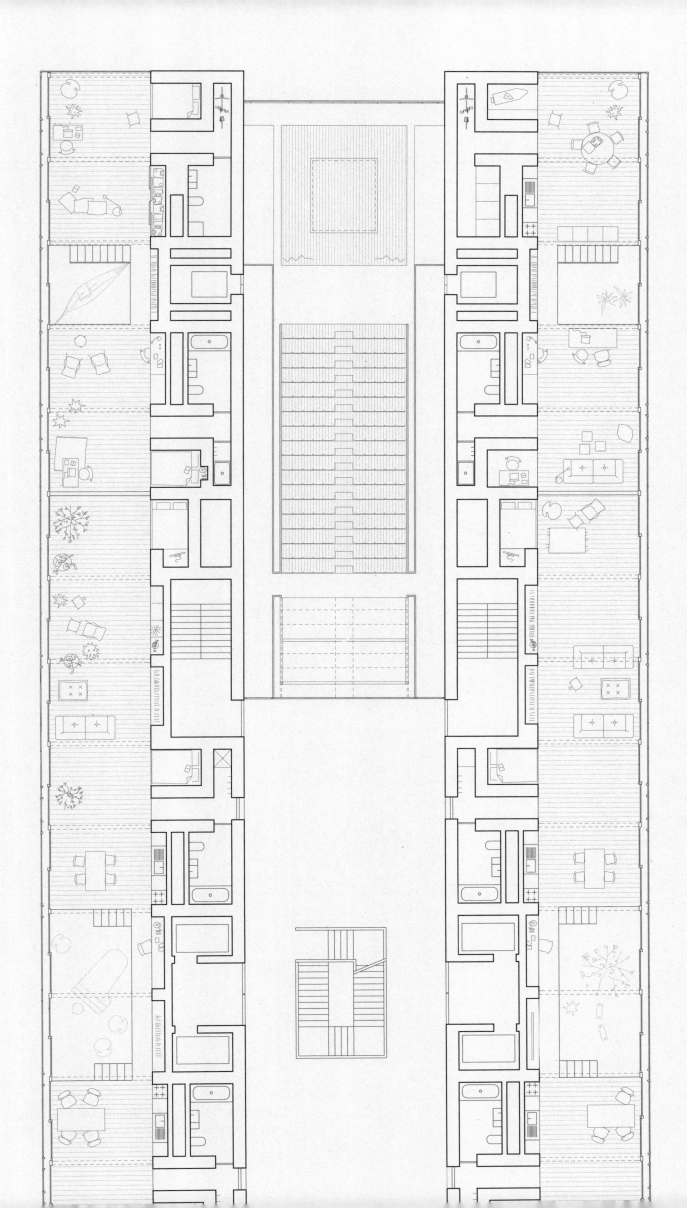

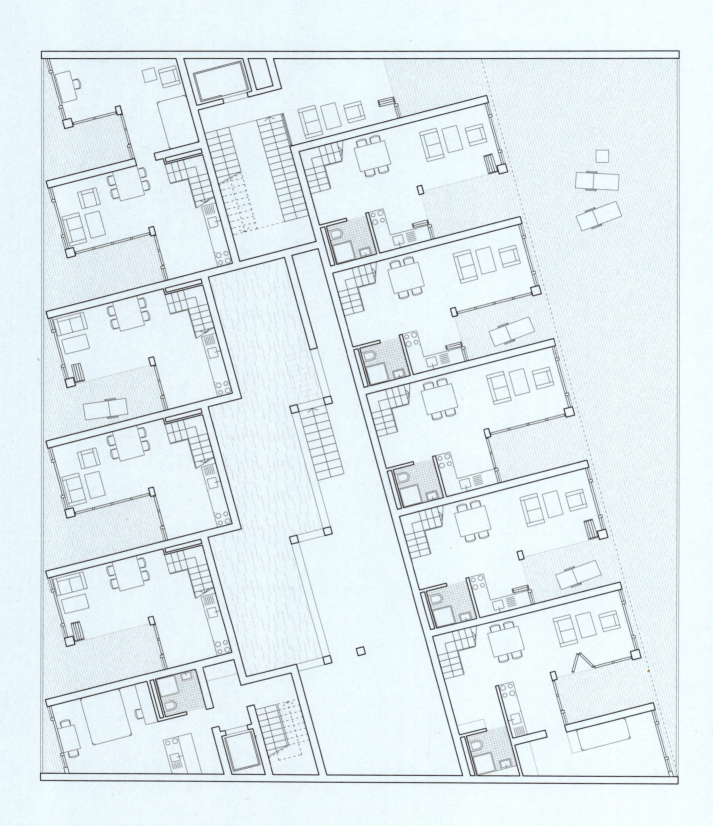

↑ Wood 13; Jannes Beulting, Dominik Schad

→ Brick 15; Sandra Schenavsky, Franziska Rüss

Students from the TU Berlin: On Housing.
Furnished Floor Plans on a Scale of 1:150

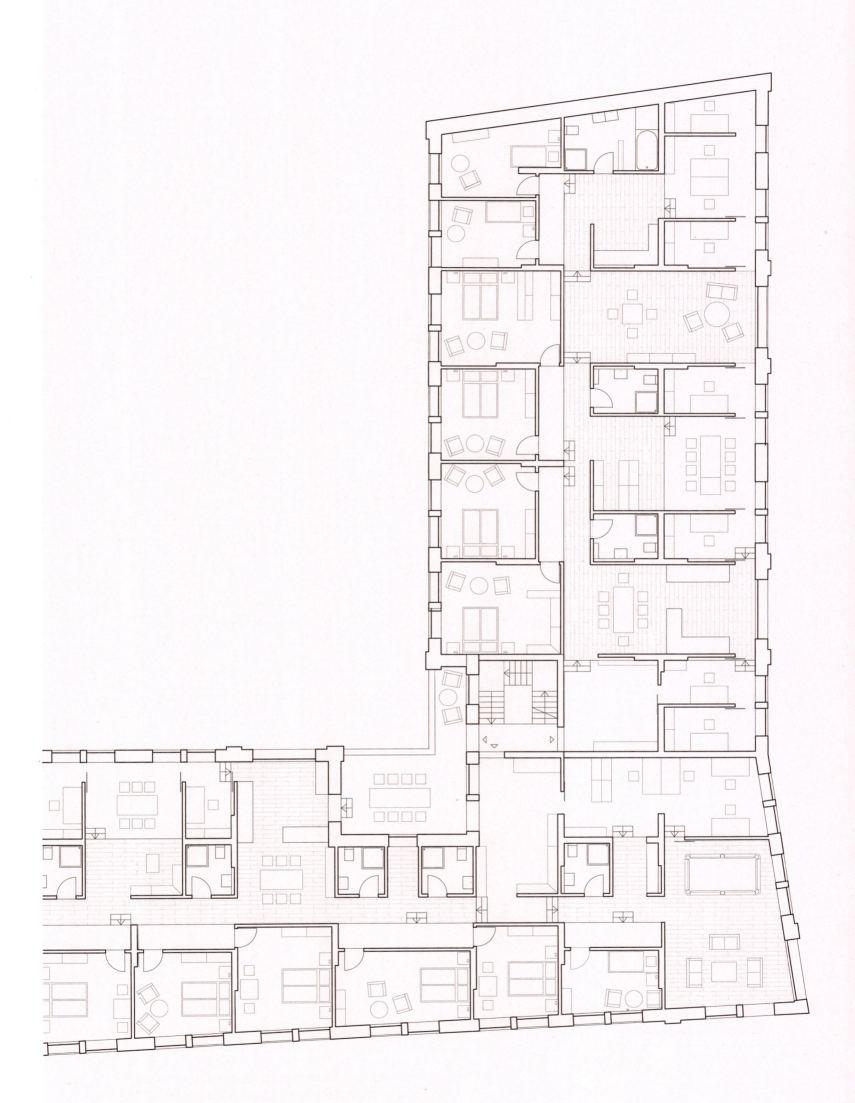

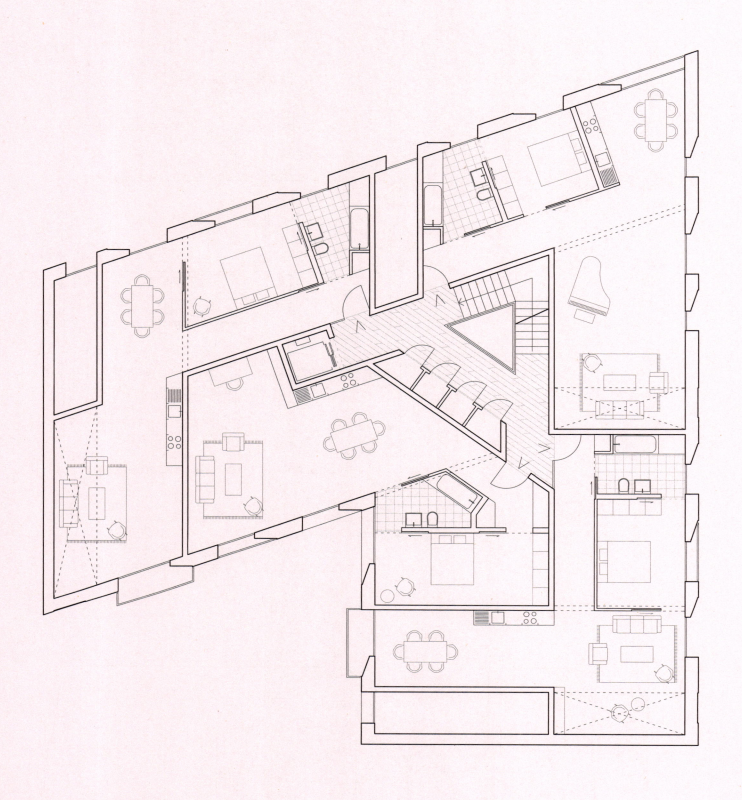

↑　Concrete 14; Tatjana Anic, Timo Lück

→　Concrete 13; Christopher Sitzler, Kristina Szeifert

Students from the TU Berlin: On Housing.
Furnished Floor Plans on a Scale of 1:150

354

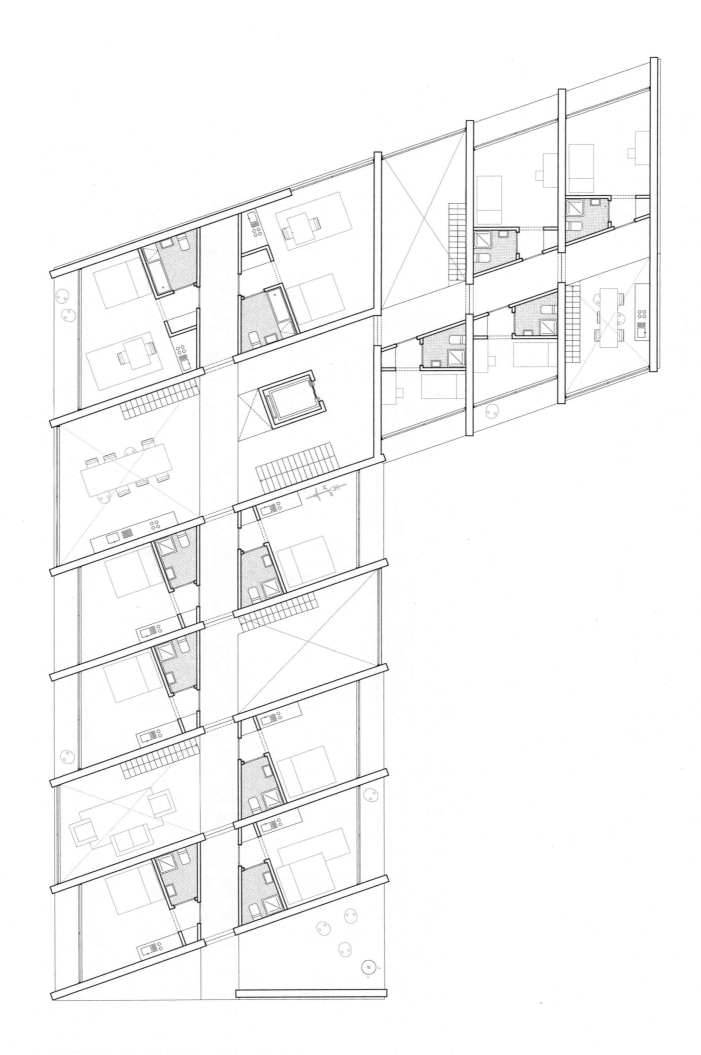

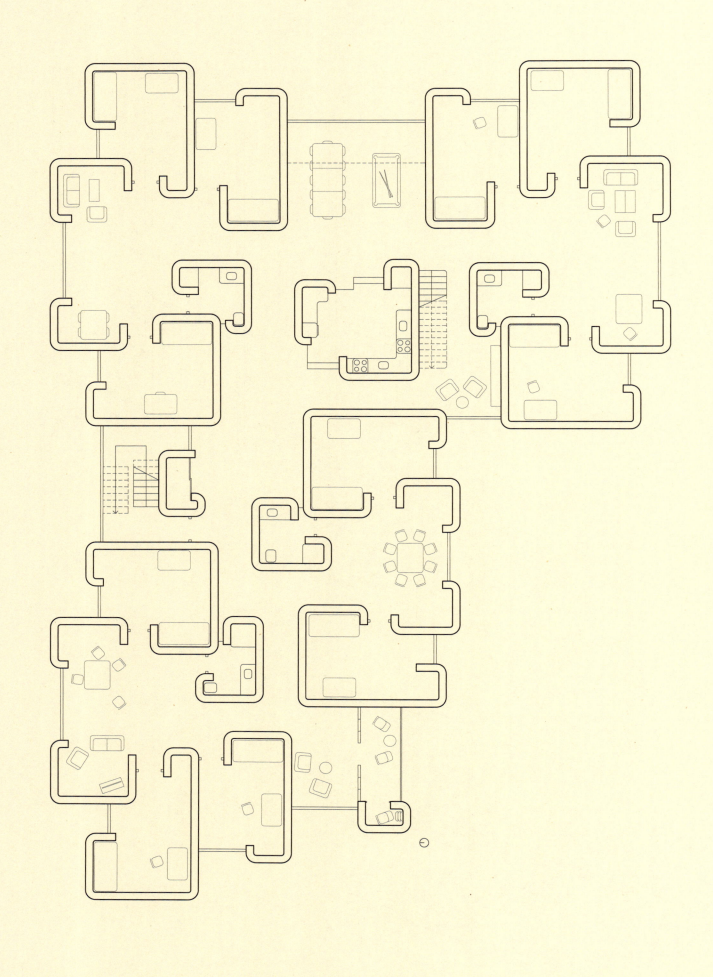

↑ College 11; Amer Eid, Michael Roth

Students from the TU Berlin: On Housing.
Furnished Floor Plans on a Scale of 1:150

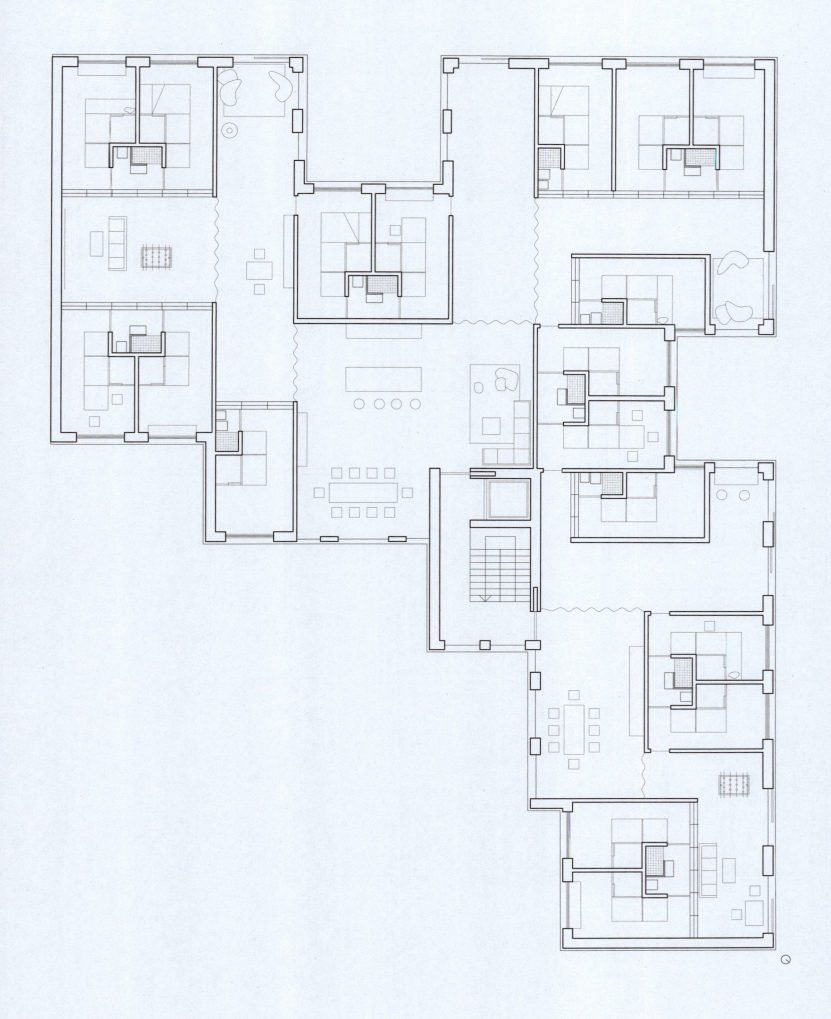

↑ Brick B04; Elizabeth Beckmann Zambrana

Studierende der TU Berlin: Vom Wohnen.
Möblierte Grundrisse im Massstab 1:150

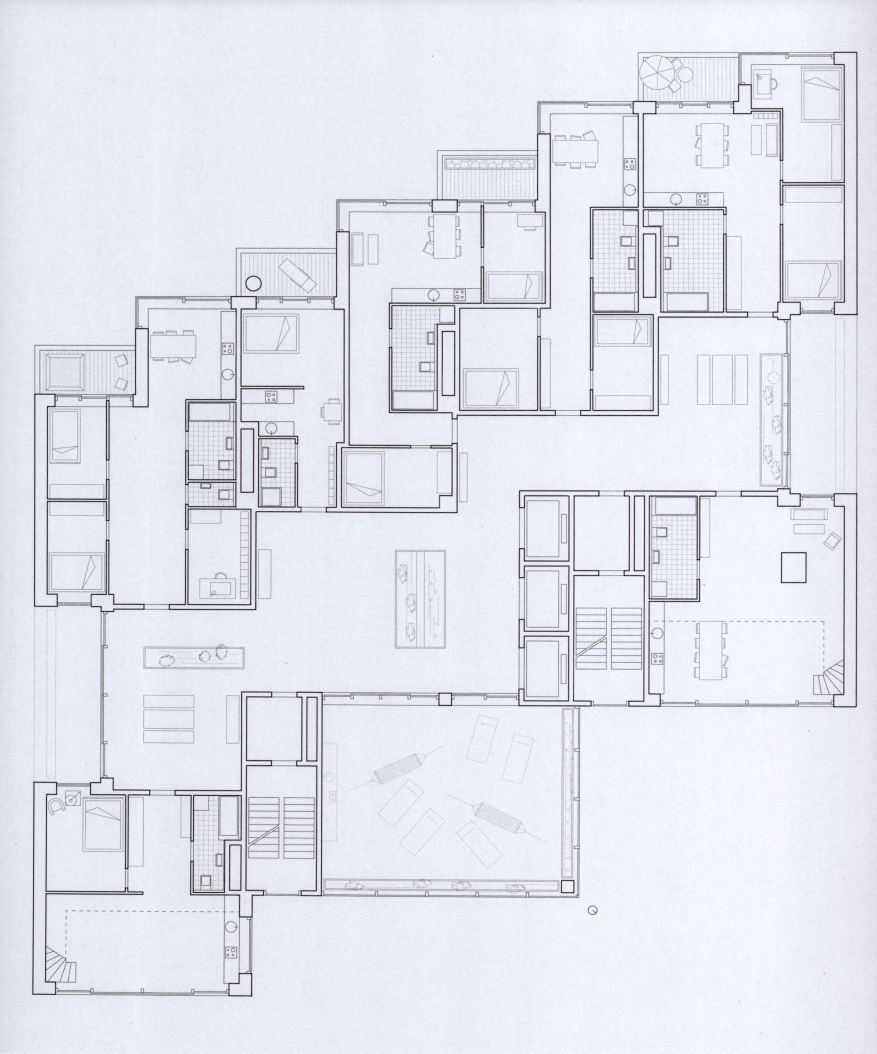

↑ High Rise 10; Paul Achter, Lorenz Preußer, Ivan Zilic

Students from the TU Berlin: On Housing.
Furnished Floor Plans on a Scale of 1:150

←

Studierende der
TU Berlin:
Vom Wohnen.
Möblierte Grundrisse
im Massstab 1:150

Students from
the TU Berlin:
On Housing.
Furnished Floor Plans
on a Scale of 1:150

Die Kultur
des Interieurs

The Culture
of the Interior

Die Kultur
des Interieurs

Das Interieur umfasst sowohl die innenräumlichen Zusammenhänge, die Raumproportionen, die Anordnung und Formulierung der strukturellen Elemente, die Gestaltung und den Umgang mit Türen, Fenstern und Übergängen, die Materialität, Beschaffenheit und Farbe der Oberflächen und den Einbau von Möbeln als auch die spätere Wohnfüllung. Dementsprechend beeinflusst das Interieur bereits in der Entwurfsphase die Auseinandersetzung mit den strukturellen und konstruktiven Elementen der Architektur. Ein Raum, der durch Stützen und Unterzüge rhythmisiert wird und über raumhohe Öffnungen mit anderen Räumen verbunden ist, hat eine andere Atmosphäre und trifft eine andere Aussage als ein Raum, der von Wänden begrenzt ist, in denen Fenster, Türen, aber auch Innenfenster einen Ausschnitt in der Wand bilden. Eine weisse Wand mit einer verputzten Oberfläche weckt andere Assoziationen als eine Wand aus Sichtmauerwerk, Beton oder Holz. Eine doppelflügelige Tür in einem «schweren» Rahmen stellt einen anderen Übergang dar als eine Schiebetür, die unsichtbar in einer Verkleidung verschwindet, oder eine kleine Tapetentür, die ein Geheimnis verbirgt.

Denkt man das Interieur mit, entsteht eine Einheit der architektonischen Elemente — von den Rohbauelementen bis zu den Möbeln. Diese Einheit beruht jedoch nicht nur oder nicht zwangsläufig auf einer Gestaltungsabsicht, sondern sie basiert auf einer Geschichte, die erzählt wird. In der Geschichte geht es um grosse oder kleine Gesten, um Geheimnisse und Offenheit, Verstecken und Zeigen.

Die Inszenierung des Interieurs

Mit dem Entstehen des aufstrebenden Bürgertums Anfang des 19. Jahrhunderts gehörte das Planen von Wohnhäusern vermehrt zum Aufgabenbereich der Architekten. John Soane war einer der Architekten, die sich dezidiert mit dem adäquaten Ausdruck von Wohninterieurs auseinandersetzten.[1] Seine Vorlesungen, die er 1809–1839 an der Royal Academy in London hielt, geben Hinweise auf seine Haltung bezüglich des Interieurs.[2] Den Gebäuden der Antike folgend, sollte die Architektur einer Skulptur gleichen, bei der sich alle Teile vereinen und ein Ganzes bilden.[3] Das galt sowohl für die äussere Erscheinung als auch für das Interieur.

1 John Soane, «Lecture VIII — The Distribution and Planning of Rooms and Staircases», in: John Soane, *Lectures on Architecture*, hrsg. von Arthur T. Bolton, Sir John Soane's Museum, London 1929, S.121ff.
2 Ebd.
3 Ebd., S. 121

Die Kultur des Interieurs

The interior of a building encompasses internal relationships, spatial proportions, the arrangement and formulation of structural elements, the design and treatment of doors, windows, and passageways, the materiality, qualities, and colors of surfaces, the installation of fixed furniture, and the addition of other furnishings and accoutrements. Even during the design process, the interior can influence the the structural and constructive elements of a project. A room that is characterized by supports and beams, and is linked to other rooms through ceiling-height openings, has a different atmosphere and makes a different statement from a room that is delimited by walls, and in which windows and doors form incisions in the walls. A white wall with a plastered surface evokes different associations than one consisting of exposed masonry, concrete, or wood. A double-wing door with a "heavy" frame effects a different type of transition to a sliding door that disappears from view into wall paneling, or a concealed door that harbors a secret.

If one thinks the interior through to the end, then a unity of architectonic elements emerges —from the building's shell all the way to its furnishings. This unity does not however necessarily rest solely on a design intention, but is instead based on a story that is being narrated. In this story, it is a question of large or small gestures, of secrets and openness, concealment and display.

The Scenography of the Interior

With the emergence of a striving, ambitious bourgeoisie during the early nineteenth century, the planning of dwellings was increasingly the responsibility of architects. John Soane is one of the architects who was preoccupied with the adequate expression of residential interiors.[1] The lectures he delivered at the Royal Academy in 1809–1839 provide clues concerning his attitude toward the interior.[2] Following the buildings of antiquity, architecture should, according to Soane, resemble a sculpture whose parts are united to form a whole.[3] This is true for the building's outer aspect as well as for its interior. Symmetry, continuity, harmony, and character should permeate even the smallest parts, and should be continued to the furnishings as well, so that the whole is deducible from the smallest part.

1 John Soane, *Lectures on Architecture*, ed. Arthur T. Bolton, London 1929, p. 121ff.
2 Ibid.
3 Ibid., p. 121.

Symmetrie, Kontinuität, Harmonie und Charakter sollten selbst die kleinsten Teile durchdringen und sich in der Möblierung fortsetzen, sodass man von jedem kleinsten Teil auf das Ganze schliessen kann.

Jenseits der angemessenen Wahl von Form, Grösse, Proportionierung und Konstruktion der Räume und ihrer einzelnen Teile ging es Soane um den Effekt oder die Wirkung, die durch die Komposition der Teile zueinander sowie durch die Lichtführung und die Bezüge entsteht. Die Komposition umfasst die Positionierung der Räume zueinander, die Raumhöhen und -proportionen, aber auch die Struktur des Gebäudes sowie die Anordnung von Fenstern, Türen und Treppen.[4] Gezielte Lichtführungen und Raumbezüge sollten den Charakter des Gebäudes unterstützen.[5] Inspiriert von den französischen Künstlerateliers mit ihrem «lumière mysterieuse» positionierte er Fenster oberhalb der Zimmergesimse oder Laternen in Deckengewölben und nutzte das mysteriöse, gedämpfte Licht zur Rauminszenierung und Unterstützung des architektonischen Ausdrucks.

Ein weiteres szenisches Element seiner Architektur bildeten die Übergänge — Flure, Treppen und Wandöffnungen dienten dem Dialog der einzelnen Teile[6] und ihre Lage, Proportion und Grösse sollten nicht nur dem Charakter und der Grösse des Ganzen entsprechen, sondern wurden gleichsam inszeniert. Dreh-, Flügel-, Schiebe- oder Falttüren in vielfältigen Ausführungen und Dimensionen, offene Wandöffnungen mit oder ohne Nischen schufen Zu-, Durch- und Übergänge, die die jeweilige spezifische Raumsituation charakterisierten.

Als Referenz für diese inszenatorische Durchbildung seiner Architektur diente ihm die griechische und römische Antike,[7] die es verstand, durch eine einheitliche Durchformung der einzelnen Teile und des Ganzen die Vorstellungskraft und die Aufmerksamkeit der Bewohner und Besucher zu wecken. Einheitlichkeit in der Materialität, die Balance in der Komposition, die auf dem ausgewogenen Verhältnis von Massivität und Leere («solidity and voids») beruht, sowie die Ausbildung von Abfolgen vielfältiger Formen und konstanter, regelmässiger Bewegungen der Teile sind Kennzeichen der klassischen Architektur, so Soane.[8]

Die Wirkung der von ihm aufgestellten Prinzipien zum Interieur veranschaulichen besonders seine Bank von England und sein eigenes Wohnhaus[9]. Das Wohnhaus und Museum besteht aus einem Netz kleiner Innen- und Aussenräume, deren vielfältige räumliche und visuelle Zusammenhänge und Bezüge sich mit der Bewegung durch den Raum verändern und immer wieder zu Überraschungen führen. Nebenräume wie Küche, Waschküche, Bedienstetenzimmer, Flure und Büro sind ebenso Teil seines räumlichen Geflechts wie die repräsentativen Räume, zu denen der Frühstücksraum, das Esszimmer, die Gemäldegalerie oder die Bibliothek gehören.

Diagonale und axiale Blickbezüge von Raum zu Raum oder über mehrere Räume hinweg — wie zum Beispiel der Blick vom Monument Court zum Monk's Hof — werden

For Soane, rooms and their individual parts should act beyond the appropriate choice of form, scale, proportions, and construction. They should contribute to the effect produced by the composition of parts in relation to one another as well as through the lighting arrangement. The composition encompasses the configuration of rooms in relation to one another, the heights and proportions of rooms, arrangement of windows, doors and staircases, and the structure of a building.[4]

Purposeful lighting and relationships between rooms should reinforce a building's character.[5] Inspired by the French artist's atelier, with its "lumière mysterieuse," Soane positions windows above a room's cornice or lamps in ceiling vaults, and uses a mysterious, muted light to characterize the room, and to support the architectonic expression.

A further scenic element of his architecture is formed by transitions. Hallways, staircases, and wall openings serve to generate dialogues between individual parts.[6] Their location, proportions, and size should not only correspond to the character and size of the whole, but should also express their own atmospheric character: revolving, winged, sliding, or folding doors in multifarious designs and dimensions; unobstructed wall openings with or without niches forming approaches; passageways, and transitions which serve to characterize the respective spatial situation.

Greek and Roman antiquity served as references for the dramatic staging of Soane's architecture.[7] These examples were capable—through the unified shaping of the individual parts and of the whole—of arousing the powers of imagination or fantasy, as well as the attention of residents and visitors. The trademarks of classical architecture were, according to Soane, consistency in materiality, compositional balance (the relation between solids and voids), as well as the articulation of sequences and the constant, regular movement of individual parts.[8]

The impact of the principles concerning the interior are particularly evident in his Bank of England and his own residence.[9] His home and museum consists of a network of small interior and exterior spaces whose multifarious spatial and visual connections are transformed by movement in space, and which repeatedly produce a sense of astonishment. Ancillary rooms such as kitchen, laundry room, service rooms, corridors, and office, are as much elements of his spatial web as the representative rooms, among them the breakfast room, dining room, painting gallery, and library.

Diagonal and axial views from room to room or across multiple rooms—the view, for example, from Monument Court to Monk's Yard—are achieved via passageways, glazed doors, or interior windows. At the same time, mirrors on walls and in cupolas extend or feign realities, generating theatrical spatial effects. Varied room heights— from one-story spaces with flat

---

4   Soane, wie Anm. 1, S. 123
5   Ebd., S. 126
6   Ebd., S. 136
7   Ebd., S. 132
8   Ebd., S. 133
9   Sein Wohnhaus und Museum in 13 Lyncoln's Inn Fields hat er zwischen 1812 und 1825 erbaut und um ein Museum ergänzt.

4   Ibid. p. 123; Soane speaks of the scale and character of the building, all of whose parts are to be subordinated in favor of symmetry. Elsewhere, he mentions French architecture and its handling of the composition and arrangement of complicated parts of architecture, with an eye toward convenience and effect.
5   Ibid., p. 126.
6   Ibid., p. 136.
7   Ibid., p. 132.
8   Ibid., p. 133.
9   Soane built his residence and museum at 13 Lincoln's Inn Fields, London, between 1812 and 1825. Beginning with a small plot, he acquired the neighboring plots over the course of the years, expanding his residence and supplementing it with a museum.

über Durchgänge, verglaste Türen oder Innenfenster hergestellt. Gleichzeitig erweitern oder verfälschen Spiegel an Wänden und in Kuppeln die Realitäten und sorgen für theatralische räumliche Effekte. Unterschiedliche Raumhöhen eingeschossiger Räume mit Flachdecken oder mehrgeschossiger Räume mit Galerien und Kuppelkonstruktionen sorgen für Kontraste und Spannungen und verstärken den dramatischen Effekt.

Selbst die Struktur des Hauses ordnete Soane der gewünschten Wirkung unter: Ebenso wie der Museumsraum aussermittig unter der Kuppel platziert ist, um einer Tribüne mit doppelter Höhe Platz zu machen, ist der rechteckige Raum des Frühstückzimmers von einer quadratischen Kuppel bekrönt, um in den verbleibenden schmalen Deckennischen Oberlichter anzuordnen. Es ist das poetische Element, das Narrative, die atmosphärische Dichte, die seine Architektur auszeichnen.[10] Soane selbst sprach von der Poesie der Architektur, als er seinen Frühstücksraum beschrieb.

Das massgeschneiderte Interieur

Dieses architektonische Feld der Auseinandersetzung mit dem Wohninterieur, das Soane Anfang des 19. Jahrhunderts eröffnete, blieb jedoch vorerst unbeachtet. Mit der Industrialisierung, dem Entstehen der Grossstädte und dem gründerzeitlichen Massenwohnungsbau wurde das Interieur auf das bewegliche Mobiliar reduziert. Erst siebzig Jahre später rückte es erneut in den Fokus der Aufmerksamkeit der Architekten — dieses Mal galt deren Interesse der gesellschaftlichen Bedeutung.

Adolf Loos kritisierte in seinen Schriften das Diktat des bürgerlichen Einrichtungsstils, der über Inklusion oder Exklusion in der Gesellschaft entschied, und propagierte das individuelle, «stillose» Interieur. Im Gegensatz zu Soane ging es ihm nicht um die Wirkung und die räumlichen Effekte, sondern um das Interieur als Spiegelbild eines individuellen Lebensstils. Seine hochspezifischen Räume zeichneten das Leben der Bewohner nach — die Essnische mit integrierten Bänken sowie Wäsche- und Geschirrschränke waren als Einbauten Teil der architektonischen Komposition. In dem massgeschneiderten Interieur choreografierte der Architekt das Leben der Bewohner, bot den grösstmöglichen Komfort und liess keine Bedürfnisse offen.

Raumbezüge, Raumproportionen, Lichtverhältnisse, Farben, Oberflächen, Materialien und strukturelle Elemente wie Stützen, Wandpfeiler oder Unterzüge bildeten bei ihm eine Gesamtkomposition, die individuell und auf die Möbel der Bewohner abgestimmt war. Vielgestaltigkeit und Raum für den persönlichen Ausdruck der Bewohner stellten die Grundlage seiner Entwürfe dar.

Diese Denkweise und Entwurfsmethodik zeichnete sich ebenso in seiner Lehre an der von ihm gegründeten Bauschule in Wien ab, deren Lehrplan ausschliesslich Inneren Ausbau, Kunstgeschichte und Materialkunde umfasste. Die Studierenden lernten bei ihm, wie Projekte

roofs to multistoried rooms with galleries and cupola constructions—generate contrast and tension, enhancing this theatrical effect.

Even the building's overall structure is subordinated to the desired effect. Just as the museum space is positioned eccentrically beneath the cupola in order to make space for a double-height tribune, the rectangular space of the breakfast room is crowned by a shallow square dome in order to configure skylights in the remaining ceiling recesses. It is this poetic element, its narrative and atmospheric density, that characterizes his architecture.[10] When describing the breakfast room, Soane himself speaks of the poetry of architecture.

The Customized Interior

The field of the residential interior which Soane opened up was, however, initially overlooked. With industrialization, the rise of large cities, and the large-scale residential development during the mid-nineteenth century "Gründerzeit" in Germany, the interior was mostly considered as movable furnishings. It took another seventy years for the interior to shift into the attention of architects, this time by virtue of its potential social significance.

In his writings, Adolf Loos criticizes the dictates of bourgeois interior furnishing, which determined social inclusion or exclusion, instead advocating a "styleless" interior.

In contrast to Soane, Loos was concerned not with spatial effects, but with the interior as a reflection of individual lifestyle. His highly specific rooms trace out the lives of their inhabitants: the dining niche with built-in benches and washing or dish cupboards are elements of the architectonic composition. In the customized interior, the architect choreographs the lives of the occupants, providing maximum comfort and leaving no function unaddressed.

For Loos, spatial relationships and proportions, lighting arrangement, colors, surfaces, and materials, as well as structural elements such as supports, wall pillars, and joists form a total composition which is coordinated individually and with specificity in relation to the furnishings of the inhabitants. Diversity and variety, along with space for personal expression on the part of inhabitants, are the foundations of his approach to design.

This way of thinking and this design methodology are in evidence as well in his teachings at the building school he founded, whose curriculum encompassed interior design, art history, and materials science. His students learned to execute a design from the interior outwards. "Floors and ceilings…were primary, the façade secondary. The primary weight was on the smallness of the axes (in ceilings and windows), on the right furnishings. In this way, I taught my students to think three-dimensionally in the cube." [11]

---

10 «[…] Some of the Poems have raised fine architectural Edifices, but most rare have been those who have discovered when they had finished their House, […] that they had built a Poem. All this you have accomplished.» Zitiert nach: *John Soane, Architect: Master of Space and Light*, Ausst.-Kat. Royal Academy of Arts, London 1999

10 "… Some of the Poems have raised fine architectural Edifices, but most rare have been those who have discovered when they had finished their House, …, that they had built a Poem. All this you have accomplished." From *John Soane, Architect: Master of Space and Light*, exhibition catalogue, London 1999.
11 Adolf Loos, "Meine Bauschule," 1913, in *Adolf Loos. Über Architektur*, Vienna 1995, p. 120.

von innen nach aussen gestaltet werden. «Fussboden und Decke [...] war das Primäre, die Fassade das Sekundäre. Auf die Kleinheit der Achsen (im Plafond und Fenster), auf die richtige Möblierung wurde das grösste Gewicht gelegt. Auf diese Weise brachte ich meine Schüler dazu, dreidimensional im Kubus zu denken.»[11]

Dieses dreidimensionale Entwickeln des Interieurs zeigt sich besonders deutlich bei der Villa Müller, die er 1930 in Prag baute. Räume mit unterschiedlichen Raumhöhen auf zueinander versetzten Niveaus werden durch Verglasungen und Wandöffnungen in Beziehung gesetzt, Treppen, in Wandnischen verborgen oder als integraler Bestandteil der eingebauten Möbel, überwinden die Ebenensprünge, strukturelle Elemente wie Stützen oder Unterzüge sind Teil der eingebauten Möbel, Decken- und Wandbekleidungen aus Marmor oder Holz gehen nahtlos in Einbauschränke und Sitzmöbel über. Jeder Raum ist ein Ereignis und die Bewegung von Raum zu Raum ist geprägt durch überraschende, neue Perspektiven, die versteckte Teile oder Bezüge und Verbindungen offenbaren.

Inspirationsquelle seiner Auffassung von Stil und Architektur sowie der von ihm propagierten «handwerklichen» Interieurs waren die einfachen Bauernhäuser sowie sein dreijähriger Aufenthalt in den USA, wo er eine von «modernen Menschen» geprägte Gesellschaft und Architektur vorfand.

Das charakteristische Interieur

Mit dem Menschen oder dem Menschlichen als Ausgangspunkt und Fluchtpunkt entwickelte Frank Lloyd Wright ebenso wie Loos seine Architektur von innen nach aussen. Jedoch war bei Wright die Einbindung der Architektur in die Umgebung ein wesentlicher Aspekt seiner Entwürfe und prägendes Element seiner Interieurs. Das Ineinandergreifen von Landschaft und Haus setzt sich im Inneren in Form fliessender Raumübergänge und als Verzahnung von Wand und Mobiliar fort. Dieses Verständnis von Raum und Raumzusammenhängen, das sich auch in der Materialität ausdrückt, subsumierte Wright unter dem Begriff des «Organischen» folgendermassen: «Organisch bedeutet wahr — im philosophischen Sinn wesentlich — überall dort, wo sich das Ganze zum Teil verhält wie der Teil zum Ganzen und wo die Natur der Materialien, die Natur des Zweckes, die Natur der gesamten Ausführung als Notwendigkeit klar wird. Aus dieser Natur ergibt sich, welchen Charakter man dem Gebäude in jeder besonderen Lage als schöpferischer Künstler verleihen kann.»[12]

Im Organischen verschmelzen Innen und Aussen zu einer Einheit — sowohl räumlich als auch im Material. Diese Haltung, diese Suche nach dem Ausdruck der Natur oder des Wesens der Dinge, der Handlungen und der Bestimmung erzeugte den Charakter in Wrights Architektur. Seine Mauern sind keine Mauern mehr, sondern «Charakteristika» oder «determinierende

This three-dimensional development of the interior is displayed with special clarity in his Villa Müller, which he built in Prague in 1930. Rooms with varied heights and on contrasting levels that are staggered in relation to one another are linked via glazing and wall openings. Staircases, concealed in wall niches or as integrated components of built-in furniture, overcome transitions between levels. Structural elements such as supports or joists are elements of the built-in furniture. Ceilings and cladding in marble or wood merge seamlessly with built-in cabinets and seating furniture.

Each room is an event and movement from room to room is characterized by astonishing new perspectives which disclose concealed elements or interrelationships and interconnections.

Simple farmhouses, and his three-year stay in America, where he discovered a society and an architecture that had been shaped by "modern people" served as inspiration for his conception of style, architecture, and the "handcrafted" interior.

The Characteristic Interior

Like Loos, Frank Lloyd Wright developed his architecture from the inside outwards, and with the human individual as a point of departure and vanishing point. With Wright, the integration of architecture into its surroundings was an essential aspect of the design and a decisive element of his interiors. The dialogue between landscape and dwelling continues on the inside in the form of flowing spatial transitions and the interlinking of walls and furnishings. Wright considered this understanding of space and spatial relationships, also explored through materiality, as follows: "Organic means—in [the] philosophic sense—entity, where the whole is to the part as the part is to the whole, and where the nature of the materials, the nature of the purpose, the nature of the entire performance becomes a necessity, and out of that comes what significance you can give the building as a creative artist."[12]

In the "organic," the interior and exterior fuse to form a unity, both spatially and materially. This attitude, the search for the expression of "nature" or the essence of things, actions, and purposes generates character in architecture. His walls are no longer walls, but instead "characteristic features," "and the features were screens grouped about interieur space."[13] The characteristic features of his interiors emerge through the untreated materiality of load-bearing and non-supporting elements as well as through fixtures and formation of transitions.

Walls are broken up into the vertical and horizontal, becoming short wall segments, wall pillars, niches, or railings. This principle is continued on the exterior, so that the garden and courtyard zones become elements of the interior. Reinforcing the horizontal organization and textile character of the wall are material

---

11 Adolf Loos, «Meine Bauschule», 1913, in: *Adolf Loos. Über Architektur*, Wien 1995, S. 120
12 Frank Lloyd Wright, *The Future of Architecture*, 1953. Dt. Fassung: *Die Zukunft der Architektur*, München 1966, S. 9

12 Frank Lloyd Wright, "A Conversation with Frank Lloyd Wright and Hugh Downs," broadcast by NBC on Sunday, May 17, 1953.
13 Frank Lloyd Wright, "Talk to the Taliesin Fellowship," 1952, from Bruce Brooks Pfeiffer, *Frank Lloyd Wright*, Cologne 2000, p. 24.

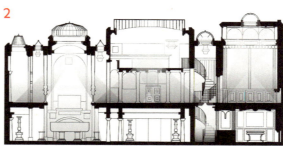

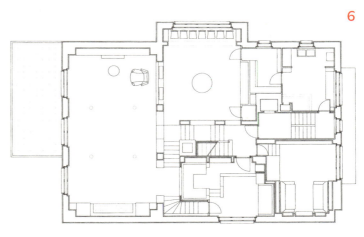

1–3 Wohnhaus und Museum, John Soane, London, 1792–1824;
     Verschmelzung von Raum und Interieur
4–6 Villa Müller, Adolf Loos, Praha, 1930; Bewegung und Blickbezüge

1–3 Residence and Museum, John Soane, London, 1792–1824; merging of space and interior
4–6 Villa Müller, Adolf Loos, Prague, 1930; movement and view axes

Die Kultur des Interieurs

7

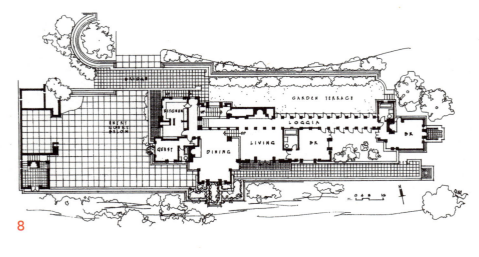

8

9 10

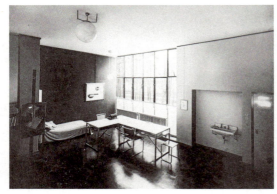

11

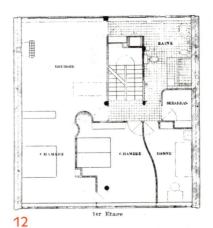

12

13

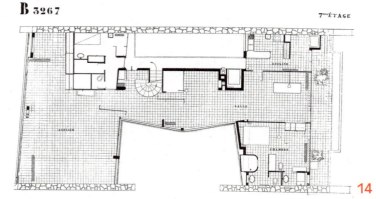

15

14

7/8   Charles Ennis House, Frank Lloyd Wright, Los Angeles/Kalifornien, 1924; textiler Charakter
9–11 Meisterhäuser am Bauhaus, Walter Gropius, Dessau, 1926; Interieur ist ein Spiegel der Gesellschaft
12/13 Maison Cook, Le Corbusier, Boulogne-sur-Seine, 1925; Durchformung der Räume
14/15 Immeuble Molitor, Le Corbusier, Paris, 1933; poetische Interieurs

7/8   Charles Ennis House, Frank Lloyd Wright, Los Angeles/California, 1924; textile character
9–11 Master's Houses at the Bauhaus, Walter Gropius, Dessau, 1926; the interior is a mirror of society
12/13 Maison Cook, Le Corbusier, Boulogne-sur-Seine, 1925; the shaping of spaces
14/15 Immeuble Molitor, Le Corbusier, Paris, 1933; poetic interior

The Culture of the Interior

Elemente, nämlich zum Innenraum geordnete Wandschirme».¹³ Das Charakteristische seiner Interieurs entsteht durch die roh belassene Materialität der tragenden und nicht tragenden Elemente und der Einbauten, dem Herausarbeiten der Funktion der jeweiligen Elemente sowie durch die Formulierung der Übergänge.

Die Wände lösen sich in der Vertikalen und in der Horizontalen auf und werden zu kurzen Wandstücken, Wandpfeilern, Nischen oder Brüstungen. Dieses Prinzip setzt sich in den Aussenräumen fort, und die Garten- und Hofräume werden so zu einem Teil des Innenraumes. Zusätzlich verstärken Materialwechsel, Einbauten oder Aussparungen die horizontale Gliederung und den textilen Charakter der Wände. Auf diese Weise entstehen Räume, die sich einem Bühnenraum gleich in der Weite oder Tiefe entwickeln und sich von den differenziert gestalteten, charaktervollen Wandschichten gegliedert als gestaffelte Raumfolgen mit unterschiedlichen Prospekten darstellen.

In den Zwischenkriegsjahren erfuhr die Auseinandersetzung mit dem Interieur eine neue Dynamik und Brisanz. Das Entstehen von Arbeiterbewegung und Gewerkschaften sowie die Politisierung der Gesellschaften und die Entwicklung von Demokratien um die Jahrhundertwende des 20. Jahrhunderts bildeten den Urgrund für das Neudenken der Gesellschaft im Privaten — Politisches und Privates waren nicht länger voneinander getrennt. Es galt, den Lebensstil und damit die Wohnung und das Interieur neu zu definieren und die Verschränkung von Individuum und Interieur als Ausdruck des Bürgertums einer monarchistisch geprägten Gesellschaft aufzulösen. «Das zwischen Innenraum und Innenleben entwickelte Netz fluktuierender Identifikationen und Analogien macht den im späten 19. Jahrhundert ausbrechenden Kampf um die Definitionsmacht des ‹guten Geschmacks› verständlich. […] Mit Diskursen um Technik, Komfort und Ästhetik wird das scheinbar stabile Verhältnis zwischen Innenraum, Dingen und Subjekten erneut zur Disposition gestellt.»¹⁴ Der Kampf um die «neue» Gesellschaft wurde über das Interieur ausgetragen.

Walter Benjamin demaskiert in seinem Essay «Spurlos Wohnen» von 1928 das Interieur mit seinen «überbevölkerten» und narrativ überlasteten Räumen, in denen kein Fleck ohne hinterlassene Spur sei, als «Falle».¹⁵ Für die Architekten im Umfeld des Neuen Bauens wurde die Wohnung zum politischen Manifest — der Wohnungsgrundriss und das Interieur sollten nicht länger Spiegelbild eines Individuums, sondern einer neuen Gesellschaft sein. Mit dem Satz «Das Haus ist eine Maschine zum Wohnen»¹⁶ postulierte Le Corbusier 1920 eine Wohnarchitektur, die sich an dem «lebensnotwendigen Minimum» orientiert und wie die Werkzeuge des Alltags — ein Ozeandampfer oder ein Flugzeug — ihre Funktion optimal erfüllt. Überlegungen zu der Minimalwohnung, die den Bedürfnissen der Kleinfamilie oder Alleinstehenden gerecht wird, oder zu der Wohnung des Existenzminimums für Arbeiter mit

13 Frank Lloyd Wright, «Talk to the Taliesin Fellowship», 1952, zitiert nach Bruce Brooks Pfeiffer, *Frank Lloyd Wright,* Köln 2000
14 Irene Nierhaus, «Störrisches Wohnen», in: *Wohnen Zeigen. Modelle und Akteure des Wohnens in Architektur und visueller Kultur,* Schriftenreihe wohnen +/- ausstellen, Bd. 1, Bielefeld 2014
15 Walter Benjamin, «Spurlos Wohnen», in: *Werke und Nachlass,* Bd. 8, Frankfurt am Main 2009, S. 111
16 «Une maison est une machine à habiter», schreibt Le Corbusier 1920 in einem Aufsatz in der Zeitschrift *L'Esprit Nouveau.*

contrasts, installations, and recesses. Emerging as a consequence are spaces which develop in breadth and depth like the stages of theaters, and which, subdivided by the differentiated design of characterful wall layers, are shaped as staggered spatial sequences with varying prospects.

During the interwar years, the theme of the interior acquired a new dynamism and explosiveness. The emergence of the worker's movement and labor unions, as well as the politicization of society and the introduction of democratic institutions around the turn of the twentieth century led to a rethinking of the social aspects of private life—political and private were no longer as segregated from one another. Lifestyles were redefined, as were apartments and their interiors with the intertwining of individual and interior as an expression of the bourgeoisie and of the disintegration of monarchical society. "The network of fluctuating identifications and analogies developed between the interior space and inner life renders comprehensible the struggle over 'good taste' that was incipient in the late nineteenth century […] Through discourses on technology, comfort, and aesthetics, the seemingly stable relationship between interior space, objects, and subjects, was now accessible to change."¹⁴ The struggle for a "new" society was enacted in relation to the interior.

In his essay *Spurlos Wohnen* (1928), Walter Benjamin unmasks the interior, with its "overpopulated" spaces, overloaded in narrative terms, where no "spot" fails to leave behind a "trace," as a kind of "trap."¹⁵ For architects in the milieu of the Neues Bauen, the apartment became a political manifesto. The apartment floor plan and the interior would no longer function as mirrors of the individual, but would instead represent a "new" society. In 1920, Le Corbusier declared "The house is a machine for living." He proposed a residential architecture that would be oriented toward the "minimum that was essential to life," and would fulfill its function optimally as a tool of everyday life; not unlike an ocean liner or an airplane.¹⁶ During the 1920s, architectural design was driven towards a minimum apartment that would satisfy the requirements of small families or singles, or to apartments designed to provide the existential minimum for workers with low incomes. Such apartments were primarily characterized by room sizes determined by functional requirements (contemporary guidelines concerning room sizes in social housing development are relics of this era). Activities such as cooking, eating, sleeping, play, and convivial gatherings were analyzed and assigned to tailor-made rooms. The Frankfurt kitchen as a space-optimized, efficient workspace for housewives is paradigmatic of this architectural approach. The functional apartment became a generally valid model for an entire stratum of society.

The work of the Neues Bauen was also characterized by strong interiors. But in contrast to the bourgeois residential architecture of the nineteenth

14 Irene Nierhaus, "Störrisches Wohnen", *Wohnen Zeigen. Modelle und Akteure des Wohnens in Architektur und visueller Kultur,* Bielefeld 2014
15 Walter Benjamin, "Spurlos Wohnen/Speisesaal", *Werke und Nachlass,* vol. 8, Frankfurt am Main 2009, p.111
16 "Une maison est une machine à habiter," wrote Le Corbusier in 1920 in an essay that appeared in the magazine *L'Esprit Nouveau.*

geringem Einkommen bestimmten die Architekturentwürfe der 1920er-Jahre. Gekennzeichnet waren die Wohnungen in erster Linie durch funktionsgebundene Raumgrössen, die dem jeweiligen Zweck entsprechend exakt austariert wurden (heutige Richtlinien zu Raumgrössen im sozialen Wohnungsbau sind Relikte aus dieser Zeit). Die jeweiligen Aktivitäten wie Kochen, Essen, Schlafen, Spielen und gemeinschaftliches Zusammensein wurden erfasst und spezifisch zugeschnittenen Räumen zugeordnet — die Frankfurter Küche als flächenoptimierter, effizienter Arbeitsraum der Hausfrau ist paradigmatisch für diesen architektonischen Ansatz. Die funktionale Wohnung wurde zum allgemeingültigen Modell einer ganzen Gesellschaftsschicht.

Jenseits dieses funktionalistischen Ansatzes war die Architektur der Protagonisten des Neuen Bauens jedoch gleichzeitig gekennzeichnet und geprägt von starken Interieurs. Doch in Abgrenzung zu der bürgerlichen Wohnarchitektur des 19. Jahrhunderts oder der Reformarchitektur des beginnenden 20. Jahrhunderts fussten die Interieurs auf neuen Raumkonzepten und entwickeln sich vertikal und horizontal im Volumen des ganzen Hauses.

Die Poesie des Interieurs

Besonders die Interieurs von Le Corbusiers Villen sind Zeugnisse dieser Denkweise. Auch wenn sein architektonischer Ansatz wesentlich puristischer und in diesem Sinne radikaler ist als der seiner Vorgänger, so kann sein Umgang mit dem Interieur dennoch als Fortsetzung gelesen werden.

Fern jeglicher Rationalität und Standardisierung sind seine Wohnungsgrundrisse geprägt von gekrümmten, geschwungenen oder diagonal angeordneten Wänden, eingeschobenen Räumen oder Raumteilen, die Nischen schaffen, Stützen, die in Abhängigkeit von ihrer Lage zur Wand unterschiedliche Formen und Dimensionen haben, Fassaden, die sich ausstülpen oder eine Schräge ausbilden sowie Treppen und Rampen mit skulpturalem Charakter. Diese individuelle Durchformung der Räume und Raumfolgen wird unterstützt oder unterstrichen durch die Wahl der Materialien und Farben. Rau oder glatt verputzte Oberflächen werden kombiniert mit Wänden aus Sichtmauerwerk und Glasbausteinen, mit Stahlstützen oder -fassaden sowie mit den Holzoberflächen der Einbauschränke und Schiebewände. Die Wand-, Decken- und Fussbodenoberflächen bilden Kompositionen aus kräftigen Farbtönen. Fenster- und Türöffnungen sind individuell, den jeweiligen Situationen entsprechend als raumgrosse Dreh- oder Schiebetür, mannshohe schmale Drehtür, Tapetentür oder schlicht ohne Tür ausgeformt.

Le Corbusiers Interieurs sind Zeugnisse eines Poeten. Es ist lyrische Ergriffenheit, die den Menschen veranlasst, sich in Bewegung zu setzen. Und das, was am Ende bleibt, ist nicht das, «was nützlich ist, sondern was bewegt»,[17] so Le Corbusier.

17 Le Corbusier, wie Anm. 16, S. 12

368

century and to the reformed architecture of the early twentieth century, the Neues Bauen approach to the interior was based on new spatial concepts developed in relation to the volume of the house as a whole.

The Poetry of the Interior

The interiors of Le Corbusier's villas in particular are testimonials to this way of thinking. Although his approach is often more purist, and so more radical, then that of his predecessors, his approach to the interior may nonetheless be regarded as a continuation of their work.

Devoid of any "rationality" or standardization, his apartment floor plans are characterized by bending, curving, or diagonally configured walls, interpolated rooms, supports of varied forms and dimensions, slanting façades, and sculptural staircases and ramps. This individual shaping of spaces and spatial sequences is reinforced and underscored by his choice of materials and colors. Untreated or smoothly plastered surfaces are combined with walls of exposed masonry or glass bricks, with steel supports or façades, as well as with the wooden surfaces of built-in cabinets and sliding walls. Walls, ceilings, and floor surfaces form chromatic compositions which display powerful tones. Windows and doors are adjusted in accordance with their respective positions. For example, doors can be ceiling-height, revolving, sliding, head-height, concealed, or simply absent.

His interiors have the touch of a poet. They hold a lyrical emotion that induces people to move through them. They are not, as Le Corbusier says, "what is useful, but what moves us…"[17]

17 Ibid., p. 12.

The Culture of the Interior

Das Interieur und das kulturelle Gedächtnis

Doch die Innenräume von Le Corbusier waren eine Ausnahme im Umfeld des Neuen Bauens und bereits Ende der 1920er-Jahre kritisierten insbesondere Kulturschaffende wie Walter Benjamin, Bertolt Brecht oder Siegfried Kracauer, aber auch Architekten wie Alvar Aalto die Sachlichkeit oder das diktatorische Prinzip des neuen Stils. Der Text «‹Nordseekrabben› oder Die moderne Bauhauswohnung» von Bertolt Brecht und Elisabeth Hauptmann, 1927 veröffentlicht, verstand sich als Kritik am Stilisierungsprozess des Neuen Wohnens.[18] Erneut hatte sich ein Stil mit normativem Charakter entwickelt: Stil in diesem Sinne steht für Kontrolle, Anpassung, Exklusion und das Diktat des Geschmacks.

Aalto formulierte seine Gegenposition zu den Architekten der Moderne erstmals 1922 in «Motifs from Times Past»[19]. Statt eines totalen Bruchs mit der Vergangenheit sollten die ästhetischen Werte der traditionellen Architektur in der zeitgemässen Architektur ihre Fortsetzung finden. Architektur war für ihn nicht eine Frage der Form, sondern der emotionalen Werte, die unter anderem über das Material, räumliche und akustische Qualitäten, Lichtverhältnisse[20], kulturelle Kontinuität sowie das architektonische Motiv vermittelt werden. Die Oberflächen des Materials, die Patina und die Reinheit oder Einfachheit («purity») sind dabei wesentliche Aspekte, und «die Natur mit dem Wohnen in Kontakt zu bringen»[21] war eine seiner Hauptprämissen.

Aaltos Interieurs spiegeln einen «humanen» Funktionalismus wider, bei dem es vorrangig um das Wohlbefinden der Bewohner und die Reflexion der gesellschaftlichen Veränderungen wie zum Beispiel das Rollenverständnis der erwerbstätigen Frau oder alleinerziehenden Mutter ging.[22] Für ihn gab es «in der Architektur [...] keine einsamen Probleme; alles hängt mit allem zusammen». Dementsprechend ist auch das Interieur keine nachträgliche Verschönerung, sondern es ist das Ergebnis der Einheit von Idee, Form und Lebensweise.

Sein Entwurf der universalen Wohnung von 1930, die sich auf kleinstem Raum entwickelt und intern in Zonen oder Halbräume für die «biodynamischen Funktionen» wie Essen, Schlafen, Arbeiten und Spielen unterteilt ist, veranschaulicht die Idee des humanen Funktionalismus. Jenseits des überholten Raumbegriffs, sentimentaler Grundrisslayouts und axialer Symmetrien besteht die Wohnung aus nischenartigen Räumen, die sich über bewegliche und faltbare Möbel flexibel und variabel verknüpfen oder isolieren lassen und so den sich ändernden Bedürfnissen der Bewohner nach Rückzug oder Interaktion gerecht werden.

18 In der Geschichte «zerstört» Müller, der seinen Freund in der stilsicheren, aufgeräumten Wohnung besucht, in seiner rauen, ungeschickten Art das Interieur.
19 Alvar Aalto, «Motifs from Times Past», in: Göran Schildt (Hrsg.), Alvar Aalto. Sketches, Cambridge, Mass./London 1978, S. 2
20 Alvar Aalto, «The Dwelling as a Problem» (Original-Veröffentlichung «Asuntomme probleemina»), in: Domus, 1930, S. 30
21 Alvar Aalto, «Das Gewissen des Architekten», in: Alvar Aalto, Bd. II, Zürich 1957, S. 33
22 «Wenn wir vom technischen Funktionalismus ausgehen, werden wir sehen, dass vieles in unserer heutigen Architektur in psychologischer und psychologisch-physiologischer Hinsicht unfunktionell ist.» Alvar Aalto, «Für eine Humanisierung der Architektur», in: Bernhard Hoesli (Hrsg.), Synopsis. Malerei, Architektur, Skulptur, Basel/Stuttgart 1970, S. 32. Original in: The Technology Review 11/1940

The Interior and Cultural Memory

But Le Corbusier's interiors are exceptional in the context of the Neues Bauen. By the late 1920s intellectuals such as Walter Benjamin, Bertolt Brecht, and Siegfried Kracauer, as well as architects such as Alvar Aalto, expressed criticisms of the objective character and the dictatorial principal of the new style. The text North Sea Shrimps or The Modern Bauhaus Dwelling by Bertholt Brecht and Elisabeth Hauptmann, which was published in 1927, was intended as a critique of the stylization process of the "Neuen Wohnens" (new housing).[18] Developing now once again is a style with normative character: style in this sense stands for control, adaptation, exclusion, and the dictates of taste.

In Motifs from Times Past, written in 1922, Alvar Aalto first formulated his position against the architecture of modernism.[19] Rather than making a total break with the past, contemporary architecture should perpetuate the aesthetic values of traditional architecture. For him, architecture is not a question of form but instead of the emotional values which are conveyed by the material, spatial, and acoustic qualities, by lighting arrangement, by cultural continuity, and by architectonic motifs.[20] One of his principal premises is that the surface of materials, their patina and their purity and simplicity, are essential aspects that make it possible to bring "nature into close contact with the home."[21]

His interiors reflect a "humane" functionalism that is concerned primarily with the well-being of residents and with reflections on societal change: for example an understanding of the roles played by the working wife or single mother.[22] For him, there are no "isolated problems in architecture; everything is interrelated." Accordingly, the interior is not an embellishment, but the result of the unified idea, form, and way of life.

Aalto's 1930 design for a universal apartment was developed in relation to the smallest room and subdivided internally into zones or half-rooms devoted to "biodynamic functions" such as eating, sleeping, work, and play. The universal apartment illustrates his notion of a humane functionalism. The apartment consists of niche-like spaces which can be linked together or isolated from one another flexibly and variably by means of movable or collapsible furniture, doing justice to the changing needs of residents for retreat or interaction.

At the same time, Aalto's humanism and the search for the "nature" of humans and objects is displayed in the richness and variety of the materials and surfaces that individualize his interiors. He combines steel, natural stone, wood, and concrete, deploying their atmospheric and haptic qualities by allowing them to age naturally.

Aalto's angled floor plans, which frame or enclose surrounding landscapes, were also influenced by his understanding of architecture as an extension of

18 In this story, Müller "destroys" the stylistically assertive, immaculate apartment of a friend he is visiting, introducing instead his own awkward style of decorating.
19 Alvar Aalto, "Motifs from Times Past," in Göran Schildt (ed.), Alvar Aalto: Sketches, Cambridge 1978, p. 2.
20 Alvar Aalto, "Asuntomme probleemina," Domus, 1930, pp.176–89.
21 Karl Fleig (ed.), Alvar Aalto, vol. 2: 1963–1970, Basel 1995, p. 8.
22 "If we proceed from technical functionalism, we shall discover that a great many things in our present architecture are not functional from the point of view of psychology or a combination of psychology and physiology." Alvar Aalto, "The Humanizing of Architecture," in Synopsis: Painting Architecture Sculpture, Basel 1980, p. 32.

Zusätzlich zeigen sich Aaltos' Humanismus und die Suche nach der «Natur» des Menschen und der Dinge in dem Reichtum und der Vielfalt der Materialien und Oberflächen, die die Interieurs individualisieren und deren Patina natürlichen Alterungsprozessen unterliegt. Er kombinierte Stahl, Naturstein, Holz und Beton und setzte sie ihren atmosphärischen und haptischen Qualitäten entsprechend ein.

Winkelförmige Grundrisse, die die landschaftliche Umgebung rahmen oder einschliessen, gründen ebenfalls auf seinem Verständnis von Architektur als Fortsetzung der Natur, wie etwa die bildhafte Umsetzung eines Stützenwaldes. Bei der Villa Mairea verwandelte er das Interieur in einen metaphorischen Wald aus scheinbar ungeordneten schlanken oder dicken, gebündelten oder vereinzelten Säulen und Holzstangen, der sich bis in den Innenhof ausweitet und in der Landschaft fortsetzt.

→ 16 17

Die in der Natur eingebundene Hütte als archaische und kulturell verankerte Form des Wohnens setzte sich als Thema auch in Aaltos mehrgeschossigen Wohnungsbauten fort. Der Balkon, die Loggia oder die Terrasse sind hier wesentliche Elemente, die den Garten oder Hof eines Einfamilienhauses ersetzen. Die Blumenbank als Naturmotiv, aber auch das Textile als Symbol für die Rückbindung an die Natur finden sich in seinen Interieurs wieder.[23]

Gleichzeitig sind Flexibilität und eine räumliche Weite selbst in kleinen Grundrissen von Bedeutung und Kennzeichen von Aaltos Architektur. Seine Grundrisse entwickeln sich häufig um einen zentralen, grosszügigen Raum herum, der über vorgelagerte Nischen oder Wandscheiben in die privateren Räume führt. Verborgenheit und Sichtbarkeit, Abgeschlossenheit und Offenheit stehen sich gegenüber und werden den Bedürfnissen der Bewohner nach Privatheit, Zurückgezogenheit und Interaktion gerecht.

→ 18 19 20

Das interaktive Interieur

Technikeuphorie, Überbevölkerung, aber auch der Zusammenbruch traditioneller Familien- und Lebensmodelle führten ab den 1960er-Jahren abermals zu neuen Architekturmodellen und Interieurs, die diese Strömungen widerspiegelten. Die Raum- und Architekturvorstellungen einer technikgläubigen Architektengeneration, zu der Frederick Kiesler und John M. Johansen ebenso gehörten wie die Archigram-Gruppe in Grossbritannien, stellten nahezu ein Gegenkonzept zu dem humanistisch geprägten Ansatz Aaltos dar. Die Architekten entwickelten Wohnungen aus schalengleichen, zellenartigen Räumen, in denen Wände, Boden und Dach als Kontinuum ineinander übergehen. Möbel, Treppenstufen, Regale und Schränke sind Teil dieses Kontinuums und wachsen quasi aus der Struktur heraus. «Living Pod», die Muttermaschine von David Greene, die ihre Bewohner reinigt, kleidet und füttert,

23 Textilien als ursprüngliches Material für die ersten Interieurs und frühen Behausungen im Zelt sind ein Symbol für die Rückbindung an die Natur.

nature. In the Villa Mairea, he transforms the interior into a metaphorical forest consisting of seemingly random slender or thick, bundled or individual columns and wooden slats which extend from the inner courtyard out into the landscape.

→ 16 17

With his multi-level apartment buildings Aalto also addresses the theme of the cottage as an archaic and culturally anchored form of dwelling that is integrated into nature. Here, balconies, loggias, and terraces are essential elements that replace the gardens or courtyards of single-family homes. He uses the flower as a natural motif and textiles as symbols of a reconnection with nature.[23]

At the same time, flexibility and spatial expansiveness, even in small floor plans, are important elements, and are characteristic of his architecture. His floor plans often develop around a central, spacious room that gives access to more "private" rooms via niches or wall panels that are set in front. Concealment and visibility, seclusion and openness coexist, doing justice to the needs of occupants for privacy, reclusiveness, and interaction.

→ 18 19 20

The Interactive Interior

Beginning in the 1960s, technological euphoria, overpopulation, but also the collapse of traditional familial structures led again toward new architectural models and interiors. As a generation who shared a passionate faith in technology, Frederick Kiesler and John M. Johansen, along with the British Archigram group, represented a counterpoint to Aalto's humanistic approach. These architects developed apartments from shell- or cell-like spaces in which walls, floors, and ceilings could flow into one another as a continuum. Furniture, stairs, shelves, and cabinets, also elements in this continuum, would "grow" out of the structure. The "living pod," David Greene's so-called "mother machine," which cleans, dresses, and feeds occupants, is one of the highpoints of this architectural orientation where the interior becomes a computer-guided, quasi-living organism that interacts with residents.

→ 21 22

Influenced by Brutalism and systems theory, John M. Johansen based his architecture on the organization of processes, actions, and patterns of behavior which were to be accommodated in a maximally simple fashion. Alongside the "technological imperative" and the "organic imperative" formulated by Johansen, architecture was now to become attentive to "psychosocial" aspects.[24] The cave, the house, the forest, the labyrinth, and the tower as Jungian archetypes served Johansson as models and sources of inspiration for the design of his Labyrinth House, and served as spatial symbols.[25]

23 As a primordial material for the first interiors and ancient tent dwellings, textiles are a symbol of a connection to nature.
24 John M. Johansen, "An Architecture for the Electronic Age," *Design*, vol. 35, no.3, 1966, pp. 461–471. Among other things, the technological imperative demanded the imitation of electronic equipment in the forms of architecture, as well as the adaptation of organization principles from electronic systems.
25 John M. Johansen, "Architecture: Three Imperatives", in: *Architecture — the AIA Journal*, March 1984, pp. 156–164.

16

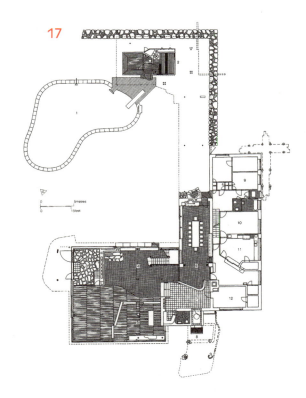

17

18

21

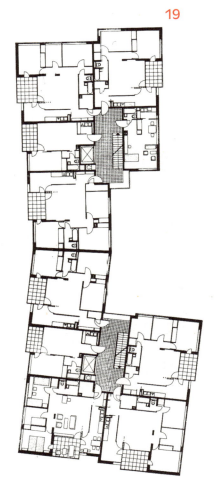

19

20

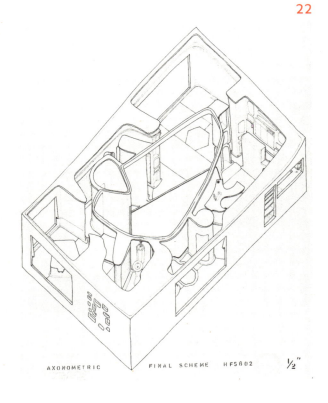

22

16/17 Villa Mairea, Alvar Aalto, Noormakku, 1939; in die Natur eingebunden
18–20 Wohnhaus im Hansaviertel, Alvar Aalto, Berlin, 1955; Weite trotz kleiner Flächen
21/22 House of the Future, Peter und Alison Smithson, London, 1956; autarke Wohnzelle

16/17 Villa Mairea, Alvar Aalto, Noormakku, 1939; integration with nature
18–20 Apartment building in the Hansaviertel, Alvar Aalto, Berlin, 1955; expansiveness despite small-scale surfaces
21/22 House of the Future, Peter and Alison Smithson, London, 1956; autarkic residential cell

Die Kultur des Interieurs

23

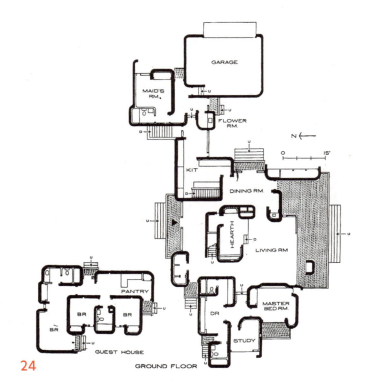

24

25

26

27

28

23	Student work, Image of the Space S14-07, Myungjin Choi/Elena Schneider, TU Berlin 2014; model photo of Labyrinth House, John M. Johansens, Southport/Connecticut, 1966
24	Labyrinth House — Taylor House, John M. Johansens, Southport/Connecticut, 1966
25	Student work, Image of the Space S15-01, Elsa Albrecht/Nikolaus Schmid, TU Berlin 2015; model photo of Thalmatt 1, Atelier 5, Herrenschwanden, 1974
26	Student work, Image of the Space W13/14-01, Jinglin Cai/Xiangyue Guan/Hang Yuan, TU Berlin 2013/14; model photo of Casa Ruben de Mendonça, João Batista Vilanova Artigas, São Paulo, 1958
27	Student work, Image of the Space W15/16-10, James Horkulak/Marko Shllaku, TU Berlin 2015/16; model photo of Villa Noailles, Robert Mallet-Stevens, Hyères, 1923
28	Student work, Image of the Space W15/16-02, Tobias Scholz/Tobias Bräunig, TU Berlin 2015/16; model photo of Appartement Rue Raynouard, Auguste Perret, Paris, 1933

The Culture of the Interior

war einer der Höhepunkte dieses architektonischen Ansatzes. Das Interieur wurde zu einem technoiden, computergesteuerten und gewissermassen lebendigen Organismus, der mit dem Bewohner interagierte.
→ 21 22

Beeinflusst von Brutalismus und Systemtheorie basierte John M. Johansens Architektur auf der Organisation von Prozessen, Handlungen und Verhaltensmustern, die auf eine möglichst einfache Weise beheimatet werden sollten. Neben dem «technologischen Imperativ»[24] und dem «organischen Imperativ», die er formulierte, sollte die Architektur «psychosoziale» Aspekte berücksichtigen.[25] Die Höhle, das Haus, der Wald, das Labyrinth und der Turm als jungianische Archetypen dienten Johansen als Vorlage und Inspiration für den Entwurf seines Labyrinth House und wurden zu räumlichen Symbolen.

Der Baukörper besteht aus einer Komposition von turmartigen, gekrümmten Betonschalen, die durch raumhohe Glasscheiben miteinander verbunden sind. Im Grundriss werden die Betonschalen zu höhlenartigen Nischen, die sich in einem offenen, fliessenden Raum ineinander verschränken oder zueinander in Beziehung treten. Aus dem Spannungsfeld von gross und klein, transparent und opak, massiv und leicht, hart und weich, geschlossen und offen entsteht eine räumliche Dramaturgie, die durch die «chaotische» Anordnung der gekrümmten Wandelemente zu einer Dramaturgie der Bewegung wird: einer Bewegung im Raum, die gleichzeitig spiralförmig und unbestimmt ist. Die Spiralform, nach C. G. Jung Symbol für den Prozess der Bewusstwerdung und Ausdruck des Individuationsprozesses, aber auch die Höhlen- und Turmmotive verweisen auf das übergeordnete Thema des Interieurs, das als Katalysator auf die Psyche des Bewohners einwirken und Entwicklungsprozesse fördern soll. In diesem offenen, ausschliesslich durch schalenartige Nischen unterteilten Raumgefüge wird die Interaktion zwischen dem Bewohner und der Architektur «intim und unvorhersehbar».[26]
→ 23 24

Das Interieur als Abbild

Die oben beschriebenen architektonischen Konzepte und Haltungen zum Interieur zeigen ein Gegenbild auf zum standardisierten Wohnungsbau, der bis heute üblich ist, und verdeutlichen das architektonische Potenzial, das verloren geht, wenn das Interieur nicht mitgedacht und mitentworfen wird.

Um dieses Terrain zurückzuerobern und sich dem Interieur als wesentlichem architektonischem Thema anzunähern, haben die Studierenden an der TU Berlin anhand von Fotografien berühmte Innenräume der

[24] John MacLane Johansen, «An Architecture for the Electronic Age», in: Design 09/1966, S. 19–22. Der technologische Imperativ fordert unter anderem die Imitation von elektronischem Equipment in den Formen der Architektur sowie die Adaption der Organisationsprinzipien elektronischer Systeme.
[25] John M. Johansen, «Architecture: Three Imperatives», in: Architecture — the AIA Journal 03/1984, S. 156–164
[26] Lebbeus Woods beschreibt in «Johansens Present Tense» den architektonischen Ansatz von Johansen folgendermassen: «Composition is gone, because the thing continually recomposes itself within an almost infinite range of possibilities. Function is gone, because it is unknown in advance. Structure […] is gone, because it is entirely fluid-dynamic, nonlinear, even mathimatically chaotic. All that remains is an intimate and unpredictable interaction between the inhabitant and the architecture.» In: John M. Johansen: A Life in the Continuum of Modern Architecture, Turin 1996

Die Kultur des Interieurs

The structure is composed of tower-like, curvilinear concrete shells linked together with room-height glass panels. The concrete shells become cave-like spatial niches which are interlocked with one another in an open, flowing space. A spatial dramaturgy emerges from the tension between transparent and opaque, solid and lightweight, hard and soft, closed and open elements. The "chaotic" configuration of curvilinear, cave-like wall elements creates a passage through space that is also spiral-shaped and indeterminate. The spiral form, according to C. G. Jung, symbolizes the process of becoming conscious and the expression of individuation, while the motifs of the cave and tower, point toward the theme of the interior. This is intended to act as a catalyst to the occupant's psyche and to promote developmental processes. In this open spatial structure interaction between resident and architecture becomes intimate and unpredictable.[25]
→ 23 24

The Interior as Image

These projects centered around the interior as an architectural concept represent a counterpoint to contemporary standardized housing development, and clarify the potential that is lost when the interior is not conceived and designed in an integrated way.

In order to reconquer this terrain and approach the interior as an essential architectural topic, students at the TU Berlin reconstructed celebrated interiors from the past 150 years on a scale of 1:20, and then photographed the resultant models.

The source of inspiration for this procedure was the artistic oeuvre of Thomas Demand. His photographs display reconstructions of rooms—typically crime scenes or settings of historically significant events. He then constructs these in paper or cardboard on a 1:1 scale. For example, he reconstructed and photographed the ruins of Hitler's headquarters, the bathroom where the body of Uwe Barschel was discovered, and the farm kitchen where Saddam Hussein hid from US-American troops. His "stories" about moments that occurred after historic events are, like the calm after a storm, filled with emptiness. They are documents of a mute horror and it is precisely this emptiness that is reinforced by the materiality—or precisely the non-materiality—of his cardboard models. These rooms are reduced to their essential structural features and details which appear in the original journalistic photographs are omitted: a typewriter lacks its keyboard, pages of a manuscript are devoid of letters, a tissue box lacks its label. These can lead to a simultaneous irritation and truth on the part of the viewer around the construction of a constructed reality. This raises questions which every beholder must answer independently.

[26] In "Johansens Present Tense," Lebbeus Woods characterizes Johansen's approach as follows: "Composition is gone, because the thing continually recomposes itself within an almost infinite range of possibilities. Function is gone, because it is unknown in advance. Structure... is gone, because it is entirely fluid-dynamic, nonlinear, even mathimatically chaotic. All that remains is an intimate and unpredictable interaction between the inhabitant and the architecture." From John M. Johansen (ed.), John M Johansen: A Life in the Continuum of Modern Architecture, Turin 1996

letzten 150 Jahre im Massstab 1:20 nachgebaut und die Modelle der Vorlage folgend abfotografiert. Inspirationsquelle für diese Vorgehensweise war die Arbeit des Künstlers Thomas Demand; seine Fotografien zeigen Nachbildungen von Räumen —Tatorte oder Räume, in denen historisch bedeutsame Ereignisse stattgefunden haben —, die er im Massstab 1:1 aus Pappe oder Papier herstellt. Das zerstörte Hauptquartier Hitlers nach dem Anschlag vom 20. Juni 1944 hat er ebenso nachgebaut und abfotografiert wie das Badezimmer, in dem Uwe Barschel tot aufgefunden wurde, oder die Bauernküche, in der sich Saddam Hussein vor den amerikanischen Truppen versteckt hielt. Seine «Erzählungen» über den Moment nach dem historischen Ereignis, der wie die Ruhe nach dem Sturm per se mit Leere gefüllt ist, sind Zeugnisse des stummen Entsetzens und eben dieser Leere, die durch die Materialität oder eben Nicht-Materialität des Pappmodells verstärkt wird. Die Reduktion der Räume auf das Wesentliche oder das Strukturelle der ursprünglichen Fotografie der Journalisten durch das Weglassen von Details — der Schreibmaschine fehlt die Tastatur, die Manuskriptseiten haben keine Buchstaben und dem Taschentuchbehälter fehlt das Label — führt gleichzeitig zu einer Irritation des Betrachters und zu der Wahrheit hinter der Wahrheit: die Konstruktion einer konstruierten Wirklichkeit. Dies wirft Fragen auf, die jeder Betrachter für sich selbst beantworten muss.

Bei den Arbeiten der Studierenden ging es ebenfalls um Fragen. Fragen nach Zusammenhängen von atmosphärisch «dichten» Interieurs und ihrem Verhältnis zu den architektonischen Elementen wie räumlichen Proportionen, Wahl und Formulierung der strukturellen Elemente wie Pfeiler, Stützen, Wandscheiben, Wandvorsprünge, Nischen, Materialität und Oberflächenbeschaffenheit, Anordnung und Grösse der Wandöffnungen und Fenster und die dazugehörige Lichtregie sowie Raum- und Blickbezüge. Während das Nachbilden der Räume und die Übersetzung von der Zweidimensionalität in die dritte Dimension den Blick schärft und das genaue Hinsehen und Verweilen erfordert, wirft das Abfotografieren des Modells Fragen auf, die zu einer Auseinandersetzung mit der Anordnung von Fenstern und deren Lichtwirkung für den Raum und die Oberflächenbeschaffenheiten der architektonischen Elemente führt. Während Streiflicht, das durch ein verborgenes Fenster in den Raum fällt, etwas geheimnisvolles und gleichzeitig «anheimelndes» haben kann, lässt Zenitlicht, das über Oberlichter den Raum erfüllt, wenig Raum für Schatten; Fenster als Gegenüber einer Tür tauchen den Raum in ein gleichmässiges Licht und erweitern ihn optisch in den Aussenraum.

Raumnischen, Wandvorsprünge und Stützen sowie Wandöffnungen und Fenster sind nicht länger ausschliesslich Strukturelemente, sondern sie sind Teile des Interieurs, die Geschichten erzählen und dem zukünftigen Bewohner ein Angebot machen. Diese räumlichen Dispositionen, bei denen es um Verstecken und Sichtbarmachen, Rhythmisierung und Bewegung, Offenheit, Diffusität, Klarheit, Raumfluss und Nischenbildung geht, entsprechen nicht nur den seelischen Zuständen und Bedürfnissen des Menschen, sondern sie sind gleichzeitig Archetypen und Symbole.
→ 25 26 27 28

The purpose of the student projects is to raise questions. Questions concerning the coherence or atmospheric "density" of interiors and their relationship to architectural elements. Elements such as spatial proportions, pillars, columns, wall panels, wall projections, niches, materiality, and surface qualities, the configuration and sizes of wall openings and windows, lighting design, and connections between rooms. These reproductions and the translation of two-dimensionality into three dimensions hones the gaze and demands precise observation and thought. Photographing the models also raises questions around lighting and the surface qualities of the architectonic elements. While diffuse light, which enters a room through a concealed window, can be somehow mysterious and at the same time "cozy," zenithal lighting, which fills a room through a skylight from above, tends to banish shadow; a window as a counterpart to a door submerges a room in a homogenous light, extending it optically into external space.

Niches, wall projections and supports, as well as wall openings and windows, are no longer exclusively structural elements, but become aspects of the interior that narrate stories and make overtures to future occupants. These spatial dispositions, which are concerned with concealing or making visible, with rhythm and movement, with openness, diffuseness, clarity, spatial flow, and the formation of niches, not only correspond to the mental states and needs of human beings, but are at the same time archetypes and symbols.
→ 25 26 27 28

The Interior as a Mirror of the Soul

This aspect of architecture, that of space, of the interior, which is so difficult to grasp, becomes immediately comprehensible when we consider the relationship between interiority and spatiality in literary works. To "read" a house or a room means to follow the poet's analysis of interiority, for the room and the house are psychological diagrams. Gaston Bachelard says as much in his book *La poétique de l'espace,* which was published in 1958. In this work, Bachelard investigates the poetic powers of imagination with reference to images created by literature. "The poetic image stands at the origin of consciousness; in the poetic space of the image, the subject inscribes itself without reserve; alive in it are solutions to problems that are hopelessly insoluble for thought."[26] After setting up a Jungian symbolic interpretation of images, Bachelard distances himself from this approach, describing an immediate access to image spaces beyond the rationality of analytical language. He calls this "topoanalysis," the systematic psychological study of the places of our interior life. For him, the image is a language that eludes words.

Bachelard strives to trace out the "significance of the hut" and to uncover the "primary virtues" that "reveal an attachment that is native in some way to the primary function of inhabiting."[27] Independent of the type of dwelling, it is a question of "the effort needed to seize upon the essential, sure, immediate well-being it encloses." When Walter Benjamin speaks of "the abode of the human being as the maternal womb," he is perhaps speaking of something similar.[28] For Benjamin, the home is an enclosure within which the human individual is encased and embedded—it bears "the impression of its occupant."

"We should therefore have to say how we inhabit our vital space, in accord with the dialectics of life, how we take root, day after day, in a 'corner of the world.' For our house is our corner of the world. As has often been said, it is our first universe, a real cosmos in every sense of the word. If we look at it intimately, the humblest dwelling has beauty. Authors of books on the 'humble home' often mentioned this feature of the poetics of space."[29]

The house integrates thoughts, memories, and dreams. And reverie is its binding principle. The house is body and soul. The house is the place of the 'inside,' of well-being, intimacy. It stands for childhood and motherliness, and is a repository of our memories and of the unconscious. The cellar, attic, nook, and corridor are characteristic sanctuaries of our memories, our reveries.

The house as a symbol or metaphor of the human soul can supply valuable references for the handling or design of the interior. The rational and irrational, the airy and the heavy, the bright and the dark, are the poles between which the human soul stretches itself out; attic and cellar as representatives of these

27 Gaston Bachelard, *The Poetics of Space,* London 1958.
28 Ibid., pp. 25–26.
29 Walter Benjamin, *The Arcades Project,* London 2000, p. 220.
30 Bachelard 1958, p. 26.

Das Haus als Symbol oder Metapher der menschlichen Seele kann wertvolle Hinweise geben auf den Umgang oder die Gestaltung des Interieurs. Das Rationale und das Irrationale, das Luftige und das Schwere, das Helle und das Dunkle sind die Pole, zwischen denen sich die menschliche Seele aufspannt; der Dachboden und der Keller als Repräsentanten dieser Pole sollten sich auch in einer horizontal organisierten Wohnung widerspiegeln. Jedes bauliche Element kreiert einen Ort, der unweigerlich mit unseren Erinnerungen, Träumereien und dem Unbewussten in einen Dialog tritt. Das Hinabsteigen einer Treppe, und seien es nur wenige Stufen, eröffnet andere innere Räume als das Hinaufsteigen. Ebenso hat die Ausführung, die Art einer Treppe eine Symbolkraft: eine gewendelte, enge oder steile Treppe steigt man empor, um dem Geheimnisvollen oder dem Versteckten in der Einsamkeit zu begegnen, während man eine breite, ausladende Treppe in aller Offenheit entlangschreitet. Raumgefüge, die zum Schreiten einladen, eröffnen dem Bewohner einen Denkraum und verbinden ihn mit dem «Sein von drinnen und dem Schicksal im Draussen».[31]

Will man der menschlichen Seele gerecht werden, braucht es Schlupfwinkel und Nischen. Die sprichwörtliche Schmollecke ist ein wichtiger Ort der Einsamkeit und des Rückzugs. Für Gaston Bachelard wie für Walter Benjamin hat das Wohnen weniger mit dem Erfüllen von Funktionen zu tun, sondern es ist ein Spiegelbild der menschlichen Seele und Verkörperung der inneren Befindlichkeiten und Seinszustände.

Fragen des Topo-Analytikers wie: «War das Zimmer gross? War der Speicher überfüllt? War der Winkel heiss? Woher kam das Licht? Wie verhielt sich in diesen Räumen das menschliche Wesen zur Stille? Wie schmeckten ihm diese verschiedenen, so besonders gearteten Formen der Stille in den verschiedenen Schlupfwinkeln der einsamen Träumereien?»[32] sind Fragen, die dem Architekten beim Denken oder «Träumen» von Interieurs behilflich sein können. Es sind Fragen, die über das Räumliche hinausgehen, die die Sinnlichkeit des Menschen einbeziehen und diese an die Räumlichkeit binden.

Das dichterische Bild als Ursprung des Bewusstseins gilt in gleichem Mass für den Dichter wie für den Architekten. Während sich der Dichter der Worte als Werkzeug bedient, um Bilder oder Bildräume zu schaffen, steht dem Architekten durch das Kreieren von Räumen eine wesentlich direktere Sprache zur Verfügung. Denn der geschaffene Raum ist ein Bild. Ob sich dieses Bild jedoch reichhaltig zu einer Geschichte entwickelt, ist das Thema des Interieurs. Das Interieur füllt den Raum mit Geschichten.

Durch das Interieur wird die Wohnung nicht nur individualisiert und zu einem hohen Grad spezifisch, sondern sie wird im Sinne Jungs dem kollektiven Unbewussten gerecht. Die «Renaissance» des Interieurs ist also nicht nur eine Antwort auf die Diversität der Bedürfnisse der Bewohner, sondern sie bietet durch ungewöhnliche räumliche Ausprägungen eine Reibungsfläche und der Seele eine Heimat.

poles should be mirrored as well in the horizontal configuration of the apartment. Every constructive element creates a place, one that enters unavoidably into a dialogue with our memories, reveries, and with the unconscious. To descend a staircase—even if it is just a matter of few steps—opens up inner spaces that differ from those that are opened up by ascending a staircase. Likewise, the structural type of the staircase, its style, possesses a symbolic force: we climb a spiral, narrow, or steep staircase in order to encounter the mysterious or the concealed in solitude, while we stride up a broad, sweeping staircase with a sense of expansiveness. Spatial structures that invite us to stride open up a thought space for occupants, making it possible to "give an exterior density to the interior being."[30] Required in order to do justice to the human soul are "retreats" and niches. The proverbial sulking corner is an important place of solitude and withdrawal. "Every corner in a house, every angle in a room, every inch of secluded space in which we like to hide, or withdraw into ourselves, is a symbol of solitude for the imagination, that is to say it is the germ of a room, or of a house."[31] For Bachelard, as for Benjamin, dwelling has less to do with the fulfillment of functions, and is instead a mirror of the human soul, and an embodiment of interior mental states and states of being.

The "topoanalyst" asks questions such as: "Was the room a large one? Was the garret cluttered up? Was the nook warm? How was it lit? How too, in these fragments of space, did the human being achieve silence? How did he relish the very special silence of the various retreats of solitary daydreaming?"[32] Their questions go beyond the spatial. They integrate the sensuous qualities of human beings and connect these to spatiality.

The poetic image as the origin of consciousness applies to the architect as much as it does to the poet. While the poet employs words as tools in order to create images or imagine spaces, the architect, by creating spaces, has access to a far more direct language. For the created space is an image. Whether or not this image, however, develops substantially into a story is the theme of the interior. The interior fills the space with stories.

Through the interior, the apartment not only becomes individualized and specific, it also does justice to the collective unconscious, in Jung's sense of the term. The "renaissance" of the interior, then, is not merely a reply to the diverse needs of city-dwellers. Instead, it offers, through unconventional spatial characteristics, a frictional surface at the soul of a home.

---

31 Bachelard, wie Anm. 30, S. 43
32 Ebd., S. 41

31 Ibid., p. 32.
32 Ibid., p. 155.
33 Ibid., p. 31.

←

Die Kultur
des Interieurs

The Culture
of the Interior

Studierende
der TU Berlin:
Interieurs.
Semesterentwürfe
im Modell

Students from
the TU Berlin:
Interiors.
Semester Designs
in Model Form

↑ College 10; Lysann Geller, Monika Pawlak, Kassandra Sarantis

Studierende der TU Berlin: Interieurs.
Semesterentwürfe im Modell

← Brick 02; Kai Hikmet Canver, Sina Pauline Riedlinger ↑ Brick 06; Larsen Berg, Harald Niessner

Studierende der TU Berlin: Interieurs.
Semesterentwürfe im Modell

High Rise 16; Lisa Beyer, Justus Preyer, Max Werner

Wood 16; Cem Baykal, Yuki Hanfeld

← Brick 02; Kai Hikmet Canver, Sina Pauline Riedlinger   ↑ Brick 14; Theodora Constantin, Vanessa Vogel

Studierende der TU Berlin: Interieurs.
Semesterentwürfe im Modell

↑ High Rise 18; Tobias Bräunig, Tobias Scholz → College 04; Marie-Louise Leeck, Lisa Thürer

Students from the TU Berlin: Interiors.
Semester Designs in Model Form

← College 12; Daniel Dieren, Helena Reischel, Ann-Kathrin Salich   ↑ High Rise 14; Franziska Käuferle, Louisa Wahler

Studierende der TU Berlin: Interieurs. Semesterentwürfe im Modell

↑ High Rise 01; Robert Bauer, Christa Elizabeth Beckmann
→ Brick 05; Vera Marie Glas, Rafael Lozykowski, Florian Rizek
→→ High Rise 05; Catherine Folawiyo, Clara Jereczek
→→→ College 14; Paul Harries, Ana Richter de Arce, Florian Tropp

Students from the TU Berlin: Interiors.
Semester Designs in Model Form

← College 05; Isabel de Palacios, Julia Ratsch, Florian Tudzierz   ↑ Brick B03; Judith Bartsch, Alexandr Minkin

Studierende der TU Berlin: Interieurs. Semesterentwürfe im Modell

← Brick 07; Luca Gericke, Franco Scheuplein, Carolin Trahorsch   ↑ College 13; Antoan Antonov, Jakob Fischer, Maurice Luft

Studierende der TU Berlin: Interieurs.
Semesterentwürfe im Modell

↗ Brick 15; Sandra Schenavsky, Franziska Rüss
→ Brick 16; Simon Kiefer, Shaghayegh Moghaddasi Sikaroudi, Elena Wickenhöfer

↑ High Rise 13; Maija Gavare, Johanna Sieberer

Students from the TU Berlin: Interiors.
Semester Designs in Model Form

↑ Steel 04; Thomas Pracht, Guang Xue

→ Steel 10; Jana Morgenstern, Jennifer Moser

Students from the TU Berlin: Interiors.
Semester Designs in Model Form

← Grandhotel 03; Hanna Rohst ↑ Grandhotel 09; Nikolaus Schmid

Studierende der TU Berlin: Interieurs.
Semesterentwürfe im Modell

↑ Urbanity and Production M03; Jana Morgenstern → Brick B02; Stefan File, Anne Kummetz

Students from the TU Berlin: Interiors.
Semester Designs in Model Form

↑ Urbanity and Production M02; Julia Rathmann Löcker
↗ Concrete 14; Tatjana Anic, Timo Lück
→ Brick B01; Catherine Folawiyo, Gesa Holzbrecher

Students from the TU Berlin: Interiors. Semester Designs in Model Form

↑ High Rise 10; Paul Achter, Lorenz Preußer, Ivan Zilic → Steel 11 ; Jialiang Cui, Liane Rosenthal

Students from the TU Berlin: Interiors.
Semester Designs in Model Form

Grandhotel 06; Julia Rathmann Löcker

←

Studierende
der TU Berlin:
Interieurs.
Semesterentwürfe
im Modell

Students from
the TU Berlin:
Interiors.
Semester Designs
in Model Form

pool Architekten: Wohnbauprojekte 1998–2018. Ein Werkverzeichnis

pool Architekten: Residential Projects 1998–2018. A Catalogue Raisonné

poolscher Wohnungsbau

Wohnbauprojekte entstehen aus unzähligen Erfahrungen und entwickeln sich von Projekt zu Projekt. Trotz der auf den ersten Blick ähnlich erscheinenden Programme, die sich durch die konstanten Bedürfnisse nach Schutz, Behaglichkeit, Individualität und Funktionalität in eng umrissenen Grenzen bewegen, generiert die Summe der Faktoren eine kaum fassbare Vielgestaltigkeit, die zu einem evolutionären Prozess führt. Die Herangehensweise als Architektenkollektiv, in dem jeder die eigene Wohnerfahrung und sein fachliches Wissen in die Projekte einbringt und diese im Dialog mit den andern adaptiert und weiterentwickelt, verstärkt den evolutionären Prozess. Diese diskursive Annäherung, die ein gemeinsames Vokabular voraussetzt und entwickelt, ist pool Architekten wichtiger als stilistische Einheit.

Der Entwurfsprozess ist die Suche nach der erfolgversprechenden Lösung, aber auch «Bricolage» aufgespürter und angeeigneter Konzepte. Die daraus entstehenden Haustypen werden also von einer bestimmten Idee getragen und sind durch ihre Verwandtschaft zu Vorläuferprojekten zugleich hybrid. Beides ist Ausdruck einer Recherche, die auf möglichst undogmatische Weise Ansätze aus der Architekturgeschichte nutzt und mit aktuellen Trends im Wohnungsbau kombiniert.

Der direkte Vergleich ermöglicht es, retrospektiv Themen und Querbezüge zwischen den einzelnen Entwürfen auszumachen. Besonders der konkrete, von vielen Faktoren bestimmte Grundrisstyp wird dadurch mehrdimensional. Die Projekte sind im Folgenden beispielhaft mit unterschiedlichen übergeordneten Themenfeldern verknüpft.

Grossformen werden durch ihre unübersehbare Eindeutigkeit als Identitätsträger und Orientierungspunkte im Stadtgefüge wahrgenommen. Die klar gefassten Figuren sind nicht auf schematische Reihung oder Wiederholung in anderen Kontexten angelegt, denn sie sind Ausdruck eines konkreten Siedlungsumfelds und einer Topografie. Deshalb vermeiden sie auch formale Beliebigkeit. Sie sind präzise morphologische Setzungen, die durch ihre bewusst gewählte Gestik in den Raum ausgreifen und Siedlungsräume bilden. Ihre Ausdehnung erlaubt es, sie als Gefäss für ein lebendiges Aussen- und Innenleben zu konzipieren.

Charakteristische Architektur, die benennbar und wiedererkennbar ist, will im Dialog mit ihrem unmittelbaren Siedlungskontext stehen. Bauweise, Programm und Gestaltungswille führen zu einem Vokabular, das sich in Materialität und Tektonik artikuliert, aber auch eine Haltung zur lokalen Tradition ausdrückt. Ein Gebäude verbindet sich dadurch mit einem Ort und wird zu einem unverwechselbaren Orientierungspunkt in seiner Nachbarschaft.

Spezifische Raumfiguren sind besonders geformte Einzelräume oder Raumfolgen, die eine vielfältige Benutzung zulassen und fördern. Gemeint sind Räume, die sich durch ihre Bestimmtheit als sehr robust gegenüber Veränderungen erweisen und dennoch durch die Bewohner in Beschlag genommen werden wollen, diese gar animieren, auch unkonventionelle Ideen der Einrichtung zu realisieren und dadurch über das vom Architekten Vorgesehene hinauszugehen.

Privatsphäre wird gerade im Zuge der inneren Siedlungsentwicklung immer wichtiger. Das Individuum will wählen können, ob es sich von kollektiven Räumen und Nachbarschaften zurückziehen oder mit diesen in Kommunikation treten will. Projekte mit einer graduellen Differenzierung zwischen Öffentlichem und Privatem und entsprechend gestalteten Schwellen dazwischen bieten zudem die Chance für eine explizite städtebauliche und architektonische Ausformulierung.

Lärmschutz wurde mit zunehmender Bewohnerdichte und Mobilität zur Alltagsaufgabe. Die Politik tut sich schwer, Massnahmen an den Lärmquellen durchzusetzen, dementsprechend verändern neue typologische Lösungen auf den Bauparzellen die Erscheinung der Siedlungsräume. In die Tiefe gestaffelte, offene Raumstrukturen wirken der Abgrenzung zum lärmbelasteten öffentlichen Raum entgegen und geben den Bauten ein Gesicht zur Strasse.

Nachhaltiges Bauen beinhaltet mehr als hochgedämmte Kompaktheit. Mindestens so wichtig ist die Dauerhaftigkeit von Konstruktionen durch hochwertige Materialien und qualitätsvolle Details. Energieeffiziente und bauphysikalisch leistungsfähige Bauweisen begünstigen den Einsatz von robusten Materialien wie Dämmbeton, Backstein und Massivholz. Ein ausgewogener, sozial verträglicher Nutzungsmix, die Bevorzugung kurzer Transportwege und die sorgfältige Integration neuer Umwelttechnologien geben gesellschaftliche, regionalökonomische und baukulturelle Impulse.

Residential Development

Residential developments emerge out of countless experiences that develop from project to project. Although at first glance, the respective programs seem to resemble one another. They share narrowly delimited boundaries through the requirements of protection, comfort, individuality, and functionality. However, constantly superimposing these factors generates an almost inconceivable variety and results in an evolutionary process as programs develop. This evolutionary process is reinforced via the architectural collective's approach of dialogically exploring personal residential experiences and professional expertise. This discursive rapprochement, which presupposes and develops a shared vocabulary, is more important to pool Architekten than stylistic unity.

The design process is the search for promising solutions, but also consists of a kind of "bricolage" of concepts that have been ferreted out or appropriated. Resultant building types are simultaneously borne by a specific idea and are hybrids, by virtue of their affinities with previous projects. Both, however, are expressions of research into architectural history combined with contemporary trends in residential development.

Through direct comparisons, different themes can be identified across varying designs. For example, concrete floor plans are determined by numerous themes, and so become multidimensional. In the following, projects are linked across a range of overarching themes:

Large forms, by virtue of their conspicuous singularity, have been perceived as bearers of identity and points of orientation within the urban fabric. These large figures are rarely conceived for schematic sequencing or repetition in other contexts. They respond to a specific development context and a specific topography. For this reason, they also avoid formal arbitrariness. They are precise morphological configurations which expand into space through deliberate gestures, shaping the development area. Their size makes it possible to conceive them as containers for a lively exterior and interior life.

Characteristic architecture that is nameable and recognizable. This is found in dialogue with its immediate surroundings. Construction method, program, and design produce a vocabulary that is articulated in materiality and tectonics, but also acknowledges local tradition. As a consequence, a building is connected to a place, and becomes an unmistakable point of orientation within its environs.

Specific spatial figures are specially-shaped individual spaces or sequences that facilitate and promote a diverse range of uses. These spaces are highly flexible and lend themselves to being appropriated by inhabitants, who implement unconventional ideas around furnishings, thereby going beyond the designs envisioned by the architects.

Private spheres are of utmost important when developing the interior of a settlement. Individuals should be free to choose whether they want to withdraw from collective spaces and proximity to neighbors, or instead enter into communication with them. Projects that feature a graduated differentiation between public and private spheres, and thresholds between the two, also offer new opportunities for their explicit urban and architectural formulation.

Noise protection has become an everyday issue with increasing residential densities. Since it is difficult to implement political solutions to reduce noises such as traffic at source, new typological solutions are transforming the appearance of settlement areas. Open spatial structures which are staggered in depth impact isolation from noise-burdened public spaces while giving buildings a striking appearance from the street.

Sustainable building means more than well-insulated, compact structures. At least as important is a structure's longevity, which can be influenced through the use of high-grade materials and high-quality details. Energy-efficient and structurally high-performing building methods facilitate the employment of robust materials such as insulating concrete, brick, and solid timber. A well-balanced, socially compatible mix of uses, a preference for short transport routes, and the careful integration of new environmental technologies can also benefit social cohesion, regional economics, and building culture.

Projektliste

→ Regelgeschosse im Massstab 1:500, S. 68
→ Fotografien realisierter Projekte, S. 120
→ Möblierte Grundrisse im Massstab 1:150, S. 154
→ Das tägliche Leben, S. 190

List of Projects

→ Standard Stories on a Scale of 1:500, p. 68
→ Photographs of Realized Projects, p. 120
→ Furnished Floor Plans on a Scale of 1:150, p. 154
→ Daily Life, p. 190

0004
Mehrfamilienhaus/
Multifamily dwelling
  Kirchdorf
Eigeninitiative/
Self-initiated
  1998/99
Fünf Eigentumswohnungen mit Einfamilienhausqualität/
Five owner-occupied units with detached house
Arbeitsgemeinschaft mit/
Joint venture with
  Frei Architekten

0007
Genossenschaftssiedlung/
Cooperative housing estate
  Wallisellenstrasse Süd
  Zürich-Oerlikon
Projektwettbewerb/
Project competition
  1998
Siedlung mit ca. 90 Wohnungen/
Housing estate with 90 units
Veranstalter/Organizer
  Amt für Hochbauten der Stadt Zürich/
  Department of Public Works of the City of Zurich
Auftraggeber/Client
  Baugenossenschaft GISA

0012
Areal Brüggli
  Romanshorn
Ideenwettbewerb, 1. Preis/
Ideas competition, 1st prize
  1999
Weiterbearbeitung für Gestaltungsplan/
Further treatment of design plan
  2000–2005
Wohnquartier mit ca. 200 Wohneinheiten/
Residential district with ca. 200 residential units
Auftraggeber/Client
  Gemeinde Romanshorn

0024
Wohnüberbauung/
Residential development
  Aarepark, Aarau
Projektwettbewerb/
Project competition
  1999
Siedlung mit ca. 100 Miet- und Eigentumswohnungen/
Housing estate with ca. 100 rental and owner-occupied units
Veranstalter/Organizer
  Stadt Aarau

0025
Siedlung für Studierende/
Housing estate for students
  Bülachstrasse, Zürich
Projektwettbewerb/
Project competition
  1999
266 Studentenzimmer
266 Student rooms
Veranstalter/Organizer
  Stiftung für Studentisches Wohnen Zürich

0032
Wohnüberbauung/
Residential development
  Unterdorf, Fällanden
Studienauftrag
Commissioned study
  1999
220 Eigentums- und Mietwohnungen
220 owner-occupied and rental units
Veranstalter/Organizer
  Göhner Merkur GU AG

0048
Genossenschaftssiedlung/
Cooperative housing estate
  Jasminweg, Zürich-Oerlikon
Studienauftrag
Commissioned study
  2000
Ersatzneubau mit 65 Familienwohnungen, Ateliers und Kinderkrippe
Replacement building with 65 family apartments, studios, and day care center
Veranstalter/Organizer
  ABZ Allgemeine Baugenossenschaft Zürich

0072
Genossenschaftssiedlung/
Cooperative housing estate
  Leimbachstrasse, Zürich-Leimbach
Wettbewerb, 1. Preis
Competition, 1st prize
  2001
Realisierung/Realization
  2002–2005
Siedlung mit 116 Wohnungen, Kinderkrippe, Kindergarten
Housing estate with 116 apartments, day care center, kindergarten
Veranstalter/Organizer
  Stadt Zürich
Auftraggeber/Client
  Baugenossenschaft Zurlinden, Baugenossenschaft Freiblick
Auszeichnungen/Awards
  best architects 12
  Gute Bauten im Kanton Zürich 2006
  Hase in Gold 2005
  AR Award for Emerging Architecture 2005 (Honourable Mention)

0079
Haus Buscaglia
  Altendorf
Direktauftrag/Direct commission
Realisierung/Realization
  2001–2003
Einfamilienhaus/
Single-family dwelling
Auftraggeber/
Client
  Privat/Private

0095
Wohnhaus/
Multifamily dwelling
  42 Homes
  Windisch
Konzeptstudie/
Conceptual study
  2002
Wohnhaus/
Apartment building
Auftraggeber/Client
  Kunz Textil Windisch AG

0097
Alterswohnungen/
Apartments for seniors
  Hirzenbach, Zürich
Projektwettbewerb/
Project competition
  2002
55 Wohnungen mit Gemeinschaftsräumen und Spitexeinrichtungen/
55 units with common rooms and Spitex facilities
Auftraggeber/Client
  Stiftung Alterswohnen der Stadt Zürich

0113
Wohnüberbauung/
Residential development
  Aspholz Nord, Zürich-Affoltern
Studienauftrag 1. Preis
Commissioned study, 1st Prize
  2003
Siedlung mit 119 Wohnungen/
Housing estate with 119 units
Realisierung/Realization
  2005–2007
Auftraggeber/Client
  BVK Zürich
Auszeichnungen/Awards
  best architects 12
  Auszeichnung für gute Bauten der Stadt Zürich 2006–2010

0128
Genossenschaftssiedlung/
Cooperative housing estate
  Hofgarten
  Zürich-Leimbach
Projektwettbewerb/
Project competition
  2004, 4. Rang/4th place
Veranstalter/Organizer
  Amt für Hochbauten der Stadt Zürich
Auftraggeber/Client
  Genossenschaft Hofgarten

0132
Terrassenhäuser/
Terrace Buildings
  Am Sonnenberg
  Würenlingen
Direktauftrag/Direct commission
Realisierung/Realization
  2006–2008
Eigentumswohnungen/
Owner-occupied units
Auftraggeber/Client
  J. Stocker
  Hoch- und Tiefbau AG

0151
Genossenschaftssiedlung/
Cooperative housing estate
  Sihlbogen
  Zürich-Leimbach
Projektwettbewerb/
Project competition
  2005
Wohnsiedlung und Gewerbezentrum/
Housing estate and commercial center
Veranstalter/Organizer
  Amt für Hochbauten der Stadt Zürich
Auftraggeber/Client
  Baugenossenschaft Zurlinden

0152
Atriumhäuser am Friedweg
  Lenzburg
Direktauftrag/Direct commission
  2004
Fünf Reihenhäuser
Five town houses
Auftraggeber/Client
  Richter ARCH

0154
Genossenschaftssiedlung/
Cooperative housing estate
  Kronwiesenweg
  Zürich-Schwamendingen
Studienauftrag/
Commissioned study
  2004
Siedlung mit 43 Reihenhäusern/
Housing estate with 43 town houses
Veranstalter/Organizer
  Vitasana Bau- und Siedlungsgenossenschaft

0156
Wohnüberbauung/
Residential development
    Grünwald
    Zürich-Höngg
Studienauftrag/
Commissioned study
    2005
Arbeitsgemeinschaft mit/
Joint venture with
    Gmür & Steib Architekten
Siedlung mit 250 Wohnungen/
Housing estate with 250 units
Veranstalter/Organizer
    Amt für Hochbauten der
    Stadt Zürich
Auftraggeber/Client
    Baugenossenschaft
    Sonnengarten,
    Gemeinnützige Bau- und
    Mietergenossenschaft
    Zürich, Stiftung
    Alterswohnungen
    der Stadt Zürich

0159
Wohnüberbauung/
Residential development
    Im Blumenfeld
    Zürich-Affoltern
Wettbewerb/Competition
    2005, 1. Preis/1st prize
Realisierung/Realization
    2006–2008
Siedlung mit 69
    Eigentumswohnungen/
Housing estate with 69 owner-
    occupied units
Auftraggeber/Client
    Generalunternehmung
    Allreal AG

0163
Genossenschaftssiedlung/
Cooperative housing estate
    Triemli, Zürich
Projektwettbewerb/
Project competition
    2005
Siedlung mit 194 Wohnungen,
    Gemeinschafts- und Atelier-
    räumen, Kinderkrippe/
Housing estate with 194 units,
    common and studio rooms,
    day care center
Veranstalter/Organizer
    Amt für Hochbauten der
    Stadt Zürich
Auftraggeber/Client
    Baugenossenschaft
    Sonnengarten

0166
Genossenschaftssiedlung/
Cooperative housing estate
    Tägelmoos,
    Winterthur-Seen
Projektwettbewerb/
Project competition
    2006
Siedlung mit 150 Wohnungen
Housing estate with 150 units
Veranstalter/Organizer
    ASIG Wohngenossenschaft,
    gaiwo Genossenschaft
    für Alters- und
    Invalidenwohnungen

0169
Terrassenhäuser/
Terraced housing
    Auhalde
    Untersiggenthal
Direktauftrag/Direct commission
Realisierung/Realization
    2007–2010
12 Eigentumswohnungen/
12 owner-occupied units
Auftraggeber/Client
    Feldmann Immobilien AG

0172
Wohnhaus/
Multifamily dwelling
    auf der Forch, Küsnacht
Projektwettbewerb/
Project competition
    2006
Fünf-Familien-Haus/
House for five families
Veranstalter/Organizer
    Eigenheimgenossenschaft
    Küsnacht

0175
Wohn- und Geschäftshaus/
Residential and Commercial
    Building
    Am Bahnhof, Wohlen
Studienauftrag/
Commissioned study
    2006, 1. Preis/1st prize
Realisierung/Realization
    2013–2015
Siedlung mit 39 Wohnungen/
Housing estate with 39 units
Auftraggeber/Client
    Feldmann Generalbau AG
Auszeichnungen/Awards
    best architects 17

0176
Genossenschaftliches Wohn-
    und Geschäftshaus/
Cooperative residential and
    commercial building
    Badenerstrasse, Zürich
Studienauftrag/
Commissioned study
    2006, 1. Preis/1st prize
Realisierung/Realization
    2008–2010
54 Wohnungen in Massiv-
    holzbauweise, Standard der
    2000-Watt-Gesellschaft,
    Grossverteiler im EG/
54 units in solid timber
    construction, standard of
    the 2000 Watt Society,
    major distributors on
    ground floor
Auftraggeber/Client
    Baugenossenschaft
    Zurlinden
Auszeichnungen/Awards
    best architects 13
    Prix Lignum 2012
    Auszeichnung für Gute
    Bauten der Stadt Zürich
    2006–2010 (Anerkennung)

0177
Genossenschaftssiedlung/
Cooperative housing estate
    Im Sydefädeli
    Zürich-Wipkingen
Studienauftrag/
Commissioned study
    2006, 1. Preis/1st Prize
Realisierung/Realization
    2013–2016
Ersatzneubauten mit 176
    Wohnungen, Gemein-
    schaftsräumen, Gewerbe
    und Kindergarten/
Replacement building with
    176 units, common rooms,
    commercial spaces, and
    kindergarten
Auftraggeber/Client
    Baugenossenschaft
    Denzlerstrasse Zürich BDZ

0178
Wohnüberbauung/
Residential development
    Badenerstrasse 707
    Zürich-Altstetten
Studienauftrag/
Commissioned study
    2006
Überbauung mit 81
    Mietwohnungen/
Residential development
    with 81 rental units
Veranstalter/Organizer
    Peter Halter Liegen-
    schaften AG, Halter
    Generalunternehmung AG
Auftraggeber/Client
    Grundeigentümer/
    Property owners

0179
Wohnüberbauung/
Residential development
    Im Gries, Volketswil
Studienauftrag/
Commissioned study
    2006, 2. Rang/ 2nd rank
Wohnsiedlung mit
    ca. 50 Wohnungen/
Housing estate
    with ca. 50 units
Auftraggeber/Client
    BAHOGE Wohnbau-
    genossenschaft

0180
Alterswohnungen/
Apartments for seniors
    Siedlung Frieden
    Zürich-Affoltern
Projektwettbewerb/
Project competition
    2006, 1. Preis/1st. Prize
Realisierung/Realization
    2009–2013
Siedlung mit 93 Alters-
    wohnungen, Spitexein-
    richtungen, Kinderkrippe,
    Eltern-Kind-Zentrum/
Housing estate with 93 units
    for elderly residents, Spitex
    facilities, day care center,
    parent-child-center
Auftraggeber/Client
    Stiftung Alterswohnungen
    der Stadt Zürich
Auszeichnungen/Awards
    best architects 15

0181
Genossenschaftssiedlung/
Cooperative housing estate
    Sonnenhalde
    Zürich-Leimbach
Studienauftrag/
Commissioned study
    2006
Studie für Ersatzneubauten/
Study for replacement building
Auftraggeber/Client
    Baugenossenschaft
    Freiblick

0182
Wohnüberbauung/
Residential development
    Dietlimoos, Adliswil
Studienauftrag/
Commissioned study
    2006
Siedlung mit 300 Wohnungen/
Housing estate with 300 units
Auftraggeber/Client
    Allreal Generalunter-
    nehmung AG

0190
Wohnüberbauung/
Residential development
    Dammstrasse, Horgen
Privater Studienauftrag/
Privately commissioned study
    2007, 1. Preis/1st prize
Vier Wohngebäude
    mit 32 Wohnungen
Four apartment buildings
    with 32 units
Auftraggeber/Client
    Erbgemeinschaft
    Ehrismann

0195
Reihenhäuser/town houses
    blue notes
    Richterswil
Studienauftrag/
Commissioned study
    2007, 1. Preis/1st prize
Realisierung/Realization
    2009/10
14 Reihenhäuser/
14 town houses
Auftraggeber/Client
    Fincasa AG,
    vertreten durch Halter AG
Auszeichnungen/Awards
    best architects 13

0199
Wohn- und Gewerbe-
    überbauung/
Residential and Commercial
    Development
    Spätzstrasse, Horgen
Direktauftrag/Direct commission
Gestaltungsplan/Design plan
    2007–2010
Realisierung/Realization
    2015–2017
Auftraggeber/Client
    Bantry Beteiligungs ag,
    vertreten durch/represented
    by Markstein AG

0200
Hochhaus/High-Rise
   Hardturm-Areal, Zürich
Studienauftrag/
   Commissioned study
   2007, engere Wahl/
   shortlisted
Hochhaus mit 136 Wohnungen
   und Dienstleistungsflächen
High-rise with 136 units and
   areas for services
Auftraggeber/Client
   Konsortium Pfingstweid,
   Hardturm AG

0201
Haus an der Bickelstrasse
   Oberrieden
Direktauftrag/Direct commission
   2007
Realisierung/Realization
   2008–2009
Einfamilienhaus/
Single-family dwelling
Auftraggeber/Client
   Privat/Private

0203
Dreifamilienhaus/
Three-Family House
   Im Dörfli/Oberrieden
Direktauftrag/Direct commission
   2007
Realisierung/Realization
   2013/14
Drei Mietwohnungen
   in Holzbauweise/
Three rental units in timber
   construction
Auftraggeber/Client
   Privat/Private
Auszeichnungen/Awards
   Architekturpreis Kanton
   Zürich 2016,
   best architects 16,
   Prix Lignum 2015
   (Anerkennung/Recognition)

0216
Wohnüberbauung/
Residential development
   Laufenburg, Aargau
Studienauftrag/
   Commissioned study
   2008, 1. Preis/1st prize
Studie für ein nachhaltiges
   Quartier/
Study for a sustainable district
Veranstalter/Organizer
   Kanton Aargau

0219
Mehrfamilienhaus/
Multifamily dwelling, Loft/Split
   Horgen
Direktauftrag/Direct commission
   2008
Realisierung/Realization
   2011/12
Sechs Loft-Wohnungen in
   umgebautem Gewerbehaus,
   acht Split-Wohnungen in
   Neubau/
Six loft units in converted com-
   mercial building, eight split
   apartments in new building
Auftraggeber/Client
   Bantry Beteiligungs
   AG, vertreten durch/
   represented by Markstein AG

0222
Wohnüberbauung/
Residential development
   Brunnmatt-Ost, Bern
Projektwettbewerb/
   Project competition
   2008
Wohnbau mit 84 Wohnungen
Auftraggeber/Client
   Emil Merz AG
   Liegenschaften/
   Bauprojekte, Hans Merz

0225
Wohnüberbauung/
Residential development
   Zellweger Park, Uster
Studienauftrag/
   Commissioned study
   2008
140 Wohnungen in
   zwei Gebäuden
140 units in two buildings
Auftraggeber/Client
   Firmenpark Uster AG

0229
Wohnhaus/Apartment Building
   Laur-Park, Brugg
Studienauftrag/
   Commissioned study
   2009, 1. Preis/1st prize
Realisierung/Realization
   2010–2013
Mehrfamilienhaus
   mit 11 Wohnungen/
Multifamily dwelling
   with 11 units
Auftraggeber/Client
   Planungskonsortium
   Laur-Park

0230
Genossenschaftssiedlung/
Cooperative housing estate
   Kalkbreite, Zürich
Wettbewerb/Competition
   2009, 9. Preis/9th prize
Gemeinschaftliche Wohn-
   formen über Tramdepot,
   gewerbliche und kulturelle
   Nutzungen/
Cooperative living arrange-
   ments above tram depot,
   commercial and cultural
   utilizations
Veranstalter/Organizer
   Amt für Hochbauten
   der Stadt Zürich
Auftraggeber/Client
   Genossenschaft Kalkbreite

0231
Genossenschaftssiedlung/
Cooperative housing estate
   Hunziker Areal
   Zürich-Leutschenbach
Projektwettbewerb/
   Project competition
   2009, 4. Preis/4th prize
Planung eines zukunft-
   weisenden Quartiers/
Planning of a future oriented
   district
Folgeauftrag zur Realisierung
   von drei Wohngebäuden
   (→0243 «mehr als wohnen»)/
Successor commission for
   the realization of three
   residential buildings
   (→0243 "mehr als wohnen")
Veranstalter/Organizer
   Amt für Hochbauten
   der Stadt Zürich
Auftraggeber/Client
   Baugenossenschaft mehr
   als wohnen

0237
Wohnsiedlung/Residential Estate
   Areal Teiggi, Kriens
Projektwettbewerb/
   Project competition
   2009
32 Wohnungen und Gewerbe-
   flächen als Umnutzung und
   Neubau/
32 units and commercial surface,
   conversion and new building
Veranstalter/Organizer
   Gemeinde Kriens,
   Luzerner Pensionskasse

0239
Genossenschaftssiedlung/
Cooperative housing estate
   Tram-/Funkwiesenstrasse
   Zürich-Schwamendingen
Projektwettbewerb/
   Project competition
   2009, 3. Preis/3rd prize
Ersatzneubauten
   mit 63 Mietwohnungen
Replacement building
   with 63 rental units
Veranstalter/Organizer
   Amt für Hochbauten
   der Stadt Zürich
Auftraggeber/Client
   BAHOGE
   Wohnbaugenossenschaft

0243
«mehr als wohnen», Haus G
   Zürich-Leutschenbach
Folgeauftrag aus Wettbewerb/
   Follow-up commission
   from competition
   2009
Realisierung/Realization
   2012–2015
Genossenschaftliches Wohnhaus
   in Dämmbetonbauweise
   mit 30 Wohnungen
   und Gewerbeflächen
Cooperative residence
   with 30 residential units
   and commercial areas
Auftraggeber/Client
   Baugenossenschaft mehr
   als wohnen

0243
«mehr als wohnen», Haus J
   Zürich-Leutschenbach
Folgeauftrag aus Wettbewerb/
   Follow-up commission
   from competition
   2009
Realisierung/Realization
   2012–2015
Genossenschaftliches
   Wohnhaus in Massivholzbauweise mit 24 Wohn-
   ungen und Gewerbeflächen
Cooperative residence with
   24 residential units and
   commercial areas
Auftraggeber/Client
   Baugenossenschaft mehr
   als wohnen
Auszeichnungen/Awards
   best architects 17 Gold

0243
«mehr als wohnen», Haus L
   Zürich-Leutschenbach
Folgeauftrag aus Wettbewerb/
   Follow-up commission
   from competition
   2009
Realisierung/Realization
   2012–2015
Genossenschaftliches Wohnhaus mit 45 Wohnungen
   und Gewerbeflächen
Cooperative residence with 45
   residential units
   and commercial areas
Auftraggeber/Client
   Baugenossenschaft mehr
   als wohnen

0251
Genossenschaftssiedlung/
Cooperative housing estate
   Muggenbühl
   Zürich-Wollishofen
Projektwettbewerb/
   Project competition
   2010
Ersatzneubauten
   mit 89 Wohnungen/
Replacement building
   with 89 units
Auftraggeber/Client
   Baugenossenschaft
   St. Jakob

0253
Wohnüberbauung/
Residential development
   Wuhrmatt, Bottmingen
Studienauftrag/
   Commissioned study
   2010
53 Wohnungen/53 units
Auftraggeber/Client
   National Suisse Immobilien,
   vertreten durch/repre-
   sented by Emch + Berger AG

0254
Wohnhaus/
Multifamily dwelling
  Limmattalstrasse
  Zürich-Höngg
Studienauftrag/
Commissioned study
  2010, 1. Preis/1st prize
Realisierung/Realization
  2011–2013
Ersatzneubau Limmattalstrasse
  mit 21 Wohnungen/
Replacement building on Limmattalstrasse with 21 units
Auftraggeber/Client
  Zürich Versicherungsgesellschaft AG, Zürich IMRE AG

0256
Wohnhaus/Multifamily dwelling
  Sittenweg, Amden
Direktauftrag/Direct commission
  2010
Wohnhaus mit drei
  Eigentumswohnungen/
Residence with three
  owner-occupied units
Auftraggeber/Client
  HEKA AG

0263
Wohnüberbauung/
Residential development
  Zollfreilager
  Zürich-Albisrieden
Wettbewerb/Competition
  2010
Wohnüberbauung aus
  Zeilenbauten und Türmen
  mit 298 Wohnungen
Residential development with
  298 units
Auftraggeber/Client
  Zürcher Freilager AG

0269
Genossenschaftssiedlung/
Cooperative housing estate
  Toblerstrasse
  Zürich-Fluntern
Studienauftrag/
Commissioned study
  2011
Ersatzneubauten
  mit 160 Wohnungen/
Replacement building
  with 160 units
Auftraggeber/Client
  ABZ Allgemeine
  Baugenossenschaft Zürich

0274
Genossenschaftliches
  Wohnhaus/
Cooperative Residence
  Seestrasse, Meilen
Studienauftrag/
Commissioned study
  2010
Wohnhaus in Massivholzbauweise mit 27 Wohnungen/
Residence with 27 units
Auftraggeber/Client
  Baugenossenschaft
  Zurlinden

0276
Mehrfamilienhaus/
Multifamily dwelling
  Kosakenweg
  Zürich-Oerlikon
Direktauftrag/Direct commission
  2010
Realisierung/Realization
  2012–2014
Acht Wohnungen/
Eight units
Auftraggeber/Client
  Privat/private

0280
Genossenschaftssiedlung/
Cooperative housing estate
  Am Glattbogen
  Zürich-Schwamendingen
Studienauftrag/
Commissioned study
  2011, 1. Preis/1st prize
Realisierung/Realization
  2016–2019
Ersatzneubauten mit 227
  Wohnungen, Kindergarten,
  Gewerbeflächen
Replacement buildings
  with 227 residential units
  and a nursery
Auftraggeber/Client
  ASIG Wohngenossenschaft

0282
Wohnüberbauung/
Residential development
  Landolt-Areal, Zürich
Studienauftrag/
Commissioned study
  2011
66 Wohnungen/
66 residential units
Auftraggeber/Client
  Agruna AG

0283
Alterszentrum Neuer Gehren
  Erlenbach
Projektwettbewerb/
Project competition
  2011
Alterszentrum
  mit 75 Einheiten/
Retirement center
  with 75 residential units
Auftraggeber/Client
  Gemeinde Erlenbach

0285
Städtische Siedlung
  Areal Hornbach, Zürich
Projektwettbewerb/
Project competition
  2011
Stadthäuser mit 127 Wohnungen, Gewerbe, Werkhof
  und Betreuungsstätte/
Town houses with 127
  residential units, business
  space and care center
Auftraggeber/Client
  Stadt Zürich

0289
Wohnüberbauung/
Residential development
  Richi Areal, Schlieren
Studienauftrag/
Commissioned study
  2012
192 Wohnungen und Gewerbe/
192 residential units
  and commercial areas
Auftraggeber/Client
  Richi Immobilien AG

0291
Wohnsiedlung für Studierende/
Housing estate for students
  ETH, Zürich-Hönggerberg
Projektwettbewerb/
Project competition
  2012, 4. Rang/4th rank
446 Studentenzimmer/
446 student rooms
Auftraggeber/Client
  ETH Immobilien

0298
Wohnhochhäuser Vulcano Areal
Zürich-Altstetten
Wettbewerb/Competition
  2012, engere Wahl/shortlisted
Wohntürme und Bürohaus/
Residential tower and office
  building
Auftraggeber/Client
  Crédit Suisse
  Anlagestiftung

0309
Studentisches Wohnen
  Binz-Ü111, Zürich
Wettbewerb/Competition
  2013
331 Studentenzimmer/
331 Student rooms
Auftraggeber/Client
  Stiftung Abendrot –
  Pensionskasse, Basel

0315
Genossenschaftssiedlung/
Cooperative housing estate
  Glattpark, Opfikon
Studienauftrag/
Commissioned study
  2013
Realisierung/Realization
  2014–2019
286 Wohnungen, Kinderkrippe,
  Kindergarten und
  Gewerbeflächen/
286 residential units and
  nursery
Auftraggeber/Client
  ABZ Allgemeine
  Baugenossenschaft Zürich

0318
Mehrfamilienhaus/
Multifamily dwelling
  Renggerstrasse
  Zürich-Wollishofen
Projektstudie/Project study
  2014
Vier Wohnungen/Four units
Auftraggeber/Client
  Baugenossenschaft
  Homelab

0319
Studentisches Wohnen/
Student housing
  Areal Rosengarten
  Zürich-Wipkingen
Projektwettbewerb/
Project competition
  2014
Wohngemeinschaften, Kindergarten, Kinderkrippe, Musikzimmer, Gemeinschaftsraum/
Shared apartments, kindergarten, music room, and
  common room
Auftraggeber/Client
  Stiftung für Studentisches
  Wohnen Zürich

0322
Genossenschaftliches
  Wohnhaus/
Cooperative residential
  building
  Stadterle, Basel
Projektwettbewerb/
Project competition
  2014
24 Gruppen- und Singlewohnungen,
  4 Clusterwohnungen/
24 group and single apartments,
  4 cluster apartments
Auftraggeber/Client
  Wohngenossenschaft
  Zimmerfrei

0323
Alterswohnen/Retirement home
  Erikastrasse, Zürich
Projektwettbewerb/
Project competition
  2014
61 Alterswohnungen,
  Spitexeinrichtungen und
  Gewerbeflächen/
61 retirement homes and
  commercial space
Auftraggeber/Client
  Stiftung Alterswohnen der
  Stadt Zürich

0324
Areal Kälin
  Oberwinterthur
Direktauftrag/Direct commission
Gestaltungsplan/Design
  2014–2016
Realisierung/Realization
  2017–2021
45 Mietwohnungen, 30
  Eigentumswohnungen,
  Co-Working und
  Gewerberäume
45 rented units, 30 owneroccupied units, co-working
  space and warehouse
Auftraggeber/Client
  Stadtbauentwicklungs AG

0331
Wohnüberbauung/
Residential development
　Eggbühl-Areal
　Zürich-Seebach
Projektwettbewerb/
Project competition
　2014/15, 1. Preis/1st prize
Realisierung/Realization
　2018–2020
135 Mietwohnungen und
　Gewerbeflächen/
135 rental apartments and
　commercial space
Auftraggeber/Client
　Diethelm Keller Holding AG

0335
Genossenschaftssiedlung/
Cooperative housing estate
　Zollhaus, Zürich
Projektwettbewerb/
Project competition
　2015
Wohngemeinschaften,
　Clusterwohnungen,
　Hallenwohnen, Pension,
　Gewerbeflächen, Kultur/
Shared apartments, cluster
　apartments, indoor living
　quarters, guest house,
　commercial space
Veranstalter/Organizer
　Amt für Hochbauten der
　Stadt Zürich
Auftraggeber/Client
　Genossenschaft Kalkbreite

0340
Wohnüberbauung/
Residential development
　Rütistrasse, Adliswil
Studienauftrag/
Commissioned study
　2015
Ersatzneubauten
　mit 71 Wohnungen/
Replacement building
　with 71 residential units
Auftraggeber/Client
　Zürich Versicherungsgesell-
　schaft AG, Zürich IMRE AG

0343
Wohnüberbauung/
Residential development
　Letzibach D
　Zürich-Altstetten
Projektwettbewerb/
Project competition
　2015
252 Wohnungen und
　Gewerbeflächen/
252 residential units
Veranstalter/Organizer
　Amt für Hochbauten der
　Stadt Zürich
Auftraggeber/Client
　Liegenschaftenverwaltung
　der Stadt Zürich,
　Stiftung Alterswohnungen
　der Stadt Zürich,
　Stiftung Wohnungen für
　Kinderreiche Familien

0347
Genossenschaftssiedlung/
Cooperative housing estate
　Areal Hardturm, Zürich
Investoren-Studienauftrag/
Commissioned study
　2016
174 Wohnungen mit Gemein-
　schaftsräumen, Ateliers,
　Gewerbe und Kindergarten/
174 residential units with
　common rooms, studios,
　commercial space, and
　kindergarten
Veranstalter/Organizer
　Finanzdepartement
　der Stadt Zürich
Auftraggeber/Client
　ABZ Allgemeine
　Baugenossenschaft Zürich

0351
Haus Mühlerain
　Meilen
Direktauftrag/Direct commission
Realisierung/Realization
　2016–2019
Fünf Mietwohnungen, Atelier/
Five apartments and studio
Auftraggeber/Client
　Privat/Private

0354
Wohnüberbauung/
Residential development
　Effretikon
　Illnau-Effretikon
Studienauftrag/
Commissioned study
　2017
Siedlung mit ca. 130
　Wohnungen/
Housing estate with
　ca. 130 units
Auftraggeber/Client
　Zürich Anlagestiftung,
　Zürich IMRE AG

0355
Wohnüberbauung/
Residential development
　Manegg
　Zürich-Manegg
Studienauftrag/
Commissioned study
　2017
250 Mietwohnungen
　und Gewerbeflächen/
250 apartments
Auftraggeber/Client
　Logis Suisse AG, Mobimo AG

0357
Cité internationale du Grand
　Morillon
　Le Petit-Saconnex, Genève
Studienauftrag/
Commissioned study
　2017
Studentisches Wohnen/
Student housing
Auftraggeber/Client
　Institut de Hautes Études
　Internationales
　et du Développement

0364
Gemeinnütziger Wohnungsbau
　Guggach Areal III
　Zürich-Oerlikon
Projektwettbewerb/
Project competition
　2018, 2. Preis/2nd prize
120 Mietwohnungen mit
　Schulhaus und Quartierpark/
120 apartments with
　schoolhouse and park
Veranstalter/Organizer
　Amt für Hochbauten
　der Stadt Zürich
Auftraggeber/Client
　Immobilien Stadt Zürich,
　Grün Stadt Zürich, Stiftung
　Einfach Wohnen

0365
Neubau Parkend Fonds
　Zürich-Hirslanden
Studienauftrag/
Commissioned study
　2018, 2. Preis/2nd prize
47 Mietwohnungen/
47 apartments
Auftraggeber/Client
　Stiftung Gemeinnützige
　Gesellschaft von
　Neumünster GGN

pool Architekten: Wohnbauprojekte 1998–2018. Ein Werkverzeichnis

pool Architekten: Residential Projects 1998–2018. A Catalogue Raisonné

pool an der TU Berlin:
Entwurfsseminare
2013–2016.
Aufgabenstellungen
und Projektlisten

pool at the TU Berlin:
Design Seminars
2013–2016.
Assignments
and Project Lists

→

Abbild des Raumes

TU Berlin, Semestervorübung,
Sommer 2013 bis Sommer 2016
→ Historische Interieurs im Modell, S. 14

Das Bild als Darstellungsmittel, das eine vorerst noch immaterielle architektonische Konzeption gegenüber Dritten fassbar macht, blickt auf eine lange Tradition zurück. Mit den heutigen technischen Mitteln ist es einfacher geworden, Bilder herzustellen. Rücken diese unsere Projekte jedoch ins rechte Licht, in dem Sinne, in dem wir sie verstanden haben wollen? Die beeindruckenden Skizzen, Perspektiven und Fotomontagen unserer Architektenvorbilder zeugen von einem umfassenden Bildwissen der damaligen Verfasser. Die Fähigkeiten, die nötig sind, um auf diesem Niveau mithalten zu können, müssen wir uns aber zuerst aneignen.

Im Rahmen der Vorübung «Abbild des Raumes» wurden in jedem Semester verschiedene Eigenschaften des Architekturbilds und dessen Zusammenhang mit dem architektonischen Konzept untersucht. Neben der Darstellungstechnik wurden inhaltliche Aspekte wie Verständnis von Struktur- und Raumkonzepten, Bildtradition und kulturelle Codes sowie die Bilddramaturgie anhand von Architekturfotografien diskutiert.

Der Bildhauer und Fotograf Thomas Demand ist berühmt für seine grossformatigen Fotografien von Innenräumen aus Papier und Karton. Seine Papier-Räume sind Nachbildungen realer (Tat-)Orte, die, nachdem sie fotografisch festgehalten sind, zerstört werden.

Inspiriert von den Arbeiten des Künstlers bauten die Studierenden Innenräume architektonischer Ikonen aus Papier, Karton und Farbe nach, um diese anschliessend zu fotografieren. Dabei galt es, dem künstlerischen Vorbild entsprechend an ausgewählten Stellen Abstraktionen vorzunehmen. Als Vorlage dienten Fotografien in Schwarz-Weiss sowie Grundrisse und Schnitte des Hauses. Das Modellfoto war dem Originalfoto in seinen wesentlichen Aspekten nachzuempfinden: Perspektive, Licht- und Schattenverhältnisse, Oberflächenqualitäten und Texturen sowie Einrichtungsgegenstände. Die Atmosphäre des Originalfotos sollte dabei mit minimalem Einsatz digitaler Nachbearbeitungswerkzeuge übertragen werden. Auf diese Weise übten wir einerseits das Sehen und Verstehen der Qualitäten ausgewählter Wohnräume, die von den Raumproportionen ebenso bestimmt werden wie von der Anordnung der Raumöffnungen, der Lichtsituation, dem Bezug zum Aussenraum, der Materialität, aber auch vom Vorhandensein von Artefakten des Gebrauchs. Andererseits lernten wir von den Meistern der Architekturfotografie die Inszenierung des Raumes und die Komposition der Darstellung. Das Abbild des Abbilds führt uns zum Modellfoto als Abstraktion des gebauten Innenraumes.

Imaging Spaces

TU Berlin Semester Preliminary Exercise,
summer 2013 to summer 2016
→ Models of Historic Interiors, p. 14

The use of images to communicate an immaterial architectonic concept enjoys a long tradition. Today, technical resources have of course made it simpler to generate images. But do the images we create position our projects in the desired light, allowing them to be understood in the ways we intend? The impressive sketches, perspective views, and photomontages produced by our architectural predecessors testify to a comprehensive understanding of images by their authors. One's ability to keep pace at this high level, however, necessitates the acquisition of the requisite tools.

Each semester, various characteristics of architectural images and their connection to architectonic concepts were explored in the exercise *Abbild des Raumes* (Imaging Spaces). Techniques of representation with reference to architectural photographs were discussed alongside the understanding of structural and spatial concepts, building traditions, cultural codes, and the dramaturgy of images.

The sculptor and photographer Thomas Demand is famous for his large-format photographs of interior spaces created using paper and cardboard. His paper spaces are reconstructions of real (crime) scenes, which are destroyed after being photographically documented.

Inspired by the work of Demand, students used paper, cardboard, and paint to reconstruct the interior spaces of architectonic icons in order to photograph them. Important here was the exploration of abstractions in selected areas in ways that corresponded to the artistic model. Black-and-white photographs, ground plans and sections of buildings were used as models. The model photo was, in its most essential aspects, a recreation of the original photo: through perspective, relations of light and shadow, surface qualities and textures, as well as furnishings. The atmosphere of the original photograph was transferred via the minimal employment of digital post-processing tools. We first practiced viewing and comprehending the qualities of selected residential spaces: the spatial proportions, arrangement of the openings, lighting, the relationship to external space, materiality, and artifacts of use. We also learned about the scenography of space and the composition of images from the masters of architectural photography. The study of images guides us toward the model photograph as an abstraction of a built interior space.

Abbild S13-03
Casa Niemeyer,
　Oscar Niemeyer,
　Rio de Janeiro, 1953
Lisa Hannes
Alexander Markau

Abbild S13-04
Maison de Verre,
　Pierre Chareau,
　Paris, 1931
Cem Baykal
Yuki Hanfeld

Abbild S13-05
Frey House 2,
　Albert Frey,
　Palm Springs/
　California, 1964
Carolin Lehnerer
Aydin Sunar

Abbild S13-06
Via Dezza,
　Gio Ponti,
　Milano, 1957
Timo Büscher
Olivier Laydevant

Abbild S13-07
Palais Stoclet,
　Josef Hofmann,
　Bruxelles, 1911
Veronika Mosser
Nico Steinacker

Abbild S13-08
Fisher House,
　Louis Kahn,
　Hatboro/Pennsylvania,
　1967
Mathias Lehmann
Torbjørn Våge

Abbild S13-09
Maison Jaoul,
　Le Corbusier,
　Neuilly-sur-Seine, 1956
Daniela Knappe
Yasha Anil Kuhn

Abbild S13-11
Casa Butantã,
　Paulo Mendes da Rocha,
　São Paulo, 1964
Murat Erman Aksoy
Jana Wecker

Abbild S13-12
Villa Tugendhat,
　Mies van der Rohe,
　Brno, 1930
Christobal Lambertini Herrera
Miguel Angel Reyes Benz
Jiajun Tan

Abbild S13-15
Villa Seynave,
　Jean Prouvé,
　Grimaud, 1961
Tatjana Anic
Timo Lück

Abbild S13-16
Kanzler-Pavillon,
　Sep Ruf,
　Bonn, 1964
Marco Migliavacca
Friedrich Neukirchen

Abbild S13-17
Howe House,
　Rudolph Schindler,
　Los Angeles/California,
　1925
Yvonne Fissel
Katharina Woicke

Abbild S13-18
House in a curved road,
 Kazuo Shinohara,
 Tokyo, 1978
Jan Blifernez

Abbild S13-19
Casa Beires,
 Alvaro Siza,
 Pavoa de Varzim, 1976
Kerstin Krüger
Elisabeth Bork

Abbild W13/14-01
Casa Ruben de Mendonça,
 João Batista Vilanova
  Artigas,
 São Paulo, 1958
Jinglin Cai
Xiangyue Guan
Hang Yuan

Abbild W13/14-02
Casa Martirani,
 João Batista Vilanova
  Artigas,
 São Paulo, 1970
Tatjana Anic
Timo Lück

Abbild W13/14-04
Casa do Jardim de Cristal,
 Lina Bo Bardi,
 São Paulo, 1958
Mikal Skodjereite
Jakob Ulbrych

Abbild W13/14-05
Casa Ugalde,
 José Antonio Coderch,
 Caldes d'Estrac, 1953
Ahmed Michael Abd Alla
Eva-Maria Thinius

Abbild W13/14-06
Villa Engström,
 Ralph Erskine,
 Nynäshamn, 1956
Johanna Backhaus
Tetyana Nesterenko

Abbild W13/14-07
Haus Beer,
 Josef Frank,
 Wien, 1931
Sebastian Blatter
Zaneta Choroba

Abbild W13/14-08
Haus Schmitz,
 Hugo Häring,
 Biberach, 1950
Jennifer Moser
Fabian Trapp

Abbild W13/14-09
Stevens Residence,
 John Lautner,
 Malibu/California, 1968
Marina Kolovou-Kouri
David Scharf

Abbild W13/14-10
Maison Jaoul,
 Le Corbusier,
 Neuilly-sur-Seine, 1956
Apostolos Klontzaris
Anja Kokott

Abbild W13/14-11
Landhaus Khuner,
 Adolf Loos,
 Payerbach, 1930
Sophie Baum
Theresa Piechottka

Abbild W13/14-12
Villa Müller,
 Adolf Loos,
 Praha, 1930
Marlene Bühner
Cassandra Donath

Abbild W13/14-13
Sea Ranch,
 Moore Lyndon Turnbull
  Whitaker,
 Sonoma/California, 1965
Julia Schmidt
Sebastian Welzel

Abbild W13/14-14
Haus Freudenberg,
 Hermann Muthesius,
 Berlin, 1908
Christopher Sitzler
Kristina Szeifert

Abbild W13/14-15
Lovell Beach House,
 Rudolph Schindler,
 Newport Beach/
  California, 1926
Julia Domanska
Mariana Ferreira

Abbild W13/14-16
Wohnhaus Schlup,
 Max Schlup,
 Biel/Bienne, 1959
Sebastian Genzel
Christobal Lambertini Herrera

Abbild W13/14-17
Umbrella House,
 Kazuo Shinohara,
 Tokyo, 1961
Kamila Marta Kojder
Cyrell Boehm

Abbild W13/14-18
Upper Lawn Pavillion,
 Alison and Peter Smithson,
 Wiltshire, 1962
Aydin Sunar
Tobias Wolski

Abbild W13/14-19
Can Lis,
 Jørn Uzon,
 Mallorca, 1972
Nicole Redmer
Claudia Schwiethale

Abbild W13/14-20
Vanna Venturi House,
 Robert Venturi,
 Philadelphia/
  Pennsylvania, 1964
Dimitra Megas
Harald Niessner

Abbild S14-01
Villa Kokkonen,
 Alvar Aalto,
 Järvenpää, 1967
Daniela Tankova
Vedran Zonic

Abbild S14-02
Own House,
 Luis Barragan,
 Mexico City, 1948
Patryk Kujawa
Martyna Aleksandra
  Wojnarowska

Abbild S14-03
Case Study House No. 8,
 Charles and Ray Eames,
 Los Angeles/
  California, 1948
Hanna Grabmaier
Julia Henning
Lisa Nagy

Abbild S14-04
Hunt House,
 Craig Ellwood,
 Malibu/California, 1955
Thomas Pracht
Guang Xue

Abbild S14-05
Pope Leighey House,
 Frank Lloyd Wright,
 Alexandria/Virginia, 1941
Cela Adamescu
Madalina Uram

Abbild S14-07
Labyrinth House,
 John M. Johansen,
 Southport/
  Connecticut, 1966
Myungjin Choi
Elena Schneider

Abbild S14-08
Maison Cook,
 Le Corbusier,
 Boulogne-sur-Seine, 1925
Jialiang Cui
Liane Rosenthal

Abbild S14-09
Werkbund-Siedlung,
 Adolf Loos,
 Wien, 1932
Ana Garcia Gasquet
Ignasi Querol Diez

Abbild S14-10
Highpoint II,
 Berthold Lubetkin,
 London, 1938
Sebastian Genzel
Harald Niessner

Abbild S14-11
Haus Moll,
 Hans Scharoun,
 Berlin, 1935
Felix Bardou
Carlo Fischer

Abbild W14/15-01
Casa Milà,
 Antoni Gaudí,
 Barcelona, 1910
Luca Gericke
Franko Scheuplein
Carolin Trahorsch

Abbild W14/15-02
Bridge House,
 John Johansen,
 New Canaan/
  Connecticut, 1956
Larsen Berg
Teymur Osmanov
Judith Schiebel

Abbild W14/15-03
Maison Jaoul,
 Le Corbusier,
 Neuilly-sur-Seine, 1956
Julius Blencke
Caspar Kollmeyer
Jan Wind

Abbild W14/15-04
Immeuble Molitor,
 Le Corbusier,
 Paris, 1933
Marlene Bühner
Cassandra Donath
Anika Weidlich
Franziska Wich

Abbild W14/15-05
Haus Rudolph,
 Lux Guyer,
 Küsnacht, 1931
Juan Cequera
Kays Elbeyli
Arthur Schmock
Marc Wendland

Abbild W14/15-06
Lipman Residence,
 George Matsumoto,
 Richmond/Virginia, 1957
Vera Marie Glas
Rafael Lozykowski
Florian Rizek

Abbild W14/15-07
Russell House,
 Erich Mendelsohn,
 San Francisco/
  California, 1951
Josephine Brillowski
Oskar Ellwanger
Jana Morgenstern

Abbild W14/15-08
Maison Gaut,
 Auguste Perret,
 Paris, 1923
Jessica Ganghofer
Anne-Katrin Schulz
Sarah Stein

Abbild W14/15-09
Villa Schroeder,
 Gerrit Rietveld,
 Utrecht, 1924
Kai Canver
Franziska Polleter
Simone Prill
Sina Riedlinger

Abbild W14/15-10
Miller House,
 Eero Saarinen,
 Columbus/Indiana, 1957
Alisa Joseph
Franziska Rüss
Sandra Schenavsky

Abbild W14/15-11
Haus Baensch,
　Hans Sharoun,
　Berlin, 1935
Simon Kiefer
Shaghayegh Moghaddasi
　Sikaroudi
Elena Wickenhoefer

Abbild W14/15-12
Uehara House,
　Kazuo Shinohara,
　Tokyo, 1976
Ilkin Akpinar
Veronique Baustert
Elena Petkova

Abbild W14/15-13
John Soane House,
　John Soane
　London, 1792–1823
Anna Gert
Cemile Kolgu
Ewa Kostecka

Abbild W14/15-14
The Orchard,
　Charles Voysey,
　Winchester, 1899
Theodora Constantin
Vanessa Vogel

Abbild W14/15-15
Ennis Housel,
　Frank Lloyd Wright,
　Los Angeles/
　California, 1924
Léo Frederic Schulz
Alara Tokcan

Abbild S15-01
Thalmatt 1,
　Atelier 5,
　Herrenschwanden, 1974
Elsa Albrecht
Nikolaus Schmid

Abbild S15-03
Hanna House,
　Frank Lloyd Wright,
　Stanford/California, 1937
Annett Donat
Jakob Pawlowski

Abbild S15-04
Dachwohnung,
　Herman Hertzberger,
　Laren, 1967
Mario Muñoz
Azad Saleem

Abbild S15-05
Own House,
　Mary Otis Stevens,
　Thomas McNulty,
　Lincoln/Massachusetts,
　1965
Fabian Koschowsky
Hanna Rohst

Abbild W15/16-01
La Fábrica,
　Ricardo Bofill,
　Sant Just Desvern,
　Barcelona, 1975
Niki Apostolopoulcu
Johanna Sieberer

Abbild W15/16-02
Appartement Rue Raynouard,
　Auguste Perret,
　Paris, 1933
Tobias Scholz
Tobias Bräunig

Abbild W15/16-03
Haus Hohen Pappeln,
　Henry van de Velde,
　Weimar, 1912
Cansu Cantas
Elina Kolarova

Abbild W15/16-04
Haus Stohrer,
　Paul Stohrer,
　Stuttgart, 1961
Robert Bauer
Fidias Curiel Casteson
Bernhard Weikert

Abbild W15/16-05
Maison Lange,
　Auguste Perret,
　Paris, 1930
Julien Engelhardt
Simon Lehmann
Merle Sudbrock

Abbild W15/16-06
Villa Mairea,
　Alvar Aalto,
　Noormarkku, 1939
Elizabeth Beckmann
Catherine Folawiyo
Clara Jereczek

Abbild W15/16-07
The Colonnade Condominiums,
　Paul Rudolph,
　Singapur, 1987
Maija Gavare
Kristine Kazelnika

Abbild W15/16-08
Haus Hohenhof,
　Henry van de Velde,
　Hagen-Eppenhausen, 1908
Tina Krause
Denitsa Todorova

Abbild W15/16-09
Entelechy 1,
　John Portman,
　Atlanta/Georgia, 1964
Paul Achter
Lorenz Preusser
Ivan Zilic

Abbild W15/16-10
Villa Noailles,
　Robert Mallet-Stevens,
　Hyères, 1923
James Horkulak
Marko Shllaku

Abbild W15/16-11
Haus Schmitthenner,
　Paul Schmitthenner,
　Stuttgart, 1953
Franziska Käuferle
Max Vesely
Louisa Wahler

Abbild W15/16-12
Maison Hexacore,
　Pierre Forestier,
　Buthiers, 1954
Sarah Meier
Maximilian Quick

Abbild W15/16-13
Kleinwohnhaus
　Weltausstellung Brüssel,
　Georg Metzendorf,
　Bruxelles, 1910
Annett Donat
Jakob Pawlowski

Abbild W15/16-14
Arcosanti,
　Paolo Soleri,
　Arcosanti/Arizona,
　1970er-Jahre
Azad Saleem
Martin Ulitzka
Olivia Valenzuela

Abbild W15/16-15
Mandalay House,
　Cliff May,
　Los Angeles/
　California, 1956
Amélie Barande
Qin Qian

Abbild S16-01
House for an Artist,
　Giuseppe Terragni,
　Milano 1933
Leonardo Jochim
Lukas Stadelmann
Samuel Yeboa

Abbild S16-02
Casa Varela,
　Alejandro de la Sota,
　Collado-Mediano, 1968
Diana Aleksowa
Nikoleta Nikolova
Tsvetomila Neshtereva

Abbild S16-03
Oliver Residence,
　Rudolph Schindler,
　Los Angeles/
　California, 1934
Marie-Louise Leeck
Lisa Thürer

Abbild S16-05
Haus Steiger-Crawford,
　Rudolf Steiger,
　Flora Steiger-Crawford,
　Zürich, 1959
Lysann Geller
Monika Pawlak
Kassandra Sarantis

Abbild S16-06
Saffa Haus,
　Lux Guyer,
　Stäfa, 1928
Ellionor Förster
Christine Feistl
Mai Tran

Abbild S16-07
Casa Tabarelli,
　Carlo Scarpa, Sergio Los,
　Cornaiano, 1969
Amer Eid
Michael Roth
Tan Phong Nguyen

Abbild S16-08
Casa Ricci,
　Leonardo Ricci,
　Monterinaldi, 1964
Paul Harries
Ana Richter de Arce
Florian Tropp

Abbild S16-09
Harumi-Apartments,
　Kunio Maekawa,
　Tokyo, 1958
Isabel de Placios
Jukia Ratsch
Florian Tudzierz

Abbild S16-10
Rue Franklin,
　Auguste Perret,
　Paris, 1904
Vadim nBelow
Katharina Zull
Timo Strauch

Abbild S16-11
Casa Luzi,
　Sergio Jaretti, Elio Luzi,
　Torino, 1966
Ann-Kathrin Salich
Helena Reischel
Daniel Dieren

Urban Wood

TU Berlin Master's Program, summer semester 2013

→ Standard Stories on a Scale of 1:500, p. 294
→ Plans 1:150, p. 324
→ Semester Designs in Model Form, p. 378

For our first semester at the TU-Berlin, we selected the Lohmühleninsel at the eastern exit of the Landwehr Canal in the Kreuzberg district of Berlin as our urban point of departure. The island-like character of the terrain was ideal for the assigned task: student groups were to develop a profile designed to strengthen a sense of identity for an entire urban quarter. Today, the island, which measures approximately 600 m in length and 100 m in breadth, is predominantly used for recreational and commercial purposes. Three historic bridges link the island with Kreuzberg toward the west and with Görlitzer Park on the eastern side. During the GDR era, the terrain lay along the inner German border. Here, we found a location, typical for Berlin, where a homogenous urban district was abruptly truncated, allowing it to be transformed into a less densified and rather undefined area. In his *The City in the City—A Green Archipelago* Oswald Mathias Ungers compares this location within Berlin to Manhattan. The "urban island" of Kreuzberg appears as a stringent structure and a fragment of a far larger complex and urban configuration.

As a starting point, students were asked to submit proposals for a masterplan involving 20 small parcels of land designed to enhance the character of this fractured place. It was a question of developing an autonomous urban pattern without infringing on the broader development pattern of Kreuzberg. Historic urban structures served as morphological references which could be adapted to the specific situation. For example, the Gratte-Ciel, a 1930s structure in Villeurbanne near Lyon, was used as a reference for a radical double-spaced complex in the center of the site. Along the central axis, a supplementary building regulation defined a rigorous façade with Berlin eaves heights of 22 m. In contrast, the canal-facing outer sides decreased in height and facilitated a variety of volumetric forms.

The enormous depth of the development could be mastered only through ingenious incisions. Building regulations also specified wooden construction to be visible both on the interior and exterior. Underpinning this requirement was the question of whether an urban identity can be generated using wood (→ p. 234 wooden construction in the chapter "Material").

The needs of urban populations can no longer be satisfied solely through apartments that are tailored to the classical family structure. To do justice to the apartment types now in demand, we define the spatial program not in relation to residential surface, nor in relation to a predetermined number of rooms, but instead in relation to spatial needs per person. This volume is set at a significantly lower level than the individual minimum requirement, and suffices for a quite tightly delimited sleeping, residential, and eating area, as well as for a bathroom. The resultant basic offering, consisting of private main living area and secondary service spaces, is supplemented by externally situated "third rooms" (→ p. 48 "Working with Typologies") designed to cover a multiplicity of additional requirements. The narrow spatial constraints of such residential units are complemented by spatial conceptions that are conceived in three-dimensional terms. Small surface — expansive sense of space!

---

1 Ein Manifest (1977) von Oswald Mathias Ungers und Rem Koolhaas mit Pieter Riemann, Hans Kollhoff und Arthur Ovaska, *Die Stadt in der Stadt. Berlin: Ein grünes Archipel*, hrsg. von Florian Hertweck und Sébastien Marot, Zürich 2013

Wood 01
Lisa Hannes
Alexander Markau

Wood 02
Pia Malina Kettler
Julia Schmidt

Wood 03
Tatjana Anic
Timo Lück

Wood 04
Debora Mendler
Nicole Redmer

Wood 05
Elisabeth Bork
Kerstin Krüger

Wood 06
Christina Höller
Jakob Kress

Wood 07
Veronika Mosser
Nico Steinacker

Wood 08
Katja Heieis
Lydia Kittelmann

Wood 09
Mathias Lehmann
Torbjørn Våge

Wood 10
Christobal Lambertini Herrera
Miguel Angel Reyes Benz
Jiajun Tan

Wood 11
Jan Blifernez

Wood 12
Marco Migliavacca
Friedrich Neukirchen

Wood 13
Jannes Beulting
Dominik Schad

Wood 14
Carolin Lehnerer
Aydin Sunar

Wood 15
Yvonne Fissel
Katharina Woicke

Wood 16
Cem Baykal
Yuki Hanfeld

Wood 17
Murat Erman Aksoy
Jana Wecker

Wood 18
Timo Büscher
Olivier Laydevant

Wood 19
Daniela Knappe
Yasha Anil Kuhn

Wood 20
Evelyn Gröger
Darina Palazova

Wood 21
Philipp Steinmetz
Andreas Woyke

pool an der TU Berlin: Entwurfsseminare 2013–2016

Urban Concrete

TU Berlin, Master-Studiengang, Wintersemester 2013/14
→ Regelgeschosse im Massstab 1:500, S. 294
→ Möblierte Grundrisse im Massstab 1:150, S. 324
→ Semesterentwürfe im Modell, S. 378

Jede Grossstadt charakterisiert sich aus überlagernden und widersprüchlichen Strukturen. Bestenfalls einzelne Stadtteile sind in sich homogen, mit einer einheitlichen Struktur und einem lokalen Zentrum. Dort, wo die Strukturen aufeinandertreffen — an den Übergängen und Rändern —, entstehen Brüche, entlang denen sich Nutzungen ansiedeln, die innerhalb der einzelnen Stadtteile keinen Platz haben. Hier finden sich auch häufig Bauten der Infrastruktur wie Verkehrshauptachsen und Eisenbahntrassen. Für uns interessanter sind aber neue, quartiersunspezifische Nutzungsmischungen, die sich an diesen Übergängen anlagern und einen ganz eigenen architektonischen Ausdruck hervorbringen, eine eigene Sprache, die die Brüche lesbar macht.

Das zu bearbeitende Areal befindet sich an einer solchen städtischen Bruchstelle, auf dem ehemaligen Gelände des 1871 in Betrieb genommenen Moabiter Güterbahnhofs, südlich des Berliner S-Bahn-Rings. Aufgrund des verkehrsgünstigen Standorts war der Bahnhof für die Versorgung der umliegenden Industriegebiete in Moabit und Charlottenburg von grosser Bedeutung. Nördlich der Gleise erstreckt sich das Westhafenareal, das 1914–1927 zum zweitgrössten Binnenhafen Deutschlands ausgebaut wurde und sich durch grossmassstäbliche Gebäudestrukturen auszeichnet. Aufgrund der Zerstörungen während des Zweiten Weltkriegs und der Abrissmassnahmen nach der Teilung Berlins sowie für die Neubebauung des Gebiets seit 2007 ist der Güterbahnhof aus dem Stadtbild verschwunden.

Wie im vorangehenden Semester veranstalteten wir unter den Studierenden als Vorübung einen städtebaulichen Wettbewerb. Die Beiträge hatten wiederum auf morphologischen Referenzen aufzubauen. Als Grundlage für den Masterplan wählten wir ein mäandrierendes Bebauungsmuster mit einer Abfolge von Halbhöfen nach dem Vorbild der Casa Convenzionata von Mario de Renzi aus den 1930er-Jahren an der Piazza Bologna in Rom. Jeder Studierendengruppe wurde eine Eckparzelle zugewiesen, auf der winkelförmige Gebäudetypen mit einer Traufhöhe von 22 Metern zu entwickeln waren. An diesen konnte exemplarisch untersucht werden, wie sich ein Grundrissprinzip um die Ecke entwickeln lässt — wird die Ecke betont oder heruntergespielt, ist sie symmetrisch oder hierarchisch, bildet sie eine Ausnahme oder folgt sie der Regel? Zusätzlich waren in einem vorgegebenen Sockel ergänzende, gemeinschaftliche und dem Quartiersleben dienende Nutzungen unterzubringen. Dieser Sockel sollte überhohe Räume mit grösseren Spannweiten enthalten (→ S. 48 «Typologien»). Die Höfe waren alternierend als Wohn- und Gewerbehöfe auszubilden.

Die einzelnen Gebäude waren durchgängig in vorgefertigten Betonelementen zu planen, sowohl die tragende Struktur als auch die Fassade (→ S. 262 «Material: Beton»). Durch die einheitliche Materialität sollte das Quartier als identifizierbarer «Stadtbaukörper» in Erscheinung treten. Strukturelle Prinzipien wie Skelettbauweise, Tafelbauweise oder Zellenbauweise und deren Gesetzmässigkeiten mussten in der Konzeption berücksichtigt werden. Plastizität, Modularität und Tektonik der Fassade waren als wesentlicher Bestandteil des Entwurfs zu untersuchen und zu gestalten, zudem sollten die Gebäude einen spezifisch urbanen Charakter erhalten.

Urban Concrete

TU Berlin Master's Program, winter semester 2013/2014
→ Standard Stories on a Scale of 1:500, p. 294
→ Plans 1:150, p. 324
→ Semester Designs in Model Form, p. 378

Every large city is characterized by the presence of overlapping and contradictory structures. Ideally, each individual urban district would be internally homogenous, with a unified structure and a local center. Where such structures converge—along transitional zones and borders—fractures emerge where new typologies can be accommodated that do not fit within individual urban districts. Infrastructural facilities such as main arteries and rail lines are often situated in these spaces. Of greater interest for us, however, are new mixes of use that are not specific to individual districts, which are situated along such transitional zones, and which generate singular forms of architecture, manifest singular languages, and render these fractured zones legible.

The fractured zone under consideration in this case is on the premises of the Moabiter Güterbahnhof (Moabit Freight Depot). It is located to the south of Berlin's S-Bahn ring train and first began operating in 1871. By virtue of its location, the site was vital as part of a supply chain to the surrounding industrial areas of Moabit and Charlottenburg. Extending north of the tracks is the Westhafen facility, constructed in the years 1914–1927 as the second largest inland harbor in Germany and characterized by large-scale structures. As a consequence of destruction during World War II, demolition measures carried out after the division of Berlin, and new construction in the district since 2007, the Güterbahnhof has all but vanished from the cityscape.

As in the previous semester, we organized an urban planning competition for the students as a preliminary exercise. As before, contributions were to build upon morphological references. As the basis for the masterplan, we chose a meandering developmental pattern with a sequence of semi-courtyards based on Mario de Renzi's Casa Convenzionata at Piazza Bologna in Rome. Each student group was assigned a corner plot and assigned the task of developing an angular building type with eaves heights of 22 m. Students were required to investigate how a floor plan principle could be developed around a corner. Is the corner emphasized or downplayed? Is it symmetrical or hierarchical? Does it represent an exception, or does it follow a rule? At a stipulated pedestal level were supplementary and community uses that would enhance life in the quarter. This level was meant to contain very tall spaces with large spans (→ p. 48 "Working with Typologies"). The courtyards were to have been shaped to serve residential and commercial purposes.

The individual buildings were to be planned with prefabricated concrete elements, both load-bearing structures as well as façades (→ p. 262 the section on concrete in the chapter "Material"). By virtue of its unified materiality, the quarter would appear as an identifiable "urban structure." Structural principles such as skeleton construction, panel construction, and modular cell construction were also to be taken into consideration in the concept. On top of these essential components of the project, students were required to consider plasticity, modularity, and façade tectonics, so that the buildings would have a specifically urban character.

Concrete 01
Jinglin Cai
Xiangyue Guan
Hang Yuan

Concrete 02
Julia Domanska
Mariana Ferreira

Concrete 03
Evamaria Christel
Marta Salomó Col

Concrete 04
Cyrell Boehm
Kamila Marta Kojder

Concrete 05
Ahmed Michael Abd Alla
Eva-Maria Thinius

Concrete 06
Christobal Lambertini Herrera
Miquel Angel Reyes Benz

Concrete 07
Apostolos Klontzaris
Anja Kokott

Concrete 08
Sophie Baum
Theresa Piechottka

Concrete 09
Jennifer Moser
Fabian Trapp

Concrete 10
Marina Kolovou-Kouri
David Scharf

Concrete 11
Rusi Ichev
Darina Palazova

Concrete 12
Johanna Backhaus
Tetyana Nesterenko

Concrete 13
Christopher Sitzler
Kristina Szeifert

Concrete 14
Tatjana Anic
Timo Lück

Concrete 15
Nicole Redmer
Claudia Schwiethale

Concrete 16
Aydin Sunar
Tobias Wolski

Concrete 17
Mikal Skodjereite
Jakob Ulbrych

Concrete 18
Julia Schmidt
Sebastian Welzel

Concrete 19
Sebastian Genzel
Christobal Lambertini Herrera

Concrete 20
Marlene Bühner
Cassandra Donath

Concrete 21
Sebastian Blatter
Zaneta Choroba

pool an der TU Berlin: Entwurfsseminare 2013–2016

Urban Steel

TU Berlin, Master-Studiengang, Sommersemester 2014
→ Regelgeschosse im Massstab 1:500, S. 294
→ Möblierte Grundrisse im Massstab 1:150, S. 324
→ Semesterentwürfe im Modell, S. 378

Die «Magistrale des Berliner Ostens», einst Teil der historisch bedeutsamen mittelalterlichen Handelsstrasse nach Frankfurt/Oder und Einmarschstrasse der Roten Armee, war 1945 infolge erbitterter Kriegshandlungen weitgehend zerstört. Der Wiederaufbau dieser Allee, der Stalinallee, war das Prestigeprojekt des 1951 ausgerufenen Nationalen Aufbauprogramms. Die ersten Entwürfe von Hermann Henselmann, Hanns Hopp, Richard Paulick und Kurt W. Leucht erfüllten die politischen Ambitionen der SED-Führung nicht und wurden wegen «formalistischer Tendenzen» kritisiert, nach sowjetischen Vorbildern überarbeitet und schliesslich mit hohem Tempo realisiert. Die einander gegenüberliegenden, mehrheitlich sieben- bis neungeschossigen Wohnblöcke mit einer Länge von bis zu 300 Metern und einer durchgängigen Gewerbezone in den unteren ein oder zwei Geschossen bilden ein geschichtsträchtiges Ensemble und beeindrucken noch heute durch ihre Monumentalität und Homogenität. Nach der Wiedervereinigung der Stadt wurde die Allee in Karl-Marx-Allee umbenannt, unter Denkmalschutz gestellt und gilt als grösstes Baudenkmal Europas.

Die Studierenden hatten die Aufgabe, sich mit den flankierenden Rückseiten der Karl-Marx-Allee bis zur nächsten Parallelstrasse auseinanderzusetzen. In der zweiten Reihe weicht die strenge urbane Setzung der Hauptachse einem orientierungslosen, oft nur der Ausrichtung zur Sonne geschuldeten Städtebau. Monotone Plattenbauten wechseln sich ab mit vom Krieg verschonten Blockfragmenten und dazwischen gestreuten Quartiernutzungen. Jede Studierendengruppe hatte einen selbst gewählten Interventionsort durch Annex- oder Zwischenbauten zu verdichten. Lediglich die Wohnnutzung war vorgegeben. Der Massstab des Eingriffs und die Art des Wohnens waren aus dem jeweiligen Konzept zu bestimmen und zu begründen. Das Raumprogramm war mit unterstützenden Nutzungen zu vervollständigen, die das Gebäudekonzept, die gewählte Gemeinschaftsform, aber auch das Quartier ergänzen.

Als Material war Stahl vorgegeben (→ S. 280 «Material: Stahl»). Stahlstrukturen sollten zwischen der repräsentativen, feingliedrigen Fassadenordnung stalinistischer Architektur und der Rigorosität der Nachmoderne vermitteln. Der Rhythmus eines strukturellen Rasters hatte die einzelnen Arbeiten zusammenzuhalten und Bauten unterschiedlicher Stile zu verbinden und zu ergänzen. Das Spektrum der Maschenweite einer Raumstruktur reicht von einer Zimmergrösse über die Dimension einer Raumgruppe bis zu der eines Hauses und darüber hinaus. In Referenzen ausgedrückt bedeutet dies: vom Case Study House oder Pavillon-Wohnen bis zu den Megastrukturen von Cedric Prices Fun Palace oder Yona Friedmans Urbanisme spatial. Für die Raumstruktur war ausschliesslich Stahl zu verwenden, während für die raumabschliessenden Elemente auch andere Materialien gewählt werden konnten. Uns interessierte, inwieweit der Stahlbau, der im Wohnungsbau nahezu vergessen ging, sich diesen wieder aneignen kann. Dabei standen bauphysikalische und feuertechnische Problemstellungen weniger im Vordergrund als die Frage, welche räumlichen und atmosphärischen Qualitäten sowie typologischen Potenziale in einer Konstruktionsweise schlummern, die das vergangene Jahrhundert entscheidend mitgeprägt hat.

Urban Steel

TU Berlin Master's Program, summer semester 2014
→ Standard Stories on a Scale of 1:500, p. 294
→ Plans 1:150, p. 324
→ Semester Designs in Model Form, p. 378

In 1945, as a result of merciless military operations, the Magistrale (Grand Boulevard) of East Berlin—formerly a section of a medieval trade route leading to Frankfurt/Oder, and the route of entry of the Red Army—was largely destroyed. The reconstruction of this boulevard, then known as Stalinallee, was the prestige project of a program of national construction which began in 1951. The initial designs proffered by Hermann Henselmann, Hans Hopp, Richard Paulick, and Kurt W. Leucht failed to fulfill the political ambitions of the SED leadership, and were criticized for their "formalist tendencies" before being reworked according to Soviet models and realized at great speed. The largely seven- to nine-story apartment blocks that confront one another on opposite sides of the avenue, with lengths up to 300m, and a continuous commercial zone in the lower one or two stories, form a historically significant ensemble that remains striking today by virtue of its monumentality and homogeneity. After the reunification of the German capital, the boulevard was renamed Karl Marx Allee and placed under landmarks protection. It is one of Europe's largest architectural monuments.

Students were confronted with the task of grappling with the flanking rear zones of Karl Marx Allee all the way to the next parallel street. The rigorous urban arrangement of the main axis gives way to urban development in the second row that lacks orientation and is often guided only by the alignment of the sun. Monotonous prefab buildings alternate with blocks that were spared by the war. Various neighborhood uses are scatter in between. Each student group chose a point of intervention which they would then densify through annexes or intermediate buildings. The only stipulation was residential utilization. The scale of the intervention and the character of the residences were to be determined and justified in relation to the overall concept. The spatial program was to be rounded off with auxiliary uses designed to complement the building concept, the chosen forms of community, but also the residential quarter as a whole.

The prescribed material was steel (→ p. 280 "Material: Steel"). Steel structures were meant to mediate between the grand, finely-articulated façade arrangement of the Stalinist architecture and the rigorous qualities of late modernism. The rhythm of a structural grid was meant to pull the individual buildings together, unifying and supplementing architectural elements which display a variety of styles, sizes, and scales. Specific references included the Case Study Houses, the megastructures of Cedric Price's Fun Palace, or Yona Friedman's Urbanisme Spatial. Steel was meant to be used exclusively for the spatial structure while other materials were available for interior surfaces. We were interested in the degree to which steel construction—virtually forgotten in relation to residential development—could be reinterpreted for such building tasks today. Standing in the foreground were not so much problems pertaining to construction physics or fire safety, but instead a question: What spatial and atmospheric qualities, as well as technological potentialities, might lie dormant in a manner of construction that has shaped the past century in such decisive ways?

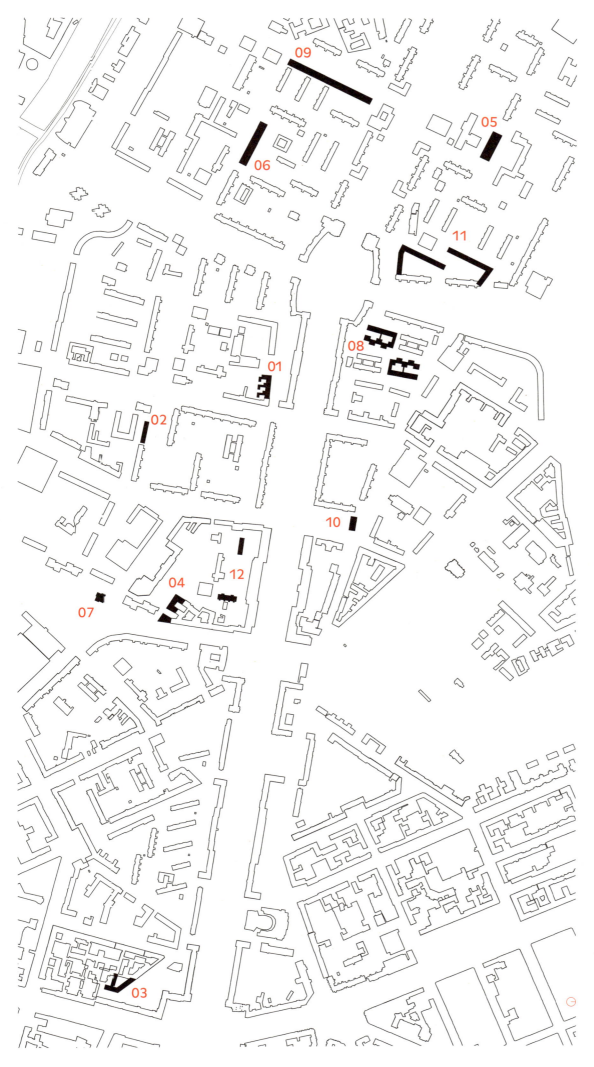

Steel 01
Ignasi Querol Diez
Ana Garcia Gasquet

Steel 02
Patryk Kujawa
Martyna Aleksandra
 Wojnarowska

Steel 03
Hanna Grabmaier
Julia Naomi Henning
Lisa Nagy

Steel 04
Thomas Pracht
Guang Xue

Steel 05
Felix Bardou
Carlo Fischer

Steel 06
Vedran Zonic

Steel 07
Daniela Tankova

Steel 08
Myungjin Choi
Elena Schneider

Steel 09
Sebastian Genzel
Harald Niessner

Steel 10
Jana Morgenstern
Jennifer Moser

Steel 11
Jialiang Cui
Liane Rosenthal

Steel 12
Vanesa Cela Adamescu
Madalina Uram

Urban Brick

TU Berlin Master's Program,
winter semester 2014/2015
→ Standard Stories on a Scale of 1:500, p. 294
→ Plans 1:150, p. 324
→ Semester Designs in Model Form, p. 378

In the fourth semester we concluded the series devoted to individual building materials. For the semester on brick, we selected the former Gaswerk Schöneberg, an industrial park characterized by brick buildings. As a consequence of adjacent railway lines, the terrain is isolated in the midst of Wilhelminian-era building development and so again forms an island-style site within the urban fabric. As an alternative to the campus found there today, then in the process of construction, we wanted to demonstrate that a mix of residential and commercial uses, as essential components of life in this urban context, would be a valid solution. The unified materiality of the site endowed it with an emphatic expressiveness that harked to the listed industrial architecture of the nineteenth century.

At a two-day urban planning workshop held at the beginning of the semester, we tested various plot sizes and layouts and determined a few rules: the number of stories, desired density, and the desired qualities of the outdoor environment. In conjunction with the prescribed brick construction method, the proposed development pattern reflected the organic ensemble of medieval urban structures. The buildings developed on the various sites were to be planned as a dense configuration. They had to touch the boundaries of the plot on all sides and be linked with buildings on neighboring plots. Since neither building depths nor heights were prescribed, the interfaces between buildings had to be negotiated in the design process in conjunction with neighboring plots. Brick was to be deployed visibly inside and outside, for both loadbearing structures and interior surfaces (→ p. 238 section on brick in the chapter "Material"). The plasticity and tectonics of the façade were to be investigated as essential elements of the design, and were to reflect the specific identity of the individual building.

Through the additional theme of large, multi-room residences, well-adapted residential types—which have been forgotten over time—were to be "rediscovered" for cohabitation in communities (→ p. 48 "Typologies"). Residential forms consist of spatial groupings that are combined to form large households. With the help of such considerations, building concepts were to be developed that embodied characteristic features of urban life and the needs of contemporary urbanites through forms that go beyond conventional family or studio apartments.

If sociological aspects played a role in the preparation of the spatial program at the beginning of the semester, then the focus during project planning was primarily on an investigation of architectonic, spatial, and typological aspects. The aim was to produce a building design that was more than the sum of its individual units, but would instead, as a unity, give expression to a strong sense of identity. Useful models during the process of structural and formal invention included stately palaces and socialist community buildings, but also commercial structures and studio buildings.

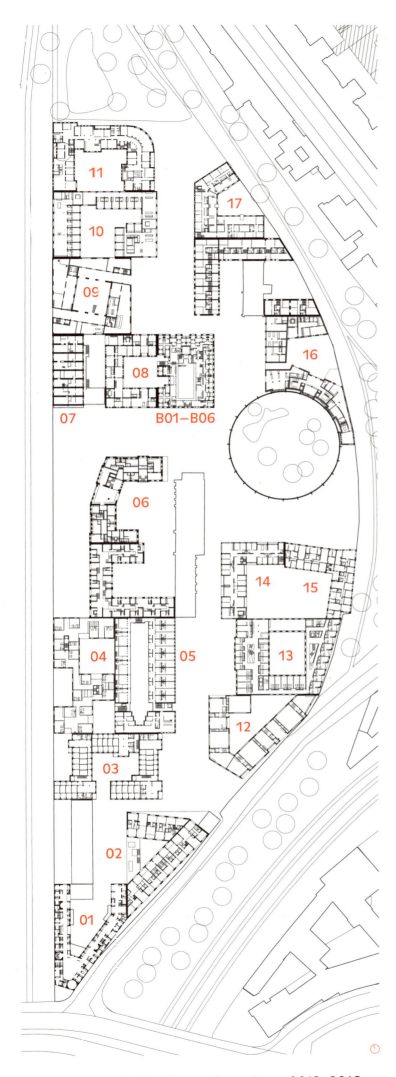

Brick 01
Julius Blencke
Caspar Kollmeyer
Jan Wind

Brick 02
Kai Hikmet Canver
Sina Pauline Riedlinger

Brick 03
Anna Gert
Cemile Kolgu

Brick 04
Franziska Polleter
Simone Prill

Brick 05
Vera Marie Glas
Rafael Lozykowski
Florian Rizek

Brick 06
Larsen Berg
Harald Niessner

Brick 07
Luca Gericke
Franco Scheuplein
Carolin Trahorsch

Brick 08
Jessica Ganghofer
Anne-Katrin Schulz
Sarah Stein

Brick 09
Kays Elbeyli
Arthur Schmock
Marc Wendland

Brick 10
Marlene Bühner
Cassandra Donath

Brick 11
Anika Weidlich
Franziska Wich

Brick 12
Véronique Baustert
Elena Petkova

Brick 13
Oskar Ellwanger
Ewa Kostecka
Judith Schiebel

Brick 14
Theodora Constantin
Vanessa Vogel

Brick 15
Sandra Schenavsky
Franziska Rüss

Brick 16
Simon Kiefer
Shaghayegh Moghaddasi
  Sikaroudi
Elena Wickenhöfer

Brick 17
Josephine Brillowski
Alisa Joseph
Jana Morgenstern

Bachelorthesis
Brick B01
Catherine Folawiyo
Gesa Holzbrecher

Brick B02
Stefan File
Anne Kummetz

Brick B03
Judith Bartsch
Alexandr Minkin

Brick B04
Christa Elizabeth Beckmann
  Zambrana

Brick B05
Cansu Cantas
Sebastian Henschke

Brick B06
Mona Hartmann
Lukas Kesler

pool an der TU Berlin: Entwurfsseminare 2013–2016

Grandhotel

TU Berlin Master's Program
summer semester 2015,
TU Berlin Master Thesis Projects 2015/2016:
Collective Courtyards,
Urbanity and Production,
Supermarkets

→ Standard Stories on a Scale of 1:500, p. 294
→ Plans 1:150, p. 324
→ Semester Designs in Model Form, p. 378

With Grandhotel, following the essay Die Grandhotel-Verschwörung von 2014 (The Grand Hotel Conspiracy of 2014), written by Hans Widmer (alias p.m.)—a pioneer of Zurich residential collectives whose work inspired new housing cooperatives—we continued our investigation of multi-room residential forms that we had begun during the previous semester (→ p.102 "Utopias," → p.48 "Typologies"). His utopian text describes the amalgamation of architecture, society, and politics, of tradition and vision. At first glance, the grand hotel could hardly be more remote from the problems facing contemporary housing development. The functional and economic pragmatism of mass housing construction seems ostensibly opposed to the glamour of such palatial buildings. But which aspects of the spatial and functional structures of the grand hotel could potentially be transferred to residential construction? Broad, street-style corridors, prominent staircases, entrance halls and lobbies, spacious external areas, cafés, and salons point beyond the small-cell, repetitive floor plan canon of residential construction. And if grand hotels once offered a stage for self-presentation on the part of guests, then as an innovative residential concept, they can now serve as a platform for urban life.

For the Grand Hotel semester, we offered a selection of three building sites in Berlin featuring extremely large construction volumes: the Humboldthafen (Humboldt Harbor) near Hamburger Bahnhof; die Prinzessinnengärten (Princess Gardens) at Moritzplatz; and the inlet next to the Strandbad Wannsee (Wannsee Bathing Beach). Each of these (varied) contexts corresponds to a specific hotel type: the train station hotel, the city hotel, and the panorama hotel.

Subsequently, three assignments for master's thesis projects, formulated by the students themselves, were based on similar thematic definitions, which also involved supplementary utilizations and spatial offerings:

Investigated for Supermarkets were underused sites with monofunctional, single-story structures. As an alternative development scheme, students proposed residential complexes that would integrate a supermarket as one aspect of the program. These would simultaneously endow the location with an urban presence by virtue of the inhabitants, density, and specific mix of uses.

With Urbanity and Production, we investigated the spatial juxtaposition of work and dwelling at Nordhafen (North Harbor). Prior to the functional zoning of cities during the twentieth century, industrial and agricultural production in the midst of residential districts was the rule.

Collective Courtyards recalls the history of large-scale residential construction in city center contexts. The value of collective spatial programs in connection with a clear architectural language was explored, with case studies from the 1920–30s including the housing estates of Red Vienna or Kay Fisker's mega-blocks. Building on this tradition, an exemplary project was produced for the Tacheles site in the Mitte district of Berlin.

---

[2] Hans Widmer (alias p.m.), «Die Grandhotel-Verschwörung von 2014», in: *Das Magazin* 36/2014

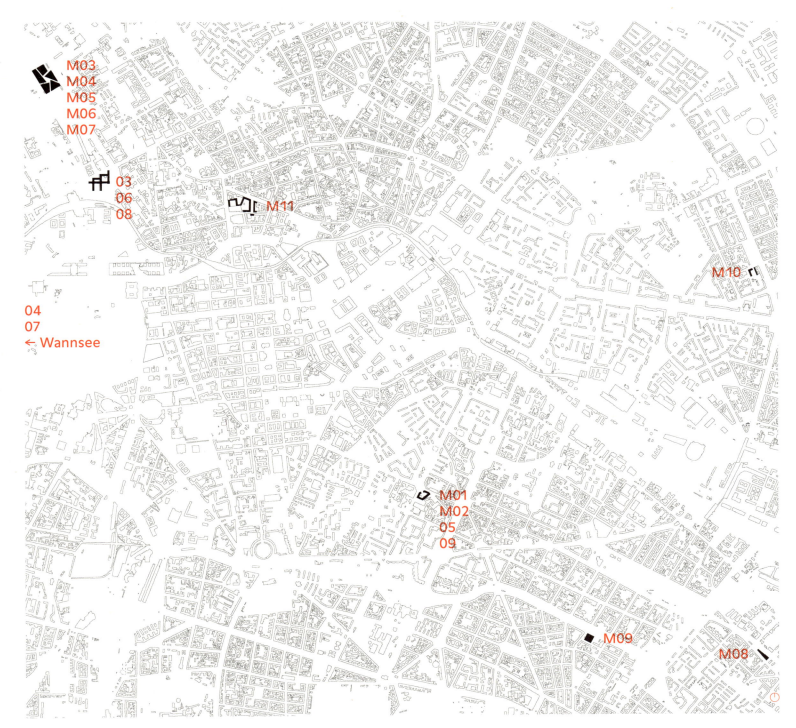

Masterthesis	Masterstudiengang	Masterthesis	Masterthesis
Grandhotel M01 Jennifer Moser	**Grandhotel 03** Hanna Rohst	**Urbanity and Production M03** Tobias Wolski	**Supermärkte M08** Harald Niessner
Grandhotel M02 Aydin Sunar	**Grandhotel 04** Robert Essen	**Urbanity and Production M04** Julia Rathmann Löcker	**Supermärkte M09** Felix Bardou
	Grandhotel 05 Siemen Andreas Aas	**Urbanity and Production M05** Jana Morgenstern	**Supermärkte M10** Sebastian Genzel
	Grandhotel 06 Julia Rathmann Löcker	**Urbanity and Production M06** Robert Essen	**Kollektive Höfe M11** Timo Büscher
	Grandhotel 07 Jakob Pawlowski	**Urbanity and Production M07** Fidias Curiel Casteson	
	Grandhotel 08 Paul Achter		
	Grandhotel 09 Nikolaus Schmid		

pool an der TU Berlin: Entwurfsseminare 2013–2016

High Rise

TU Berlin, Master-Studiengang, Wintersemester 2015/16
→ Regelgeschosse im Massstab 1:500, S. 294
→ Möblierte Grundrisse im Massstab 1:150, S. 324
→ Semesterentwürfe im Modell, S. 378

Der Schriftsteller James Graham Ballard beschreibt in seinem Roman *High-Rise* (1975) das Zusammenleben in einem Hochhaus, das seinen zweitausend Bewohnern luxuriösen Komfort bietet. Nach dem Verkauf des letzten Apartments beginnt in der Erzählung jedoch ein Prozess der Verwahrlosung und des Verfalls. Die Bewohner des Hochhauses degenerieren zu gewalttätigen, instinktgesteuerten Nachbarn, die sich gegenseitig bekriegen. Soziale Spannungen entladen sich im Kampf um Nutzungsrechte der gemeinschaftlichen Schwimmbäder, Schulen und Supermärkte. Es entsteht eine Dreiklassengesellschaft, die sich über die vertikale Verteilung im Haus definiert. Obwohl die Situation eskaliert, verharren die Bewohner in der Abgeschlossenheit ihres Hochhauses – die totale Anarchie gibt ihnen die Möglichkeit, aus gesellschaftlichen Zwängen auszubrechen. Mittels der übersteigerten Bilder des Romans erkundet Ballard eine unmittelbar hinter der Realität verborgene Welt, die keine Sicherheit bietet und sich in jedem Augenblick verändert. Ähnlich wie Rem Koolhaas in *Delirious New York* (1978) legt Ballard die Architektur und seine Nutzer auf die Couch und unterzieht sie einer Psychoanalyse, die den Blick für die irrationalen Phänomene der Stadt schärft und uns in einer eigentümlichen Ambivalenz zwischen Bewunderung und Schaudern schweben lässt. Auf der einen Seite die Errungenschaften der Moderne mit ihrer analytischen Einfachheit und auf der anderen Seite die Komplexität der realen Welt mit ihrer Vielfalt an Formen, sozialen Bedürfnissen und kulturellen Bezügen.

Der dystopische Text als Ausgangspunkt des Entwurfs verweist auf die Frage nach der Verbindung von Architektur, Gesellschaft und Politik, von Tradition und Vision sowie der Wechselwirkung zwischen Nutzern und Objekt. Inwieweit eignen sich Hochhäuser, um den Bedürfnissen der Bewohner zu begegnen und diese in architektonischen Projekten adäquat auszudrücken? Grosse Bauvolumen treten im Stadtgefüge markant in Erscheinung und lassen auch einen entsprechenden gesellschaftlichen Beitrag im Quartier erwarten.

Das Gebiet zwischen Alexanderplatz und Spree ist mit seiner bewegten Vergangenheit und den daraus resultierenden Brüchen äusserst komplex und vielschichtig. Die im Semester verfolgte städtebauliche Strategie basierte auf einer Planung aus dem Vorjahr im Fachgebiet von Prof. Jörg Stollmann an der TU Berlin. Die Massstäblichkeit der DDR-Planung sowie die Gegenwart der historischen Fragmente machen den besonderen Charakter des Ortes aus. Durch die Einfügung von Wohnhochhäusern, die den riesigen Freiraum zwischen Fernsehturm und Schloss begleiten, wird die Geschichtlichkeit des Ortes artikuliert. Die Aufgabenstellung basierte auf hypothetischen Annahmen, bei denen nicht die Realisierbarkeit, sondern die Auslotung der städtebaulichen und typologischen Potenziale des Hochhauses im Vordergrund stand.

Zu Semesterbeginn wurden Raumgruppen historischer Vorbilder analysiert und von der horizontalen Anordnung in die Vertikale übersetzt, ohne dabei ihre spezifischen räumlichen und funktionalen Beziehungen zu verlieren. Kombiniert mit Strukturtypen von Hochhäusern entstanden daraus architektonisch spannungsvolle Entwürfe, die mit einem zeitgemässen Raumprogramm versehen die ursprünglichen Vorbilder in die heutige Zeit übertrugen.

High Rise

TU Berlin Master's Program, winter semester 2015/2016
→ Standard Stories on a Scale of 1:500, p. 294
→ Plans 1:150, p. 324
→ Semester Designs in Model Form, p. 378

In his novel *High-Rise* (1975), the author J.G. Ballard describes cohabitation in a skyscraper that offers its 2,000 residents a luxurious level of comfort. After the last apartment has been sold, however, the novel begins to narrate a process of neglect and decay. Violence spreads and instinct-driven residents make war against one another. Social tensions explode in struggles over the right to use communal swimming pools, schools, and supermarkets and a three-class society emerges that is defined in relation to the vertical subdivision of the building. Although the situation escalates, the residents remain in their insular high-rise as total anarchy makes it possible for them to break free from societal constraints. Through the novel's exaggerated imagery, Ballard explores a world that is hidden immediately behind reality, one that offers no security, and which changes moment by moment. Not unlike Rem Koolhaas in *Delirious New York* (1978), Ballard lays architecture and its users on the couch and subjects them to psychoanalysis. Through his gaze, the phenomena of urban life appear irrational and readers are left suspended in a peculiar ambivalence between admiration and repulsion. On one side, there exists the achievements of modernism, with its analytical simplicity; on the other, the complexity of the real world, with its multiplicity of forms, social needs, and cultural references.

As a point of departure for design work, this dystopian text calls our attention toward questions concerning the relationship between architecture, society, and politics, between tradition and vision, as well as toward the reciprocal interplay between users and objects. To what extent are high-rises suited to satisfying the requirements of inhabitants? Large construction volumes make a striking appearance within the urban fabric and raise expectations for a corresponding social contribution to the residential quarter.

With its turbulent history and resultant fractures, the area that lies between Alexanderplatz and the River Spree is extremely complex and multilayered. The urban strategies pursued in this semester were based on planning undertaken during the previous year in the studio of Prof. Jörg Stollmann at the TU-Berlin. GDR planning and the presence of historic fragments account for the specific character of this site. The historicity of the location is articulated through the insertion of apartment towers, which occupy this enormous open space between the Fernsehturm (TV Tower) and the Berlin Palace. This assignment was based on exploring the urban and typological potential of the high-rise,

At the beginning of the semester, the spatial layouts of historical references were analyzed and translated from horizontal into vertical configurations without sacrificing their specific functional relationships. Students subsequently produced enthralling architectural designs which, furnished with contemporary spatial programs, translated the historical references into the present day.

High Rise 01
Robert Bauer
Christa Elizabeth Beckmann

High Rise 02
Amélie Barande
Qin Qian

High Rise 03
Niki Apostolopoulou
Fidias Curiel Casteson
Bernhard Weikert

High Rise 04
Merle Sudbrock
Roberta Zucchetti

High Rise 05
Catherine Folawiyo
Clara Jereczek

High Rise 06
Tina Krause
Denitsa Todorova

High Rise 07
Azad Saleem
Martin Ulitzka
Olivia Valenzuela

High Rise 08
Julien Engelhardt
Simon Lehmann

High Rise 09
James Horkulak
Marko Shllaku

High Rise 10
Paul Achter
Lorenz Preußer
Ivan Zilic

High Rise 11
Annett Donat
Jakob Pawlowski

High Rise 12
Kristine Kazelnika
Maximilian Vesely

High Rise 13
Maija Gavare
Johanna Sieberer

High Rise 14
Franziska Käuferle
Louisa Wahler

High Rise 15
Cansu Cantas
Elina Kolarova

High Rise 16
Lisa Beyer
Justus Preyer
Max Werner

High Rise 17
Sarah Meier
Maximilian Quick

High Rise 18
Tobias Bräunig
Tobias Scholz

pool an der TU Berlin: Entwurfsseminare 2013–2016

College: Die Uni als Kiez

TU Berlin, Bachelor-Studiengang, Sommersemester 2016
→ Regelgeschossen im Massstab 1:500, S. 294
→ Möblierte Grundrisse im Massstab 1:150, S. 324
→ Semesterentwürfe im Modell, S. 378

Die angelsächsische College-Tradition unterscheidet sich grundsätzlich von der in Mitteleuropa verbreiteten Trennung zwischen monofunktionalen Hochschularealen auf der einen und durchmischten Stadtquartieren auf der anderen Seite. Hier wird gelehrt und geforscht — dort wird gewohnt, gehandelt, konsumiert, gefeiert und gearbeitet. Die Folge sind Areale, die sich tagsüber beleben und nachts praktisch vollständig menschenleer sind, oftmals jedoch grosse Nutzungsreserven aufweisen. Die Colleges in Oxford und Cambridge, wie sie seit dem 12. Jahrhundert gewachsen sind, folgen hingegen einem völlig anderen Siedlungs- und Lebensmodell. Eine dichte Abfolge von Raumzellen bildet den Rahmen für einen 24-Stunden-Betrieb, bei dem sich Wohnen und Arbeiten, Studium und Freizeit überschneiden.

Der von Bernhard Hermkes 1955 entwickelte Bebauungsplan für den Ernst-Reuter-Platz bildet den Ausgangspunkt für die weitere Entwicklung des Nordgeländes der TU Berlin. Die räumliche Konzeption sieht Baukörper unterschiedlichster Höhe vor, die als plastische Gebilde frei im Raum angeordnet sind und in rhythmischer, spannungsreicher Beziehung zueinander stehen. Die Baukörper öffnen den Platzraum ganz im Sinne des modernen Städtebaus in die Weite, anstatt diesen räumlich zu schliessen. Die erste Ausbauphase des neuen TU-Geländes erfolgte 1958–1968 auf Basis des städtebaulichen Entwurfs von Kurt Dübbers, der dem Grundgedanken von Hermkes folgte und diesen in einem orthogonalen, lockeren Bebauungsmuster weiterentwickelte. Mit der Moderne als Leitbild und dem amerikanischen Campus als Sinnbild für Demokratie zum Vorbild sollte die Architektur sachliche Bedürfnisse befriedigen und Spielraum für künftige Erweiterungen zulassen. Noch heute, nach mehreren Ausbauphasen, sind diese Prinzipien deutlich erkennbar.

Als Ausgangspunkt für das Entwurfsseminar «College — Die Uni als Kiez» wurde die Siedlungs- und Raumstruktur der angelsächsischen Collegetradition auf das TU-Areal am Ernst-Reuter-Platz adaptiert. Der Masterplan zeigt zeilen- und winkelförmige Baukörper, die in das bestehende orthogonale System eingefügt werden, die Durchlässigkeit der Anlage erhalten, jedoch eine Abfolge von kleinmassstäblicheren Raumzellen aus Plätzen um einen zentralen Hof bilden. Die unmittelbare Nähe von bestehenden Institutsbauten und zusätzlichen Wohngebäuden schafft neue Nachbarschaften und generiert die kritische Masse, die für qualitätsvolle Stadträume und Urbanität erforderlich ist.

Die Studierenden entwickelten auf den ihnen zugelosten Bauplätzen studentische Wohnhäuser, aber auch Wohnungen für Forschende, Lehrende und andere Beschäftigte. Ergänzende Nutzungen sollten die Nahversorgung gewährleisten und das Quartier aufwerten. Als Inspirationsquelle dienten wiederum Referenzbeispiele zum zimmerreichen Wohnen (→ S. 48 «Typologien»), unter anderem die klösterlichen Kollegien, die schon Vorbild für die englischen Colleges waren. Die Studienreise zu Semesterbeginn nach Oxford und Cambridge zeigte eindrücklich die urbanen Qualitäten von Siedlungsstrukturen, die seit dem 14. Jahrhundert den gleichen räumlichen Prinzipien folgen und in die sich selbst moderne und brutalistische Architekturen harmonisch einfügen.

College: The University as Neighborhood

TU Berlin Bachelor's Program, summer semester 2016
→ Standard Stories on a Scale of 1:500, p. 294
→ Plans 1:150, p. 324
→ Semester Designs in Model Form, p. 378

The Anglo-Saxon college tradition differs fundamentally from the segregation—so prevalent in central Europe—of mono-functional university areas from mixed urban districts. In one, teaching and research; in the other, residence, commerce, consumption, socializing, and labor. As a consequence, we find neighborhoods that are lively during the daytime but virtually deserted at night, and which often harbor enormous potential for use. In contrast, the colleges of Oxford and Cambridge, as they have evolved since the twelfth century, follow a completely different model of settlement and lifestyle. A dense sequence of spatial cells forms the framework for a 24-hour operation where residence and work, study, and leisure activities overlap.

The development plan developed by Bernhard Hermkes for Ernst Reuter Platz, Berlin in 1955 was the point of departure for the subsequent development of the northern sector. The spatial concept incorporates structures with a wide variety of heights that are freely arranged as sculptural forms connected through a rhythmic, highly-charged dialogue. In the spirit of modern urban planning the structures are open to the surrounding space, instead of being closed to it. The first construction phase of the new TU premises proceeded in 1958–68 according to an urban design by Kurt Dübbers, who followed Hermkes' basic ideas and developed them in an orthogonal, loosely arranged developmental pattern. With modernism as a guiding principle and the model of the American campus as exemplary of democracy, this architecture is intended to satisfy objective requirements while allowing leeway for future extensions. Even today, after a number of building phases, these principles are readily legible.

As a point of departure for the design seminar *College – Die Uni als Kiez* (College—the University as Neighborhood), the settlement and spatial structure of the Anglo-Saxon college tradition was adapted to the TU premises at Ernst Reuter Platz. The masterplan features linear and angular structures. These are inserted into the preexisting orthogonal system in order to preserve the permeability of the complex while at the same time forming a sequence of smaller-scale spatial cells as squares around a central courtyard. New neighborhoods and a high quality urban environment are generated through the immediate proximity to other university buildings and additional residential structures.

On the building sites assigned to them, student participants developed housing for students, researchers, instructors, and other staff members. The municipality also ensured further uses on the site such as shopping, common areas, and spaces for culture and leisure. Serving as sources of inspiration, once again, were references pertaining to the *large, multi-room residence* (→ p. 48 "Typologies"), among them the cloistral colleges of England. A student trip to Oxford and Cambridge at the beginning of the semester highlighted the urban qualities of settlement structures that have followed the same spatial principles since the fourteenth century, and which are able to adapt themselves harmoniously to modern and Brutalist architecture.

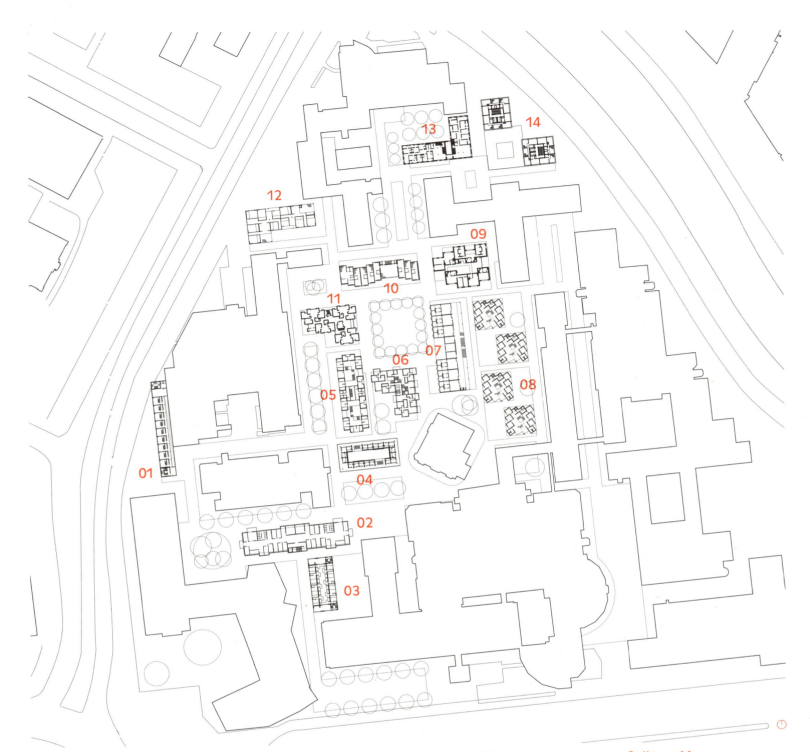

College 01
Leonardo Jochim
Lukas Stadelmann
Samuel Yeboa

College 02
Tycho Brand
Viktor Parijer
Felix Rottka

College 03
Tan Phong Nguyen
Mai Tran

College 04
Marie-Louise Leeck
Lisa Thürer

College 05
Isabel de Palacios
Julia Ratsch
Florian Tudzierz

College 06
Vadim Below
Timo Strauch
Katharina Zull

College 07
Paulina Grabowska
Luciana Lagoa de Nobile
Dilara Uzgeldi

College 08
Diana Aleksova
Tsvetomila Neshtereva
Nikoleta Nikolova

College 09
Christine Feistl
Ellinor Förster

College 10
Lysann Geller
Monika Pawlak
Kassandra Sarantis

College 11
Amer Eid
Michael Roth

College 12
Daniel Dieren
Helena Reischel
Ann-Kathrin Salich

College 13
Antoan Antonov
Jakob Fischer
Maurice Luft

College 14
Paul Harries
Ana Richter de Arce
Florian Tropp

Biografien

pool Architekten

Das Zürcher Architekturbüro pool Architekten formierte sich 1994 als Diskussionsplattform mit Workshops und Debatten über Architektur und Städtebau. 1996 nahm die praktische Tätigkeit als Architektengemeinschaft ihren Anfang und führte 1998 zur Gründung der pool Architekten Genossenschaft mit acht Partnern. Die zehn Partner Dieter Bachmann, Floris Besserer, Raphael Frei, Thomas Friberg, Mathias Heinz, Philipp Hirtler, David Leuthold, Andreas Sonderegger, Mischa Spoerri und Matthias Stocker sowie die sechs Associates Bettina Komminoth, Danijela Jovicic, Maja Markovic, Martin Gutekunst, Martin Trefon und Peter Wassmer leiten heute die Geschicke von pool.

pool macht seit gut 20 Jahren mit seiner interdisziplinären und undogmatischen Arbeitsweise auf sich aufmerksam. Schwerpunkte der Tätigkeit umfassen vor allem Wohnungsbauten, Schulen und Sportbauten sowie städtebauliche Planungen. 2014 erhielten pool Architekten den renommierten Grand Prix Kunst/Prix Meret Oppenheim vom Bundesamt für Kultur.

Die praktische Tätigkeit ergänzend, engagierten sich die Partner in den letzten zehn Jahren als Dozenten und Professoren an diversen Hochschulen wie der ETH Zürich, der TU Berlin, der TU Wien, der Universität Liechtenstein und den Fachhochschulen Winterthur, Luzern und Burgdorf.

Zudem vertreten sie aktiv die Anliegen der Architektur in diversen Gremien, Berufsverbänden und Fachkommissionen.

Simone Jeska

Simone Jeska ist Mitautorin der Buchpublikation *Poolologie des Wohnens*. Als Architektin und Autorin umspannt ihr Arbeitsfeld sowohl die praktische als auch die theoretische Auseinandersetzung mit Architektur. Sie realisierte eigene Projekte und Projekte für Hascher Jehle Achitektur; ihre Arbeit als wissenschaftliche Mitarbeiterin an der TU Berlin, Vorträge zum Thema Material in der Architektur sowie mehrere Publikationen im Bereich Architektur — unter anderem der Entwurfsatlas *Bürobau* und die Bücher *Transparente Kunststoffe* sowie *Neue Holzbautechnologien* — zeugen von ihrem Spektrum. Sie lebt und arbeitet in Berlin.

Biographies

pool Architekten

The Zurich-based architectural practice pool Architekten was formed in 1994 as a platform for workshops and debates on architecture and urban planning. Practical work as an architectural collective began in 1996 which led to the founding of pool Architekten Genossenschaft with eight partners in 1998. The fortunes of pool are guided by our 10 partners Dieter Bachmann, Floris Besserer, Raphael Frei, Thomas Friberg, Mathias Heinz, Philipp Hirtler, David Leuthold, Andreas Sonderegger, Mischa Spoerri, and Matthias Stocker, joined by our six associates Bettina Komminoth, Danijela Jovicic, Maja Markovic, Martin Gutekunst, Martin Trefon, and Peter Wassmer.

For 20 years now, pool has attracted attention by virtue of its interdisciplinary and undogmatic approach. Areas of particular focus include residential development, schools, sports facilities, and urban planning. In 2014, pool Architekten received the prestigious Grand Prix Kunst /Prix Meret Oppenheim from the Swiss Federal Office of Culture.

To complement our built work, our partners have worked over the past 10 years as instructors and professors at a variety of institutions of higher learning, among them the ETH Zurich, the technical universities in Berlin and Vienna, Liechtenstein University, and the technical colleges in Winterthur, Lucerne, and Burgdorf.

At the same time, our partners serve as active advocates for architectural concerns in various committees, professional associations, and expert commissions.

Simone Jeska

Simone Jeska is the co-author of the publication *Poolology of Housing*. As an architect and author, her sphere of activity encompasses practical as well as theoretical issues in architecture. She has worked independently and on projects for Hascher Jehle Achitektur. She worked as an academic associate at the TU Berlin, lectured on materials in architecture at the TU Berlin, and has worked on a number of architecture publications including the *Office Buildings: A Design Manual*, *Transparent Plastics* and *Emergent Timber Technologies*. She lives and works in Berlin.

Bildnachweis/Image Credits

Alle Grundrisse und Pläne
von pool Architekten, Zürich,
ausser anders vermerkt.
© pool Architekten, Zürich

All floor plans and sections
by pool Architekten, Zürich,
unless otherwise noted.
© pool Architekten, Zürich

Fotografien und Pläne
von Studierendenprojekten
von den Studierenden selbst,
wie in den Bildunterschriften vermerkt.
© die Studierenden

All photos and floor plans
of student projects by the students
as noted in the captions.
© the students

Umschlag vorne/
Front cover:
© Thomas Pracht, Guang Xue;
© Ralph Feiner, Malans

Umschlag hinten/
Back cover:
© Ralph Feiner, Malans;
© Patryk Kujawa, Martyna
Aleksandra Wojnarowska

Umschlag Innenseite/
Inside cover:
© Giuseppe Micciché, Zürich
© Annett Donat, Jakob Pawlowski

Abbild des Raumes/
Imaging Spaces

S./pp. 15–46:
Fotografiert von den Studierenden,
wie in den Bildunterschriften
vermerkt./Photographs taken by
students as noted in the captions

Das Arbeiten
mit Typologien/
Working
with Typologies

S./p. 58, 21/22:
© Stadt Wien MA 18/R. Christanell
S./p. 61, 27/28:
Courtesy Politecnico di Torino, Sezione
Archivi Biblioteca Roberto Gabetti,
Fondo Mollino
S./p. 61, 31:
Aus/taken from: Werner Blaser,
Bauernhaus der Schweiz — Eine
Sammlung der schönsten ländlichen
Bauten, Birkhäuser, Basel 1983
S./p. 61, 32/34:
pool Architekten, Zürich
S./p. 61, 33:
Staatsarchiv des Kantons Bern, T.A.
Dürrenroth 8

Utopien und Erfindungen/
Utopias and Inventions

S./p. 110, 7:
Aus/taken from: Manfredo Tafuri,
Progetto e Utopia, Bari 1973;
© Eredi Aldo Rossi, courtesy of
Fondazione Aldo Rossi
S./p. 110, 8:
© 2019 Gaetano Pesce
S./p. 110, 9:
Aus/taken from: p.m., bolo'bolo,
Paranoia City, Zürich 1983
S./p. 110, 10/11:
© Martin Stollenwerk, Zürich
S./p. 110, 12/13:
Aus/taken from: Peter Sloterdijk,
«Architekturen des Schaums»,
in: ARCH+ 169/170, 2004

pool Architekten:
Das charaktervolle Haus
in der Stadt/
pool Architekten:
The Characterful House
in the City

S./pp. 121, 123–124, 127–128, 135–137,
139–140, 142–145, 148, 150–151:
© Andrea Helbling, Zürich
S./pp. 122, 125, 146–147, 149:
© Ralph Feiner, Malans
S./pp. 126, 129–134:
© Niklaus Spoerri, Zürich
S./pp. 138, 152:
© Giuseppe Micciché, Zürich
S./p. 141:
© Martin Stollenwerk, Zürich

pool Architekten:
Interieurs/
pool Architekten:
Interiors

S./p. 191:
© Sander Lückers, Zürich
S./pp. 192, 197–199, 206, 211–212, 215–217,
220–221, 223:
© Ralph Feiner, Malans
S./p. 193:
© Georg Aerni, Zürich
S./pp. 194–196, 208, 224:
© Niklaus Spoerri, Zürich
S./p. 200:
© Giuseppe Micciché, Zürich
S./pp. 201–202, 204, 210, 218–219, 225–226:
© Andrea Helbling, Zürich
S./p. 203:
© Walter Mair, Basel
S./pp. 205, 207, 209, 213–214:
© pool Architekten, Zürich
S./p. 222:
© Martin Stollenwerk, Zürich

Holz — Stäbe und Platten/
Wood—Posts and Panels

S./p. 237, 1:
Aus/taken from: Gottfried Semper,
Der Stil in den technischen und
tektonischen Künsten (Bd. 2),
Bruckmann, München 1863, S. 263
S./p. 237, 2:
Aus/taken from: Marc-Antoine Laugier,
Essai sur l'architecture, 1755
S./p. 237, 6/7:
Aus/taken from: Teiji Itoh, Alte Häuser
in Japan, DVA, Stuttgart 1984, S. 85/87
S./p. 239, 8–10:
pool Architekten, Zürich
S./p. 239, 11–13:
© Niklaus Spoerri, Zürich
S./p. 239, 14:
© Georg Aerni, Zürich;
S./p. 239, 16:
© Andrea Helbling, Zürich

Backstein — vom
Weben und Fügen/
Brick—of Weaving
and Joining

S./p. 247, 26/27:
Library of Congress Prints and
Photographs Division Washington,
D.C., 20540 USA
S./p. 249, 33–35:
© Cemal Emden; © 2019 Louis I. Kahn
Collection, The Architectural Archives,
University of Pennsylvania and the
Pennsylvania Historical and Museum
Commission, Philadelphia, USA
S./p. 252, 41/42/45:
Für die Werke von/for all works by Frank
Lloyd Wright © 2019, ProLitteris, Zurich
S./p. 252, 46–48:
Swedish Centre for Architecture
and Design
S./p. 255, 49/50/52:
Aus/taken from: Giancarlo De Carlo,
Urbino — la storia di una città e il
piano della sua evoluzione urbanistica,
Marsilio Editori, Padua 1966
S./p. 257, 56/57, 58–60, 61/62:
pool Architekten, Zürich

Beton — das Feine
im Rohen/
Concrete—the Fine
within the Rough

S./p. 265, 71:
Für die Werke von/for all works
by Walter Gropius
© 2019, ProLitteris, Zurich
S./p. 265, 74:
Aus/taken from: Kenneth Frampton,
Studies in Tectonic Culture. The
Poetics of Construction in Nineteenth
and Twentieth Century Architecture,
MIT Press, Cambridge 1995
S./p. 266, 78–80:
Für die Werke von/for all works
by Le Corbusier © FLC/2019,
ProLitteris, Zurich
S./p. 266, 81–84:
Aus/taken from: Team 10: 1953–1981.
In Search of a Utopia of the Present,
NAi Publishers, Rotterdam 2005
S./p. 276, 113:
© Niklaus Spoerri, Zürich
S./p. 276, 114:
pool Architekten, Zürich
S./p. 276, 115/117:
© Niklaus Spoerri, Zürich
S./p. 276, 116, 118–120:
pool Architekten, Zürich

Stahl — der
«unsichtbare» Stoff/
Steel—the
'Invisible' Material

S./p. 283, 125–127, 128/129:
Für die Werke von/for all works
by Ludwig Mies van der Rohe
© 2019, ProLitteris, Zurich
S./p. 284, 130:
© Eames Office, LLC (eamesoffice.com),
photo by Timothy Street-Porter
S./p. 284, 134/135/136:
Für die Werke von/for all works
by Jean Prouvé
© 2019, ProLitteris, Zurich
S./p. 287, 137–139:
© Casterman, Tournai 1985
S./p. 287, 140–142:
Für die Werke von/for all works
by Le Corbusier
© FLC/2019, ProLitteris, Zurich
S./p. 287, 143–145:
Jochen Brandi und Partner, Stahl und
Form, Stahl-Informationszentrum,
Düsseldorf 1976
S./p. 288, 146/147:
Für die Werke von/for all works
by Le Corbusier
© FLC/2019, ProLitteris, Zurich.
147 Aus/taken from: Bruno Krucker/
Arthur Rüegg, Konstruktive Konzepte
der Moderne, Niggli Verlag, Sulgen/
Zürich 2001
S./p. 288, 148:
Für die Werke von/for all works
by Yona Friedman
© 2019, ProLitteris, Zurich
S./p. 288, 151/152/153:
Für die Werke von/for all works
by Le Corbusier
© FLC/2019, ProLitteris, Zurich
S./p. 288, 154:
© Richard J. Dietrich

Die Kultur des Interieurs/
The Culture of the Interior

S./p. 365, 1–3:
© Sir John Soane's Museum London
S./p. 366, 7/8:
Für die Werke von/for all works
by Frank Lloyd Wright
© 2019, ProLitteris, Zurich
7: © Andrea Helbling, Zürich
S./p. 366, 10/11:
Für die Werke von/for all works
by Lucia Moholy
© 2019, ProLitteris, Zurich.
Für die Werke von/for all works
by Walter Gropius
© 2019, ProLitteris, Zurich
S./p. 366, 12–15:
Für die Werke von/for all works
by Le Corbusier
© FLC/2019, ProLitteris, Zurich
S./p. 371, 16:
Foto: Maija Holma, Alvar Aalto Museum,
2001; für die Werke von/for all works
by Maija Holma
© 2019, ProLitteris, Zurich;
S./p. 371, 17:
Scan: Alvar Aalto Museum
S./p. 371, 18–20:
Hansaviertel, Interbau Berlin 1957,
1955–1957, Berlin, Germany;
18: House 16, Apartment 3, Kitchen
and living room. Foto: Heikki Havas,
Alvar Aalto Museum, 1957.
19: Plan, Scan: Alvar Aalto Museum.
20: House 16, Apartment 3, balcony
and living room. Foto: Heikki Havas,
Alvar Aalto Museum, 1957

Studierende
der TU Berlin: Interieurs/
Students from
the TU Berlin: Interiors

S./pp. 379–410:
Fotografiert von den Studierenden,
wie in den Bildunterschriften
vermerkt/Photographs taken by
students as noted in the captions

Dank/Acknowledgments

pool bedankt sich herzlich bei allen, die zur Entstehung dieses Buches beigetragen haben!

An erster Stelle sind dies alle ehemaligen und aktuellen Mitarbeiter von pool, die mit viel Herzblut an der Entwicklung der zahlreichen Wohnungsgrundrisse mitgewirkt haben und ohne die eine solche typologische Diversität nicht entstanden wäre.

Ausdrücklich mit eingeschlossen sind die Studierenden der TU Berlin, die auf dem poolschen Fundus aufbauend die Thematik in oft überraschende Richtungen lenkten und uns dabei unterstützten, das eigene Wissen zu reflektieren.

Ein besonderer Dank geht auch an die Professorenkollegen der TU Berlin, die uns motivierten, unsere *recherche architecturale* zum Wohnungsbau voranzutreiben, sowie an unsere Mitarbeiter im Fachgebiet: die wissenschaftlichen Mitarbeiter Simone Jeska, Ingo Turtenwald und ganz am Anfang Beate Boenicke sowie im Sekretariat Bertien Götsche-Pons und als Tutoren Mathias Lehmann und Oskar Ellwanger.

Einen wesentlichen Beitrag geleistet haben alle, die in unserem Büro direkt an der Produktion des Buches mitwirkten: Simone Jeska mit ihrer Textarbeit und ihren inhaltlichen Fragen, die es uns erlaubten, das Denken zum Wohnungsbau nochmals zu schärfen; ausserdem Oskar Ellwanger mit dem Aufarbeiten der Grafiken, mit Unterstützung von Dorothée Müller, Lona Boxleitner, Wojciech Hryszkiewicz, Thomas Klinkhammer, Monica Küng, Anna Plückbaum und Samila Sydiq.

Sponsoren und Partners

Ohne Auftraggeber und Planungspartner können Architekten weder planen noch realisieren. Wir sprechen an dieser Stelle allen einen grossen Dank aus, die uns vom ersten Gedanken bis zum fertigen Bau begleiten und unterstützen.

Namentlich erwähnt sein sollen die Firmen und Institutionen, die das vorliegende Buch mit einem finanziellen Beitrag ermöglicht haben:

Amstein + Walthert AG
ASIG Wohngenossenschaft
Baugenossenschaft Freiblick Zürich
Baugenossenschaft mehr als wohnen
Bhend Elektroplan GmbH
Bivgrafik GmbH
Caretta + Gitz AG
Diethelm Keller Holding AG
Dr. Deuring + Oehninger AG
dsp Ingenieure & Planer AG
Eduard Truninger AG
Elprom Partner AG
enerpeak ag
ewp
Forster & Burgmer Architekten & GU AG
Gode AG Zürich
Gruenberg + Partner AG

pool would like to express our heartfelt thanks to everyone who contributed to the production of this book!

Thanks first and foremost to all of our former and present colleagues at pool, who contributed with such passion to the development of numerous residential floor plans, and without whom such typological diversity would never have emerged.

This unequivocally includes the students at the TU Berlin, who—building on the material generated by pool—guided the topic in astonishing directions, thereby encouraging us to reflect on our own knowledge.

A special thanks to our colleagues on the faculty of the TU Berlin, who provided us with an impetus to advance our *recherche architecturale* on housing development, as well as to our colleagues in the field: the academic associates Simone Jeska and Ingo Turtenwald, as well as, at the very start, Beate Boenicke, along with Bertien Götsche-Pons in the secretariat, and as tutors, Mathias Lehmann and Oskar Ellwanger.

An essential contribution was made by all of those in our architectural practice who worked directly on the production of this publication: our sincere thanks to Simone Jeska for her work on the texts and her questions which allowed us, once again, to hone our thinking on residential development. Thanks also to Oskar Ellwanger, with support from Dorothée Müller, Lona Boxleitner, Wojciech Hryszkiewicz, Thomas Klinkhammer, Monica Küng, Anna Plückbaum, and Samila Sydiq, for preparing the graphics.

Sponsors and Partners

Without clients or planning partners, architects wouldn't be able to plan, let alone realize, buildings. Therefore, we would like to thank all the people who take part in our projects from first inception to finished building.

Listed below are the companies and institutions that with their generous contributions have made this book possible:

Implenia Schweiz AG
Kopitsis Bauphysik AG
Leideritz Bauleitungen GmbH
Makiol Wiederkehr AG
Meier+Steinauer Partner AG
Müller Illien Landschaftsarchitekten
schaerholzbau ag
SJB Kempter Fitze AG
Takt Baumanagement AG
Urech Bärtschi Maurer AG
Waldhauser + Hermann AG

Impressum/Imprint

Konzept/Concept
pool Architekten, Zürich

Übersetzung/Translations
Ian Pepper

Lektorat/Copy editing
Sandra Leitte, George Kafka

Korrektorat/Proofreading
Karin Prätorius, Anna Roos

Gestaltung/Design
Bonbon — Valeria Bonin,
Diego Bontognali, Mirko Leuenberger,
Zürich

Lithografie, Druck und Bindung/
Lithography, printing, and binding
DZA Druckerei zu Altenburg, Thüringen

© 2019 pool Architekten, Zürich, und/and Park Books AG, Zürich

© für die Texte: bei den Autoren/
for the texts: the authors
© für die Bilder: siehe Bildnachweis/
for the images: see image credits

Park Books
Niederdorfstrasse 54
8001 Zürich
Schweiz/Switzerland
www.park-books.com

Park Books wird vom Bundesamt für Kultur mit einem Strukturbeitrag für die Jahre 2016–2020 unterstützt.

Park Books is being supported by the Federal Office of Culture with a general subsidy for the years 2016–2020.

Alle Rechte vorbehalten; kein Teil dieses Werks darf in irgendeiner Form ohne vorherige schriftliche Genehmigung des Verlags reproduziert oder unter Verwendung elektronischer Systeme verarbeitet, vervielfältigt oder verbreitet werden.

All rights reserved; no part of this publication may be reproduced, stored in a retrieval system or transmitted in any form or by any means, electronic, mechanical, photocopying, recording, or otherwise, without the prior written consent of the publisher.

ISBN 978-3-03860-088-6

Umschlag/Front cover
← Craig Ellwood, Hunt House, Malibu/California, 1955
  Abbild S14–04: Thomas Pracht, Guang Xue
← pool 0203; Dreifamilienhaus/Three-Family House, Im Dörfli, Oberrieden, 2013/14

Umschlag Innenseite/Inside cover
← pool 0176; Genossenschaftliches Wohn- und Geschäftshaus/Cooperative residential and commercial building Badenerstrasse, Zürich, 2008–2010

Umschlag Innenseite/Inside cover
→ High Rise 11; Annett Donat, Jakob Pawlowski

Umschlag/Back cover
→ pool 0201; Haus an der Bickelstrasse, Oberrieden, 2008–2009
→→ Luis Barragan, Own House, Ciudad de México, 1948
  Abbild S14–02: Patryk Kujawa, Martyna Aleksandra Wojnarowska